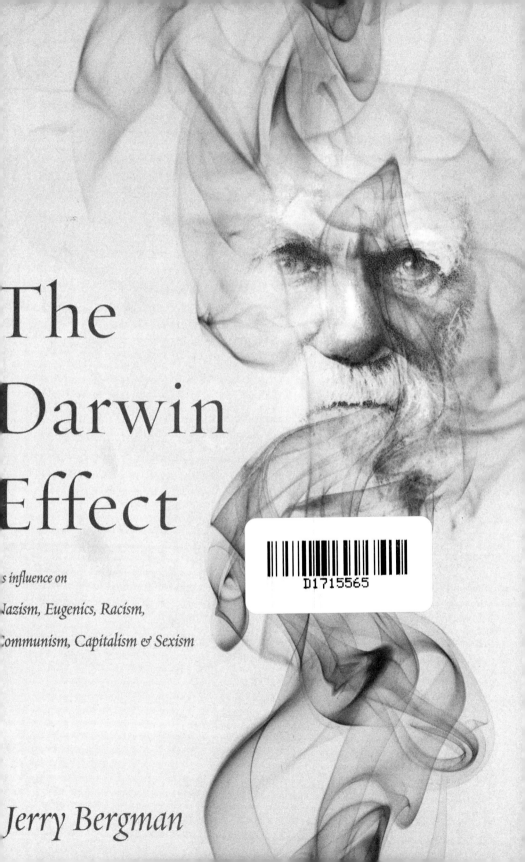

The
Darwin
Effect

s influence on

Nazism, Eugenics, Racism,

Communism, Capitalism & Sexism

Jerry Bergman

D1715565

What Others Are Saying about *The Darwin Effect* . . .

Those who enjoy having their "scholastic taste buds" stimulated will experience this book like a smorgasbord of mind-grabbing topics. As you read, you will appreciate the depth and breadth of the subject and continue looking forward to more and more intriguing material on the nefarious influence of Darwinism on modern society.

> — Wayne Frair, PhD, Professor Emeritus of Biology
> The Kings College, New York

Jerry Bergman's *The Darwin Effect* is both comprehensive and compelling. The book is revealing in its detail and at the same time damning with its evidence of a totally destructive worldview. I highly recommend it.

> — Emerson Thomas McMullen, PhD, Department of History
> Georgia Southern University

The Darwin Effect is a sobering look at the grim reality of what happens to societies whose people really come to believe that all that exists is the result of nothing more than chance and time. Bergman pulls no punches in this eye-opening history of the consequences of the 19th century's most destructive idea.

> — Steven E. Woodworth, PhD, Associate Professor of History
> Texas Christian University, Fort Worth, TX

This book is a tale of a reverse "Midas touch." Instead of turning to gold, everything the Darwinian worldview touches turns filthy and corroded. Bergman documents a plethora of examples that show the dark side of Darwinism — racism, sexism, communism, hate, and more. Yet, unlike the Midas fable where Midas learns a lesson and all is made right, there is no happy ending to Bergman's tale . . . so far. But perhaps there is hope — if enough people come to realize what Darwinism and evolution are doing to mankind.

> — Professor David J. Oberpriller, Computer Science Department
> Arizona Christian University

Acknowledgments

I want to thank Emerson Thomas McMullen, PhD, Steven E. Woodworth, PhD, Wayne Frair, PhD, Dr. David Herbert, Professor David Oberpriller, Bryce Gaudian, Bert Thompson, PhD, Clifford Lillo, MA, Robert Kofahl, PhD, Jody Allen, RN, and Professor Aeron Bergman, MA for their feedback on earlier drafts of this work. Needless to say, all mistakes that remain are mine. I also want to thank Bolton Davidheiser, PhD, John Woodmorappe, MA, and Ian Taylor for their comments on earlier drafts of this book.

Photo Credits

First printing: September 2014

ISBN: 978-0-89051-837-3
Library of Congress Number: 2014948502

Cover by Diana Bogardus

Please consider requesting that a copy of this volume be purchased by your local library system.

Printed in the United States of America

Please visit our website for other great titles:
www.masterbooks.net

For information regarding author interviews,
please contact the publicity department at (870) 438-5288

Master
Books®
A Division of New Leaf Publishing Group
www.masterbooks.net

Table of Contents

Foreword

In the spring of 2008 outside the gates of the University of Western Ontario, I approached a second-year philosophy student and asked if he would complete a questionnaire relating to my book, *Charles Darwin's Religious Views* (2009). In an ensuing conversation, he, being an avowed atheist and evolutionist, declared in no uncertain terms that all moral values were totally relativistic. I asked him if a man molested a seven-year-old girl (the ages of my two granddaughters at that time), was such an act wrong? He calmly replied, "Absolutely not! Remember, we are nothing more than animals."

Dr. Jerry Bergman's newest book, *The Darwin Effect*, traces the roots of this university student's heinous mode of reasoning. Dr. Bergman correctly identified the evolutionary writings of Charles Darwin, especially *The Origin of Species* (1859) and *Descent of Man* (1871), as a major contributing factor. Evolutionism, ensconced within a naturalistic worldview, emerged as a dominant religious perspective in the 20th century. Within this time frame, eugenics — the application of evolutionary dogma upon humans — left an unspeakable carnage in its wake.

Francis Galton, Charles Darwin's cousin, was the founder and publicist of the eugenics movement. Having died in 1911, he never witnessed the untold worldwide suffering that his villainous philosophy caused. Eugenics, placed in the hearts and hands of such maniacal autocrats as Adolf Hitler, Joseph Stalin, and Chairman Mao, resulted in a predictable maelstrom. Dr. Bergman has estimated that this diabolical trio caused 400 million people to perish.

H.G. Wells, a prolific writer of some 100 books, is renowned for his *The Outline of History* (1920) of which, remarkably, some two million copies have been sold. One is not surprised with his ardent evolutionary bias in view of the fact that Wells was a student of T.H. Huxley, Darwin's bulldog. But most disconcerting was his firm commitment to eugenics. He publicly advocated the elimination of the so-called "unfit" — those with incurable diseases, the mentally ill, and the disabled. Furthermore, he sympathized with Nazism and its desire to form a white superior Aryan race.

Dr. Bergman's portrayal of Ota Benga poignantly illustrates the disastrous effects that Darwinism can have on an individual. The mistreatment and eventual suicide of this Congolese Pygmy has to be one of the darker moments of American racism. This well-researched book is an excellent companion volume to Dr. Bergman's *The Dark Side of Charles Darwin* (2011).

Dr. David Herbert, historian (www.diherbert.ca) (Dr. Herbert earned his doctorate from the University of Toronto.)

References

Herbert, David. *Charles Darwin's Religious Views*. Kitchener, Ontario, Canada: Joshua Press, 2009.

Chapter 1

Introduction

This book documents how often — and how easily — Darwinism has been exploited for sinister political ends by a wide assortment of persons and movements (Sebastian and Bohlin 2009). Since the turn of the last century, a large number of professors and scientists became Darwinists, and, as a result, had an enormous influence and effect on society.

For example, historian Professor Aziz wrote that "with the exception of several isolated cases of courage, the German University as a whole accepted without protest the notion that the medical people should be accomplices to the massacre" of so-called less fit humans during the Nazi rule in Germany (Aziz 1976, 113). Aziz added that "almost a third of the psychiatry department chairmen [in Nazi Germany] were participating in the [eugenics] program as experts in the selection and elimination of the mentally ill" (Aziz 1976, 113). Worldwide, even many Jews were involved in/or supported eugenics, although in contrast to the German eugenists conclusion, the ethnic groups they thought were inferior were all non-Jews, not Jews (Glad 2011).

This book, and my two other books in this series, *The Dark Side of*

Charles Darwin and *Hitler and the Nazis Darwin-ian Worldview: How the Nazis Eugenic Crusade for a Superior Race Caused the Greatest Holocaust in World History* document the fact that Darwin was responsible, directly and indirectly, for more holocausts, suffering, and destruction of property than any other man in history. As this book documents, his ideas inspired not only Nazism, but also communism and ruthless capitalism, costing the lives of an estimated up to one-quarter billion persons. Barrett et al has documented that in the last century 45.5 million Christians were martyred, a large number specifically by movements inspired by Charles Darwin, who in turn was a major influence on the former-Christian-turned-atheist Karl Marx, as documented in chapters 14 and 15 (2001). It is sometimes argued that someone else would have come along to achieve what Darwin did, which may be true, but this rationalization is like saying that if Hitler did not exist, someone else would have caused the same horrors in Germany that he did. Therefore, Hitler was not a bad guy because the Holocaust that he and his close followers brought about would have occurred anyway.

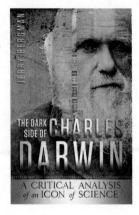

Darwinism is the view of origins first popularized by Charles Robert Darwin (1809–1882). This view is now often called neo-Darwinism because many modifications were made in Darwin's theory, including the view that the main source of variety is mutation instead of Darwin's semi-Lamarckian theory. Neo-Darwinism teaches that simple molecules, such as methane, water, hydrogen, and ammonia, evolved into all life forms from bacteria to humans by the natural selection of genetic mistakes called mutations by natural selection (survival of the fittest), chance, the outworking of natural law, plus enormous amounts of time.

The political persuasions of those who have harnessed Darwin for evil range from the so-called radical right to the extreme left. The history of Darwinism's critical role in communism, capitalism, eugenics, Nazism, and sexism is told in the following pages in engaging prose that reads like a historical novel (except it is fact). As will be documented, although racism existed before Darwin published his 1859 work *Origin of Species*, Darwinism gave the human inferior-superior racial hierarchy theory the respectability and authority of science, increasing the racism problem in the Western world by several orders of magnitude (Gould 1977, 127). Part of the problem was that the 19th-century world had created a new god — Science. Such creeds as Scientism and the even more rational Positivism held that science would wrest all cosmological mysteries from the churches and that science itself would then take on [the direction of society]. . . . All mankind's problems would be solved through the knowledge of natural and social processes (Jones 2002, 299–300).

This book elucidates what has happened as a result of creating this new god.

A major objection to my conclusions is the correct observation that other factors also contributed to the evils discussed in the following pages. I have no quibble with this observation. This work, though, is about the important influence of Darwinism on eugenics, racism, sexism, capitalism, Nazism, and communism. Many other books and articles have evaluated the other factors influencing these "isms," but these factors are not the focus of this work. It is well documented in the scholarly literature that Darwinism had a major influence on all of these 20th-century evils, and this work attempts to understand some of the details of this influence (Bergman 2012).

Darwinism did not make any major contributions of practical benefit for humanity, at least compared to the discovery of DNA, antibiotics, the invention of the transistor, the computer chip, or MRI. It has been placed at the pinnacle of media and scientific esteem, not by scientific fact or history, but rather by a vast and expensive public-relations program paid for by tax dollars (Sewell 2009).

The focus here is on the practical and political results of applying Darwinism to society, not its validity. One specific focus in most chapters is on the Darwinian-inspired eugenics movement that has swept the world for major parts of the last two centuries and still influences many today. In researching eugenics, one issue is to understand

how a tightly knit group of scientists (and most of the main actors in this story were scientists — biologists, zoologists, psychologists and doctors) went about trying to sell an esoteric idea to the general public; how they organized, mobilized, and influenced politicians; and how they succeeded in getting laws enacted to suit their ideological purposes (Sewell 2009, xi–xii).

This work details the enormous harm that this esoteric movement has caused society, and carefully documents this conclusion with hundreds of references.

Daniel Dennett wrote that evolution is a universal acid that dissolves every ethical and moral system it encounters (1995). The extent that evolution is indeed such a "universal acid" which helps in explaining societal decay is covered in some detail. For some persons, evolution even explains, and to some evolutionists justifies, rape (Thornhill and Palmer 2000).

Evolution teaches that nature selects those organisms which leave more offspring, and the more sexually aggressive a person, the more offspring he will usually produce, passing on the genes that cause sexual aggression to a disproportionate number of offspring. As a result, Darwinists teach that this trait will become more common in the population.

Many scholarly tomes cover the adverse influence of Darwinism on society, but the goal of this work is a readable, hard-hitting, well-supported account that documents this connection. One major adverse influence of Darwinism is the idea of eugenics, a term coined by Darwin's cousin Francis Galton (1822–1911). Eugenics is the belief that improvements in society require breeding better people using techniques similar to breeding better animals. Eugenics teaches that, as humans are animals, use of forced sterilization or, in extreme cases euthanizing inferior people as the Nazis did, will cause the human race to evolve in desirable directions. There is "no doubt about the [Darwinian] lineage of eugenics itself," and in the "years leading up to the First World War, the eugenics movement looked like a Darwin family business." Specifically

> Darwin's son Leonard replaced his cousin Galton as chairman of the national Eugenics Society in 1911. In the same year an offshoot of the society was formed in Cambridge. Among its leading members were three more of Charles Darwin's sons, Horace, Francis and George. The group's treasurer was a young economics lecturer at the university, John Maynard Keynes, whose younger brother Geoffrey would later marry Darwin's granddaughter Margaret. Meanwhile, Keynes's mother, Florence, and Horace Darwin's daughter Ruth, sat together on the committee of the Cambridge Association for the Care of the Feeble-Minded . . . a front organization for eugenics (Sewell 2009, 54).

The author has endeavored not to misrepresent Darwinism, but also felt compelled to cover details that are often sorely neglected in much of the evolution literature. The picture documented in this work is not pretty — but both sad and tragic. The words of leading Darwinian scientists, such as Charles Darwin and Ernst Haeckel, whose racist ideas were crystal clear in their writings, were often allowed to speak for themselves.

Richard Dawkins has also convinced many persons that a "slam-dunk case [exists] for giving up any search for meaning, purpose or direction in human affairs" (Sewell 2009, 8). Historian Dennis Sewell is not so confident of the validity of Dawkins's case:

> Eugenics might have remained where it began, on the margins of British political life, something to be discussed in draughty temperance halls at meetings of the Rationalist Association (for the Darwinist/atheist axis had already become well established). However, unlike many other esoteric theories of the day . . . the eugenics movement could count on the support not only of cranks, but of Cambridge academics, fellows of the Royal Society and large numbers of the medical profession itself (Sewell 2009, 55).

Sewell then concluded that the Darwinism/atheist axis launched

> what would prove to be an impressive political lobbying campaign. In a remarkably short space of time, the vocabulary and basic principles of eugenics spread through the middle class, becoming almost the rule rather than the exception. This rapid mainstreaming of what began as a quirky set of ideas was rather like the way that the environmental movement developed in our own times (Sewell 2009, 55).

Hitler and the Nazis

The best and one of the most extreme examples of the attempt to apply eugenics to humans is the National Socialist Workers Party, or Nazi, movement. Hitler made it clear in his writings and speeches that he believed

> only a tiny part of what is usually regarded as mankind consists of human beings — notably those whom he imagined to be of Nordic descent. . . . The rest — what he called racial mish-mash — belongs not to mankind but to an inferior species . . . simply animals disguised as human beings (Cohn 1967, 187).

Professor Norman Cohn documents that this racist idea was "disguised as scientific truth" by the German government, the racial scientists, and the academics at leading German universities. This idea was then used to terrorize "Europe from the English Channel to the Volga" (Cohn 1967, 187). To support this conclusion, Cohn quotes from a document issued by the German government that concludes non-Nordics or non-Aryans were subhuman creatures that biologically look as though

> it were of absolutely the same kind, endowed by Nature with hands, feet and a sort of brain, with eyes and mouth — is nevertheless a totally different, a fearful creature, is only an attempt at a human being, with a quasi-human face, yet in mind and spirit lower than any animal (Cohn 1967, 188).

The document explained that inside of these quasi-humans is "a cruel chaos of wild, unchecked passions: a nameless will to destruction, the most primitive lusts, the most undisguised vileness" (quoted

Adolf Hitler and Benito Mussolini in October of 1936, with Germany and Italy declaring their alliance.

in Cohn 1967, 188). They concluded that these inferior people must be destroyed for the good of society and, as chapters 1–11 of this book will explain, Hitler's view was firmly grounded in Darwinism (Bergman 2012). The movement of eugenics from theory to politics, then to social control

> required an expansion of state agencies and an expansion of their scope for prying into — and ultimately directing — the lives of the poor. "A system will also be established for the examination of the family history of all those placed on the register as being unquestionably mentally abnormal," said Leonard Darwin, "especially as regards the criminality, insanity, ill health and pauperism of their relatives. . . . If all this were done, it can hardly be doubted that many strains would be discovered which no one could deny ought to be made to die out in the interests of the nation [in what in Germany became a short step to the holocaust] (Sewell 2009, 54–55).

The result was the Holocaust. The Nazi concentration camp Dachau was liberated by the U.S. Army about a month before the 15th Engineer

Battalion arrived in May of 1945. Part of that battalion was U.S. soldier Martin Gaudian. He wrote that the first thing he saw when he arrived in Dachau was an

> 8 to 10 year-old boy standing by a furnace talking to another soldier. He was showing him some pictures of bodies that had been placed into the furnace. He had many pictures that he sold to the soldier. He mentioned that his parents had also been gassed and burned. The same day I remember seeing the water tower. It had been used by Dr.'s who performed experiments to see how long humans could survive during the cold months in freezing water. Then I remember seeing this huge warehouse not far from the brick building where we were housed. I walked over to the building and went inside. The first part I entered was like a small entry room with shelves on the wall. One large shelf had jars with human body parts in the jars in a liquid solution. I remember seeing an eye, ear, heart, sexual organs, fingers, etc. Then I entered the warehouse section of the building. There were huge tables loaded with all kinds of precision tools — protractors, measuring instruments, tools, pliers, other gripping devices, bayonets . . . the room was huge, maybe 200 feet long, 50 feet wide (Gaudian 2010, 1).

Darwinian racism contributed not just to eugenics but also to the Holocaust. In a speech given March 5, 1943, German commander of occupied Ukraine Erich Koch said the Aryans

> are the Master Race and must govern hard . . . I will draw the very last out of this country. I did not come to spread bliss. . . . The population must work, work, and work again. . . . We have come here to create the basis for victory. We are a master race, which must remember that the lowliest German worker is racially and biologically a thousand times more valuable than the population here [in Ukraine] (quoted in Piotrowski 1998, 30).

Historian Tadeusz Piotrowski concluded that the "sheer enormity and horror of that attempt at genocide will forever haunt mankind." The same Darwinian motivations were also shared by Stalinism, producing similar results, only worse (Geyer and Fitzpatrick 2009). Among the worst examples of the application of Darwinism was done by the scientific establishment, especially the medical profession.

A doctor in the Auschwitz camp, Dr. Miklos Nyiszli, wrote that Nazi doctors hoped studying twins would solve the problem of faster reproduction of superior races by advancing

> one step in the search to unlock the secret of multiplying the race of superior beings destined to rule was a "noble goal." If only it were possible, in the future, to have each German mother bear as many twins as possible! The project, conceived by the demented theorists of the Third Reich, was utterly mad. And it was to Dr. Mengele, chief physician of the Auschwitz KZ [concentration camp], the notorious "criminal doctor," that these experiments had been entrusted (Nyiszli 2011, 60).

He added that among the many

> malefactors and criminals, the most dangerous type is the "criminal doctor," especially when he is armed with powers such as those granted to Dr. Mengele. He sent millions of people to death merely because, according to a racial theory, they were inferior beings and therefore detrimental to mankind (Nyiszli 2011, 60).

To make this claim, Dr. Nyiszli relied on his own first-hand experience and knowledge to draw his conclusion about doctors and Nazism. He writes that Mengele

> spent long hours beside me, either at his microscopes, his disinfecting ovens and his test tubes or, standing with equal patience near the dissecting table, his smock befouled with blood, his bloody hands examining and experimenting like one possessed. The immediate objective was the increased reproduction of pure Germans in numbers sufficient to replace the Czechs, Hungarians, Poles, all of whom were condemned to be destroyed, but who for the moment were living on those territories declared vital to the Third Reich (Nyiszli 2011, 60).

Much has been written about the Jewish Holocaust, but this event was only part of the ugly fruits of eugenics. Close to the staggering number of

> 12,000 Polish people died in the occupied territories as a result of the Nazi euthanasia program. Of this total, 10,000 were from hospitals for the mentally impaired. That this was only the beginning of the Nazi plan for achieving a superior race of human beings is borne

out by Gauleiter Arthur Greiser's intention to exterminate 25,000 to 35,000 Poles in Kraj Warty (Piotrowski 1998, 28).

The excuse given for these murders was because the victims "suffered from tuberculosis," a contagious disease that the Nazis incorrectly believed was a hereditary disease. One often-ignored example of Darwinian racism is that not only many Jews and Poles died in the Nazi concentration camps, but also

> Gypsies, who, like the Jews, were slated for total extermination. Although the king of the European Gypsies and president of the Gypsies in the General Government, Rudolf Kwiek, in 1942 offered collaboration in exchange for better treatment of his people, his proposal went unanswered. Of the 75,000 to 85,000 Gypsies in prewar Poland, over 50,000 died (Piotrowski 1998, 29).

Piotrowski speculated that if Germany had "won the war, there is no doubt that the scope of the Nazi euthanasia program would have been eventually broadened to include all those who, for whatever reason, were not able to contribute to the economic well-being of the Third Reich" (Piotrowski 1998, 28). From the evidence, Professor Michael Burleigh concluded that

> Hitler's objectives were almost without limit. Nor was his planning hampered by questions of cost, human or otherwise, for war in his eyes had a positive, regenerative value for the "health" of the race and nation. As he said, "We may have a hundred years of struggle before us; if so, all the better — it will prevent us from going to sleep" (Burleigh 1999, 343).

Although the racist conclusion was once almost universal among Darwinian scientists, such as the assertion that "black people were closer in the evolutionary scale to apes than white people," this belief is recognized "by scientists today as a ghastly mistake." Unfortunately, evolutionary scientists have not taken responsibility for this mistake, and traces of Darwinian eugenics still "linger in the minds of millions, affecting attitudes of race everywhere" (Sewell 2009, 20).

As evidence of this fact, Sewell noted that Nobel Laureate James Watson "explained his gloomy prognosis for Africa's social and economic development" by arguing that we could not expect "the intellectual capacities of people graphically separated in their evolution should prove to have evolved" to the level of the more highly evolved, technologically sophisticated whites (Sewell 2009, 19).

Darwinism's Importance to Communist Movement

The importance of Darwinism to the success of the communist movement, as outlined in chapters 14 and 15, was documented by Oxford University history professor Niall Ferguson who wrote

Ernst Haeckel was a German naturalist, biologist, and philosopher of evolution.

just as doubts had begun to assail the Marxists, a breakthrough in an unrelated field of science provided a vital new source of validation for their model of social change. Darwin's revolutionary statement of the theory of natural selection was immediately seized upon by Engels as fresh evidence for the theory of class conflict — though it was not long before the same claims were being made by theorists of racial conflict, who crudely misinterpreted and distorted Darwin's complex (and at times contradictory) message. Writers like Thomas Henry Huxley and Ernst Haeckel took the earlier racial theories of Gobineau and modernized them with a simplified model of natural selection in which competition between individual creatures became a crude struggle between races (Ferguson 1999, 41–42).

He added that "Darwin's revolutionary statement of the theory of natural selection" soon "became the common currency of much political debate at the turn of the century" and

"Social Darwinism" rapidly took on a host of different forms: the pseudoscientific work of eugenic theorists . . . and ultimately, of course, the violent, anti-Semitic fantasies of Hitler which combined racialism and socialism in what was to prove the most explosive ideology of the twentieth century. But what linked them was their deterministic (in some cases, apocalyptic) thrust, and indifference to the notion of individual free will. Given this apparent convergence of Marx and Darwin — despite their starkly different intellectual origins — it is hardly surprising that belief in the possibility of deterministic laws of history was so widespread during and after their lifetimes (Ferguson 1999, 42).

Ferguson documented the central role of race in the Nazi movement by detailing their plans after they won the war. All inferior races, such as the Slavic race (which is where we get our word slave), will be slaves for the superior race and will by law not be able to get an education or rule themselves in a system very much like the slavery system was in America.

Eugenics Still with Us Today

Eugenics is not dead today, just subtler. One example is the case of the self-proclaimed Social Darwinist Pekka-Eric Auvinen, an 18-year-old Finnish high school student who on November 7, 2007, murdered six students, a nurse, and the school's head teacher and wounded more than a dozen others at Jokela High School in Jokela, a town in the municipality of Tuusula, Finland (Williams 2007; Odd Culture 2007, Anonymous 2007).

Auvinen was concerned that humans had slowed, or even reversed, evolution in Western society, and was determined personally to do something about what he saw as this problem (Sewell 2009, 45). He wrote on his blog that the "stupid, weak-minded people reproduce . . . faster than intelligent, strong-minded" persons like himself (Sewell 2009, 45). Auvinen added he hated Christianity and other "enslaving religions" and, in contrast, he favored "evolution science" (Anonymous 2007, 1).

Auvinen carefully thought through the philosophical implications of Darwin's argument and concluded that humans, like every other animal, have no special value because evolution has proved that life was without long-term purpose or meaning, but rather was simply a cause-and-effect result of a long process of survival of the fittest (Sewell 2009, 45). He also wrote, "I am a cynical existentialist," a "social Darwinist," and an "atheist," adding that "Life is just a meaningless coincidence" the "result of [a] long process of evolution and many . . . factors, causes and effects" and "there are no other universal laws than the laws of nature and the laws of physics." He added:

> Evolution is both a theory and a fact, creationism is neither one. . . . Religious people, your gods are nothing and exist only in your heads. Your slave morals means nothing. . . . Human life is not sacred. Humans are just a species among other animals and the world does not exist only for humans. Death [and killing] is not a tragedy, it happens in nature all the time. . . . Not all human lives are important or worth saving (Auvinen 2007).

He further stated,

> Only superior (intelligent, self-aware, strong-minded) individu-
> als should survive while inferior (stupid, retarded, weak-minded
> masses) should perish. Today the process of natural selection is
> totally misguided. It has reversed. . . . Modern human race has not
> only betrayed its ancestors, but the future generations too. It's time
> to put Natural Selection and Survival of the Fittest back on track!
> (Auvinen 2007).

Auvinen concluded that he has "evolved a step higher" than most of the rest
of us. His special plea was that his actions would result in society taking the
role of social Darwinism more seriously. Auvinen stressed that movies, television, computer games, and music were not the source of his motivation to
murder those he judged inferior, but rather his motivation was Darwinism
(Sewell 2009, 46).

Furthermore, he chose his victims with care, "trying to weed out those
who were, in his judgment, the unfit" (Sewell 2009, 46). To those of us not
intoxicated with Darwinism, he was psychotic or, at the least, simply an evil,
misguided young man. He intended to cause maximum bloodshed, and had
with him 500 cartridges and used a total of 69 cartridge cases (Anonymous
2007). His own words, as printed in his *Natural Selector's Manifesto,* are as
follows:

> How Did Natural Selection Turn Into Idiocratic Selection? Today
> the process of natural selection is totally misguided. It has reversed.
> Human race has been devolving very long time for now. Retarded
> and stupid, weak-minded people are reproducing more and faster
> than the intelligent, strong-minded people. Laws protect the retarded
> majority which selects the leaders of society. Modern human race
> has not only betrayed its ancestors, but the future generations too.
> *Homo sapiens,* HAH! It is more like a *Homo Idioticus* to me! When I
> look at people I see every day in society, school and everywhere . . . I
> can't say I belong to the same race as the lousy, miserable, arrogant,
> selfish human race! No! I have evolved one step above!
>
>   Humans are just a species among other animals and the world
> does not exist only for humans. Death and killing is not a tragedy,
> it happens in nature all the time between all species. Not all human
> lives are important or worth saving. Only superior (intelligent, self-
> aware, strong-minded) individuals should survive while inferior

(stupid, retarded, weak-minded masses) should perish.

There is also another solution to the problem: stupid people as slaves and intelligent people as free. . . . they who have free minds, are capable of intelligent existential and philosophical thinking and know what justice is, should be free and rulers . . . and the robotic masses, they can be slaves since they do not mind it now either and because their minds are on so retarded level. The gangsters that now rule societies, would of course get what they deserve (Odd Culture 2007).

He concluded by adding, "Life is just a meaningless coincidence . . . result of a long process of evolution and many several factors, causes and effects" (Odd Culture 2007).

The Columbine killers — who Sewell described as "two amateur social Darwinists" — made similar arguments as did Auvinen (Sewell 2009, 47). The school shooting occurred on April 20, 1999, at Columbine High School in Columbine, an unincorporated area of Jefferson County, Colorado. Two senior students, Eric Harris and Dylan Klebold, embarked on a shooting spree, murdering 12 students and one teacher, and injuring 21 other students directly, and three others while attempting to escape.

The pair then committed suicide. Eric Harris wore a "Natural Selection" T-shirt on the day of the massacre he committed at Columbine High School, and both killers made remarks on a video about helping natural selection along by eliminating the weak among humankind. They also made frequent references to evolution, all which were ignored by the press (Sewell 2009, 47).

Another example is James Jay Lee, 43, who armed himself with a gun and bombs and held three hostages, two employees, and a security guard in the Discovery Channel building in Maryland. His demands included, "The Discovery Channel and its affiliate channels MUST have daily television programs at prime time slots . . . [featuring] leading scientists who understand and agree with the Malthus-Darwin science." He demanded the network "develop shows that mention the Malthusian sciences about how food production leads to the overpopulation of the Human race. Talk about Evolution. Talk about Malthus and Darwin until it sinks into the stupid people's brains until they get it!!" (Brumfield and Miller 2010).

The police shot him when he evidently attempted to murder one of the hostages. As the hostages got ready to make a break for it, the officers who were moving in on Lee heard a noise they thought could have been gunfire or a bomb detonating. In response, they shot Lee dead, ending the drama that had lasted for roughly four hours. Lee's homemade pipe bombs, one of which went off when he was shot, were propane canisters containing shotgun shells. Authorities found and detonated four more similar devices.

During the standoff, the three hostages spent most of the time lying on the floor. Lee only infrequently engaged them in conversation, but did say, "I don't care about these people," explaining that his goal of getting the network to show more Darwinism material was more important. Montgomery County Police Chief Thomas Manger said Lee did not expect to come out alive and "told us many times over the course of hours that he was ready to die" (Brumfield and Miller 2010).

The serial killer Jeffrey Dahmer's case is another example. In an interview with Stone Phillips on *Dateline NBC*, which aired November 29, 1994, Dahmer said that if a person does not believe

> that there is a God to be accountable to, then what's the point of trying to modify your behavior to keep it within acceptable ranges? That's how I thought anyway. I always believed the theory of evolution as truth, that we all just came from the slime. When we died, you know, that was it, there is nothing, and I've since come to believe that the Lord, Jesus Christ is truly God, and I believe that I, as well as everyone else, will be accountable to him (quoted in Ratcliff 2006, 55).

Reverend Ratcliff, a Madison, Wisconsin, Church of Christ minister, baptized Dahmer after he professed his Christian faith. Of note is that this segment was removed from the DVD version of the interview (Phillips 2006).

These few modern examples show how easily Darwin's writings can lead to, or at least influence, very disturbed ways of thinking and behaving. Using abortion to produce fitter humans and government programs to control medical decisions based on modern soft eugenics are other contemporary examples (Bergman 2008). Most of us do not feel comfortable leaving these judgments to scientists or politicians.

One example of abortion used to produce "fitter" children is a woman who aborted her first two children because the sonogram of each one showed an extra finger. The doctor in the case later learned that the mother was born with the same condition, which in her case had been effectively dealt with by a fairly minor operation. Yet the doctor reported that she chose to abort two children who had inherited her minor flaw, one that caused few, if any, adverse life consequences (Sewell 2009).

Behavior of those like Pekka-Eric Auvinen, James Lee, Eric Harris, and Jeffrey Dahmer is, albeit on a small scale, not unlike the attitudes once common in Nazi Germany. The explosion in evolutionary psychology that attempts to describe every human behavior, including religion, sexual orientation, occupational interests, and the work ethic as genetically determined, are other modern examples.

Darwinism has caused widespread dehumanization. It has misled us in the past and still does so today — and will likely continue to do so in the near future as a result of the genetics revolution and the ability to select so-called "fitter" children by techniques such as DNA sequencing and *in vitro* fertilization. To defend Darwin, some persons correctly argue that anything can be abused — sex, food, religion, time, evolution, and money. In the case of Darwinism, though, the abuses were often a direct and logical application of the Darwinian survival-of-the-fittest worldview.

References

Anonymous. 2007. Finland Gunman Suicide Note Found. http://news.bbc.co.uk/2/hi/europe/7085329.stm accessed April 18, 2012.

Auvinen, Pekka-Eric. 2007. The Pekka Eric Auvinen Manifesto. http://oddculture.com/odd-crime/the-pekka-eric-auvinen-manifesto/ accessed April 18, 2012.

Aziz, Philippe. 1976. *Doctors of Death. Vol 4, In the Beginning was the Master Race.* Geneva: Ferni Publishers.

Barrett, David, George Kurian, and Todd Johnson. 2001. *World Christian Encyclopedia.* New York: Oxford University Press.

BBC News. 2007. Finland Gunman Suicide Note Found. http://news.bbc.co.uk/2/hi/europe/7085329.stm accessed April 18, 2012.

Bergman, Jerry. 2008. Birth Control Leader Margaret Sanger: Darwinist, Racist and Eugenicist. *Journal of Creation* 22(3):62–67.

———. 2012. *Hitler and the Nazis Darwinian Worldview: How the Nazis Eugenic Crusade for a Superior Race Caused the Greatest Holocaust in World History.* Kitchener, Ontario, Canada: Joshua Press.

Burleigh, Michael. 1999, in Ferguson, 1999. *Virtual History: Alternatives and Counterfactuals.* New York, NY: Basic Books, ch. 6, Nazi Europe: What if Nazi Germany Had Defeated the Soviet Union.

Brumfield, Sarah, and Kathleen Miller. 2010. Police: Discovery Channel Hostages Planned Escape. http://news.yahoo.com/s/ap/us_discovery_channel_gunman. September 2, accessed April 18, 2012.

Cohn, Norman. 1967. *Warrant for Genocide.* New York: Harper and Row.

Dennett, Daniel. 1995. *Darwin's Dangerous Idea: Evolution and the Meanings of Life.* New York, NY: Simon and Schuster.

Derbyshire, John. 2010. Remarks at a Panel Discussion. University of Pennsylvania Law School,

April 5, 2010. http://www.johnderbyshire.com/Opinions/HumanSciences/upennlaw.html, accessed April 18, 2012.

Ferguson, Niall. 1999. Introduction to *Virtual History: Alternatives and Counterfactuals*. New York, NY: Basic Books.

Gaudian, Martin C. 2010. *Memories of Dachau Concentration Camp Experience — May 1945*. Unpublished manuscript. 12/9/2010.

Geyer, Michael, and Sheila Fitzpatrick. 2009. *Beyond Totalitarianism: Stalinism and Nazism Compared*. Cambridge, NY: Cambridge University Press.

Glad, John. 2011. *Jewish Eugenics*. Washington, DC: Wooden Shore Publishers.

Gould, Stephen Jay. 1977. *Ontogeny and Phylogeny*. Cambridge, MA: Harvard University Press.

Jones, J. Sydney. 2002. *Hitler in Vienna, 1907–1913: Clues to the Future*. New York: Cooper Square Press.

Odd Culture. 2007. Deadly Finnish School Shooting Pekka-Eric Auvinen Goes On Rampage. http://oddculture.com/odd-crime/deadly-finnish-school-shooting/, accessed April 18, 2012.

Nyiszli, Miklos. 2011. *Auschwitz: A Doctor's Eyewitness Account*. New York: Arcade Publishing.

Phillips, Stone. 2006. *Inside Evil: Serial Killers Jeffrey Dahmer & Son of Sam*. New York: NBC News. This is the edited DVD version of the show aired on November 29, 1994.

Piotrowski, Tadeusz. 1998. *Poland's Holocaust: Ethnic Strife, Collaboration with Occupying Forces and Genocide in the Second Republic, 1918–1947*. Jefferson, NC: McFarland & Company.

Ratcliff, Roy, with Lindy Adams. 2006. *Dark Journey Deep Grace*. Abilene, TX: Leafwood Publishers.

Sebastian, Sharon, and Raymond Bohlin, 2009. *Darwin's Racists. Yesterday, Today and Tomorrow*. College Station, TX: VBW Publishing.

Sewell, Dennis. 2009. *The Political Gene: How Darwin's Ideas Changed Politics*. London: Picador.

Thornhill, Randy, and Craig T. Palmer. 2000. *A Natural History of Rape: Biological Bases of Sexual Coercion*. Cambridge, MA: The MIT Press.

Williams, David. 2007. YouTube Massacre: Schoolboy Gunman Posts Threat on the Internet Then Kills Eight. http://www.dailymail.co.uk/news/article-492268/YouTube-massacre-Schoolboy-gunman-posts-threat-internet-kills-eight.html, accessed April 18, 2012, and http://www.dailymail.co.uk/news/article-492268/YouTube-massacre-Schoolboy-gunman-posts-threat-internet-kills-eight.html#ixzz10B9Arehw, accessed April 18, 2012.

Chapter 2

The Origins of Biological Racism

Introduction

Biological racism as we know it today did not exist throughout most of history. Racism has a surprisingly recent origin and parallels the rise of evolutionary thought. At the earliest, it can be traced back to the Renaissance. This chapter documents the importance of Darwinism in producing the concept of biological race and, along with it, the racism and strife that has flourished in America and elsewhere for the last two centuries. If all races were equally fit, as indeed they are, evolution could not occur, because whether or not a particular race survived would depend on chance, not the alleged superiority of the race. Race is not a biological but a sociological construct.

A Short History of Biological Racism

The origin of Western civilization (and many other modern civilizations) was in the Middle East–Mediterranean lands — an area of the world that, in some ways, is still similar to what it was thousands of years ago. Home to Aristotle, Plato, Moses, and Christ, this part of the world created the philosophical, cultural, religious, and scientific bedrock of our modern world. We are fortunate in having a relatively large amount of writings from those who lived in this region centuries before Christ. From this record, we can ascertain that the people living in the Middle East before Christ consisted of a mixture of racial groups.

Among those who formed part of this early melting pot were many people from nearby Africa. The African continent was in the southwestern corner of the middle-eastern world and ensured the presence of many Black Africans who ultimately played a prominent role in forming what we today know as our 21st-century society. We, though, can only guess if a specific person was of African descent. If someone is said to be from Ethiopia, we can guess with more confidence, but in the historical record there often exists only indirect hints of a person's biological race (Haller 1971). The reason for this is very simple: *for most of human history, skin color simply was not relevant to most discussions* of people any more so than eye or hair color.

Occasionally, an historical account would mention that a person was left-handed, had much body hair, or possessed brown skin, but this typically was the case *only* if this information was relevant to the situation under discussion, and these traits were rarely germane. The reason that physical traits were rarely mentioned is that *for most of history, people were not discussed by biological "racial" traits, but rather according to culture, language, religion, or other nonracial factors.* The city where a person lived was very important, as was his tribal background, such as which one of the 12 tribes of Israel one was from, but biological "race" was not important. It was not even part of the consciousness of the people.

Skin color was of little importance in most parts of the world throughout much of recorded history. One reason this was true for the Middle East was because *most* people there had naturally olive brown skin, due in part to long-term intermarriage between the various peoples there. In fact, *most* non-Oriental people in the world then and now have brown skin (Kottak 2004). Most people at that time spent long hours in the sun and tanned to the degree that inherited skin color was often of minor relevance.

In Portugal (and most other countries in that area of the world), it was often very difficult (and remains so today) to distinguish the "races" of the people

Plato's teachings greatly influenced Western philosophy.

living there. Furthermore, it is a universal trend that the *closer* to the equator a people live, the *darker* their skin color tends to be. The farther north one lives, the lighter his or her skin is likely to be. The lightest-complexioned people are northern Europeans (especially the Scandinavians and northern Germans), while the darkest Europeans are those who live in the South.

The same is true in Africa — the skin color and other racial traits of Africans vary enormously today and always have. Americans frequently have a distorted view of skin color, partially because the majority of Afro-Americans originally came from west-central Africa near the equator, while the majority of whites emigrated from northern Europe. Consequently, the two most extreme skin colors in the world have lived side by side in America for decades.

In many ways it was appropriate that Christ and the Apostles came from a part of the world where they could not be classified accurately as either Whites or Blacks, since the people in the Middle East generally had an olive-brown skin color (a color in the middle) and dark, often black, hair color. It is true that many Jews in Israel today have very white skin, but this is partially because many of the light-complexioned groups immigrated to Israel from countries such as Russia.

The Beginning of the Idea of "Biological Race"

In both the Western world and the Judeo-Christian-Muslim world, until about the time of Darwin, most people believed that all men and women were descendants of Adam and Eve — a view called **monogenism** — thus, all humans were literally brothers and sisters (Ham et al. 1999; Johnson 2000). Consequently, the *most* that can be said is that one branch of the human family had curlier hair, another had lighter skin, and yet another had certain facial features.

These differences would mean no more than if scattered members in a large family today had red hair, a trait that is often noted by comments such as, "Your daughter has Grandma's red hair." The concept of "race" as we think of it today never would have entered one's mind until about the time of the scientific revolution in the 16th century and increased significantly after Darwin. In Professor's Gould's words, "Biological arguments for racism may have been common before 1859, but they increased by orders of magnitude following the acceptance of evolutionary theory" (1977, 127).

People have historically tended to assume they were better than those who were culturally different, but most ideas of *biological* racial inferiority are fairly recent. Although some individuals developed ingenious ideas to justify the conclusion that Blacks were inferior, such as that God created them as a separate race (some argued that the "beasts of the earth" discussed in Genesis was the Black race), this view never has held much weight in historical Christian theology — Protestant, Catholic, or Orthodox (Hasskarl 1898; Hall 1977; Isherwood 2000; Evola 1970). As Proctor opined:

> Prior to Darwin, it was difficult to argue against the Judeo-Christian conception of the unity of man, based on the single creation of Adam and Eve. Darwin's theory suggested that humans had evolved over hundreds of thousands, even millions of years, and that the races of men had diverged while adapting to the particularities of local conditions. The impact of Darwin's theory was enormous (1988, 14).

Until the widespread acceptance of evolution, the only religious justification for racism was the belief that God cursed certain groups or created other men who were inferior before He created Adam — a view called **polygenism**. Some evolutionists justified condemning so-called race mixing based on the polygenism belief that Whites descended from chimps, Blacks from gorillas, and Orientals from orangutans (Crookshank 1924, 1931).

These inferior races could be identified by physical traits such as skin color. Others taught that some groups biologically degenerated more than others — but were still our brothers. As Gould notes, "Nearly all scientists were creationists before 1859, and most did not become polygenists" (1996, 75). Professors Walbank and Taylor conclude that

> Darwinism led to racism and anti-Semitism and was used to show that only "superior" nationalities and races were fit to survive. Thus, among the English-speaking peoples were to be found the champions of the "white man's burden," an imperial mission carried out by Anglo-Saxons. . . . Similarly, the Russians preached the doctrine of pan-Slavism and the Germans that of pan-Germanism (1961, 361, Vol. 2).

One of the first departures from the human family model as presented in the book of Genesis was Linnaeus's classification of humans into his binomial nomenclature system as *Homo sapiens, Homo monstrous*, and *Homo ferus* (Fiedler 1978, 240). Fiedler concluded that implicit in Linnaeus's classification was "the assumption of a hierarchal order, which beginning with 'monstrous man,' mounts to 'wild man,' and climbing upward through black, brown, yellow, and red men" then climaxed in the white Europeans. The result was a taxonomic system that contributed to creating the new "mythology of 'race' " that later culminated with social Darwinism via biological racism (Fiedler 1978, 240).

A pupil of Linnaeus named Fabricus tried to explain how he had concluded that the "inferiority of the Negroes" was the result of "cross-breeding between humans and simians. . . . Moreover, further mating between black and white, which is to say, miscegenation in the second degree, produced — according to 19th-century anthropology — mulattos, sterile offspring like the mating of horses and asses" (Fiedler 1978, 240).

Another thinker who made a major contribution to the modern concept of race was Voltaire. In the late 1700s, he taught that "the white man is to the Black as the Black is to the monkey" (quoted in Fiedler 1978, 240). Fiedler concluded that "such racist mythology did not play a major role in the [new racists'] perception of non-Europeans by Europeans until the triumph of the theory of organic evolution in Darwin's" work *The Origin of Species by Means of the Preservation of Favored Races in the Struggle for Life* and "its extension by analogy into early developmental anthropology. Darwin taught that without deviance, adaptation, and the 'survival of the fittest,' evolution would never have occurred" (Fiedler 1978, 240). Almost all of Darwin's early readers understood him as concluding that the struggle to survive does not cease when one moves from the biological to the social or cultural plane.

> This second "ascent of man," the new anthropology taught, has raised men from "primitivism" or "savagery" to "civilization," from a culture without the alphabet or the wheel to one with a printing press and an advanced technology, from, in short, the "nasty, brutish and short" life eked out in most of the world to the kind enjoyed in Europe (Fiedler 1978, 240–241).

Fiedler concludes that the new biological racists' theory was shared by "Darwin and Marx and the founding fathers of modern anthropology." This biological racism became more and more common after 1859 and was

> made brutally explicit in Thomas Dixon Jr.'s popular novel *The Leopard's Spots*. Published in 1902, it inspired in 1915 D.W. Griffith's great film *The Birth of a Nation*, which, as its subtitle, *A Romance of the White Man's Burden — 1865–1900*, makes clear, sought to justify the Ku Klux Klan. In its climactic scene, a white father says

to the Harvard-educated "mulatto" who has asked for his daughter's hand, "I happen to know the important fact that a man or woman of Negro ancestry, though a century removed, will suddenly breed back to a pure Negro child, thick-lipped, kinky-headed, flat-nosed, black-skinned. One drop of your blood in my family could push it backward three thousand years in history" (Fiedler 1978, 241–242).

In contrast, Christianity has taught (and most of the Western world historically has believed) that, regardless of what physical traits a person possesses, he or she still is part of the one human family (Ham et al. 1999). Equally important, Christianity has also taught that a person's worth is to be determined by the contents of his or her heart. The physical traits of a family member do not divide a family, but behavioral traits sometimes do.

Even during the early development of America — although conflicts clearly existed because of nationality, competition, and language differences — divisions because of "race" were rare. Large numbers of free Blacks lived in the early United States. In 1800, about 20 percent of the population were listed as "Negro," and we are just now beginning to realize the important contribution that they made to early American history.

One of the first persons to die in the American Revolutionary War was Crispus Attucks, a black male — a fact that was rarely mentioned for many years, at least by Northerners, simply because his skin color was not deemed important any more than were any of his other physical features. *What* he did was considered more noteworthy. Of course this was not true in the Southern states.

The difficulty in knowing the skin color of a historically significant person is due to the fact that skin color was most often *not* relevant and, thus, was rarely mentioned. Even for those persons about whom we know a great deal, we often know little about the traits that would help us classify them according to current biological "racial" divisions. Some evidence exists that a diverse group of well-known people may have had what we today regard as Negroid traits, including Hannibal, Grimaldi, Cheopes (most famous for his monument *The Great Pyramid of Cheopes*, one of the seven wonders of the ancient world), perhaps even Moses, and others.

Evidently, the Elamites (and possibly some Persians and Phoenicians) had "Negro" traits.

The Pentateuch, the first five books of the Bible, were given through Moses by God's Spirit.

The fact that people with "Negroid" traits existed in one of the centers of the origins of Western culture is especially apparent from historical paintings and statues. Probably the most famous example of a statue with Negroid traits is the Sphinx in Egypt. No one knows for certain the racial traits of the Elamites because it was not seen as relevant to their history.

In history as a whole, marriage between different "races" and groups occurred to the extent that all humans have a mixed racial ancestry. When the Israelites were led out of Egypt by Moses, they took a "mixed multitude" with them. The Israelites discussed in the biblical record were constantly chastised for taking "foreign wives," and King Solomon's downfall was attributed to his many foreign spouses and concubines. Yet, never once was concern expressed regarding "racial mixing." Rather, the concern was always the *adverse effect of pagan cultures* and their beliefs on the Israelites.

In fact, so much race mixing has occurred historically that even if classifications that are useful today could be applied, huge numbers of the population would be what was once described as "mulattos" (Rogers 1970). So-called race mixing (miscegenation) was common even in early America — a notable possible example being the third president of the United States, Thomas Jefferson, or his brother or nephews, was evidently the father of several mulatto children (Rogers 1970, 8). The level of race mixing existed to the degree that some historians estimate that the entire American White population today is as much as 5 percent Black (Stuart 1973). In a study of Black-White marriages in the United States from 1874 to 1965, Bruce and Rodman (1973) found that they numbered in the thousands, even where state law barred such unions.

Biological "Races" Do Not Exist

The use of quotes around the term "race" in the title stresses the fact that anthropological research today has shown that *race, in a strict biological sense, does not exist* (Kottak 2004). Barzun notes that

> contrary to common opinion, no set of fixed characteristics occurs in human beings as a constant distinguishing mark of race. So-called Nordics have long skulls, but so have many so-called Negroes, the Eskimos, and the anthropoid apes. The "Mongolian" birth-spot occurs among whites, and the Ainos of Japan frequently show features that should class them as "Nordics" (Barzun 1965, 8).

In his extensive study of race, Phillip V. Tobias of Witwatersrand University in Johannesburg, South Africa, concluded that the "term race is only a crude summary for many physiological and genetic traits that, under close scrutiny, prove to vary greatly" (quoted in Plog 1970, 196).

Even defining race is fraught with problems. One reason is that the difference between the various "races" of humans is small compared to many animals (such as various types of dogs, for example). Comparing even the most divergent humans — an Australian Aborigine and a Swede, for example — reveals that the two groups are relatively similar when compared to a Lhasa Apso and a Chihuahua or a Greyhound and a Pekingese.

People see great differences between some human groups, but objective physical comparisons of traits in animals (such as the smallest and the largest dog) reveal a hundred times more contrast than found in humans — equivalent to a short race of men being four feet tall on average, and the tallest towering over ten feet on average. Even the facial features of dogs vary enormously. Compare the Pekingese snout, which is almost nonexistent, with the long Collie snout, which is eight or more times as long.

The differences between humans are so minuscule that it is now concluded only one "breed" of humans exists — in contrast to over 206 breeds of dogs. Furthermore, greater physical differences exist between, for example, the Australian Aborigines and Afro-Americans than between the typical Afro-American and European American.

The idea that there existed three "races" of humans was perpetuated by physical anthropologists who "once held . . . that there were originally clearly differentiated Negro, Caucasoid, and Mongoloid groups and that the innumerable intermediate types which now link the extreme examples of each stock came about as a result of crossing" (Linton 1955, 21). Many saw certain races, such as "the Negro" as the "missing link" between apes and humans (Hasskarl 1898).

The "innumerable intermediate" human types that did not fit into *any* of the three stereotype races allowed acceptance of the three-race concept while limiting the many exceptions that existed. We recognize today that this idea is erroneous — there are far too many exceptions — and no evidence exists that three "races" exist or descended from three different primates, as once was commonly supposed (Montagu 1999; Williams 1997).

A century ago, a three-classification system was used — the so-called White, Black, and Yellow races. Then, further anthropological work forced researchers to add several new categories, including Polynesian, American Indian, Eskimo, Australian Aborigine, African Pygmy, and others. Further research then concluded that 12 races existed, and then 18. Soon, however, 27 different races were required to categorize all humans then known.

Eventually, our increase in knowledge made the concept of race an unworkable means of grouping humans (Kottak 2004). It was realized, in the words of the famous anthropologist Ruth Benedict, "The Bible story of Adam and Eve, father and mother of the whole human race, told centuries ago . . . related the same truth that science has shown today; that all peoples of the earth are a single family and have a common origin" (1943, 171).

Some Christians argued that separate creations of the races occurred, but "this was offensive to the faithful who preferred something which remained compatible with the Biblical original pair" (Brace and Livingstone 1999, 209). Barzun called "race" a "superstition" and added that, in the past, most scientists unfortunately supported "race-thinking." An example would be Sir Arthur Keith, who spent a "great deal of time and energy stressing the value of race-prejudice in modern life and urging the necessity of conflict among races as a means of improving the species" by survival of the fittest via evolution (Barzun 1965, 5).

Professor Richard Goldsby (1971) acknowledges the fact that *diversity* exists among humans but concludes the system that works best to partition persons into races uses traits that can be measured scientifically. Skin color is a common method but rapidly breaks down as more people are examined. Almost one-third of the world's population possesses decidedly dark, swarthy skin, yet very "white" facial features and, therefore, are classified as "white." This includes people from India and Sri Lanka and many other countries with dark-skinned people (Kottak 2004).

Because of pre-1960 American racism, thousands of light-skinned Afro-Americans were able to "pass" each year and live in the "white" world to avoid discrimination. Similar problems exist with *any* trait or method that we use (even genetic ones) to classify humans into races. Goldsby concludes that in order to be scientific, a classification scheme would require use of a blood type status system, because the science of blood-typing has provided the most reliable and objective indicator of "racial identity." This is hardly what most people think of today when they refer to race.

The difficulty of racial classification became especially prominent in countries that have endeavored to base legal status on race — such as Nazi Germany, which by law defined a person

> as Jewish who "descended from at least three grandparents who were racially fully Jews [or] . . . one who descended from two full Jewish parents if (a) he belonged to a Jewish community at the time this law was issued or he joined the community later; (b) he was married to a Jewish person at the time that this law was issued or married one subsequently; (c) is the offspring from marriage with a Jew contracted after the law for the protection of German blood and German honor became effected; (d) is the offspring of an extramarital relationship with a Jew and was born out of wedlock" (quoted in Goldsby 1971, 6–7).

This law, which defined race according to ancestry as well as current social involvement, was almost impossible to apply consistently and objectively. Since this specific law did not specify *how far back* one needed to go to determine if one had three Jewish grandparents "who were racially fully Jews" the first part of the definition applied to a large number of Europeans.

Another illustration of this is related to the author's ethnic background, Finnish — a "race" that was mixed with mongoloids originally from Mongolia — people who are not pure Europeans as is sometimes supposed. Those Orientals who remained behind in Europe to rear families after the Mongolian invasions of Europe mixed with native peoples, producing modern Finns. Most people are unaware of this fact because, due to extensive intermarriage, most Finns today only have faint indications of Mongoloid ancestry. The same is true of the Hungarians (historically called Magyar Koztarsasars).

The Origin of the Biological "Race" Concept

Many divergent theories have been postulated by evolutionists to explain human diversity. One theory that was commonly accepted for years suggested that Blacks were less evolved humans and that Whites were the highest evolved of all human races. *Hunter's Biology*, a popular American textbook that was allegedly used by John Scopes to teach evolution when he substitute taught for a biology class and, consequently, figured prominently in the Scopes trial, ranked the human races in this way.

One of the major factors that historically was used to classify race was brain size. Thorough investigation of the conclusion that the races differ in this trait (specifically, the cortex) found that, although brain size is clearly related to body size and age, far greater differences exist *within* the races than *between* the races (Plog 1970). Research on intellectually gifted persons has found that brain size varies enormously within this group (Plog 1970, 196–197).

Many evolutionists believe that the skin color of our human ancestors was originally dark brown and only recently has evolved into lighter forms. When putative human ancestors such as *Australopithecus* and others are drawn by artists, they are typically presented with black or dark-brown skin and stereotypical "Negro" facial features. In fact, scientists have no idea of the skin colors of the creatures that are hypothesized to be human ancestors. If you ever shave a gorilla, a chimpanzee, or an orangutan, you will find they *all* have white skin!

Darker skin and hair are protective against skin cancer; the lighter the complexion, the greater the likelihood of developing skin cancer. Although many skin carcinomas, such as squamous and basal, frequently are not lethal, melanoma usually is. Tanning is the body's response to dangerous ultraviolet radiation — the tan protects the skin from these rays, which are the primary cause of skin cancer. If lighter skin has evolved, this would be an example of devolution, because an important biological protective system for those living in hot, sunny latitudes has been *lost*.

The differences in the skin color of "races" is not due to the number of *melanocytes* (the cells that produce melanin pigment), but to a difference in melanin *production levels*. Whites and Blacks both have the same number of melanocytes; the difference is *only* in the *amount* of melanin that they secrete (lighter skin tones are considered "melanin deficient" by oncologists). An even greater difficulty in classifying people on the basis of skin color is the fact that the color changes due to maturation, disease, or hormonal changes:

> Many babies of all races are born with lighter skins than they will have as adults. More babies are born with light eyes and blond hair than ever reach maturity as blonds. Some babies' eyes will turn brown in the first months of life, while their hair may gradually darken over the first one to five years of childhood. Others who reach adolescence with light brown hair will have dark brown hair by middle life. A much smaller group remain light all their lives. On the other hand, no normal babies are born with dark skin, eyes, or hair and then gradually lighten as they grow up (Gorney 1973, 611–612).

Why Race Is Critical to Evolution

The complete title of Darwin's most famous work is *The Origin of Species by Means of Natural Selection or the Preservation of Favored Races in the Struggle for Life*. The concept of race was not just critical to the whole Darwinian theory but was also based on the conclusion that some races were *superior* and would therefore eventually win out in the struggle for life. Darwin first discussed human evolution in his book *The Descent of Man, and Selection in Relation to Sex*, first published in 1871. He based this conclusion on the fact that there exist observable biological differences not only between animal kinds but also within *any one* animal kind.

Darwin's "The Origin of Species" with the full title, "by Means of the Preservation of Favored Races in the Struggle for Life."

The theory went beyond this and argued that such differences can confer an evolutionary advantage which aids in the struggle against other animals for life, both those of its own animal kind and other kinds of animals. In other words, a rabbit that can run slightly faster or that has slightly better hearing than other rabbits is more likely to escape its enemies and, as a result, is more likely to survive and pass this advantage on to its offspring.

The theory of "survival of the fittest" is evolution's main support and represents the major contribution that Darwin made to the success of the concept of evolution. A key aspect of evolution was the belief that superior races would win in the competition for food, mates, and everything else needed for life. The evolutionarily "less fit" would be more apt to die, would leave fewer offspring and, as a result, would eventually become extinct. We are, evolutionists have stressed, the offspring of the survivors in the struggle for life. If there were no differences between the races, evolution could not occur, because significant differences must exist so natural selection will have something from which to select. John Koster summarizes Darwin's view on race as follows:

> Darwin . . . never considered "the less civilized races" to be authentically human. . . . his writings reek with all kinds of contempt for "primitive" people. Racism was culturally conditioned into educated Victorians by such "scientific" parlor tricks as Morton's measuring of brainpans with BB shot to prove that Africans and Indians had

small brains and hence had defects in minds and intellects (1988, 50).

Darwin's own words were clear on this point when he was comparing what he called "primitive races" with Europeans:

> I could not have believed how wide was the difference between savage and civilized man; it is greater than between a wild and domestic animal. . . . Viewing such a man, one could hardly make oneself believe that they are fellow creatures and inhabitants of the same world (1959, 141).

Darwin concluded that the "savage races" included the Negro, Australian Aborigines, and others, all of whom were inferior and, therefore, eventually would become extinct (Bergman 1993). Many saw the discovery of "strange peoples" resulting from the worldwide exploration that occurred in the 1600s and 1700s as confirming evolution — the missing link was not missing but was alive and lived in Australia and Africa.

Darwinism is racism to the degree that racism is a synonym for evolutionism. The term now used is *speciation,* although some evolutionists use more respectable terms such as "differential survival." Darwinism teaches that ultimately, our "creator" consists of mutations and the eventual extinction of the inferior races as a result of the fact that the members of these groups are less fit, that is, inferior. Many evolutionists went much further than Darwin and, in fact, *virtually all evolutionists* accepted the idea of biological race inferiority until recently (Haller 1971). Many historians of science today also recognize that nearly all scientists were creationists before evolution took hold (Gould 1980, 43).

Only after creationism lost its dominance in science could ideas about biological racism develop to the extent that they did in history. The racism perpetuated by Darwin was found in virtually every science book from the middle 1800s until the 1930s. In short, "Darwinism led to racism and anti-Semitism and was used to show that only 'superior' nationalities and races were fit to survive" (Walbank and Taylor 1961, 361). It was only in the 1940s, especially due to work like Montagu's 1953 book, *Man's Most Dangerous Myth: The Fallacy of Race,* that biological racism started to decline significantly.

Although Darwin's work was enormously important in popularizing evolution, evolutionary ideas were actually discussed extensively by scholars *before* he published his classic work, *The Origin of Species.* Darwin's own grandfather, Erasmus Darwin, in his classic work *Zoonomia,* developed a theory of evolution very similar to that which Darwin eventually elaborated. As King-Hele stated, "The credit for first propounding a well-rounded theory of evolution, with examples and support belongs [not to Charles Darwin, but] instead to Erasmus Darwin" (1963, 67). This same author concluded that Erasmus "believed in evolution for many years, probably since 1771" (1963, 67).

Partly for this reason, the evidence for evolutionary hierarchy of the races was a prominent topic of many books and articles before Darwin's work was published. Brace and Livingstone note that attempts to justify social inequalities on the basis of innate biological differences can be extended back to the Renaissance, partly because of the development of a pre-Darwinian "form of evolution by means of a crudely conceived kind of natural selection" (1999, 209). Many Christians rejected these racial views, although some attempted to accommodate them with Christianity because it was felt that they had been "proven" by science to be true.

Application of Evolution to Social Policy

The eventual outcome of the racism that Darwin taught was an attempt to apply the conclusions of Darwinian scientists to government. The best example is Adolf Hitler, who endeavored to produce a superior race by preventing the inferior races from breeding with the "superior" ones. Those that Hitler concluded were inferior included "Negroids, Jews, Gypsies," and other groups. In the words of Tennenbaum, "The political philosophy of the . . . German state was built on the ideas of struggle, selection, and survival of the fittest, all notions and observations arrived at . . . by Darwin" (1956, 211).

The importance of Darwinism to Nazism was critical, and "although it is no easy task to fully assess the conflicting motives of Hitler and his party, eugenics clearly played an important part. If the Nazi party had fully embraced and consistently acted on the belief that all humans are brothers, equal before God . . . the Holocaust probably would have never occurred" (Bergman 1992, 122).

The direct head-on conflict between Christianity and Darwinism in the field of race research was historically recognized by many scientists. Eminent British biologist Sir Arthur Keith, who was knighted for his scientific contributions, stated, "Christianity makes no distinction of race or of color; it seeks to break down all racial barriers. In this respect, the hand of Christianity is against that of Nature [evolution], for are not the races of mankind the evolutionary harvest which Nature has toiled through long ages to produce?" (1946, 72).

The opposition to religion by many scientists of the past was due to the fact that they believed Christianity worked against evolution by helping inferior races and opposing racism. Evolutionists once taught that natural selection pruned out the weak, reducing the likelihood that they reproduced and passed inferior genes on to offspring. Conversely, Christianity focused on supporting the weak, helping the needy, and protecting those who could not protect themselves. Hitler actually expressed contempt for Christians because of their aiding "Negroes" in Africa and believed that Negroes were "monstrosities half way between man and ape." Then he "lambasted the fact of Christians going to 'Central Africa' to set up 'Negro missions,' resulting in the turning of 'healthy . . . human beings into a rotten brood of bastards'" (Humber 1987, ii).

Hitler discussed this topic extensively in a chapter of *Mein Kampf* titled "Nation and Race" in which he concluded that the stronger must dominate the weaker. Marriage between inferior races was condemned, and it was considered the "natural" Darwinian right of the superior races to enslave the inferior ones. This is why Hitler enacted extensive legislation to prevent "Aryans" from "inter-breeding" with "inferior races," including "Jews, Negroes, and others" (Humber 1987, ii).

The Nazis concluded that their theory had been proven by science, which was one reason why they opposed Christianity (Burleigh 2000). German scientists published a whopping *13* scientific journals devoted to "racial hygiene" and also set up numerous "scientific institutions," many of which were connected with major universities or research centers devoted to "racial science" (Proctor 1988). Racism was not a German fascination alone. In fact, German eugenicists actually relied heavily upon the scientists doing research in Britain and America, since in many ways eugenics research was more advanced in the United States (in spite of the enormous attention that the German government gave to it). A major focus of this research was to determine which races had the most "primitive racial traits," that is, those traits that were prominent in inferior races such as the Neanderthals.

A 1934 edition of Hitler's *Mein Kampf* (My Struggle).

Interracial Marriage and Biology

Most evolutionists once condemned what was called miscegenation (interracial marriage) because they thought that marrying a member of an "inferior race" would produce children who, likewise, were inferior. Miscegenation only would bring the race down and pollute it, they feared, causing devolution. Reducing miscegenation was part of the *eugenics* (meaning well-born) movement. Most scientists in the early 1900s accepted this conclusion and, because of this belief, many states and countries passed laws against miscegenation. Not uncommonly, even mixed sex interracial socialization was strongly condemned by many communities (Gallagher 1999).

We now know that so-called interracial marriages tend to produce children that are physically *healthier* than average. The reason is because the *closer* a married couple is genetically, the greater the likelihood is that both will have the same recessive mutations (which may show up in the offspring as disease). However, if two people who are racially mixed marry, because they are genetically further apart, the likelihood of both of them having a mutation on the same gene is extremely small. Sickle cell anemia, a major problem among Blacks, is extremely rare among first-generation interracial marriages. Once again, scientific research has shown that the Darwinian race hypothesis is wrong.

Unfortunately, Christians are all too often influenced by the society around them and for years condemned interracial marriage. This is why the Scriptures teach that Christians should be "without spot from the world" (1 Peter 1:19) and their life wholly guided by the Scriptures. In addition, some condemn interracial marriage for a very pragmatic reason; namely, if the frequency of interracial marriage continues to be high, the obliteration of a group's unique physical differences will eventually occur. Because brown features are dominant, in time, high levels of interracial marriage will produce a population with predominantly brown hair, brown skin, and brown eyes. Intermarriage already has reduced many of the ethnic differences that originally existed in the American population. Most Americans are a mixture of several races — a trend that is especially common in the darker races.

Once condemned by the science of the day, we now know that interracial marriages tend to produce children that are physically healthier than average.

What Does This History Tell Us?

It is my conclusion that if the biblical record of human origins was fully accepted and put into practice, much of the grief and tragedy that has resulted from "racial" conflicts in America, Germany, and elsewhere never would have occurred:

> Adam and Eve are the traditional human pair in Christendom, but they hardly help if one is looking for distinct races in mankind. One pair of ancestors would obviously make us all of one race. How [to] account for the "striking differences" that caught our attention earlier [was a problem]? (Barzun 1965, 9).

The idea of biological race is a recent idea that evolved, in part, from evolutionary naturalism and "was a mode of thought endemic in Western civilization [and is] a Western phenomenon" (Barzun, 6). Unfortunately, "the greatest, as well as the weakest, minds of the past century have yielded to its lure" (Barzun, 6). The tragedy of race, the Holocaust, and the slaughter of an estimated one billion persons since 1900 alone by nations in wars, purges, genocides, and other organized killings could have been avoided if people had fully internalized the biblical teaching that all humans, as children of Adam, are brothers and sisters. It is only when we recognize that biological races do not exist — and that all humans are one species that manifests much variety — will full "racial" harmony be achieved (Ham et al. 1999). Race is a social construction.

References

Barzun, Jacques. 1965. *Race: A Study in Superstition.* New York: Harper and Row.

Benedict, Ruth. 1943. *Race, Science and Politics.* 2nd ed. New York: The Viking Press.

Bergman, Jerry. 1992. "Eugenics and the Development of Nazi Race Policy." *Perspectives on Science and Christian Faith*, 44(2):109–123.

———. 1993. "Evolution and the Origins of the Biological Race Theory." *CEN Tech. Journal* 7(2):155–168.

Brace, C. Loring, and Frank Livingstone. 1999. "On Creeping Jensenism," in Montagu, 1999.

Bruce, James D., and Hyman Rodman. 1973. "Black-white Marriage in the United States: A Review of the Empirical Literature." Chapter 9 in Stewart and Abt 1973.

Burleigh, Michael. 2000. *The Third Reich; A New History.* New York: Hill and Wang.

Crookshank, F.G. 1924. *The Mongol in Our Midst; A Study of Man and His Three Faces.* New York: E.P. Dutton and Company.

———. 1931. *The Mongol in Our Midst: A Study of Man and His Three Faces, Greatly Revised Edition.* London: Kegan Paul, Trench, Truber & Co.

Darwin, Charles. 1959. *The Voyage of the Beagle.* New York: Harper and Row.

Evola, Julius. 1970. *Race as a Revolutionary Idea.* Arab, LA: Western Unity Research Institute.

Fiedler, Leslie. 1978. *Freaks: Myths and Images of the Secret Self.* New York: Simon and Schuster.

Gallagher, Nancy. 1999. *Breeding Better Vermonters; The Eugenics Projects in the Green Mountain State.* Hanover, VT: University Press of New England.

Goldsby, Richard A. 1971. *Race and Races.* New York: The Macmillan Company.

Gorney, Roderic. 1973. *The Human Agenda.* New York: Bantam Books.

Gould, Stephen J. 1977. *Ontogeny and Phylogeny.* Cambridge, MA: Belknap-Harvard.

———. 1980. "Wallace's Fatal Flaw." *Natural History*, January, 89(1).

———. 1996. *The Mismeasure of Man.* New York: Norton.

Haller, John S., Jr. 1971. *Outcasts From Evolution; Scientific Attitudes to Racial Inferiority, 1859-1900.* Urbana, IL: University of Illinois Press.

Hall, Marshall, and Sander. 1977. *The Connection Between Evolution, Theory and Racism.* Lakeland, FL: P/R Publishers.

Ham, Ken, Carl Wieland, and Don Batten. 1999. *One Blood: The Biblical Answer to Racism.* Green Forest, AR: Master Books.

Hasskarl, G.H. 1898. *The Missing Link; or the Negroes Ethnological Status.* Chambersburg, PA: The Democratic News.

Humber, Paul. 1987. "The Ascent of Racism." *Impact*, Feb., 1–4.

Isherwood, H.B. 2000. *Man's Racial Nature.* Metairie, LA: Sons of Liberty.

Johnson, Phillip. 2000. *The Wedge of Truth.* Downers Grove, IL: InterVarsity.

Keith, Arthur. 1946. *Evolution and Ethics.* New York: G.P. Putnam and Sons.

King-Hele, Desmond. 1963. *Erasmus Darwin: Grandfather of Charles Darwin.* New York: Charles Scribner's Sons.

Koster, John. 1988. *The Atheist Syndrome.* Brentwood, TN: Wolgemuth and Hyatt Publishers.

Kottak, Conrad. 2004. *Anthropology: The Exploration of Human Diversity.* New York: McGraw Hill.

Linton, Ralph. 1955. *The Tree of Culture.* New York: Alfred A. Knopf.

Montagu, Ashley. 1953. *Man's Most Dangerous Myth: The Fallacy of Race.* New York: Harper.

——— (editor). 1999. *Race and I.Q.* New York: Oxford University Press.

Plog, Fred. 1970. "Anthropology," in *1971 World Book Yearbook.* Chicago, IL: Field Enterprises Educational Corporation.

Proctor, Robert N. 1988. *Racial Hygiene; Medicine Under the Nazis.* Cambridge, MA: Harvard University Press.

Rogers, J.A. 1970. *100 Amazing Facts About the Negro: With Complete Proof.* New York: Helga M. Rogers.

Stuart, Irving R., and Lawrence E. Abt. 1973. *Interracial Marriage: Expectations and Realities.* New York: Grossman Publishers.

Tennenbaum, Joseph. 1956. *Race and Reich.* New York: Twayne Publishers.

Walbank, T. Walter, and Alastair M. Taylor. 1961. *Civilizations Past and Present.* 4th ed. New York: Scott Foreman Company.

Williams, David. 1997. "Race and Health: Basic Questions, Emerging Directions." *Annals of Epidemiology.* 7:322–333.

Chapter 3

Darwin's Cousin, Sir Francis Galton, and the Eugenics Movement

A central plank in Nazism, communism, and other totalitarianism movements was eugenics (Bergman 2012). Eugenics, the "science" of improving the human race by scientific control of breeding, was viewed by a large percentage of all life scientists, professors, and social reformers for over a century as an important, if not a major, means of accomplishing the goal of producing paradise on earth (Sewell 2009).

The formal founder of this new science was Sir Francis Galton, a cousin and close associate of Charles Darwin. Galton's work was critical in providing the foundation for a movement that culminated in contributing to the loss of tens of millions of lives, and untold suffering of hundreds of millions of people.

The now-infamous eugenics movement grew from the core concepts of biological evolution — primarily those ideas expounded by Charles Darwin

(Gould 1996; Himmelfarb 1959; Shannon 1920; Haller 1971; Barzun 1958). In fact, all the leading figures in the eugenics movement, including Pearson, Davenport, Forel, Ploetz, Schallmayer, etc., not just Galton, consistently maintained that Darwinism was central to their eugenics.

Eugenics took a firm hold in most western European nations and the United States, where it was translated into social policy, and remnants still exist in an academic field called sociobiology (Sahlins 1977). Eugenics was the "legitimate offspring of Darwinian evolution, a natural and doubtless inevitable outgrowth of currents of thought that developed from the publication in 1859 of Charles Darwin's *The Origin of Species*" (Haller 1984, 3). The best example is from Darwin's 1871 book:

> We civilized men . . . do our utmost to check the process of elimination; we build asylums . . . we institute poor laws. . . . vaccination has preserved thousands, who from a weak constitution would formerly have succumbed to small-pox. Thus the weak members of civilized societies propagate their kind. No one who has attended to the breeding of domestic animals will doubt that this must be highly injurious to the race of man. It is surprising how soon a want of care, or care wrongly directed, leads to the degeneration of a domesticated race; but excepting in the case of man himself, hardly anyone is so ignorant as to allow his worst animals to breed (1871, Vol 1, 168).

An example of the racism that Darwin produced is illustrated in the following quote from a widely used zoology text in the 1920s:

> The gulf between the most highly civilized and capable races of Europeans and the degraded brute-like African pygmies is so vast that some authorities are impelled to conclude that they belong to distinct species, or at least to subspecies (Newman 1925, 403).

This tragic application, some would argue misapplication, of Darwinism eventually contributed to the Nazi Holocaust and other destructive social movements such as eugenics (Proctor 1988). A critically important player in this movement was Francis Galton (1822–1911), the nephew of Erasmus Darwin, and the younger cousin to Charles Darwin. Galton was independently wealthy and never held a scientific or teaching post. Best known for his work as the founder of eugenics, he argued that it was largely genetics ("nature") that determined human intellect. Thus, our destiny was fixed at conception and, in the belief that certain people were superior, he strongly advocated controlled breeding to maintain the finest ruling classes (Taylor 2001).

Galton's lifelong eugenic crusade began with his acceptance of macro-evolution (Bynum 2002, 379). The publication of Darwin's *Origin of Species* transformed Galton's life and removed "any lingering religious sentiments" he had had before reading Darwin (Bynum 2002, 379). Galton wrote in his autobiography that reading

> the *Origin of Species* by Charles Darwin made a marked epoch in my own mental development, as it did in that of human thought generally. Its effect was to demolish a multitude of dogmatic barriers by a single stroke, and to arouse a spirit of rebellion against all ancient authorities whose positive and unauthenticated statements were contradicted by modern science (1908, 287).

Pearson claimed that Galton was loyal to Darwin's ideas "with a loyalty far rarer" than existing today (1914, vii). Galton accepted Darwinism for several reasons, saying that Darwin's theory "drove away the constraint of my old superstition" and

> allowed the acceptance of a purely secular faith in progress. Traditional spiritual beliefs in a fallen creation and human redemption through divine grace gave way to a materialistic view of humanity rising through evolutionary development (Larson 1995, 18–19).

Understanding why the eugenics movement grew so large so rapidly requires a knowledge of how evolution was viewed in America and Europe during the late 1800s and early 1900s. Many scientists used Darwinian analysis to evaluate various human "racial" groups and concluded that some "races" had evolved further than others. They then reasoned that the presence of certain racial groups in the United States and Europe constituted a threat to the long-range biological quality and health of the nation. Consequently, it was concluded that "selective breeding was a necessary step in solving many major social problems" (Haller 1984, x).

We are today keenly aware of the tragic results of this belief. Most people are horrified by such statements when expressed by modern-day White supremacists and racist groups, such as the Aryan Nation and Ku Klux Klan. Yet many of the extremist groups today often quote from, and also reprint and extensively distribute, the scientific and eugenic literature of this time.

Although the eugenics movement dates back to Darwin's original work, several discoveries around 1880 caused it to become scientifically respectable. After a basic understanding of the mechanism of heredity, and the rediscovery of Mendelian genetics that occurred soon after the turn of the 20th century, more scientists than ever before became convinced that they had unlocked the secret of heredity, and thus the key to evolution (Cravens 1978, 39–47).

Farmer William Donta holds a gun after a KKK rally and cross burning on his property in Jackson County, Ohio, 1987.

These discoveries opened up a whole new understanding about humankind's place in nature, and were the key to a method that many felt offered a major potential for societal improvement. Just as variations in animal species made them more or less fit for evolutionary survival, so too it was argued that the variations within the human racial groups made a group more or less fit than other groups — an idea translated to inferior or superior rankings of the races (Haller 1984, x–xi).

The Founder of Eugenics, Darwin's Cousin Francis Galton

In the late 1850s when Francis Galton was in his late thirties, he began his lifelong quest to quantify human traits that he grouped into "races." His goal was to genetically improve the human race. Strongly influenced by his older second cousin Charles Darwin, Galton concluded that the key to human progress was the direct application of Darwinism to society by law and national programs (Gallagher 1999).

So important was the eugenic doctrine, that within six years of the publication of *The Origin of Species,* "Galton had arrived at the doctrine that he was to preach for the remainder of his life . . . this became for him a new ethic and a new religion" (Haller 1984, 10). He then set out to find convincing evidence for his "new religion" of eugenics. The wealth that Galton inherited from his father at the young age of 22 allowed him to

> broaden his familiarity with various racial types through extensive world travels that included explorations of parts of Africa unknown to Europeans. . . . Galton brought back from his travels a firm conviction that there was a natural hierarchy of the human races that placed Anglo-Saxons above all others. His cousin's masterpiece *On*

the Origin of Species . . . stimulated Galton to investigate how the human species had developed through variation, selection, and inheritance, which were the driving forces of Darwinian evolution (Larson 1995, 18).

In 1865, Galton first published his eugenic ideas in a two-part series of articles for *Macmillan's Magazine,* which he eventually expanded into a book titled *Hereditary Genius* (1869). His articles focused on the source of various human traits, including intellect, personality, and even moral qualities, especially those that enabled one to become an effective leader. He also researched the skills required to excel in the arts, sciences, and literature, and in positive human endeavors in general.

Galton openly stated that his goal was to "produce a highly gifted race of men by judicious marriages during several consecutive generations." He reasoned that because one can "obtain by careful selection a permanent breed of dogs or horses gifted with peculiar powers of running, or of doing anything else, so it would be quite practicable to produce a highly-gifted race of men by judicious marriages during several consecutive generations" (Galton 1869, 1).

Galton proposed in his 1865 *Macmillan's* article that the state sponsor competitive "examinations" to identify the "best" humans, and that the male winners be given the female winners as brides. He later even went so far as to suggest that the state rank people by evolutionary superiority levels, and then use monetary rewards to encourage those who ranked high to have more children. Those ranked toward the bottom would be segregated into monasteries and convents in order to prevent them from propagating more of their kind (Kevles 1985, 4). One reason Galton was conservative in his comments compared to the Nazis was because he realized, as did Darwin, that radical claims would ensure that their eugenic cause would fail:

> Shaw's later proselytizing of the eugenics cause was not to be looked upon by Galton with much favour: he was too extreme and deliberately provocative, while Galton was preaching caution to elicit public acceptance (Forrest 1974, 258).

Galton knew that, for his goals to be successful, he needed to avoid what the common people regarded as extreme statements. For his research, Galton relied on a methodology to study genius that has been used by many others since (see Goertzel and Goertzel 1962). The source of his sample population, which spanned two centuries, was the bibliographical encyclopedia

Dictionary of Men of Time published in 1865. Not unexpectedly, he found that many of those included in this massive reference work, presumably the most distinguished statesmen, scientists, painters, and jurists of his day, were blood relatives.

Galton concluded that families with eminent members were far more likely than others to produce offspring of ability due to genetics. Later researchers, such as Karl Pearson, concluded that fully 90 percent of one's intelligence was inherited (Hofstadter 1955). A commonly cited estimate today is 70 percent, meaning that a good environment could raise the IQ of a child from average (IQ 100) to as much as 130, which would qualify the child for gifted programs in most cities.

Galton's end goal was to produce a super race to control tomorrow's world, a dream about which he not only wrote, but actively promoted for his entire life. To describe his use of evolution to improve humans, Galton coined the word *eugenics* (from two Greek words meaning *well born*). He also introduced the terms *nature* and *nurture* into scientific discussions, fueling the nature/nurture debate that still rages today. The term eugenics was important because by

> giving a popular name to theories that he had already begun developing from the evolutionary concepts of his cousin Charles Darwin, Galton founded a movement that swept throughout Europe and North America during the ensuing half century (Larson 1995, 18).

In 1901, he founded the Eugenics Education Society, housed in the Statistics Department at the University College of London (Jones 1980). This organization flourished, later even producing the journal *Biometrika,* which was founded and edited by Galton, and later Karl Pearson. Although still a leading journal today, its editors have since rejected the basic philosophy behind its founding.

Galton concluded that not only intelligence but also many other human traits were primarily, if not almost totally, the product of heredity and thus were determined by "nature." He also believed that virtually every human trait could be evaluated statistically and that human beings could be quantitatively compared using many hundreds of traits. Galton also was fully convinced that the survival of the fittest law applied to humans and that reproduction should be limited to those who were most intelligent and responsible (Pearson 1914, 1924, 1930).

The social class ethos was that a laborer's son should not aspire to a better station in life because most labor families were assumed to be genetically inferior. Greene, after noting that many British were influenced heavily by the writings of people like Adam Smith and Thomas Malthus, concluded that it is no

A portrait of Thomas Malthus from 1833.

> coincidence that all of the men who arrived at some idea of natural selection the first half of the nineteenth century — one thinks of William Wells, Patrick Mathew, Charles Lyell, Edward Blyth, Charles Darwin, A.R. Wallace, and Herbert Spencer — were British. Here, if anywhere in the history of science, we have a striking example of the influence of national habits of thoughts on the development of scientific theory (Greene 1981, 49).

Galton, a child prodigy himself, soon set out looking for other superior men to study — by measuring the size of their heads, bodies, and brains. He devised sophisticated measuring equipment for this purpose that supposedly quantified not only the brain and intelligence but also virtually every other human trait that could be measured without surgery. He even designed a whistle to measure the upper range of human hearing, now called a *Galton whistle,* a tool that still is standard equipment in a physiological laboratory.

His work was usually extremely thorough. He relied heavily on the empirical method and complex statistical techniques, many that he developed specifically for his eugenic work. In fact, Galton and his coworker, Karl Pearson, are regarded as the founders of the modern field of statistics, both having made major contributions. Their thorough, detailed research was extremely convincing, especially to academicians. German professors were among the first to embrace wholeheartedly not only Darwinian evolution but also the eugenics worldview that eventually led to the Holocaust. The obsessional quality of Galton's interest in quantifying every conceivable human activity was reworked by Eliot Slater, a psychiatrist, in his Galton lecture for 1960 (Slater 1960).

Eugenics in America

Eugenics was advocated not only by British scientists but also by American scientists. The eugenic journal *Biometrika* had far more subscribers in the

United States than in Great Britain. Eugenicist Karl Pearson (1857–1936) at one time even considered moving to the United States, where he assumed people would be more receptive to his eugenic ideas. A foremost goal of the founders since America was settled was to avoid a repeat of the wars that tore Europe apart for almost 500 years. In an attempt to reduce cultural conflicts, after about 1890 vigorous efforts were made to ensure that American society was homogenous, often White, Anglo-Saxon, and Protestant (Taylor 2001). If racist arguments

> could be backed by science then the appearance of bigotry would be avoided. Eugenics was thus the perfect answer and vigorously applied at immigration ports such as New York. . . . Would-be immigrants were often refused entry on the basis of head measurements or finger-tip to knee-cap distance (if too short, the individual was clearly insufficiently evolved!) (Taylor 2001, 1).

The idea that humans could achieve biological progress and eventually breed a superior race was not seen as heretical to the Victorian mind, nor did it have the horrendous implications of Nazism that it does today. Galton saw the fruits of recent advances in technology and the results of the Industrial Revolution, both of which had proved to him that humans could achieve mastery over inanimate nature (Kevles 1985, 2). People understood that farmers could obtain better breeds of both plants and animals by careful breeding selection, and so it was logical that the human race likewise could be improved in the same way (Jones 1980).

Galton's conclusion was that, for the sake of the human future, pollution of the precious superior gene pool of certain classes *must be stopped* by preventing interbreeding with inferior stock. The next step was that humans must intelligently direct their own evolution, rather than leaving such a vital process to chance alone. It is significant that Galton was not alone in this conclusion; all of the major supporters of evolution, including Charles Darwin, Alfred Russel Wallace (often called the cofounder of the modern theory of evolution), E. Ray Lancaster, and Erasmus Darwin, believed that "evolution sanctioned a breeding program for man" (Haller 1984, 17).

The route to produce a race of gifted humans was to use science to control who marries whom (Galton 1869, 1). In an effort to be tactful in his discussions of race breeding, Galton used terms such as "judicious marriages" and "discouraging breeding by inferior stock." He did not see himself as cruel, at least in his writings, but believed that his proposals were for the long-term good of humanity.

Galton utterly rejected, and wrote much against, the Christian doctrine of helping the weak and showing charity toward the poor. In contrast, Eugenics' cofounder Karl Pearson has been described as a cold, mathematical man without feeling and sympathy. Galton received numerous honors for his work, including not only the prestigious Darwin and Wallace Medals, but also the Huxley and Copley Medals. He even was knighted by the British government, thus his title Sir Francis Galton (Galton 1908).

Brain Size and Intelligence

To prove his theory, Galton first had to show how radically the races of mankind differed from each other. Then he had to demonstrate that these differences were inherited. Galton was influenced considerably by French physician Paul Broca, who maintained that human intelligence was directly related to brain size. Galton was aware that some brilliant men had small heads and that many ignorant men had large heads, but he endeavored to explain away these cases, stressing that *in general* the relationship held.

These views must be considered in relationship to the dominant scientific climate of the time (Kevles 1985, 8). If a relationship between brain size or race and intelligence exists, it is not for the racist reasons that Galton supposed. Better diets and environmental conditions produced children who were physically larger and consequently had larger brains. Children of the upper classes also were often better fed, better educated, and had more leisure time to pursue intellectual interests. Children reared in the slums more often had poorer diets and lived in adverse mental and physical environments. As a result, they often were of smaller stature and, consequently, faced other disadvantages. As is recognized today, children from eminent families are far more likely to have intellectually stimulating home environments, attend better schools, and receive better educations. They also may have more support, encouragement, and motivation to achieve eminence.

For these reasons, many cases existed that Galton used to support his eugenic theory. A high correlation between brain size and intelligence *does not* prove causation, a well-recognized statistical fallacy that Galton ignored. Although the absolute average size of the brain varies, it tends to be correlated primarily with maturity and body size. Except in cases of disease or abnormal development, gross brain size has little to do with intelligence or any other observable trait and thus is evidently a nonfunctional characteristic that fails to affect survival. Some of the most brilliant men in history have had very small brains, while others with large brains were mentally retarded, a fact that, as noted, did not dissuade Galton from promoting his theory

(Birdsell 1972, 516; Lorber 1980).

Galton thought that intelligence or "talent" is hereditary (inborn) and will develop regardless of the environment, because he believed it is "rarely impaired by social disadvantage." He assumed that for a child to develop his intelligence or talents does not require "a privileged family and . . . other social advantages." To prove that talent rarely was impaired by social disadvantage, Galton selected examples of individuals that came from humble families who succeeded (Kevles 1985, 4). He concluded that because a few children from humble backgrounds *did* become successful, most of them *could have* if they had the required genes. Galton did not adequately deal with the possibility that those persons of high ability who rose from poverty might have done far better if they had been born in a privileged family and had other social advantages.

One "proof" of the theory of eugenics was America where Galton concluded the rigid class structure that existed in Great Britain had been virtually eradicated. If culture prevented talented people from greater achievement, then the number of persons in the arts and sciences in America certainly would far surpass those in Britain. Galton concluded that the number did not, and therefore if "the hindrances to the rise of genius were removed from English society as completely as they have been removed from that of America," Britain would not become richer in highly eminent persons (Galton 1869, 40–43).

A serious problem with this generalization was the difficulty in judging a "first class work of literature, philosophy, or art." Galton largely ignored the fact that America and Europe possessed different art values and norms, a fact that blocked the rise of people born into lower social classes in Europe. Many Americans produced art that was appreciated in the United States but not in Britain. Not many British would conclude that America had more superior artists, writers, etc. (Chase 1980).

The Making of Galton

Francis Galton's own upbringing in many ways belied his theory. He was born in 1822 into an old family that originally earned its wealth by manufacturing guns. Galton's father was a banker when he married the daughter of Erasmus Darwin, Charles Darwin's grandfather. His family invested considerable time and energy in Francis's intellectual development. Although Francis Galton was obviously a gifted child, much of the credit for his precocity was due to the work of his sister, who was 12 years his senior, and who tutored Galton so effectively that, at age two-and-a-half, he mastered basic reading, and at four he could write. In contrast to Francis Galton, his two brothers did not do very well as adults; he was the only one in his family who achieved any measure of success.

The Galton family admired Erasmus Darwin and often extolled his eminence in the field of medicine and biology. The family's religious background was Quaker, but Francis's father converted to the Anglican Church at the insistence of his wife, Violetta. This later worked to Francis's advantage, since he was able to attend England's leading universities, which at the time still were restricted to Anglicans.

Although Galton was a precocious child, he did not do well in school. He was sent to medical college at age 16 but did not do well there either (Pearson 1914). He was bored, unmotivated, and often partied, attending many social gatherings late into the night. He traveled extensively to find himself. In 1844, when Francis was 22, his father died, leaving him a large inheritance.

Even with a world waiting for him and the financial means to explore it, Galton's inclination to do so likely came not from his genes, but from the influence of those around him. Brooding, depressed, and without goals, Galton consulted a phrenologist who reported that men of his head type were best suited for activities such as colonizing and exploring (Kevles 1985, 6). Believing this obviously erroneous advice to be true, in 1850 Galton went off to explore a part of the world that at that time was largely unknown to Europeans — the foreboding land of dark Africa.

Galton returned to England with a renewed curiosity about both the natural world and the ranking of the races from low to high. It was only after reading Darwin's *Origin* in 1860 that he found his true vocation, and for the rest of his life applied all his considerable energies to advancing eugenics. Although his eugenics science was faulty and caused much harm, his contributions to statistics, and especially to the field of fingerprints, were scientific milestones. He soon was awarded a gold medal by the World Geographical Society and was elected as a Fellow of the Royal Society as a result of his achievements. This experience also led him to lecture and write, two tasks at which he excelled. Most of his books went through many editions during his lifetime.

From this point on, Galton's ideas about eugenics rapidly jelled. The impressions he had obtained during his African travels served to further confirm his beliefs about inferior races, and how to improve society. This conclusion strongly supported the writings of both his grandfather and his second cousin, Charles Darwin. Galton also was highly rewarded for his scientific contributions, and likely felt that his eugenics work was another way that he could attain even more honors. He concluded that this work was more important than that which he had completed for the various geographical societies, and more important than even his research that helped the fingerprint system become part of the British method of criminal identification.

Eugenics theory is intimately tied to the history of evolution. Haller (1984, ix), the author of one of the most definitive works on the history of the eugenics movement, stated: "Eugenics arose out of the Darwinian theory of evolution and attempted to apply the theory to mankind . . . eugenics . . . involved the application — or misapplication — to many of the discoveries in genetics that were then transforming scientific understanding of living organisms and the ways that evolution operated." In a letter to Darwin, Galton said, "The appearance of your *Origin of Species* formed a real crisis in my life" resulting in demolishing his Christianity "as if it had been a nightmare and was the first to give me freedom of thought" (quoted in Haller 1984, 198). Another aspect of Galton's motivation was that, as an agnostic, he

> found in eugenics an emotional equivalent for religion. "An enthusiasm to improve the race is so noble in its aim" he declared "that it might well give rise to the sense of a religious obligation." (Haller 1984, 17)

Galton even advocated the view that both "law and custom" should be utilized to support eugenics to achieve "the improvement of the race" (Haller 1984, 17). This, of course, is exactly what the Nationalist Socialist Party (Nazis) did do many years later in Germany.

The method of race analysis that Galton developed, called "statistics by intercomparison," later became a common system of scaling psychological tests. This scale permitted Galton "to make a number of general statements about the comparative abilities of different races, statements that were well in tune with," and in many ways were merely reexpressions of the prejudices of his day (Stigler 1986, 272).

Interestingly, Galton rated the ability of the ancient Athenians "very nearly two grades higher than our own — that is, about as much as our race is above that of the African Negro" (Galton 1869, 342). How Galton was able to do this is not entirely clear, but he likely relied almost totally on the writings of ancient literate Athenians.

Although biologists in Galton's day provided much of the intellectual and empirical support for the theory, the eugenics movement was supported heavily by the work of the superintendents of asylums for the feebleminded, the insane, alcoholics, plus prison wardens, physicians, sociologists, social workers, and others involved in the care of persons with mental or physical problems (Haller 1984, 5). Members of these professions generally believed that society had a responsibility to care for these persons, but they also felt that society should prevent such persons from contaminating future generations.

This conclusion is understandable: those who work with the feebleminded, the institutionalized criminals, paupers, and others found their work incredibly frustrating (Dörner 1981). It often is very difficult to help people change their ways either by conversation or exhortation. Their general failure to help these people often was explained, not on the basis of the inadequacies or ineptness of the helpers (the social workers, institutions, and doctors involved), but because the patient's condition *primarily* was the result of heredity, and consequently there was *little that one could do to help them*; the caregiver's failure was not his or her fault.

Assuming that the patients' conditions were due to heredity, the next logical step was to find ways to restrict the propagation of these people. Numerous laws were passed that required sterilization of a wide assortment of individuals who, for a variety of reasons, found themselves in some type of institution. Looking back now, we recognize the reasons for the failure of many of the so-called treatments and the institution system as a whole (Valenstein 1986; Dörner 1981).

Around the year 1900, eugenics was fully accepted as valid by the educated classes (Blacker 1952). As a result "Galton's religion [became] as much a part of the secular pieties of the nineteen-twenties as the Einstein craze" (Kevles 1985, 59). Books on eugenics became best sellers. Albert E. Wiggam wrote four popular books on eugenics, all of which sold very well (Wiggam 1922, 1924, 1925, 1927), and the prestigious Darwin family name stayed with the eugenics movement for years. Major Leonard Darwin, Charles's son, was president of the British Eugenics Society from 1911 to 1928.

The impact of the eugenics movement on American law was especially profound. In the 1920s, Congress passed numerous laws intended to restrict the influx of "inferior races," including those from southern and eastern Europe, as well as China. Eugenic beliefs were also reflected in everything from school textbooks to social policy. American Blacks especially faced the brunt of these laws (Stanton 1960). Interracial marriages were forbidden by law in most states, and discouraged by social pressure in all states.

He added the "broad, flat nose, the slanted profile of the Negro face, and the smaller, average skull capacity — so it was argued — placed the Negro closer to the anthropoids" (Haller 1984, 52), and since they were inferior, miscegenation was considered the "road to racial degeneration." The eugenicists concluded that the American belief that education could benefit everyone was unscientific, and the conviction that social reform and social justice could substantially reduce human misery was more than wrong-headed, it was openly dangerous (Haller 1984, 6).

It was primarily between 1870 and 1900 that educated Americans moved toward a wide acceptance of varying forms of eugenic-based racism (Haller 1984, 50). The year 1870 is an important date because

> before the Civil War the lack of a well-developed racist philosophy in the Western World and a general belief that all men descended from Adam and Eve retarded the growth of race concepts. Only among those defending Negro slavery from increasingly bitter attack did specific biological theories of race become at all important. In the post-Civil War period, however, the general background of evolutionary thought and the writings of European racists provided a climate of opinion that nurtured race thinking (Haller 1984, 50–51).

In his extensive travels, Galton not only spent much time studying the races but also reading widely in the field of anthropology. He was also formally involved with the Royal Anthropological Institute where he could intersect with other scientists interested in race. He concluded that the Anglo Saxons were far superior to the Negroes, who in turn were superior to the Australian Aborigines (Galton 1880, 17). While Galton did not advocate the deliberate extinction of races, he did state that the sentiment *against* the extinction of an inferior race was unreasonable, clearly setting the stage for later abuses (Galton 1897, 605–606). Galton was very open about his views about the intellectual inferiority of Negroids, writing that the number of

> negroes ... whom we should call half-witted men, is very large. Every book alluding to negro servants in America is full of instances. I was myself much impressed by this fact during my travels in Africa. The mistakes the negroes made in their own matters, were so childish, stupid, and simpleton-like, as frequently to make me ashamed of my own species (quoted in Graves 2001, 96).

Graves also noted that Galton believed "various breeds of dogs were higher in intellect than some races of humans" (2001, 96).

Many Jewish thinkers touted the same message. For example, Rabbi Henry H. Mayer expressed concern in a service in Kansas City, thundering, "our blood is being adulterated by the infusion of blood of inferior grade," namely the Negroes (quoted in Kevles 1985, 61). Even some Protestant and Catholic ministers joined the act, suggesting that the Bible taught eugenics and that we have an obligation to God to apply the "laws" that eugenics had "discovered." Of course the Bible taught all humans are descendants of Adam and Eve, thus all humans are related and no racial group is inferior (Wieland 2011).

Many of those involved "cast off Biblical religion and, some with enthusiasm, others by default or in despair, had embraced a religion of science" (Kevles 1985, 68). And "with the modern miracles went a modern priesthood: the scientists — no small number of them geneticists. In America, the eugenic priesthood included much of the early leadership responsible for the extension of Mendelism" (Kelves 1985, 69).

An example of Galton's analysis was his study of deviations from the average. He used data on traits such as height, and produced a graph using a bar and dot pattern to indicate each case. Each dot represented the height of one man, with the pattern showing a concentration in the middle, and fewer dots as deviation from the middle occurred. The same concept is expressed today in the normal curve.

By 1875, Galton developed a new way to display this data that he called an *ogive*, a term he borrowed from the field of architecture. We now refer to this distribution as an *inverse normal cumulative distribution function*. Because his goal was to show the dissimilarity of races, Galton began to explore ways of evaluating these differences. The middle (or medium) score was assigned a value of zero, the upper quartile a value of one, and the lower quartile a value of minus one. This method later developed into the standard deviation concept (Cowan 1985).

Conclusions

The allegation by some that Darwinism was misused to support eugenics, and neither Darwin nor Galton should be faulted for abuses of their theories, does not correspond to history. Furthermore, the fact is

racism was only one step away from eugenics, a school of applied Darwinism founded by Francis Galton with the aim of improving the fitness of the human race by applying the "theory of heredity, of variations, and the principle of natural selection." From eugenics, it was no large leap to genocide (Hsü 1986, 11).

Ultimately, the eugenics movement failed, partly because of the excesses arising from it such as Nazism. Galton at first encouraged only the "fittest" men and women to marry and produce children, a proposal that became known as "positive eugenics." He later suggested segregating the unfit in monasteries to prevent them from reproducing, a proposal called "negative eugenics" (Larson 1995, 19). In time, Galton's disciples put more and more attention on negative eugenics, partly because it was more easily applied.

The fact that negative eugenics became a primary focus of many later eugenicists exacerbated Hitler's eugenic program, which eventually resulted in the loss of millions of lives and widespread violations of human rights. In the words of Harvard biologist Ernst Mayr, "Eugenics was conceived by its founders as a way of lifting humans toward greater perfection. It is sadly ironic that this noble original objective eventually led to some of the most heinous crimes mankind has ever seen" (1988, 80). Although Galton founded the eugenics movement, he did not personally fulfill his own eugenical obligations; he was the scion of two prominent English families and married to the daughter of a third, but never produced offspring of his own (Taylor 1987; Gillham 2001).

Sir Francis Galton (1822–1911) at age 66

References

Barzun, Jacques. 1958. *Darwin, Marx, Wagner*. Garden City, NY: Doubleday Anchor Books.

Bergman, Jerry. 2012. *Hitler and the Nazis Darwinian Worldview: How the Nazis Eugenic Crusade for a Superior Race Caused the Greatest Holocaust in World History*. Kitchener, Ontario, Canada: Joshua Press.

Birdsell, J.B. 1972. *Human Evolution*. Chicago, IL: Rand McNally and Co.

Blacker, Charles P. 1952. *Eugenics: Galton and After*. Cambridge, MA: Harvard University Press.

Bynum, W.F. 2002. "Francis Galton," in *Encyclopedia of Evolution*. Edited by Mark Pagel. Oxford, UK; New York: Oxford University Press.

Chase, Allan. 1980. *The Legacy of Malthus: The Social Costs of the New Scientific Racism*. New York: Alfred Knopf.

Cowan, Ruth Schwartz. 1985. *Sir Francis Galton and the Study of Heredity in the Nineteenth Century*. New York: Garland Publishing.

Cravens, Hamilton. 1978. *The Triumph of Evolution: American Scientists and the Heredity-Environment Controversy 1900–1941*. Pittsburgh, PA: University of Pennsylvania Press.

Darwin, Charles. 1871. *The Descent of Man, and Selection in Relation to Sex*. London: John Murray.

Dörner, Klaus. 1981. *Madmen and the Bourgeoisie: A Social History of Insanity and Psychiatry*. Oxford, UK: Blackwell.

Forrest, D.W. 1974. *Francis Galton: The Life and Work of a Victorian Genius*. New York: Taplinger.

Gallagher, Nancy. 1999. *Breeding Better Vermonters*. Hanover, NH: University Press of New England.

Galton, Francis. 1865. "Hereditary Talent and Character." *Macmillan's Magazine*, 12: 157–166, 318–327

———. 1869. *Hereditary Genius*. London: MacMillan.

———. 1880. *Inquiries into Human Faculty and Its Development*. Second ed. New York: E.P. Dutton, Inc.

———. 1897. "Rate of Racial Change That Accompanies Different Degrees of Severity in Selection." *Nature*, 55:605–606.

———. 1908. *Memories of My Life*. London: Methuen.

Gillham, Nicholas Wright. 2001. *The Life of Sir Francis Galton*. New York: Oxford University Press.

Goertzel, Victor, and Mildred Goertzel. 1962. *Cradles of Eminence*. Boston, MA: Little Brown.

Gould, Stephen Jay. 1996. *The Mismeasure of Man*. New York: W.W. Norton.

Graves, Joseph L. Jr. 2001. *The Emperor's New Clothes: Biological Theories of Race at the Millennium*. New Brunswick, NJ: Rutgers University Press.

Greene, John C. 1981. *Science, Ideology, and World View*. Berkeley, CA: University of California.

Haller, John S., Jr. 1971. *Outcasts from Evolution: Scientific Attitudes to Racial Inferiority, 1859–1900*. Urbana, IL: University of Illinois Press.

Haller, Mark. 1984. *Eugenics: Hereditarian Attitudes in American Thought*. New Brunswick, NJ: Rutgers University Press.

Himmelfarb, Gertrude. 1959. *Darwin and the Darwinian Revolution*. New York: Doubleday.

Hofstadter, Richard. 1955. *Social Darwinism in American Thought*. Boston, MA: Beacon Press.

Hsü, Kenneth. 1986. *The Great Dying: Cosmic Catastrophe, Dinosaurs and the Theory of Evolution*. New York: Harcourt, Brace, Jovanovich.

Jones, Greta. 1980. *Social Darwinism and English Thought: The Interaction between Biological and Social Theory*. Atlantic Highlands, NJ: The Humanities Press.

Kevles, Daniel J. 1985. *In the Name of Eugenics: Genetics and the Uses of Human Heredity*. New York: Alfred A. Knopf.

Larson, Edward. 1995. *Sex, Race, and Science*. Baltimore, MD: The Johns Hopkins University Press.

Lorber, John. 1980. "Is Your Brain Really Necessary?" *Science*, 210:1232.

Mayr, Ernest. 1988. "The Origins of Human Ethics," in *Toward a New Philosophy of Biology: Observations of an Evolutionist*. Cambridge, MA: Harvard University Press.

Newman, Horatio Hacket. 1925. *Outlines of General Zoology*. New York: Macmillan.

Pearson, Karl. 1914. *The Life, Letters and Labours of Frances Galton*. Vol. 1, 1914; Vol. 2, 1924; and Vol. 3, 1930. Cambridge, MA: Cambridge University Press.

Proctor, Robert N. 1988. *Racial Hygiene: Medicine under the Nazis*. Cambridge, MA: Harvard University Press.

Sahlins, Marshall. 1977. *The Use and Abuse of Biology: An Anthropological Critique of Sociobiology*. Ann Arbor, MI: The University of Michigan Press.

Sewell, Dennis. 2009. *The Political Gene: How Darwin's Ideas Changed Politics*. London: Picador.

Shannon, T.W. 1920. *Eugenics*. Topeka, KS: Standard Publishing Company.

Slater, Eliot 1960. "Galton's Heritage." *Eugenics Review*, 52(2): 91–103.

Stanton, William. 1960. *The Leopard's Spots: Scientific Attitudes towards Race in America, 1815–1859*. Chicago, IL: University of Chicago Press.

Stigler, Stephen M. 1986. *The History of Statistics: The Measurement of Uncertainty before 1900*. Cambridge, MA: The Belknap Press of Harvard University Press.

Taylor, Ian. 1987. *In the Minds of Men*. Minneapolis, MN: TFE Publishing.

———. 2001. Personal Correspondence.

Valenstein, Elliot S. 1986. *Great and Desperate Cures*. New York: Basic Book Publishers.

Wieland, Carl. 2011.*One Human Family: The Bible, Science and Culture*. Atlanta, GA: Creation Book Publishers.

Wiggam, Albert Edward. 1922. *The New Dialogue of Science*. Garden City, NJ: Garden City Publishing Co.

———. 1924. *The Fruit of the Family Tree*. Indianapolis, IN: Bobs Merrill Company.

———. 1925. *The Marks of an Educated Man*. Indianapolis, IN: Bobs Merrill Company.

———. 1927. *The Next Age of Man*. Indianapolis, IN: Bobs Merrill Company.

Chapter 4

Racism Expounded by Leading Darwinists for Over a Century

Introduction

The racist views of early Darwinists were widely supported, not just by a few renegade scientists, but by most of the leading biologists until at least the 1950s. The extent of this support from the worldwide scientific community shows that Darwinism gave scientific justification for preexisting prejudices that allowed the classification of people according to physical traits based on evolutionary criteria at a level never seen before in history.

The Concept of Race

The biological concept of race as we know it today had its modern impetus when what is now called "social Darwinism" was embraced by many scientists and social reformers in the early to middle 1800s (Tobach et al. 1974; Davidheiser 1969). Social Darwinism was the belief that society and humanity could be improved by the application of Darwin's ideas, specifically his "survival of the fittest" ideas. This was the belief that evolution advances by the less fit dying off, leaving the fittest behind to reproduce, and thereby improving the race and society.

Darwin's theory, specifically the belief held by many in his day that some races, such as Blacks, were inferior to others, became so widely accepted by the scientific community that "the subject of race inferiority was beyond critical reach in the late nineteenth century" (Haller 1971, 132). By the beginning of the 20th century, discussions of social problems usually involved Darwinian notions of class and race. Nearly "every one of these theories had some practical application as its corollary: political, social or cultural; and meanwhile biological research, anthropology, and the science of language had intensified, not abated, the use of 'race thinking' " (Barzun 1958, xix).

Many of the major pre–civil rights era textbooks were openly racist. For example, Newman (1932, 190) defined evolution as "racial change," adding that "races are the *evolutionary units of life*" (emphasis in original) and if "there is no variation there can be no evolution" (1932, 539). He concluded (p. 539) the races are not equal, and the condition or state of equality is "supremely undesirable from the purely evolutionary point of view, because . . . organic evolution . . . depends upon the struggle between creatures possessing various variations and the consequent selection of those variations which constitute their possessors best adapted or fitted to the particular environment," that is, the survival of the fittest race. Anyone who collects old biology books soon notes that such examples are legion, especially in those with textbooks that focus on evolution.

As discussed, Darwin's cousin, Sir Francis Galton, was the founder of the eugenics movement. Galton's writing had served a critical influence in the growth of biological racism, especially in promoting biological determinism (Galton 1880). Biological determinism is the idea that a person's lot in life is largely determined by genes, not the environment. Furthermore, his racial inferiority views were widely assumed to have been proven by scientists and layman alike. These factors resulted in many, if not most, of the early Darwinists becoming outspoken racists. Historian Richard Weikert claims that before the 1890s

> almost all the influential Darwinian anthropologists and ethnologists — along with most Darwinian biologists and popularizers — embraced scientific racism. Indeed, Darwinian materialists and

monists were the leading apostles of scientific racism in Germany. While not formally depending on Darwinian theory, scientific racism appealed to Darwinists because of its stress on biological determinism and inequality (2004, 114).

As a result, eugenics and biological racism were not subjects of debate or concern by most scientists (Haycraft 1895; Stanton 1960). So strong was the racism that Marks notes when anthropologist Ashley Montagu published his early research opposing racism in biology (1941), he faced the wrath of "the most powerful mid-century physical anthropologists and biologists" (Marks 1999, 11).

The applied racism in the eugenics movement was also well-entrenched among biologists and those in related fields, especially in Germany. Historian Edward Larson noted that even in the United States, "leading biologists generally endorsed, or at least did not publicly oppose, the [eugenics] movement during its formative years" (1995, 30). He added that the scientific "professional associations typically followed suit" and that a "handful of elite philanthropists and foundations," including the Carnegie Institute and the Rockefeller Foundation, provided much of the movement's financial backing (1995, 30).

Anthropologist Pierre Van den Berghe concludes that the entire Western intelligencia "was infected by racism and Social Darwinism" from the middle of the 19th century when Darwin published his *Origin of Species* (1859) until the 1920s (1967, 2). He notes that one of the few exceptions was anthropologist Franz Boas.

Historian John Haller concluded that "science became an instrument which verified the presumptive inferiority of the Negro and rationalized the politics of disenfranchisement and segregation into a social-scientific terminology" and that understanding the "attitudes of racial inferiority in the context of nineteenth-century science and social science is a first step in fathoming the depth of race prejudice in our own day" (Haller 1971, x).

He adds that belief in the inferiority of certain races "was at the very *foundation* of their evolutionary framework and, remaining there, rose to the pinnacle of 'truth' with the myth of scientific certainty. To see racial prejudices in their scientific robes is to understand why . . . attitudes of racial inferiority have continued to plague western culture" (Haller 1971, x–xi, emphasis mine).

Although only in Germany did biological racism reach the extent of mass genocide, eugenics did strongly influence racist governmental policies and court decisions in America and elsewhere (Gallagher 1999). Historian Michael Burleigh even argued "the distinguishing characteristic of Nazi Germany was its obsession with race" and "the professional intelligentsia including anthropologists, doctors, economists, historians, lawyers, and psychiatrists" were committed to Darwinian racism to the extent that they were involved in both the "formation and implementation of Nazi policies" (Burleigh 2001, 507).

Racism existed in the West before Darwin, but it was largely due to ideas that emanated from the developing anti-Christian secular movement, the so-called "enlightenment." As Weikart explains, one fruit of the enlightenment that presaged scientific racism was polygenism, the idea that the human "races did not descend from common ancestors," an idea that

> arose in the eighteenth century and clashed with monogenism, which had been dominant for centuries, because Christian teaching up to this time traced all human ancestry to a single pair created in the not-so-distant past. Voltaire and some other Enlightenment thinkers used polygenism as a weapon to attack Christianity's allegedly outmoded dogmas. Polygenism would continue to wield influence in the nineteenth century, until late in the century, when it was swamped by Darwinian explanations for the origin of races (2004, 104).

Opposing this biological view was the environmentalist view that was espoused by many 19th-century intellectuals. They argued "that the human mind was a blank slate (a *tabula rasa*, to use Locke's terminology)," and human disparities were due

> to differences in experiences, training, and education. Because of this, they thought "uncivilized" races could be elevated to the same level as Europeans through education. Many leaders of German anthropology in the late nineteenth century, especially the dominating figures of Rudolf Virchow, Adolf Bastian, and Johannes Ranke, reflected this liberal perspective and vigorously opposed incursions of biological racism (and Darwinism, too, for that matter) into their field (Weikart 2004, 104).

In the battle for ideas these intellectuals eventually lost out to Darwinism.

The Importance of Darwin's Writings and Ideas

Darwin's writings were critical in the development of evolutionary theory. His thoughts on the application of his theory are also crucial to understanding the history of racism. Although known as a kind and gentle man, Darwin openly supported many eugenic ideas, as well as the racism to which his theory gave birth. He was fully convinced that the eugenic theory was valid and "canonized Galton with the words; 'we now know, through the admirable labours of Mr. Galton, that genius . . . tends to be inherited' " (Kevles 1985, 20). Heredity is one factor in the development of certain traits, such as musical ability. Galton and the eugenicists extended this factor far beyond a specific discrete ability to a wide variety of factors that clearly have a major environmental component.

Although Darwin was far less racist than many of his disciples (such as Spencer, Haeckel, Hooton, Pearson, and Huxley), his theory provided the *basis* for their extreme racism as expressed in the eugenics movement, an idea he openly supported even though he opposed the extreme forms of eugenics such as forced sterilization espoused by many in his day. Darwin ended his book on human evolution, noting that the "advancement of the welfare of mankind is a most intricate problem" and

> as Mr. Galton has remarked, if the prudent avoid marriage, whilst the reckless marry, the inferior members tend to supplant the better members of society. Man, like every other animal, has no doubt advanced to his present high condition through a struggle for existence consequent on his rapid multiplication; and if he is to advance still higher, it is to be feared that he must remain subject to a severe struggle. Otherwise he would sink into indolence, and the more gifted men would not be more successful in the battle of life than the less gifted. . . . There should be open competition for all men; and the most able should not be prevented by laws or customs from succeeding best and rearing the largest number of offspring (1896, 618).

This idea gradually won acceptance within the scientific community in Europe, the United States, and elsewhere. The "one race" creationism belief slowly lost favor. For example, Darwin still believed that all humans had a common ancestry but this belief

> by no means implied racial equality. Far from it. Indeed many Darwinists claimed that Darwinism proved human inequality, including racial inequality. Darwin and most Darwinists . . . emphasized

biological variation within each species. When explaining human evolution, Darwin needed to respond to those who insisted that human rationality, speech, and morality were unique to humans and could not be the product of evolution (Weikart 2004, 105).

In order to deal with these valid concerns, Darwin tried to show that animals, especially primates, also have some level of reasoning power, speech, and even morality. Conversely, Darwin taught that certain

> races have much lower intellectual and moral faculties than Europeans. Emphasizing racial inequality thus served an important function in Darwin's attempt to bridge the chasm between primates and humans. Even though he opposed slavery and sometimes expressed sympathy for non-European races, nonetheless he believed a wide gap separated the "highest races" from the "lowest savages," as he called them, who were inferior intellectually and morally . . . to Europeans. This was not just a peripheral point of *Descent*, for in the introduction Darwin clearly stated that one of the three goals of his book was to consider "the value of the differences between the so-called races of man" (Weikart 2004, 105).

Darwin was also keenly aware of the implications for racism based on his evolution theory. In the sixth chapter of *Descent of Man*, he speculated that survival-of-the-fittest pressures eventually would eliminate not only the Negro race but also all other "lower races." He concluded that "with savages, the weak in body or mind are soon eliminated" (1896, 133) and that "the civilized races have extended, and are now everywhere extending their range, so as *to take the place of the lower races*" (1896, 135, emphasis mine). Darwin taught that natural selection has done, and is doing, much "for the progress of civilization" (1887, 316). An example he gives is the

> risk the nations of Europe ran, not so many centuries ago of being overwhelmed by the Turks, and how ridiculous such an idea now is! The more civilized so-called Caucasian races have beaten the Turkish hollow in the struggle for existence. Looking to the world at no very distant date, what an endless number of the lower races will have been eliminated by the higher civilized races throughout the world (Darwin 1887, 316).

Darwin's primary spokesman in Germany, biologist Ernst Haeckel, was "the great ancestor" of Nazi biology theoreticians (Poliakov 1974, 284). Four decades of research on Nazism has clearly shown that the "Nazi obsession with racial Utopia" was "rooted in Darwinism" (Laquer 2001, 282). It is important to note that Darwin did little to oppose the racists' conclusions of his work and writings, which spread like wildfire among the educated classes (see chapter 7, "On the Races of Man" in his *The Descent of Man*).

Darwin's Racism

Although Darwin personally opposed all forms of slavery, he *did* conclude that one of the strongest evidences for evolution was the existence of living "primitive races," which he believed were evolutionarily in between the "civilized races of man" and the gorilla. He also believed, as noted above that in the not too distant future, the advanced "civilized" human races

> will almost certainly exterminate, and replace, the savage races throughout the world. At the same time, the anthropomorphous apes . . . will no doubt be exterminated. The break between man and his nearest allies will then be wider, for it will intervene between man in a more civilized state, as we may hope, even than the Caucasian, and some ape as low as a baboon, instead of as now between the Negro or Australian and the gorilla (Darwin 1896, 156).

As this quote makes clear, Darwin saw the "savage races" as biologically in between apes and humans. For this reason, many evolutionists of the time concluded that the missing link wasn't missing but lived in Australia and other far-off lands (de Laubenfels 1949). The existence of these races was openly viewed as irrefutable evidence of a gradation of living creatures "linking" humans to the apes. The expression used today is "linking humans to our common primate ancestor" instead of to apes. This "scientific conclusion" was interpreted as compelling evidence for evolution and, as a result, most biology textbooks of the time discussed the "hierarchy of the races." As John Koster notes, Darwin

> never considered "the less civilized races" to be authentically human. For all his decent hatred of slavery, his writings reek with all kinds of contempt for "primitive" people. Racism was culturally conditioned into educated Victorians by such "scientific" parlor tricks as Morton's measuring of brainpans with BB shot to prove that Africans and Indians had small brains, and hence, had deficient minds and intellects. Meeting the simple Indians of Tierra del Fuego, Darwin wrote: "I could not have believed how wide was the difference

between savage and civilized man; it is greater than between a wild and domesticated animal. . . . Viewing such man, one can hardly make oneself believe that they are fellow creatures and inhabitants of the same world" (1988, 50).

Darwin also concluded that the more advanced apes, the "anthropomorphous apes," will also go extinct.

Darwin's Contemporaries

Many of Darwin's evolutionary contemporaries were also racists. Alfred Russel Wallace, the man who is credited with codiscovering evolution by natural selection along with Darwin, espoused essentially the same ideas as Darwin, but only relative to nonhumans (Brooks 1984; Wallace 1890). In his words, "on the whole the best fitted live . . . [and] this self-acting process" would "*improve the race*," because in "every generation the inferior would inevitably be killed off" and the "superior" would remain — that is, "*the fittest would survive*" (quoted in Ward 1927, 288, emphasis his). This was the essence of Darwinism, and the relative fitness caused by race differences (racism) was at its core.

British biologist, naturalist, and geographer Alfred Russel Wallace, circa 1895.

Robert Chambers concluded in his classic *Vestiges of the Natural History of Creation*, about which Darwin reportedly said that without *Vestiges* he might never have written *The Origin of Species*, that the Negro was "at the foot of" the Mongol (the Yellow race) and Caucasians were at the top (Crookshank 1931, 4, 6). Chambers also taught that the "various races of

Robert Chambers, Scottish editor, bookseller, and scientist, circa 1863.

mankind, are simply . . . stages in the development of the highest or Caucasian type" and that the Negroes were the least developed, and the Caucasians were the highest, most evolved race (Crookshank 1931, 4). Weikart also noted that the connection between

Darwinism and scientific racism appears all the more striking when we compare the Darwinian anthropologists and ethnologists with their non-Darwinian counterparts. The dominating figures in the German anthropological community in the late nineteenth century were the famous pathologist (and liberal political leader) Rudolf Virchow, Adolf Bastian, and Johannes Ranke, all of whom opposed Darwinian theory (2004, 114–115).

He added that Virchow caused his former student, Haeckel, to become angry in 1877 "by questioning the appropriateness of teaching evolution in schools, when the theory was so highly speculative" and for rejecting

Neanderthal Man as a primitive human ancestor, claiming instead that it was merely a pathological specimen. Ranke was also known for his anti-Darwinian stance, astonishing Hermann Klaatsch at the 1899 Anthropological Congress by calling his Darwinian views on human evolution fantasy, not science. Along with rejecting Darwinism, Virchow, Bastian, and Ranke also rejected biological racism. Instead, they stressed racial equality, monogenism, and the influence of the environment and education on people. Scientific anthropology did not necessarily spawn theories of biological inequality, as German anthropology shows (2004, 114–115).

Why So Many Scientists Became Outspoken "Racists"

The success in breeding cattle, dogs, and other animals with certain desired characteristics gave empirical support to the concept of "racial breeding" as first advocated by early eugenicists and later made into public policy by Hitler and others (Stein 1988; Weinding 1989). Eugenics, the notion that humans could improve the race by selective breeding, also was widely accepted by the educated public, especially in Europe and the Americas (Gallagher 1999; Chase 1980; Cravens 1978; Campbell 1955). Most important was the eugenics movement, which was supported by most of the more prominent scientists after Darwin (Kevles 1985; Hofstadter 1955).

That many examples illustrate the fact that living humans can be ranked from the most evolutionary advanced to the least evolutionarily advanced was a major feature of Darwinism. One typical example was a response to Smithsonian Institution biologist Austin H. Clark, who proposed that evolution proceeds in "jumps" (Funk 1929, 28). Note that the quote draws support from the now discredited *Piltdown Man* as well as from the *Neanderthal* and *Cro-magnon* men, both of which have now been shown to be different variations of humans, for evidence.

> Dr. Clark calmly reverses the old saying that nature never proceeds by leaps, and assures us that this is her only method of procedure. Yet man, as the skull history shows us so clearly, proceeded by slow steps from the Pithecanthropus, the Piltdown man, the Neanderthal Man, to the Cro-magnon Man, who distinctly represents the modern type (Funk 1929, 28).

In response to Clark, Funk argues if evolution proceeded in broad jumps

> as Dr. Clark believes, the first man should have shown the high, civilized type of to-day. But we do not have to go back to fossils. *The lowest type of men now living, the Australian savages, are at a sufficiently great remove from the civilized type to overthrow Dr. Clark's theory,* which, instead of embodying the good points of the creational and developmental theories, actually combines the difficulties of both (Funk 1929, 28, emphasis mine).

The scientist primarily responsible for the widespread acceptance of Darwinism in the 19th century, Thomas Huxley, wrote that soon after the Negro slaves were freed in America

> no rational man, cognizant of the facts, believes that the average negro is the equal, still less the superior, of the average white man. And, if this be true, it is simply incredible [to assume] that, when all his disabilities are removed . . . he will be able to compete successfully with his bigger-brained and smaller-jawed rival, in a contest which is to be carried out by thoughts and not by bites (1871, 20).

Negroes were viewed by evolutionists as being, in many ways, irrevocably inferior to Caucasians (Mintz 1972, 387). One work that documented this fact beyond question noted that after 1859

> the evolutionary scheme raised additional questions, particularly whether or not Afro-Americans could survive competition with their white near-relations. The momentous answer [from the scientists] was a resounding no. . . . The African was inferior — he represented the missing link between ape and Teuton (Burnham 1972, 506–507).

The racism that developed in America from Darwinism was by no means focused only on African-Americans. One of the leading American racists, Harvard-educated Charles Davenport, founder and director of the world-famous Cold Spring Harbor Biological Laboratory, concluded that races that were inferior to Caucasians included "the Poles, the Irish, the Italians . . . the Hebrews" and even Serbians, Greeks, Swedes, and Bohemians (Kevles 1985, 46–47). He attributed a wide variety of negative racial characteristics to each of the groups that he concluded were inferior: Poles tended to be independent (although self-reliant), the Italians tended to commit crimes of personal violence, and the Swedes, Germans, and Bohemians were all given to "thriving." A major concern of his was that the immigrants then flooding the United States would rapidly cause Americans to become darker in pigment, smaller in stature, and more involved in crimes of larceny, kidnapping, assault, rape, and murder.

Professor Davenport taught that a woman should not marry without a thorough knowledge of her betrothed's biological and genealogical history. He felt that a woman should behave like a stock breeder who carefully checks the pedigree of a potential sire for his colts or calves. Davenport argued that ideally the state should control who is able to breed, reasoning that, if the state had the right to take a person's life, surely it could deny permission to reproduce. As a highly respected scientist, Davenport's ideas were very influential at the time and were no more radical than those advocated by many other scientists and intellectuals. As documented in other chapters, the policies that Germany, then among the most advanced nations in the world, advocated in the late 1930s were very similar (Kevles 1985, 46–47).

Sir Arthur Keith, one of the world's leading evolutionary anthropologists of the 20th century, stated he was proud that the "German fuhrer" was "an evolutionist" and had "consciously sought to make the practice of Germany conform to the theory of evolution" by applying eugenics to governmental policies (1946, 230). The late Harvard evolutionist Steven J. Gould concluded that human racism was so widespread at this time among biologists that Darwin's friend, Alfred Russel Wallace, was *one of the few nonracist* evolutionists of the 19th century. Wallace concluded that, in contrast to the animals, humans owed their origin to God.

Gould added that, as a result of this conclusion, Wallace firmly "believed that all human groups had innately equal capacities of intellect." Wallace defended his "decidedly unconventional egalitarianism with two arguments, one anatomical the other cultural." He claimed, in contrast to the claims of most all evolutionists of his day, that "the brains of 'savages' are neither much smaller nor more poorly organized than our own" and that in "the brain of the lowest savages, and, as far as we know, of the prehistoric races, we have an organ . . . little inferior in size and complexity to that of the highest type" (Gould 1981, 36).

Contrary to the widespread beliefs of the evolutionists around him, Wallace concluded the behavioral differences between black and white races were due to cultural conditioning, which "can integrate the rudest savage into our own most courtly life." The reason for Wallace's "unconventional egalitarianism" was explained by Gould as follows:

> Wallace, the hyperselectionist, the man who had twitted Darwin for his unwillingness to see the action of natural selection in every nuance of organic form, halted abruptly before the human brain. Our intellect and morality, Wallace argued, could not be the product of natural selection; therefore, since natural selection is evolution's only way, some higher power — God, to put it directly — must have intervened to construct this latest and greatest of organic innovations (1981, 35).

Gould also noted that Darwin was "positively aghast at Wallace's abrupt about-face at the finish line" of evolution, namely humans (1981, 35). Darwin wrote Wallace in 1869 about his heresy, stating that "I differ grievously from you, and I am very sorry for it." Wallace, sensitive to the rebuke, thereafter referred to his non-racist theory of human intellect as "my special heresy."

The End of Darwinian Racism

One of the first major researchers to fight the racism that once dominated biology and anthropology was Ashley Montagu (1941). After his highly successful work was published, the racist views of mainstream science gradually became less radical for many reasons, both social and scientific (Lewontin 1977). The civil rights movement and court decisions were a very critical factor. The change took more than 30 years but was so complete that the prominent anthropologists Ruth Benedict and Gene Weltfish stated under the topic, "One Human Race," that "the peoples of the earth are a single family and have a common origin." The reasoning behind their conclusion involves the "intricate make-up of the human body" and "all its different organs cooperating in keeping us alive, its curious anatomy that couldn't possibly have 'just happened' to be the same in all men if they did not have a common origin" (1951, 3–4).

The example they give as evidence of their conclusion is the structure of the human foot:

> When you list all of the little bones and muscles and the joints of the toes, it is impossible to imagine that it would all have happened twice. Or take our teeth: so many front teeth, so many canines, so many molars. Who can imagine finding the same arrangements in two human species if they weren't one family? The fact of the unity of the human race is proved, therefore, in its anatomy. . . . No difference among human races has affected limbs and teeth and relative strength so that one race is biologically outfitted like a lion and another biologically outfitted like a lamb (1951, 4–5).

They conclude that "all the racial differences . . . are in nonessentials such as texture of head hair, amount of body hair, shape of the nose or head, or color of the eyes and the skin" (1951, 5).

One reason for the change was the recognition that all of the differences were what Benedict classified as "non-essentials." The few differences that exist do *not* confer a Darwinian survival advantage for one race over another. The nonessentials do not by definition affect fitness and, thus, are largely irrelevant to survival. Hair texture, for example, does not relate to survival but will, at most, affect personal comfort in adjusting to certain climates — an advantage that is largely offset by technology such as clothes and houses. Since these innovations have been part of culture since earliest recorded history, these traits would *never* have had a significant selection advantage (Haller 1971).

The most obvious difference between Negroes and Caucasians is skin color (thus the terms "Blacks" and "Whites"). Dark skin gives Blacks some protection against strong sunlight and thus skin cancer, especially in the tropics, but Whites can protect themselves by the natural process of tanning and by utilizing clothes, hats, sun helmets, and, in modern times, sunscreen. This enables them to survive with few problems in tropical areas. Dark skin serves more to aid individual comfort than survival (Downs and Bleibtreu 1969). Skin color variations do not represent a quality difference, only a quantity difference — the darker the skin, the greater amount of melanin secreted by melanocytes, and the more yellow the skin, the more the carotene (the source of the yellow tinge) secreted.

All humans also have about the same concentration of melanocytes in their skin (Hole 1990, 168). The variations are due largely to the *amount* of melanin these cells produce — the darker the skin, the greater the amount of melanin secreted in the lower skin layers (Garn 1962). Except albinos, who totally lack coloring substances and appear in all races, every person, however dark or light, is affected by the sun in much the same manner (Comas 1976; Goldsby 1971).

All of these qualities have little or nothing to do with survival during and before childbearing years and, consequently, *cannot be accounted for by evolution.* These differences seem to exist primarily to increase the variety so evident in the living world — a variety that not only makes our sojourn on earth much more enjoyable but also helps us to differentiate the scores of people alive today (D'Souza 1995; Dunn 1959).

Other alleged racial differences include substances in the blood, thus the expression "blood relations" and the classifications "Aryan blood," "Chinese blood," or "Negroid blood." Most of the dozens of known blood types are found in every race. The major blood types (A, B, AB, and O) are present in all races, although in different percentages. Consequently, blood transfusions can be administered without regard to race — only a blood type match is required. Studies of other creatures have found the same problem with natural selection. For example, Leigh Van Valen, professor of biology at the University of Chicago, surprised the scientific world by documenting

> the randomness of species extinctions. . . . Working with data tabulated from the books and scientific papers of many paleontologists, Van Valen counted species and calculated their life spans over many millions of years. According to standard Darwinian theory, the better adapted species should last a long time and those not as well adapted should die out quickly. Theory would also have predicted that the longer a species survived, the lower the probability of its extinction in the next time interval. However, Van Valen's statistical

analysis of species' lifetimes indicates that there is no such difference. His research implies that the process of extinction does not distinguish between species (Raup 1979, 208; see also Raup 1991).

This scientific research has slowly demolished the view that some races are biologically inferior to others, demonstrating the brotherhood of all humans as taught in Genesis.

Conclusions

Scholarly works are increasingly supporting what is now the prevailing opinion among scientists: allowing for environment, no significant innate overall difference of consequence exists between Blacks and Whites (Bulmer and Solomos 1999). Richard Leakey, the son of the famous anthropologist Louis Leakey, noted that his father's life work has proven that racial differences are superficial (Leakey and Lewin 1978, 78).

It was for this reason, Benedict concluded, "The races of mankind are what the Bible says they are — brothers. In their body is the record of their brotherhood" (1957, 171). Darwinism, though, requires that differences *even within a very small group of people* would confer to that group of people a survival advantage (Wolpoff and Caspari 1997). Thus, that group would become larger and larger and, as selection continued, would become increasingly different from the outside population.

This, though, is not now happening with humans as shown by the fact that separate populations are not developing from the main populations. This state of affairs means that, without *any clear significant differences, there is nothing from which to select. And without selection, evolution cannot occur.* Many evolutionists attempt to deny this requirement of their theory in an attempt to deny the racism behind it (Wieland 2011).

References

Barzun, Jacques. 1958. *Darwin, Marx, Wagner*. Garden City, NY: Doubleday Anchor Books.

Benedict, Ruth. 1957. *Race, Science and Politics*. New York: The Viking Press.

———, and Gene Weltfish. 1951. *The Races of Mankind*. New York: The Public Affairs Pamphlet, No. 85.

Brooks, John Langdon. 1984. *Just Before the Origin*. New York: Columbia Univ. Press.

Bulmer, Martin, and John Solomos (editors). 1999. *Racism*. Oxford, NY: Oxford University Press.

Burleigh, Michael. 2001. "Racism," in Walter Laquer. *The Holocaust Encyclopedia*. New Haven, CT: Yale University Press, p. 507–514.

Burnham, John C. 1972. *Outcasts From Evolution* (book review). *Science,* (4021): 506–507.

Campbell, Byram. 1955. *American Race Theorists; A Critique of Their Thoughts and Methods.* San Diego, CA: The Truth Seeker.

Chase, Allan. 1980. *The Legacy of Malthus; The Social Costs of the New Scientific Racism.* New York: Alfred A. Knopf.

Comas, Juan. 1976. *Racial Myths.* Westport, CT: Greenwood Press.

Cravens, Hamilton. 1978. *The Triumph of Evolution; American Scientists and the Heredity-Environment Controversy 1900–1941.* Philadelphia, PA: University of Pennsylvania Press.

Crookshank, F.G. 1931. *The Mongrel in Our Midst; A Study of Man and His Three Faces.* Third Edition. London: Kegan, Paul, Trench, Turbner.

Darwin, Charles. 1896. *The Descent of Man, and Selection in Relation to Sex; The Works of Charles Darwin.* 2nd edition. New York, NY: D. Appleton and Company. (Reprinted by AMS Press, 1972).

———. 1887. *Life and Letters.* Edited by Francis Darwin. London: John Murry. Vol 1.

Davidheiser, Bolton. 1969. "Social Darwinism." *Creation Research Society Quarterly* 5(4):151.

de Laubenfels, M.W. 1949. *Pageant of Life Science.* New York: Prentice-Hall.

Downs, James F., and Hermann K. Bleibtreu. 1969. *Human Variation: An Introduction to Physical Anthropology.* Beverly Hills, CA: Glencoe Press.

D'Souza, Dinesh. 1995. *The End of Racism.* New York: The Free Press.

Dunn, L. C. 1959. *Heredity and Evolution in Human Populations.* Cambridge, MA: Harvard University Press.

Funk, Willard. 1929. "New Theory of Man in the Making." *Literary Digest,* Feb. 16, 100(7): 27–28.

Gallagher, Nancy L. 1999. Chapter 3: The Quest for a "Eugenic Vermont," 1925–1931, *Breeding Better Vermonters; The Eugenics Project in the Green Mountain State*, Hanover and London: University Press of New England, p. 71–126.

Galton, Francis. 1880. *Inquiries Into Human Faculty and Its Development.* Second Edition. New York, NY: Dutton.

Garn, Stanley M. 1962. *Human Race.* Springfield, IL: Charles C. Thomas.

Goldsby, Richard A. 1971. *Race and Races.* New York, NY: Macmillan Company.

Gould, Stephen Jay. 1981. "Wallace's Fatal Flaw." *Natural History,* Jan., 89(1):26–40.

Haller, John S., Jr. 1971. *Outcasts From Evolution: Scientific Attitudes to Racial Inferiority, 1859–1900.* Urbana, IL: University of Illinois Press.

Haycraft, John Barry. 1895. *Darwinism and Race Progress.* New York: Scribner.

Hofstadter, Richard. 1955. *Social Darwinism in American Thought.* Boston, MA: Bacon Press.

Hole, John W. 1990. *Human Anatomy and Physiology.* Dubuque, IA: Wm. Brown Pub.

Huxley, Thomas. 1871. *Lay Sermons, Addresses and Reviews.* New York: Appleton.

Keith, Arthur. 1946. *Evolution and Ethics.* New York: G.P. Putnam's Sons.

Kevles, Daniel J. 1985. *In the Name of Eugenics; Genetics and the Uses of Human Heredity.* New York, NY: Alfred A. Knopf.

Koster, John. 1988. *The Atheist Syndrome.* Brentwood, TN: Wolgemuth and Hyatt Publishers.

Laquer, Walter. 2001. *The Holocaust Encyclopedia.* New Haven, CT: Yale University Press.

Larson, Edward John. 1995. *Sex, Race, and Science: Eugenics in the Deep South.* Baltimore, MD: Johns Hopkins University Press.

Leakey, Richard, and Roger Lewin. 1978. *Origins.* New York: E.P. Putnam.

Lewontin, Richard C. et al. 1977. *Biology as a Social Weapon.* Minneapolis, MN: Burgess.

Marks, Jonathan. 1999. "Ashley Montagu Dies." *Reports of the National Center for Science Education,* 19(5):11.

Mintz, Sidney W. 1972. *Outcasts From Evolution.* Book review, *American Scientist* 60(3):38.

Montagu, Ashley. 1941. "The Concept of Race in the Human Species in the Light of Genetics." *Journal of Heredity* 23:243–247.

Newman, Horatio. 1932. *Evolution, Genetics, and Eugenics.* Chicago, IL: University of Chicago Press.

Poliakov, Leon. 1974. *The Aryan Myth.* New York: Basic Books.

Raup, David M. 1979. "The Revolution in Evolution." *Science Year; The World Book Science Annual, 1980.* Chicago, IL: World Book.

———. 1991. *Extinction; Bad Genes or Bad Luck?* New York: W.W. Norton & Company.

Stanton, William. 1960. *The Leopard's Spots: Scientific Attitudes towards Race in America, 1815–1859.* Chicago, IL: University of Chicago Press.

Stein, George. 1988. "Biological Science and the Roots of Nazism." *American Scientist,* Jan-Feb, 76(1): 50–58.

Tobach, Ethel, and John Gianusos, Howard R. Topoff, and Charles G. Gross. 1974. *The Four Horsemen; Racism, Sexism, Militarism, and Social Darwinism.* New York, NY: Behavioral Publications.

Van den Berghe, Pierre. 1967. *Race and Racism.* New York: John Wiley and Sons.

Wallace, Alfred Russel. 1890. "Human Selection." *Popular Science Monthly,* Nov., 38(93).

Ward, Henshaw. 1927. *Charles Darwin: The Man and His Warfare.* New York: The Bobbs Merrill Co.

Weikart, Richard. 2004. *From Darwin to Hitler: Evolutionary Ethics, Eugenics, and Racism in Germany.* New York: Palgrave Macmillan.

Weinding, Paul. 1989. *Health, Race and German Politics Between National Unification and Nazism — 1870–1945.* Cambridge, MA: Cambridge University Press.

Wieland, Carl. 2011. *One Human Family: The Bible, Science, Race and Culture.* Atlanta, GA: Creation Book Publishers.

Wolpoff, Milford, and Rachel Caspari. 1997. *Race and Human Evolution.* New York: Simon and Schuster.

Chapter 5

H.G. Wells: Darwin's Disciple and Eugenicist Extraordinaire

Introduction

After being exposed to Darwinism in school, Herbert George (H.G.) Wells converted from (he claimed) devout Christian to devout Darwinist as a young man and spent the rest of his life proselytizing for Darwin and eugenics. His journey along this path, and the factors that influenced him, have been carefully documented in his own writings (Brome 1951). For much of his life, Wells advocated a level of eugenics that was even more extreme than Hitler's, even to the point of concluding that the time would come when the only proper punishment for social deviation was death.

His Background

H.G. Wells was one of the most well-known and important late 19th and early 20th-century science-fiction and science writers in the English-speaking world. Some historians claim that he changed the mind of Europe and the world, and Wells was for this reason called the "great sage" of his time (Achenbach 2001, 112). Born in Bromley, Kent, England, on September 21, 1866 (Wells 1924), he died in London on August 13, 1946.

Although from a poor family, Wells studied at the Normal School of Science in South Kensington under Darwin's chief disciple, Thomas Henry Huxley. He completed his bachelors of science with first-class honors in zoology and second-class honors in geology. His doctoral thesis from London University was titled: "The Quality of Illusion in the Continuity of the Individual Life in the Higher Metazoa with Particular Ref-

Herbert George (HG) Wells, was a well-known British writer of fiction, with novels concerning issues of politics, social issues, and science fiction.

erence to the Species *Homo sapiens*." After teaching in private schools for four years, Wells began teaching college-level courses in 1891 and married his cousin Isabel the same year.

Wells soon became a writer and authored over 100 books in his long career, including such best-selling science fiction (a genre he made enormously popular) classics as *The Time Machine* (1895), *The Invisible Man* (1897), *The War of the Worlds* (1898), and *The First Man on the Moon* (1901). He also published much general fiction and later branched out into other areas, including history and science. His best-selling (and still in print) *Outline of History* (1920) and the four-volume *The Science of Life* (1931), in which he collaborated with his eldest son, George Phillip Wells, and Sir Julian Huxley, sold very well. *The Outline of History* alone has sold over two million copies (West 1984, 82). Both *The Outline* and *Science of Life* went into great detail to defend the Darwinist worldview (Coren 1993).

Wells wrote as many as two books a year, plus articles in such journals as *The Fortnightly Review*. While he began his career writing science fiction, he soon moved on to write books that would help solve what Wells concluded were society's "deepening social perplexities" (Wells 1979, iv). One of his specializations was predicting the future — which not only expressed itself in his science fiction but also in such books as *Anticipations* (1902, reprinted in 1999), *Mankind in the Making* (1903), *A Modern Utopia* (1905), and *A Mind at the End of Its Tether* (1945), a work in which he expressed the bleakest pessimism about humankind's future presented in any of his books. Many of his works are still in print (see http://www.online-literature.com/wellshg/.), and there even exists an H.G. Wells Society that has its own website: http://www.hgwellsusa.50megs.com/.

From Christian to Darwinian Atheist

Wells's writings also detail his conversion from theism to Darwinism. He wrote that when young, he fully believed that God created the universe but later began to conclude that "there was a flaw in this assumption" (1934, 126). Wells was both impressed and influenced by Darwin's ideas, but at first tried to reconcile them with his faith in the "simple but powerful concept, implanted by his mother's teachings when he was small, that 'somebody must have made it all' " (Mackenzie and Mackenzie 1973, 42).

As a youngster, Wells stated he had a "crude conception of Evolution" but only when in college was he fully persuaded of Darwinism (1934, 126). As a result, he rejected Christianity and eventually God. Among the books that he read was Henry Drummond's *Natural Law in the Spiritual World.* Drummond was a theistic evolutionist who wrote several best-selling books defending Darwinism and attempting to harmonize Darwinism and Christianity.

One important reason the formerly devout believer became an atheist was his difficulty accepting both theism and Christianity because, as Wells stated, when he believed in evolution, he could no longer accept Genesis (1934, 127). He logically deduced that if evolution were true, the basis of Christianity, including the Fall and the sacrificial death of Christ to redeem fallen humans, was impossible.

Wells realized that the "new science" of Darwinism "had dealt telling blows at revealed religion but offered no spiritually rewarding alternative to it" (Mackenzie and Mackenzie 1973, 42). Later, when he came across the weekly atheist magazine called *The Free Thinker,* his "worst suspicions" about Christianity were confirmed, and he became a committed atheist. He soon enjoyed mocking Christianity and theism (Mackenzie and Mackenzie 1973, 43). After Wells rejected theism, he embraced socialism and, later, even Soviet-style communism, both of which he also became disillusioned with, and eventually rejected.

Although his mentor, T.H. Huxley, was called Darwin's bulldog for his lifetime of tenaciously fighting for Darwinism, Wells might be called one of Darwin's chief apostles (Mackenzie and Mackenzie 1973, 53). Huxley, Wells, and other "eminent men of science" had an "almost fanatical faith" that science alone was the answer to "all human misery" (Mackenzie and Mackenzie 1973, 55).

Toward this end, Wells was active both in writing and in defending his new religion of Darwinism for his entire life — a "mission, as capable of arousing enthusiasm as any religious revival" (Mackenzie and Mackenzie 1973, 55). Even his fiction books actively defended Darwinism — Kemp concluded that *The Time Machine* was a "blend of Marx and Darwin" (1982, 14).

Wells was also very active in attacking all forms of Christianity, especially Catholicism. For example, he wrote an entire book criticizing the Catholic Church titled *Crux Ansata,* which attacked the Catholic Church and presented a distorted one-sided history of the church's putative crimes against humanity (1944). Another example of Wells's antichurch activities involved British Catholic Hilaire Belloc, who wrote a 119-page response to Wells's *Outline of History* titled *A Companion to Mr. Wells's Outline of History* (1926), refuting its anti-Christian and pro-Darwinism bias.

The book prodded Wells into writing a reply, published later in the same year under the title *Mr. Belloc Objects* (1926). Gardner concluded that Wells's response to Belloc was written in "a mood of amused anger" (1957, 134). Mackenzie and Mackenzie called Wells's book "vituperous" and intimated that Wells was "enraged" with Belloc (1973, 348). Belloc also produced a rebuttal to Wells's *Mr. Belloc Objects*, titled *Mr. Belloc Still Objects* (1927) in which Belloc defended his objections to Darwinism and critiqued Wells's attack on theism.

Eugenics

After Darwinism "had destroyed the conventional theology" in the minds of most British intellectuals, the question in the minds of many intellectuals was, could Darwin "provide an alternative basis for morality?" (Mackenzie and Mackenzie 1973, 55). The problem, as Mackenzie and Mackenzie note, was that the

popular and optimistic gloss on Darwin's theory of evolution had simply replaced the Divine Purpose by the process of natural selection. Man remained the supreme achievement of genetic variation. . . . But Huxley did not accept this benignly complacent view of Nature. Suppose, he asked, the emergence of the human species was merely an accident, and probably a temporary phenomenon. Suppose Nature were at best neutral and at worst hostile. Suppose the evolution of species could as easily lead to stagnation and regression as to progress. Then *Homo sapiens* might be damned as surely by the laws of evolution as by original sin. In both cases there would be a last judgment (1973, 56).

Wells and many others believed that one part of the solution to this problem was eugenics. For Wells, along with many other Darwinists of his time, eugenics became a key to human advancement. Eugenics was a field in which Wells "out-Darwined" Darwin, and one that he championed for most of his adult life. Nowhere is this revealed so vividly as in his book about his hope for the future of humankind. Titled *Anticipations,* it was Wells's first nonfiction bestseller and a "fabulous commercial success" (Achenbach 2001, 118). This work had "an enormous impact on British intellectuals and their European counterparts" (Gardner 1999, iii). Although the book contained many useful ideas, such as that all books should be "annotated by writers who held contrary opinions," in it he also defended an "extreme program of negative eugenics" (Gardner 1999, ix–x).

Wells's own words openly advocated favoring "the procreation of what is fine and efficient and beautiful in humanity — beautiful and strong bodies, clear and powerful minds . . . and to check the procreation of base and servile types . . . of all that is mean and ugly and bestial in the souls, bodies, or habits of men" (Wells 1999, 167–168). This goal was to be completed by "death" or "mercy killings," and Wells advocated that those involved in his eugenic world should have "no pity" for the unfit, and "not be squeamish" about inflicting death on the unfit because those who kill the weak will have a "fuller sense of the possibilities of life than we possess. They will have an ideal that will make killing worth the while" (Wells 1999, 169). His concern was to control the "laws of evolution so that mankind could become their master rather than their victim" (Mackenzie and Mackenzie 1973, 120).

The "unfit" that Wells added to his list included persons with "transmittable diseases, with mental disorders, with bodily defamations, the criminally insane, even the incurable alcoholic! All are to be put to death humanely — by first giving them opiates to spare them needless suffering!"

(Gardner 1999, x). Wells advocated not only killing but also sterilization and birth control as an effective way to rid the earth of "inferior" races and peoples (Gardner 1999, xi). Wells believed that evolution operating on its own was not "progressive" but needed to be "directed" by the educated elite. For this reason, he actively worked toward establishing eugenics programs.

A question on many people's minds was the place of the Jews and what Wells called "the inferior races" in society (Wells 1999, 177). Wells concluded that Jewish faces were "very ugly," but added that so are many Gentile faces. Wells also concluded that many Jews are intensely vulgar in dress, materialistic, and cunning, but added so are many Gentiles. He believed that intermarriage eventually would cause the Jews to cease to exist as a physically distinct "race."

Wells was far less charitable about the "darker races," concluding that "those swarms of blacks, and brown, and dirty-white, and yellow people . . . will have to go" (Gardner 1999, xi). Gardner comments that "Wells' statements about inferior races, and the use of killing as a tool to weed out the unfit, came perilously close to Hitler's efforts to breed a superior Aryan race, and to 'solve the Jewish question' with the aid of gas chambers" (1999, xi).

Gardner concludes that, as far as he knows, Wells never retracted or ever apologized for these statements and even called *Anticipations* the keystone to the main arch of his life work (1999). In his 1934 autobiography, Wells still advocated ridding the world of those he called the "unfit," but no longer advocated killing them; instead, he wanted to rely on sterilization. This is often called the "soft eugenicist approach" as opposed to Wells's earlier "hard eugenicist" stand.

An example of soft eugenics is found in Wells's book *The Work, Wealth, and Happiness of Mankind* (1931). In this book, Wells still advocated isolation and sterilization of the unfit, but now recognized that variety in human beings can be advantageous. Many of his works also advocated a dictatorship by the educated-elite class and disparaged the common, less-educated population. For this reason, he was opposed to democracy and felt that the world should be governed by an enlightened science-trained elite, that is, the scientists (Mackenzie and Mackenzie 1973, 59). For much of his life, he also actively advocated a world government. As Achenbach noted, Wells's "scientific utopia, led by a powerful elite, bore an uneasy relationship to the totalitarian horrors of Nazi Germany and the Soviet Union" (2001, 123).

Wells also argued that inferior humans should cause their own death, stating that, in his eugenic world, society will "naturally regard" the "suicide of incurably melancholy, or diseased or helpless persons as a high and courageous act of duty rather than a crime" (1999, 169). Wells concluded that long terms of imprisonment for those who commit crimes is "infinitely worse than death." Instead, Wells believed the state should execute all persons convicted of serious crimes (1999, 169).

For other offenders, Wells recommended if deterrent punishment is necessary, "scientifically caused pain that will leave nothing but a memory" should be utilized, but he does not go into detail on how this should be done (1999, 169). He even argued that the time would come when the *only* punishment will be killing, and because, in the future, society "will be far less disposed to torture than to kill . . . to kill under the seemly conditions science will afford is a far less offensive thing: . . . People who cannot live happily and freely in the world without spoiling the lives of others are better out of it" (1999, 169–170).

By killing themselves, Wells concluded that they could save society the trouble: "most of the human types, that by civilized standards are undesirable, are quite willing to die out . . . if the world will only encourage them a little" (1999, 171). It is true that Wells later modified this extreme stand — no doubt greater wisdom and maturity helped him comprehend the foolishness of some of his earlier ideas. Nonetheless, he continued to defend eugenics, but instead of utilizing murder, he proposed sterilization (see chapter 5 of his *Modern Utopia*, 1905).

One of his most revealing quotes was related to his idea of a utopian new republic:

And how will the new republic treat the inferior races? How will it deal with the black [race]? how will it deal with the yellow man? how will it tackle that alleged termite in the civilized woodwork, the Jew? Certainly not as races at all. It will aim to establish . . . a world state with a common language and a common rule. All over the world its . . . standards, its laws, and its apparatus of control will . . . make the multiplication of those who fall behind a certain standard of social efficiency unpleasant and difficult. . . . If the Jew has a certain incurable tendency to social parasitism, and we make social parasitism impossible, we shall abolish the Jew. . . . And for the rest, those swarms of black, and brown, and dirty-white, and yellow people, who do not come into the new needs of efficiency? Well, the world is . . . not a charitable institution, and I take it they will have to go. The whole tenor and meaning of the world, as I see it, is. . . . So far as they fail to develop sane, vigorous, and distinctive personalities for the great world of the future, it is their portion to die out and disappear (Wells 1902, 340–342).

Wells and Christianity

As an adult, Wells had very definite, strongly negative, ideas about Christianity — for example, he felt the Deity that Christians worshiped was "absurd" (1999, 160). At first he could not accept a totally atheistic worldview and he tried for years to replace the Christian God with a god of his own making — a god that allowed him to violate Christian morals, yet gave meaning to the universe and human history.

Wells himself would later repudiate God in total, declaring himself "an honest atheist" (Gardner 1999, ix). Yet his biographer concluded that Wells's youthful religious beliefs still influenced him, even if unconsciously, and he "always sought to reconcile the scientific concepts he had acquired at South Kensington with the doctrines of evangelical [Christian] belief" (Mackenzie and Mackenzie 1973, 121).

Nonetheless, Wells concluded that the ideas of Malthus "awakened almost simultaneously in the mind of Darwin and Wallace" a set of ideas that "found expression and demonstration at last in the theory of natural selection" (Wells 1999, 162). Natural selection, as it has been increasingly

> assimilated and understood by the general mind has destroyed, quietly but entirely, the belief in human equality which is implicit in all the "Liberalising" movements of the world . . . it has become apparent that whole masses of human population are, as a whole, inferior in their claim upon the future to other masses, that they cannot be given other opportunities or trusted with power as the superior peoples are trusted, that their characteristic weaknesses are contagious and detrimental in the civilising fabric, and that their range of incapacities tempts and demoralizes the strong. To give them equality is to sink to their level, to protect and cherish them is to be swamped in their fecundity (Wells 1999, 162–163).

Furthermore, Wells concluded that "Darwinism destroyed the dogma of the Fall upon which the whole intellectual fabric of Christianity rests. For without a Fall, there is no redemption, and the whole theory and meaning of the Pauline system is vain" (1999, 163). Wells continues, noting that scientific discovery has resulted in the loss of "the very habit of thought from which the belief in a Fall arose" (1999, 163). Evolution, Wells assures us, makes incomprehensible facts such as death comprehensible. It helps explain many things because natural selection causes all things to be "integral in the mighty scheme, the slain builds up the slayer, the wolf grooms the horse into swiftness, and the tiger calls for wisdom and courage out of man" (1999, 164).

Wells also predicted that Protestant Christianity would slowly decay, and many of those who abandoned Protestantism would turn to pseudo-scientific cults, such as spiritualism, Eastern religions, witchcraft, and devil worship. He surmised that the latter two activities were more of an expression of rebellion than of sincere belief. Gardner concludes that Wells was "quite accurate" in this prediction (1999, x). These anti-Christian views were reflected in numerous influential books Wells wrote, including his two 1917 classics, *God the Invisible King* and *The Soul of a Bishop*.

Wells and Morality

An ironic statement in his *Anticipations* was "God is no moralist" (1999, 160). Wells also opined that the "sexual morality of the civilized world is the most illogical and incoherent system of wild permissions and insane prohibitions, foolish tolerance and ruthless cruelty that it is possible to imagine" (Wells 1999, 170). He was an early advocate of free love, an idea that he "scandalously" put into practice (Achenbach 2001, 112). Conversely, he also felt strongly that the young should be protected from premature sexual involvement (Raknem 1962).

Soon after Wells married Isabel in 1891, his "sensual fever soon broke" and "his eye wandered" (Achenbach 2001, 115). He soon had an affair with one of his young students, Amy Katherine Robbins, who was described by a friend as "one of the prettiest girls" he had ever seen (West 1984, 210). Wells then married her and changed her name to Jane because he did not like her "Christian" name (Wells 1977, 29).

She gave him two sons, ran the family household, and edited his manuscripts to make them readable. She even typed everything Wells wrote (Achenbach 2001, 115; Wells 1977). Soon after the wedding, Wells was actively having affairs with yet other women. Jane was "infinitely tolerant" of his escapades, and they stayed together in spite of his long string of affairs.

Among his "casual affairs licensed by his understanding with Jane" was a ten-year affair with the famous writer Rebecca West (West 1984, 83). Wells's illegitimate son by her, Anthony West, explained that his father and Jane Wells had an "understanding" that would allow H.G. Wells to have "casual affairs." Wells took advantage of this arrangement by actively living his philosophy (West 1984, 83). His other casual affairs included those with Miss Rosamund Bland and Amber Reeves, both daughters of friends. Yet another paramour with whom he indulged in an affair was Margaret Sanger, the woman who spent much of her life campaigning for the sexual liberation of men and women, advocating unrestricted sales of contraceptives, and later founding Planned Parenthood (West 1984, 83).

The Influence of Darwinism

Wells noted in his autobiography that he believed both T.H. Huxley and Charles Darwin were "very great men" who "fought boldly, carefully, and simply," and "spoke and wrote fearlessly and plainly," and "were mighty intellectual liberators" (1934, 162). Wells studied both biology and zoology under Huxley, concluding that the year he spent in his class "was beyond question, the most educational year of my life" (1934, 161). Wells's admiration for Huxley was so great that he said Huxley was "the acutest observer, the ablest generalizer, the great[est] teacher, the most lucid and valiant of conversationalists" (1934, 159).

Wells's illegitimate son, Anthony West, stated that his father was "in heaven, as a freshmen" when he studied biology under "the great Thomas Henry Huxley" (West 1984, 57). After studying under Huxley, "Darwinian evolution inspired Wells' writings forever after" (Achenbach 2001, 115).

Wells spoke of evolution as uncontroversial fact, which had an "impregnable base of proof" (1934, 162). He further concluded that the Church "had always known all about Evolution and the place of man in Nature, just as it has always known about the place of the solar system in space," but the Church did not want to reveal these facts so it could keep the population in the dark. Wells's life speaks eloquently about the influence of Darwinism on his ideas and his once-conservative Christian beliefs. In turn, Wells influenced millions of others to live a life patterned after his own. Fortunately, Wells's eugenics utopia — where "the elites of the future will kill off the diseased, ill-formed or unintelligent members of the human race" — never came to pass (Achenbach 2001, 123).

In his later life, Wells became very ambivalent about science as our savior, correctly recognizing that science could also become a major means to evil as happened in Nazi Germany. In the end, Wells believed that humanity was ultimately doomed and that its prospect is not salvation, but extinction. Despite all of his hopes in science to save us, Wells knew that in the end science must be "darkness still" (Mackenzie and Mackenzie 1973, 124). Wells died in 1946, an "infinitely frustrated" and broken man. Borrello concluded that the Darwinism taught by "Darwin's Bulldog," T.H. Huxley, "imparted to Wells an understanding of life which kept alive the fires of pessimism which were to burn strongly even when Wells was hailed as the apostle of optimism. Huxley gave him that fear for man's future which precipitated the despair that darkened his final years" (1972, 6).

Conclusion

Wells's loss of his Christian faith and his unbridled philandering were all part of the result of his acceptance of Darwinism. His life, and "the despair that darkened his final years," clearly demonstrated the ultimate consequences of Darwinism (Achenbach 2001, 124; see also Smith 1986 and Borrello 1972). Yet he is still honored today by some; a Wells Society even exists to keep alive his work, and no less than 25 of his books are still in print (Borrello 1972). His memory should be kept alive, not as a hero, but as a tragic illustration of the baneful influence of Darwinism on humanity.

References

Achenbach, Joel. 2001. "The World According to Wells." *Smithsonian*, 32(1):111–124, April.

Belloc, Hilaire. 1926. *A Companion to Mr. Wells' "Outline of History."* San Francisco, CA: ESA Publisher.

———. 1927. *Mr. Belloc Still Objects.* London: Sheed and Ward.

Borrello, Alfred. 1972. *H.G. Wells: Author in Agony.* Carbondale and Edwardsville, IL: Southern Illinois University Press.

Brome, Vincent. 1951. *H.G. Wells: A Biography.* London: Longmans, Green and Co.

Coren, Michael. 1993. *The Invisible Man: The Life and Liberties of H.G. Wells.* New York: Athenaeum.

Gardner, Martin. 1957. *Fads and Fallacies in the Name of Science.* New York: Dover.

———. 1999. Introduction to the Dover edition of *Anticipations* by H.G. Wells. Mineola, NY: Dover .

Kemp, Peter. 1982. *H.G. Wells and the Culminating Ape; Biological Themes and Imaginative Obsessions.* London: The Macmillan Press Ltd.

Mackenzie, Norman, and Jeanne Mackenzie. 1973. *H.G. Wells: A Biography by Norman and Jeanne Mackenzie.* New York: Simon and Schuster.

Raknem, Ingvald. 1962. *H.G. Wells and His Critics.* Oslo, Norway: Scandinavian University Books.

Smith, David C. 1986. *H.G. Wells: Desperately Mortal.* New Haven, CT: Yale University.

Wells, Frank. 1977. *H.G. Wells: A Pictorial Biography.* London: Jupiter Books.

Wells, H.G. 1917. *God the Invisible King.* New York: Macmillan.

———. 1902. *Anticipations of the Reaction of Mechanical and Scientific Progress: Upon Human Life and Thought.* New York: Harper & Brothers. Reprinted by Dover, Mineola, NY.

————. 1903. *Mankind in the Making*. London: Chapman & Hall.

————. 1905. *A Modern Utopia*. London : Chapman & Hall.

————. 1917. *The Soul of a Bishop*. New York: Macmillan.

————. 1920. *The Outline of History*. New York: Macmillan.

————. 1924. *H.G. Wells; A Sketch of His Life and Works*. New York: Charles Scribner's Sons.

————. 1926. *Mr. Belloc Objects*. New York: Doran.

————. 1931. *The Work, Wealth, and Happiness of Mankind*. Garden City, NY: Doubleday Doran.

————. 1931. *The Science of Life*. New York: Doubleday, Doran & Co.

————. 1934. *Experiment in Autobiography*. Boston, MA: Little Brown.

————. 1944. *Crux Ansata*. New York: Agora Publishing Co.

_____. 1945. *A Mind at the End of Its Tether*. London: W. Heinemann.

_____. 1979. *The Complete Science Fiction Treasury of H.G. Wells*. New York: Crown.

_____. 1999. *Anticipations of the Reactions of Mechanical and Scientific Progress Upon Human Life and Thought*. London: Dover Publications; 1902 Leipzig: Bernhard Tauchnitz.

West, Anthony. 1984. *H.G. Wells; Aspects of a Life*. London: Hutchinson.

Chapter 6

Darwinism and the Tasmanian Genocide

Introduction

Darwin did not originate the theory of evolution by natural selection, but his 1859 book was critical in causing its wide acceptance. The story of the complete extermination of the native peoples of Tasmania in the 1800s is a well-documented example of one negative influence of the pre-Darwin racist evolutionary theories.

Tasmania, a 26,000 square mile (67,000 square-kilometers) island about the size of Ireland, is close to two hundred miles south of the Australian mainland, almost directly south of Melbourne. The island, once called Van Dieman's Land, is now part of Australia. The native Tasmanians, a highly isolated population of about 70 tribes and five language groups, had virtually no contact with other humans for thousands of years (Plomley 1983, 1991; Jones 1971). Their sole sea transportation was small rafts that were usually practical only for short trips (Mulvaney 1969).

Darwin did not publish his *Origin of Species* until 1859, but evolution in various forms was widely believed by many biologists, geologists, and others in the early 1800s (Osborn 1929). Darwin's own grandfather, Erasmus, was one of the first researchers to dig up an Aborigine from the grave to stuff and exhibit at the Royal College of Surgeons — the first of up to 10,000 bodies desecrated "to try to prove their racial inferiority" and document the "missing" link between stone age men and fully evolved Whites (Gripper 1994, 32). King-Hele (1963, 75) stated, "After 1794, statements of the principle of natural selection and evolution came fairly thick and fast." These ideas were widely discussed and influenced thinking about race, especially the place of the so-called "primitive" people in the animal kingdom.

In the early 1800s, the intelligencia believed that the native people of Australia, often called the Australian Aborigines because they were judged as primitive humans, were "the connecting link between man and the monkey tribes" (Travers 1968, 135). Many observers predicted that the "Blacks of Australia" were "a doomed race, and before many years they will be completely wiped out" (Hatton-Finch 1885, 148). Darwin himself concluded that the extinction of inferior races was part of the process of evolution that must be accepted as inevitable:

> Extinction follows chiefly from the competition of tribe with tribe, and race with race. Various checks are always in action, serving to keep down the numbers of each savage tribe, such as periodical famines, nomadic habits and the consequent deaths of infants, prolonged suckling, wars, accidents, sickness, licentiousness, the stealing of women, infanticide, and especially lessened fertility. If any one of these checks increases in power, even slightly, the tribe thus affected tends to decrease; and when of two adjoining tribes one becomes less numerous and less powerful than the other, the contest is soon settled by war, slaughter, cannibalism, slavery, and absorption (Darwin 1896, 182).

Darwin added that even when a weaker tribe is not rapidly exterminated once it

> begins to decrease, it generally goes on decreasing until it becomes extinct. When civilized nations come into contact with barbarians, the struggle is short, except where a deadly climate gives its aid to the native race. Of the causes which lead to the victory of civilized nations, some are plain and simple, others complex and obscure.

We can see that the cultivation of the land will be fatal in many ways to savages, for they cannot, or will not, change their habits (Darwin 1896, 182).

The Tasmanians as an Evolutionary Link

In the 19th century it was widely believed that the Tasmanians were a living evolutionary link between modern humans and their primate ancestors. They were a dark-skinned people, and their often-mentioned racial background included Negritic, Andamanese, and Murrayian (Birdsell 1949). Given the common presupposition of naturalistic evolution, the Tasmanian "race" was often seen as less than human and, consequently, many people felt that it was not wrong or immoral to treat Tasmanians like animals. This attitude eventually influenced behavior that resulted in the total extermination of the native Tasmanians. Today it is universally recognized that they were a distinct ethnic group similar to the Australian Aborigines and, although they possessed a unique culture, they were fully human (Mulvaney and Golson 1971).

The History of Tasmania and the Conflict

Tasmania was named after Dutchman Abel Jansen Tasman, a commander of two small Dutch vessels, who discovered the island in 1642. The island was soon visited by many others, including the French in 1772 (Castelain 1988; Plomley 1983; Garanger 1985; Hull 1870). In 1777, Captain Cook interacted with the natives, calling them "mild and cheerful, without reserve or jealousy of strangers" (Bonwick 1870, 6). He also said they behaved like "animals . . . scattered about along the coasts and in the woods" (Trollope 1873, 61). This perception would set the tone for later contacts with the native Tasmanians, sometimes called the Tasmanian Aborigines in contrast to the Australian Aborigines.

Other explorers with the benefit of more extensive contact concluded that the Tasmanians were people with cheerful dispositions, polite, kind, sincere, intelligent, and extremely skilled divers and fishermen (Plomley 1983; Bonwick 1870). The married women were described as excellent mothers, caring, affectionate, gentle, and exhibiting marked maternal tenderness (West 1987). The younger women were described as affectionate, gentle, and full of grace and wonderful spirit. Although the natives possessed a "primitive mentality," Plomley quoted an explorer who described them as

intelligent, grasping readily all my gestures. From the first moment, they seemed to understand my object perfectly, and they repeated willingly the words I had not been able to grasp the first time, and often roared with laughter when, trying to repeat what they said, I made a mistake or pronounced them badly (Plomley 1983, 64).

As a result of his extended contact with the Tasmanians, Pe´ron stated that the people had a "gentle confidence" in Pe´ron's crew as documented by their "benevolence which they never ceased to manifest toward us" and the

> frankness of their manners, the touching ingenuousness of their caresses, all concurred to excite within us sentiments of the tenderest interest. The intimate union of the different individuals of a family . . . had strongly moved us. I saw with an inexpressible pleasure the realization of those brilliant descriptions of the happiness and simplicity of the state of nature of which I had so many times in reading felt the seductive charm (Bonwick 1870, 27).

They wore necklaces and other ornaments, constructed huts, manufactured spears, waddys, spatulas, water vessels, cushions, baskets, cords and ropes, canoe rafts, and many other items (Plomley 1983). The island terrain and foliage, often described as a paradise, was

> diverse in scenery and in climate. . . . its small area [contains] tangled masses of mountains, great forests, innumerable lakes, picturesque waterfalls, fertile valleys and probably the roughest and most inaccessible country in all Australia. The climate is temperate, with a warm summer and a moderately cold winter. . . . The . . . coasts have moderate rainfall of up to 40 inches, the central tableland is drier; but within a few miles, in the western belt, the rain is at times practically continuous, and averages over 100 inches in the year (Laseron 1972, 139).

The native Tasmanians consisted of hunter-gatherers that were biologically similar to the aborigines living on the Australian mainland. Morris described them as a

> smallish but long-legged people, red-brown rather than black, with beetle brows, wide mouths, broad noses, and deep-set brown eyes. The men had rich beards and whiskers and wore their hair tightly curled in ringlets, smeared with red ochre; the women cut their hair short, but they were hirsute, too, and in old age often developed

incipient mustaches. Physically, the Tasmanians seem to have lacked stamina: their senses were uncannily acute, but they were not very strong, nor even particularly agile, though they were adept at running on all fours (1972, 62).

After reviewing the favorable early contacts with the Tasmanians, Bonwick sadly noted that the people, although at first were "almost universally" regarded positively by English colonists, a few years later, were viewed as creatures

> whose destruction would be a deed of merit, as well as an act of necessity. Smile as we may at the simplicity of Pe'ron, had our faith in the poor creatures been more like that of the kind-hearted Frenchman, the reader might have been spared the . . . mournful record of "The Last of the Tasmanians" (Bonwick 1870, 27).

This change in attitude was due to many factors including greed, economics, cultural, social and language differences, plus mistrust on both sides and the contingencies of history, but the factor we are focusing on here is the critical influence of evolution. Although it is difficult at this point in time to assess accurately the exact role Darwinism played in the events that followed the European arrival in Tasmania, it is clear that its role was not small and served to justify the many atrocities that occurred.

After the Tasmanian conflicts developed, the Europeans now described them as "ugly," some even "repulsive" with a "most hideous expression of countenance" (Morris 1972, 62). The "scientific" view of them then was summarized by Diamond who noted that the

> Tasmanians attracted the interest of scientists, who believed them to be a missing link between humans and apes. Hence when the last man, one William Lanner, died in 1869, competing teams of physicians, led by Dr. George Stokell from the Royal Society of Tasmania and Dr. W.L. Crowther from the Royal College of Surgeons, alternately dug up and reburied Lanner's body, cutting off parts of it and stealing them back and forth from each other. Crowther cut off the head, Stokell the hands and feet, and someone else the ears and nose (1988, 9).

The common attitude about the Tasmanians was expressed by David Collins, a 19th-century judge-advocate who wrote that Tasmanians were savages (Fisher 1968, 24). This belief is summarized by the eminent German

evolutionist Ernst Haeckel who concluded that "since the lower races —
such as the Veddahs or Australian Negroes — are physiologically nearer to
the mammals — apes and dogs — than to the civilized European, we must,
therefore, assign a totally different value to their lives" (1905, 390). West-
erner's perception of the Tasmanian culture was described by Mulvaney as

> so rudimentary that evolutionary theorists later judged it a store-
> house of fossil facts. Edward Tylor dubbed Tasmanians the "rep-
> resentatives of Palaeolithic Man;" John Lubbock implicitly denied
> their humanity with his mechanistic aphorism: "The Van Diemener
> [Tasmanians] and the South American are to the antiquary what the
> opossum and sloth are to the geologist" (1969, 133).

The result of this belief was well put by Diamond when he stated:

> If you ask any anthropologist to summarize in one phrase what was
> most distinctive about the Tasmanians, the answer will surely be
> "the most primitive people still alive in recent centuries." The label
> "primitive" clearly has explosive . . . racial overtones, and in the
> nineteenth century its application led to tragic consequences (1993,
> 51).

The first major skirmish with the native Tasmanians occurred on May 3,
1804. This event was the beginning of a series of conflicts that eventually
resulted in a full-scale attack on them. A British officer, for reasons that are
unclear today, ordered his men to open fire on the Tasmanians, killing or
mortally wounding at least 50. The result was that "the friendly disposition
of the natives was completely altered by this unwarranted attack and the
consequent loss of life. Animosity and revenge were engendered by this atro-
cious act of barbarity, and the result was a series of petty encounters . . . in
which of course the natives were constantly defeated, many of them losing
their lives" (Knighton 1886, 272).

Lieutenant Moore, the officer who gave the command to fire, was evidently drunk from an "over-dose of rations' of rum," and the firing seems to
have been done in order to see them flee. And flee they did, terrified "at the
execution" which left in them "a deep-rooted hatred of the white faces which
never subsequently died out" (Knighton 1886, 272). The beginning of the
slaughter came not long after the Europeans began settling in Tasmania and
is vividly summarized by Diamond:

> Whites kidnapped Tasmanian children as laborers, kidnapped

women as consorts, mutilated or killed men, trespassed on [their] hunting grounds, and tried to clear Tasmanians off their land. . . . As a result of the kidnappings, the native population of northeast Tasmania in November 1830 had been reduced to seventy-two adult men, three adult women, and no children. One shepherd shot nineteen Tasmanians with a swivel gun loaded with nails. Four other shepherds ambushed a group of natives, killed thirty, and threw their bodies over a cliff remembered today as Victory Hill (1988, 8).

The Tasmanians' ineffective attempts to defend themselves allowed Governor Sir George Arthur to order all Tasmanians to leave areas of the island settled by Europeans (Bonwick 1870). Evidently, not content to deal with the situation by this order alone, in November 1828 Arthur authorized his men to kill on sight any Tasmanian that still lived or wandered into the areas where Europeans resided (Diamond 1993, 57). The government even sponsored "roving parties" consisting of convicts led by police that

hunted down and killed Tasmanians. . . . Next, a bounty was declared on the natives: five British pounds for each adult, and two pounds for each child [that was] caught alive. "Black catching" as it was called because of the Tasmanians' dark skin, became big business pursued by private as well as official roving parties. . . . A commission . . . was set up to recommend an overall policy towards the natives. After considering proposals to capture them for sale as slaves, poison or trap them, or hunt them with dogs, the commission settled on continued bounties and the use of mounted police (Diamond 1988, 8–9).

One account of the violence that the European-Tasmanian conflicts developed into is as follows:

A party of the Richmond police were passing through the Bush in 1827, when a tribe, seeing them, got up on a hill and threw stones upon them. The others fired in return, and then charged them with the bayonet. We have Mr. G.A. Robinson's authority for stating that "a party of military and constables got a number of Natives between two perpendicular rocks, on a sort of shelf, and killed seventy of them, dragging the women and children from the crevices of the rocks, and *dashing out their brains*" (Bonwick 1870, 64, emphasis in original).

One report from an 1830 account said

> a new sport has become fashionable in Tasmania and is spreading
> through Australia: "Abo hunting." In Tasmania's largest "hunt" so
> far, a line of beaters spread across the island to push the Aborigines
> into the muzzles of the huntsmen's guns. . . . To the uneducated
> settlers they are vermin — to be subdued and slaughtered (Mercer
> 1999, 448).

The wanton brutality against what some Caucasians saw as their inferior
competitors was horrendous. Women were commonly raped and many bore
children by the early settlers. Many of the settlers allegedly "amused themselves by emasculating all of the native men that they could seize . . . and
it was the subject of mutual boasting as to the numbers that they had thus
treated" (Knighton 1886, 274).

Knighton concludes that the whole Tasmanian record was "one of outrage, torture, mutilation, murder, and robbery, relieved here and there by
noble acts of philanthropy and kindly benevolence" (1886, 283). In short,
they were "hunted down like wild beasts" because this is what many Europeans believed that they were (Bonwick 1870, 66). At the least, the biblical
teaching that all men are descendants of Adam and Eve was ignored. The
European brutality was described by Diamond as follows:

> When British settlers poured into Tasmania in the 1820s . . . racial
> conflict intensified. Settlers regarded Tasmanians as little more than
> animals and treated them accordingly. Tactics for hunting down
> Tasmanians included riding out on horseback to shoot them, set-
> ting out steel traps to catch them, and putting out poison flour
> where they might find and eat it. Shepherds cut off the penis and
> testicles of aboriginal men, to watch the men run a few yards before
> dying (1993, 57).

The Tasmanian affair was not simply a conflict between cultures but, as
vividly related by Knighton (1886, 268), was also influenced by the beliefs
of the "race expert scientists" who concluded that "attempts to civilize the
Australasians many regarded as absolutely futile. It would be easier . . . to
bring down the whites to the level of the natives than to raise the natives to
the level of the whites. Many of the whites, it may be replied, have already
sunk to the level of the black fellows, by their own unaided effort in descent"
(1886, 268).

Some rationalized the Tasmanian situation by concluding that the "struggle for life which is going on around us now, [and] as it has been ever since man made his appearance upon earth" is a fact of nature (Knighton 1886, 269). Many Christians and clergy did attempt to help them, some with much success, but their help was far too little too late (Bonwick 1869, 1870).

The foreign office in London was fully aware that a wide variety of native peoples lived in British colonies. They were far more concerned about governing their vast empire than proving evolution theories, and ordered the natives to be treated with amity and kindness. Consequently, many of the local residents — a large number of which were convicts — and the local British government, endeavored to deal with them justly and legally. Nonetheless, the people "soon learned that the best game was raping and disfiguring Tasmanian women and killing and mutilating Tasmanian men. No one censored this practice; children were murdered, men emasculated and women stolen from their tribes" (Shepherd 1990, 3).

Although some whites tried to blame the conflicts on the Tasmanians, many of the settlers were convicted felons, and the evidence supports the conclusion that most of the unprovoked violence came from the Europeans (Bonwick 1870). As Knighton notes, though, many offenses against the natives "could not be substantiated in the courts for want of witnesses. The only witnesses there were the white men who committed the outrages" (1886, 273).

The words of the biologist opposed to evolution did not help to stem the slaughter against the Tasmanians. Nor did they help to stop the genocide solution to the whole "savage tribe" problem. After relating how one person used strychnine to kill a large number of Blacks, Hatton-Finch noted that, in general, "few people are ambitious" enough to indulge

> in such wholesale slaughter, and, when the Blacks are troublesome, it is generally considered sufficient punishment to go out and shoot one or two. They are easily discouraged in their wild state, especially by anything that they cannot understand (1885, 149–150).

Even some of the mainline churches acquiesced to the view that the Tasmanians were an inferior race, loved neither by man nor God.

> Clergyman in the early days of the colony ignored the aborigines completely, believing them to be so far beneath the level of humanity as to be not worth teaching. As late as 1829, some twenty-six

years after the first settlement, Henry Widowson wrote [the Church] . . . made no attempt to convert the "poor wretches" he noted, and added: "I have never heard, nor do I believe, that any teacher of the gospel ever went half a dozen miles from Hobart Town to enquire into their conditions." In fact when Governor Arthur asked the Church Missionary Society in 1828 for a missionary he was refused (Travers 1968, 35).

The Last of the Tasmanians

In 1830, a mere 30 years after the British originally settled in Tasmania, the last 135 of the original population, estimated from 3,000 to as many as 5,000, were rounded up by George Agustus Robinson and transported to

Flinders Island 30 miles northeast of Tasmania (Jones 1971). Flinders Island, a place with few trees, no rivers, violent cold winds, frequent rain, and overrun with grass-tree scrub and tea-tree thickets, is directly north of the northeast corner of Tasmania (Fisher 1968). Robinson had long fought for the interests of the natives, even learning their language, and was thoroughly convinced that the blame for the

Photograph of the last 4 Tasmanian aborigines, with Truganini seated on the right.

native-settler conflicts lay primarily with the settlers (Bonwick 1870).

Although he was paid three hundred pounds in advance, and was to be paid seven hundred total if he ridded Tasmania of the natives, he also likely realized that this was the only chance to save the remaining Tasmanians (Hormann 1949). A "fervent Christian, he was not convinced that these so-called savages were beyond salvation" (Travers 1968, 157). His enormous success in working with them was vastly greater than the government's, partly because "he regarded them as rational humans, not savages, akin to the monkeys" (Travers 1968, 179).

Unfortunately, Robinson proved to be a mediocre administrator, and the living conditions on the island were poor, many natives were extremely homesick, and disease was rampant. The newly transported persons soon began to die from chronic pneumonia, influenza, or other respiratory illnesses, as did virtually all infants born on the island. They often felt that they were taken there to die and, 30 years later, in 1869, evidently only six pure-blooded free Tasmanians remained alive, including William Lanne (or Lanney), a woman "with sparkling features" named Truganini, and one other woman called "Mini." Lanne died of choleric diarrhea at age 34 on March 3, 1869, and the last woman died on May 8, 1876 at age 73 (Turnbull 1948). The interest of outsiders in these three persons, even at this point, was not humane, but because of

> the interests of science to secure a perfect skeleton of a male Tasmanian aboriginal. A female skeleton is now in the Museum, but there is no male, consequently the death of "Billy Lanne" put our surgeons on the alert. The Royal Society, anxious to obtain the skeleton for the Museum, wrote specifically to the Government upon the subject, setting forth at length the reasons why, if possible, the skeleton should be secured to them. The Government at once admitted their right to it, in preference to any other institution, and the Council expressed their willingness at any time to furnish casts, photographs, and all other particulars to any scientific society requiring them. . . . so valuable a skeleton would not have been permitted to remain in the grave, and possibly no opposition would have been made to its removal, had it been taken by those best entitled to hold it in the interests of the public and of science (Bonwick 1870, 397–398).

Other scientific institutions besides the Royal Society were determined to add Billy Lanne's skeleton to their collection. One determined thief entered the hospital on a Friday night and "the head was skinned and the skull carried away." To conceal the crime

> the head of a patient who had died in the hospital . . . was . . . placed inside the scalp of the unfortunate native, the face being drawn over so as to have the appearance of completeness. On this mutilation being discovered, the members of the Council of the Royal Society were greatly annoyed, and feeling assured that the object of the party who had taken the skull was afterwards to take the body from the grave, and so possess himself of the perfect skeleton, it was resolved

to take off the feet and hands and to lodge them in the Museum (Bonwick 1870, 397–398).

The demand for the bones and other body parts was primarily a result of the importance of the Tasmanians in documenting and researching evolution. The Royal College of Surgeons museum listed its Aboriginal skulls as "the most primitive of all existing forms of mankind" (Monaghan 1991, 30). Before the last pureblood Tasmanian woman, Truganini, died, Diamond noted that she was

> terrified of similar post mortem mutilation and asked in vain to be buried at sea. As she had feared, the Royal Society dug up her skeleton and put it on public display in the Tasmanian Museum, where it remained until 1947. In that year the museum finally yielded to complaints . . . and transferred Truganini's skeleton to a room where only scientists could view it. . . . Finally in 1976 — the centenary year of Truganini's death — her skeleton was cremated over the museum's objections, and her ashes were scattered at sea as she had requested (1988, 9).

The extent of the desecrating grave problem was so widespread in science that

> some of the greatest names in British science were involved in a body-snatching trade of huge proportions. Between 5,000 and 10,000 Aborigines had their graves desecrated, their bodies disinterred and parts dismembered. George Rolleson, of Oxford University's Museum of Anatomy, and Sir Richard Owen and Sir Arthur Keith, of the Royal College of Surgeons, were involved, Charles Darwin is also implicated through letters written in the 1870s and found in a Hobart archive in the mid-1970s (Monaghan 1991, 33).

A few mixed-blooded Tasmanians survived, and the claim of the last pure Tasmanian was finally settled by Parliament to be Fanny Cochrane Smith who was

> an Aboriginal lady, a very hard-working woman, who lived at Nicholls Rivulet. Fanny was taken in by a white family and was readily accepted by the white community. She married a William Smith on 2 October 1854 at the Independent Church in Hobart. They had eleven children. Fanny continued to press her claim that she, not Truganini, was the last of the full-bloods. She finally convinced

Parliament, with the result that a resolution was passed in 1884 granting her land of two hundred acres in addition to the one hundred she already had at Port Cygnet. Fanny and William belonged to the Methodist Church. Fanny had a lovely singing voice. She recorded some songs two years before she died on 25 February 1905, at seventy-four. She had been in receipt of a Government annuity of 50 pounds a year and after her death she left her property to the Methodist Church. Her descendants still live in the same area (West 1987, 91).

Travers concluded that the last full-blooded Tasmanian died in 1888. Although little is known about the last survivors after Truganini, evidence exists that at least three women were kidnapped by sailors and have presented reasonable claims as to their heritage (Mollison and Everitt 1978; Bonwick 1869).

Were the Tasmanians an Inferior Race?

That the motivation for the slaughter involved race and evolutionary beliefs cannot be debated. By the mid-1800s, the scientific "interest in the bones of Australian Aborigines was gaining popularity, as early evolution theorists sought proof. . . . The interest grew to a storm soon after Charles Darwin published his *On the Origin of Species* in 1859" (Monaghan 1991, 34). The reason was because, in his book on human evolution,

> *The Descent of Man*, Darwin positioned the Australians as crucial proof of his theories: "At some future period, not very distant as measured by centuries, the civilized races of man will almost certainly exterminate, and replace, the savage races throughout the world." Within 20 years, Darwin's prediction was to come true in Tasmania. Darwin himself wrote to one of his associate's museums, asking for pure-blood Tasmanian skulls if it would not upset the feelings of the remaining natives. There were then only four Tasmanian Aborigines left. Darwin's theories had placed Aborigines as a possible evolutionary link between man and ape. Museum curators from around the world clamored to obtain skulls. A complete set of racial crania was essential for any study. Australian Aboriginal skulls, particularly the increasingly rare Tasmanians, were much sought after (Monaghan 1991, 34).

In Darwin's words, the different human races "act on each other in the same way as different species of animals — the stronger always exterminating the weaker" (Darwin 1965, 230). A concern in understanding the contribution of the Tasmanian holocaust to evolution is that the slaughter started before Darwin published his classic work in 1859. As Altick documents, "Most of the components of what Darwin formalized as the theory of evolution were abroad in informed circles long before the *Origin* appeared" (1978, 287). When Darwin published his *Origin,* many scientists had already accepted his basic ideas. Darwin simply presented what was then one of the best-documented and most convincing cases for an idea already widely accepted by many of the intellectual elite.

While many claimed that the Tasmanians were a "primitive" race, judging by physical characteristics they were related to the Australian Aborigines (Thorn 1971). The observation that many of their cultural practices, such as burial traditions, were very similar supports this conclusion (Hiatt 1969). In a study of prehistoric Australia, Mulvaney (1969) concluded that the Tasmanian racial affiliations still remain speculative.

That the Tasmanians were not an "inferior race" was evident from the observations of many qualified researchers. In answer to the question "Were the Blacks of Tasmania capable of *true civilization?*" Bonwick answered "*Yes,* undoubtedly;" and provided the example of Walter George Arthur, a Tasmanian aboriginal whom he personally knew. Arthur

> was captured when a mere infant, and brought up and educated at the Queen's Orphan School (at Hobart Town). His ideas were perfectly English, and there was not the smallest dash of the savage in him. He was a very conversable man, fond of reading, and spoke and wrote English quite grammatically. His spelling was also quite correct. This man had a hundred acres of land, and knew his rights in relation thereto quite as well as you do yours [and he was] . . . creditable to his acuteness, sense of right, and of honorable feelings (Bonwick 1870, 353).

As late as 1926, many respected scientists were still teaching that the native Australians were "strongly reminiscent of the species Neandertalensis" and that the "former inhabitants of Tasmania [were a] . . . race probably a bit more primitive than Australians" (Wilder 1926, 341–342). Hughes even claimed "by the 1870s, Tasmania had more paupers, lunatics, orphans, and invalids than South Australia and Queensland combined, concentrated in a population less than half of theirs" (1987, 593). This was true partially because a large number of ex-convicts lived there but, according to Hughes, the nonconvict population had the worst jobs, the least capital, the lowest education, were most prone to fighting and drinking, and were more likely to be both charged and convicted of crimes.

According to historical research, little evidence exists for the commonly alleged behavioral deviancy and other so-called evidences of biological "primitiveness" of the Aborigines and the Tasmanians in general (Burnham 1980; Thomas 1981; Mulvaney 1969; Lockwood 1963; Thomas 1959; Turnbull 1962; Healy 1978; and Haydon 1980). Consequently, it is difficult to conclude from the evidence that a "superior" race of individuals conquered an "inferior" group.

In addition, the social system and the nonconvict population did little to help matters: "Australia presented them with much the same social disabilities that had pushed them [the convict population] into crime in Britain," and "the unrelenting, go-getting, land-grabbing, cash-and-gold obsessed materialism of free Australian colonists, acting in a vast geographical space, but a small social one" exacerbated matters (Hughes 1987, 588). Conditions were such that Hughes expresses surprise that "with such a social ethic . . . the conviction rate was not higher." The crime level among the convicts actually was rather low compared to the rate found in the general population in the average large American city today.

Hughes (1987) estimates that in the middle 1840s, very few of the criminal convictions in Australia — he estimates 6 percent — were for crimes committed by the natives. Part of the reason, he concludes, is that the Aborigines were "diligent family-oriented workers with a stake in their community." Bates (1973, 64) even believes that the moment the Europeans entered their lives "all native social and sexual taboos were broken" to the major detriment of the native people. They also possessed a social system that the Europeans destroyed (Brown 1988; McGrew 1987; Goede and Harmon 1983). Much of the problem was because the authorities allowed, and even encouraged, violence against the Tasmanians:

> They have been shot in the woods, and hunted down as beasts of prey. Their women have been contaminated, and then had their throats cut, or been shot, by the British residents, who . . . call [ed] themselves civilized people. The . . . Government, to its shame be it recorded, in no one instance, on no single occasion, ever punished, or threatened to punish, the acknowledged murders of the aboriginal inhabitants (*The Hobart Town Times*, April 1836, quoted in Bonwick 1870, 70).

The extermination of the Tasmanians solved the native problem by Nazi-type final solution. The same end did not befall the mainland Australian Aborigine population partially because they were far too numerous to exterminate in the same manner as the Tasmanians, although the new settlers came close. Diamond claims that after the arrival of the British colonists in 1788, the Australian Aborigine population declined from 300,000 to a mere 60,000 by 1921. The Australian Aborigines were somewhat different from the other native peoples in this part of the world such as the Polynesians (Grattan 1942, 40). As a result, they were at times "brutally slaughtered as one might slaughter vermin" and were also slaughtered for science; "murdered for the body-parts trade" to supply bones to prove evolution to the public (Monaghan 1991, 33).

One early Darwinist revealed the attitude toward genocide that the Darwinist belief structure engendered: "The Negro alone . . . of the dark races, appears to be able to hold his own in the great struggle for existence, when brought into competition with the white man. We may deplore the fact, but we cannot alter the laws of nature" (Knighton 1886, 285). The inferior races were destined to be wiped out in the great struggle for life that Darwinists then believed created all life. Like the wild animals, the Aborigines were in the way of the new settlers. Because they interfered with the new population, they were not to be shown mercy, but were to be wiped out for the benefit of the superior race.

British historian Anthony Trollope expressed the prevailing 19th-century attitude toward Australian Blacks: "It is their fate to be abolished; and they are already vanishing" (1873, 75) and, as an inferior race, "the negro cannot live on equal terms with the white man" (69). The Aborigines were even considered "infinitely lower" than the "African negro" (69). When they were killed by a White, the murder was not reported to the police because "no one but a fool would say anything about it" to them (Trollope 1873, 73). They are the "same as a tiger or a snake" that "has to go," but "should perish without unnecessary suffering" (Trollope 1873, 76):

> If you ask what sort of race the Blacks of Australia are, nine people out of ten will immediately answer . . . that they are physically and intellectually the most degraded race in the world. . . . for the purpose of gauging their physical and intellectual merits, we can only do so by comparing [races] with each other. When compared with those nations of the Old World . . . the Australian Black is, of course, a very low specimen of the human race indeed (Hatton-Finch 1885, 137).

Darwin himself used the Aborigine and the Tasmanian holocaust as prime evidence for his theory of natural selection (Monaghan 1991; Darwin 1896, 182). His words about their demise illustrate an example of the title of his 1859 work, *The Origin of Species By Means of Natural Selection or the Preservation of Favored Races in the Struggle for Life*:

> When Tasmania was first colonized, the natives were roughly estimated by some at 7,000 and by others at 20,000. Their number was soon greatly reduced, chiefly by fighting with the English and with each other. After the famous hunt by all the colonists, when the remaining natives delivered themselves up to the government, they consisted only of 120 individuals, who were in 1832 transported to Flinders Island (Darwin 1897, 183–184).

After they were forced from their homeland and transported to Flinder's Island, Darwin notes that they could not compete with the more advanced races:

> Disease and death still pursued them, and in 1864 one man (who died in 1869), and three elderly women alone survived. . . . With respect to the cause of this extraordinary state of things . . . death followed the attempts to civilize the natives. "If left to themselves to roam as they were wont and undisturbed, they would have reared more children, and there would have been less mortality." Another careful observer of the natives, Mr. Davis, remarks, "The births have been few and the deaths numerous" (1896, 184).

Darwin's words and those of his followers no doubt motivated hunting the Australian Aborigines down after 1859 and slaughtering them wholesale, and removing their "bones from their sacred graves . . . to prove the racist theory of white superiority." What occurred to them was not just massive killing and genocide, but, according to Dr. Broca, the English committed "atrocities a hundred times less excusable than the hitherto unrivaled crimes of which the Spaniards were guilty in the sixteenth century in the Antilles" (quoted in Bonwick 1870, 66).

The carnage was to the extent that proving the "racial inferiority" idea became a "new export industry" of Australia (Gripper 1994, 32). The motivation was to prove that "the Aborigines were the 'missing link' between Stone Age men and 'fully evolved' whites" (Gripper 1994, 32). In the words of Shepherd:

> Ironically, the Tasmanians were more interesting in death than they

had ever been in life. Darwin's theory placed this society so low on the evolutionary scale that their lifestyle and, concomitantly, their dead bodies became fascinating to scientists. Their graves were robbed so that physicians and anthropologists could study their anatomy; science was the excuse. The discovery of the remains of Neanderthal man paralleled the discovery of the Tasmanians, societies that were almost equally primitive. The Royal College of Surgeons in London had the largest collection of Tasmanian skeletons, and in what may be the final injustice, this collection was destroyed by a German firebomb during the Second World War (1990, 4).

The Tasmanians were commonly used as links to prove human evolution. For example, Haeckel tried to prove that "the gap between humans and their nearest animal relatives could be bridged by almost imperceptible gradations" (Weikart 2004, 106). The frontispiece of the first edition of Haeckel's popular work, *The Natural History of Creation* (1868), consisted of a set of 12 male facial profiles, beginning with a European and "descending" in order, an East Asian, a Fuegian, an Australian, a Black African and, last, a Tasmanian. The "lowest human," the Tasmanian, looked very similar to the gorilla in the seventh profile.

After the gorilla came five other simian species. The six "steps" between the "highest" and "lowest" human races and only a single "step" between the "lowest" human race and gorillas, demonstrated Haeckel's point about how close the lowest humans were to apes. To ensure no one missed the point, Haeckel noted in his caption that his illustrations demonstrated graphically that "the differences between the lowest humans and the highest apes are smaller than the differences between the lowest and highest humans" (quoted in Weikart 2004, 106). Weikart adds that the

> proximity of "inferior" or "lower" races to simians is a frequent theme in Haeckel's writings. He referred to the Australian Aborigines and the Bushmen of South Africa as similar to apes (*affenähnlich*). He further described some races in Africa and Asia as having no concept of marriage or the family; like apes, they live in herds, climb trees, and eat fruit. These races are not capable of learning European culture, for "it is impossible to want to plant human education (*Bildung*), where the necessary ground for it, human brain development, is lacking. . . . They have scarcely elevated themselves above that lowest stage of transition from anthropoid apes to apemen" (2004, 106).

Conclusions

The Tasmanian genocide is a good example of the influence of Darwinism even before Darwin published his first book espousing evolution in 1859. In the concatenation of social, cultural, religious, and other influences, evolutionary beliefs played a clear, if not a major role, in the demise of the Tasmanian natives (Wieland 1995). Darwin taught that the "inferior" races would become extinct, and these teachings influenced many important scientists and political leaders (Bergman 1992).

Many Christians of this era also were heavily influenced by inferior race ideas, and some even attempted to try to use biblical arguments to justify their racial inferiority beliefs, such as the conclusion that some races were pre-Adamites, created before Adam and thus were not humans. Another example is the conclusion that certain races were "the beasts of the earth" or black skin was a sign of the curse that God put on Ham and all his descendants mentioned in Genesis 3:14, 7:21, and 8:17 (Buswell 1964).

The negative role that Darwin's theory played in history is clear, and the suffering caused by Darwinism has been, and continues to be, enormous (Chalk and Jonassohn 1990). If the British fully believed and acted consistently on the belief that all humans were children of Adam, and were all brothers and sisters as Genesis teaches, the Tasmanian holocaust would likely never have occurred. Never would the "long series of cruelties and misfortunes" that befell these people have happened (Bonwick 1870, 56). As Diamond noted, "While the Tasmanians were few in number, their extermination was disproportionately influential in Australian history because Tasmania was the first Australian colony to solve its native problem . . . by . . . getting rid of all its natives" (1988, 9).

References

Altick, Richard. 1978. *The Shows of London*. Cambridge, MA: Harvard University Press.

Bates, Daisy. 1973. *The Passing of the Aborigines: A Lifetime Spent Among the Natives of Australia*. New York: Pocket Books.

Bergman, Jerry. 1992. "Eugenics and the Development of Nazi Race Policy." *Perspectives on Science and Christian Faith*, June, 44(2):109–123.

Birdsell, J.B. 1949. "The Racial Origin of the Extinct Tasmanians." *Records of the Queen Victoria Museum*. 2:223–231.

Bonwick, James. 1869. *The Last of the Tasmanians*. London: Samson Low, Son and Marston.

———. 1870. *Daily Life and Origin of the Tasmanians; or The Black War of Van Diemen's Land*. London: Samson Low, Son and Marston.

Brown, Dorothy. 1988. Review of "Pride Against Prejudice — Reminiscences of a Tasmanian

Aborigine, by Ida West." *Journal of the Polynesian Society* 97(2):225–226.

Burnham, John C. 1980. "Psychotic Delusions as a Key to Historical Cultures: Tasmania, 1830–1940. *Journal of Social History,* Spring, 13(3):368–383.

Buswell, James O. 1964. *Slavery, Segregation and Scripture.* Grand Rapids, MI: Eerdmans.

Castelain, Anne Marie. 1988. "In Search of the Australian Continent: The Baudin Expedition [1801–1804]. *Cahiers de Sociologie Economique et Culturelle, Ethnopsychologie,* June, 9:9–36.

Chalk, Frank, and Kurt Jonassohn. 1990. *The History and Sociology of Genocide.* New Haven: Yale University Press.

Darwin, Charles. 1896. *Descent of Man, and Selection in Relation to Sex.* New York: D. Appleton.

———. 1897. *The Origin of Species By Means of Natural Selection or the Preservation of Favored Races in the Struggle for Life.* New York: D. Appleton and Company.

———. 1965. "Journey Across the Blue Mountains to Bathurst in January 1836." *Fourteen Journeys Over the Blue Mountains of New South Wales 1813–1841.* Ed. by George Mackaness. London: Harwitz-Grahame.

Diamond, Jared. 1988. "In Black and White; How Have Ordinary People, So Often throughout Human History, Brought Themselves to Commit Genocide?" *Natural History,* Oct., 97(10):8–14.

———. 1993. "Ten-Thousand Years of Solitude." *Discover,* March, 14(3):49–57.

Fisher, John. 1968. *The Australians: From 1788 to Modern Times.* New York: Taplinger Publishing Company.

Garanger, J. 1985. "The Baudin Expedition and the Tasmanian Aborigines 1802, by N.J.B. Plomley." *Anthropologie,* 89(3):434–435.

Goede, A., and R.S. Harmon. 1983. "Radiometric Dating of Tasmanian Speleothems — Evidence of Cave Evolution and Climatic Change. *Journal of the Geological Society of Australia* 30(1-2):89–100.

Grattan, C. Hartley. 1942. *Introducing Australia.* New York: The John Day Company.

Gripper, Ali. 1994. "Blacks Slain for Science's White Superiority Theory." *The Daily Telegraph Mirror* (Sydney, Australia), April 26, p. 32.

Haeckel, Ernst. 1868. *Natürliche Schöpfungsgeschichte.* Berlin: Georg Reimer.

———. 1905. *The Wonders of Life.* New York: Harper.

Hatton-Finch, Harold. 1885. *Advance Australia! An Account of Eight Years Work, Wondering and Amusement in Queensland, New South Wales and Victoria.* London: W.H. Allen & Company.

Haydon, Tom. 1980. *The Last Tasmanian.* Del Mar, CA: CRM-McGraw Hill Films; Pt. I, Ancestors, Pt. II, Extinction.

Healy, J.J. 1978. *Literature and the Aborigine in Australia 1770–1975.* New York: St. Martin's Press.

Hiatt, Betty. 1969. "Cremation in Aboriginal Australia." *Mankind,* Dec., 7(2):104–119.

Hormann, B.L. 1949. *Extinction and Survival: A Study of the Reaction of Aboriginal Populations to European Expansion.* Ph.D. Thesis. Chicago, IL: University of Chicago.

Hughes, Robert. 1987. *The Fatal Shore: The Epic of Australia's Founding.* New York: Alfred A. Knopf.

Hull, Hugh M. 1870. *Lecture on the Aborigines of Tasmania.* Hobart, Tasmania: Mercury Steam

Press.

Jones, Rhys. 1971. "The Demography of the Hunters and Farmers in Tasmania." Chapter 19, p. 271–287, in Mulvaney and Golson 1971.

King-Hele, Desmond. 1963. *Erasmus Darwin; Grandfather of Charles Darwin.* New York: Charles Scribner's Sons.

Knighton, William. 1886. *Struggles for Life.* London: Williams and Norgate.

Laseron, Charles Francis. 1972. (J.N. Jennings, editor). *The Face of Australia; The Shaping of a Continent.* Sydney, Australia: Angus and Robertson.

Lockwood, Douglas. 1963. *We, The Aborigines.* Westport, CT: Greenwood Press.

McGrew, W.C. 1987. "Tools to Get Food: The Subsistent of Tasmanian Aborigines and Tanzanian Chimpanzees Compared." *Journal of Anthropological Research,* 43(3):247–258.

Mercer, Derrik. 1999. *Millennium Year by Year.* New York: Dorling Kindersley. "European Settlers Kill Tasmanian Natives."

Mollison, B., and C. Everitt. 1978. *The Tasmanian Aborigines and Their Descendants.* Hobart: University of Tasmania.

Monaghan, David. 1991. "The Body-Snatchers. *The Bulletin* (Sydney, Australia), November 12, 113(5795):33–38.

Morris, James. 1972. "The Final Solution, Down Under," in *Horizon* Winter 1972, 9(1):61–70. New York: American Heritage.

Mulvaney, D.J. 1969. *Ancient Peoples and Places; The Prehistory of Australia.* Vol. 65 in the series, Daniel, Glyn, editor. London: Thames and Hudson.

Mulvaney, D.J., and J. Golson, editors. 1971. *Aboriginal Man and Environment in Australia.* Canberra: Australian National Press.

Osborn, Henry Fairfield. 1929. *From the Greeks to Darwin; The Development of the Evolution Idea Through Twenty-Four Centuries.* New York: Charles Scribner's Sons.

Plomley, N.J.B. 1983. *The Baudin Expedition and the Tasmanian Aborigines, 1802.* Hobart, Tasmania: Blubber Head Press.

———, editor. 1991. *Jorgen Jorgenson and the Aborigines of the Van Dieman's Land.* Sandy Bay, Tasmania: Blubber Head Press.

Shepherd, Ann. 1990. *The Last Tasmanian.* Instructors Guide for the CRM/McGraw-Hill Film. Del Mar, CA.

Thomas, Elizabeth Marshall. 1959. *The Harmless People.* New York: Alfred A. Knopf.

Thomas, Nicholas. 1981. "Social Theory, Ecology and Epistemology; Theoretical Issues in Australian Prehistory." *Mankind,* December, 13(2):165–177.

Thorn, A.G. 1971. "The Racial Affinities and Origins of the Australian Aborigines." Chapter 21, p. 316–325 in Mulvaney and Golson 1971.

Travers, Robert. 1968. *The Tasmanians: The Story of a Doomed Race.* Sydney: Cassell Australia.

Trollope, Anthony. 1873. *Australia and New Zealand.* London: Chapman and Hall. Chapter 4: "Aboriginals," p. 59–76.

Turnbull, Colin M. 1962. *The Forest People.* New York: Simon and Schuster, Inc.

Turnbull, Clive. 1948. *The Black War: The Extermination of the Tasmanian Aborigines.* Melbourne: F.W. Cheshire.

Weikart, Richard. 2004. *From Darwin to Hitler: Evolutionary Ethics, Eugenics, and Racism in Germany.* New York: Palgrave Macmillan.

West, Ida. 1987. *Pride Against Prejudice.* Canberra, Australia: Australian Institute of Aboriginal Studies.

Wieland, Carl. 1995. "Culture Class." *Creation,* June-August 17(5):42–44.

Wilder, Harris Hawthorne. 1926. *The Pedigree of the Human Race.* New York: Henry Holt and Company.

Chapter 7

The Eugenics Movement Comes to America

Introduction

It is commonly assumed that the eugenics movement, which began and took hold primarily in Europe, was introduced by the Nazis. The movement actually originated in Great Britain, and one of the first countries where Darwin's ideas on eugenics took hold and flourished aside from Germany was in America (Ordover 2003; Jones 1980). The American eugenics movement heavily influenced not only new legislation but also court decisions. The result was that science influenced a new worldview that resulted in a large number of human rights abuses that even rivaled some of those that existed in Nazi Germany (Green 1981).

The eugenics movement developed from the core ideas of biological evolution, primarily those expounded and popularized by Charles Darwin (Barzun 1958). The eugenics movement grew rapidly soon after Darwin published his *Origin* book in 1859. The basic eugenics theory was formulated by Darwin's cousin, Sir Francis Galton (1869, 1880). It has been well documented that "eugenics was the legitimate offspring of Darwinian evolution, a natural and doubtless inevitable outgrowth of currents of thought that developed from the publication in 1859 of Charles Darwin's *The Origin of Species*" (Haller 1984, 3).

Eugenics, the science of improving the human race by scientific control of breeding, was viewed by many if not most scientists for over a century as a major means of producing paradise on earth. These scientists concluded that most human traits, including behavior, were genetic in origin, and that persons who came from genetically "good families" tended to turn out far better than those who came from genetically inferior families. A major way to achieve this paradise, therefore, was to encourage genetically good families to have more children, and genetically poor families to have few or no children.

From these simple observations developed one of the most far-reaching movements in recent history, which resulted in the loss of untold millions of lives and enormous suffering, primarily in Nazi Germany. It discouraged building hospitals for the mentally ill or even aiding the sick, the poor, and all those who were believed to be in some way "genetically inferior," which included persons afflicted with an extremely wide variety of unrelated physical and even psychological maladies. The end goal was to save society from the "evolutionarily inferior humans" (Haller 1984, 17).

The means to achieve this goal included sterilization, permanent custody of "defective" adults by the state, marriage restrictions, and, in Germany, even the elimination of the unfit through means that ranged from refusal to help them to outright murder. In modern times, this movement probably had a greater adverse influence on society than virtually any other ideology except Marxism that developed from an idea touted as scientific. It culminated with the infamous Holocaust, and afterward rapidly declined until today — and now is held in disrepute by most persons, including most scientists. Eugenics movements spanned the political spectrum from conservative to radical socialists; what they had in common was a belief in Darwinism and a faith that science, particularly evolutionary genetics, held the key to improving humanity.

The Growth of the Eugenics Movement in America

The first eugenics movement in America was founded in 1903 and included many of the most eminent biologists in the country: David Star Jordan (a prominent biologist and chancellor of Stanford University) was its chairman,

American horticulturist Luther Burbank, 1915.

and Luther Burbank (the famous plant breeder), Vernon L. Kellogg (a world-renowned biologist at Stanford), William E. Castle (a Harvard geneticist), Roswell H. Johnson (a geologist and a professor of genetics), and Charles R. Henderson of the University of Chicago were all active members.

One of the most prominent eugenicists in the United States was a Harvard PhD, Charles Benedict Davenport (Witkowski and Inglis 2008). Davenport served as instructor of biology at his alma mater until he became an assistant professor at the University of Chicago in 1898 (Chase 1980, 118). In 1904, he became director of a new station for experimental evolution at Cold Spring Harbor on Long Island.

Other people active in the new American eugenics society were Planned Parenthood founder Margaret Sanger and the inventor of the telephone, Alexander Graham Bell, who became "one of the most respected, if not one of the most zealous" eugenic advocates of the last century (Cravens 1978; Haller 1984, 33; Haller 1971). Bell published numerous papers in scholarly journals, specifically on heredity and its effect on some cases of deafness.

Many American geneticists who are today recognized as major genetic pioneers include Thomas Hunt Morgan, William Bateson, and Herman J. Muller (Kevles 1985, 69; Shannon 1920; Goertzel and Goertzel 1962). Professors were prominent among both the officers and members of various eugenics societies that sprang up in most large American cities. According to Haller, the eugenics movement

> was the creation of biological scientists, social scientists, and others with a faith that science provided a guide for human progress. Indeed, during the first three decades of the present century, eugenics was a sort of secular religion for many who dreamed of a society in which each child might be born endowed with vigorous health and an able mind (1984, 3).

Virtually every college and university had professors "inspired by the new creed," and most major colleges offered credit courses on eugenics (Haller

1984, 72–73). These classes typically were well attended, and their content was widely accepted as part of proven science. Many eugenicists also lectured widely and developed new courses, both at their institutes and elsewhere, to help educate the public about eugenics (Stanton 1960).

The eugenics movement also attacked the idea of democracy itself. Many eugenicists concluded that letting inferior persons participate in government was naive, if not dangerous. Likewise, providing educational opportunities and governmental benefits for every citizen seemed to be a misuse of resources: one saves only the best cows for breeding, slaughtering the inferior ones and, to improve the race, these laws of nature must also be applied to "human animals."

The movement generally concluded that the primary determinant of humankind's behavioral nature is genetic; therefore, environmental reforms are largely useless or worse. Furthermore, persons at the "bottom" of society are in this position as a result of their own biological inferiority, and not because of social injustice, their freely made choices, or discrimination (Chase 1980).

The American Eugenics Movement Prospers

Few individuals were more important in the field of educational psychology and educational measurement and evaluation than Edward Lee Thorndike of Columbia University. He wrote many of the college texts that were the standard for years, not only in educational psychology, but also in educational measurement and child psychology. Thorndike's work is still today regarded as central to the field, and his textbook on test and measurements set the standard for the field. Yet he was largely unaware of (or ignored) the massive evidence that had accumulated against many of the basic eugenic views.

When Thorndike retired from Columbia Teacher's College in 1940, he wrote a 963-page book titled *Human Nature and the Social Order*. In it, he reiterated virtually all of the most blatant misconceptions and distortions of the eugenicists. As Chase states,

> at the age of sixty-six, he was still peddling the long discredited myths about epilepsy that Galton had revived when Thorndike was a boy of nine. . . . Despite Thorndike's use of such twentieth-century scientific words as "genes" and his advocacy of the then current Nazi Eugenics Court's practice of sterilizing people who got low marks on intelligence tests and for "inferior" morals, this

[book] was, essentially, the 1869 gospel of Galton, the eugenical orthodoxy that all mental disorders and diseases were at least 80 percent genetic and at most 20 percent environmental (1980, 354–355).

Margaret Higgins Sanger was an American birth control activist, and founder of what has become the Planned Parenthood Federation of America.

As methods of mechanically controlling human reproduction progressed, Havelock Ellis and others argued that sexual satisfaction should be separated from procreation. Ellis taught that birth control could not only help couples control their family size but also could enable the state to participate actively in physically improving the human race. Many eugenicists realized that few people would refrain from sexual activity or even marriage solely for the good of the race; therefore, the state must intervene. Havelock Ellis, Margaret Sanger, and many of the other founders of the birth-control movement concluded that if sex were purely a matter of personal pleasure — and not related to either marriage or procreation — reproduction could be regulated by the state for the good of society.

Although many eugenicists did not support state control of procreation, they often supported widespread use of birth control. However, many were concerned that use of contraceptive methods would separate passion from the responsibility of procreation and, as a result, foster promiscuity and licentiousness (Proctor 1988).

In addition, many who supported birth control were involved in the women's movement, which many eugenicists opposed because they feared that the movement would result in the eugenically *superior* women having *smaller* families (or no families at all). They argued that better educated, intelligent women should have *larger* families, even though the current trend for this social class was to have smaller families. For this reason, many eugenicists opposed the higher education of women because they perceived that schooling would direct the energy of superior women away from procreation into education.

Support for these views included a study that found female college graduates were less likely to marry, and those who did had fewer than two children, less than half of that necessary to maintain their eugenic line. Those who supported both higher education for women and the eugenics movement often argued that social class and education were separate issues. When social class was controlled, they felt that most of the differences that the eugenicists cited would disappear. They produced studies of their own that purported to show that college-educated women were as likely to marry, and also to have as many children, as their less educated sisters (Himmelfarb 1959).

Conversely, those who advocated free access to birth control argued that denying it openly encouraged the increase of syphilitics, epileptics, cripples, criminals, dipsomaniacs, and a variety of other genetic degenerates. Both Margaret Sanger in America and Marie Stopes in Great Britain increasingly used eugenic arguments to rally support for free access to birth control information. They stressed that many of the poor want to control their sexual urges, but their genetically caused, weak-willed temperament adversely interfered with both their work and sex habits. Furthermore, genes accounted for *both* their poverty and lack of sexual control, and thus large families resulted.

As their movement grew, both Margaret Sanger and Marie Stopes increasingly tied conception to eugenics concerns (Grant 1988). They felt that society could do much more to help people by giving them the means of family control that they needed so as not to reproduce indiscriminately. They also stressed that the rich had the means of controlling their families but the poor did not, and consequently, dysgenics resulted. By giving the poor birth control equipment and encouraging its use, the fit would have more children and the unfit fewer children (Hofstadter 1955).

Charles Davenport, a Major American Eugenic Leader

One of the most important figures in the American eugenics movement was Charles Davenport. While a zoology instructor at Harvard, he read some of Karl Pearson's and Darwin's works on eugenics and soon converted. During a trip to England, he visited Galton, Pearson, and Weldon, and returned to Boston an enthusiastic true believer. In 1904, he convinced the Carnegie Institute to establish a station for "the experimental study of evolution" at Cold Spring Harbor, about 30 miles from New York City. Davenport then recruited a staff to work there on various genetic research projects.

Fortunately, Davenport was not as autocratic as were many other eugenicists, including Karl Pearson. As a result, Davenport's students worked in a variety of fields besides eugenics. To study human genetics, they set up a data-gathering system that included sending hundreds of "family record" forms to institutions ranging from medical to mental, and also to numerous individuals. Each form required three generations of data, and the results were published in a 1911 book titled *Heredity in Relation to Eugenics.*

Among the many serious problems with Davenport's research was his assumption that all traits were a result of single Mendelian characters, whereas we now know that most are polygenetic in origin. This error caused him to greatly oversimplify his interpolations from the genotype to the phenotype. He argued that heritability was a major influence in everything from criminality to epilepsy, and from alcoholism to pauperism.

Davenport ignored the effects of the environment to such a degree that he labeled those who "loved the sea" as suffering from *thalassaphilia*, and concluded that this trait was sex-linked recessive because it was virtually always exhibited in males! Davenport even concluded that prostitution was caused, not by social, cultural or economic factors, but by a dominant genetic trait that caused a woman to become a nymphomaniac.

Davenport tended to classify traits on the basis of symptoms, not etiology. This was especially a serious problem with his classification of mental aberrations. We now know that tremors, for example, can be caused by everything from infections to drinking, and that even head injuries or physical diseases can contribute. Davenport and many others of the time were "blinded by eugenic prejudice" (Kevles 1985, 49).

They had an enormous amount of data for their ideas — from the time his Cold Spring Harbor laboratory was founded in 1904 until it closed in 1924, more than 250 field workers were employed to gather data, and about three-quarters of a million case histories were completed. These data served as the source of bulletins, memoirs, articles, and books on eugenics. Raised a Congregationalist, Davenport rejected his father's faith and replaced it with a worship of

> Science, Humanity, the Improvement of Mankind, Eugenics. The birth control crusader, Margaret Sanger, recalled that Davenport, in expressing his worry about the impact of contraception on the better stocks, "used to lift his eyes reverently and, with his hands upraised as though in supplication, quiver emotionally as he breathed, Protoplasm. We want more protoplasm" (Kevles 1985, 52).

Davenport believed that sexual immorality caused eugenically negative personality traits. Ironically, he opposed birth control because it reduced the natural inhibitions against sex. A hard worker to the point of excess, he was extremely demanding and was quick to label a staff member who complained, legitimately or otherwise, as disloyal.

Some Reasons Why American Eugenics Grew so Rapidly

Part of the reason why the eugenics movement caught on so rapidly was because of the failures of the many innovative reformatory and other programs designed to help the poor, criminals, and people with mental and physical problems. The high rate of failures in even the best programs caused many of those who worked in these institutions to become convinced that most of the poor possessed inferior genes that handicapped them in the struggle for life and should not be allowed to breed indiscriminately. Evolution gave them an answer to the difficulties that they faced.

Charles Loring Brace labored hard for New York's poor and became so "fascinated by evolution that he read and reread the *Origin of Species* thirteen times" and

> reported that during the depression winter of 1873–74 those connected with charity work had warned against indiscriminate giving to the poor. But the warnings went unheeded, with the result that tramps converged on New York, many poor families abandoned their jobs, and many laborers lost the habit of steady industry (Haller 1984, 33).

In short, he argued that instead of helping people, charity was hurting them by destroying their positive habits of industry and enabling them to breed more genetically inferior persons. Those who began their careers helping the poor often concluded that many, if not most, of their programs were doing more harm than good.

A major problem with the eugenics movement is that many of its leaders assumed that almost *every* behavior of which they disapproved was genetically based and, therefore, those who displayed such behavior were biologically inferior. People were inferior who were not easy going, were religious, were shy, were lazy, and those who displayed any other behavior that the labeler concluded was undesirable! The next step was to translate eugenics into both programs and policy.

From Theory to Social Policy

Translating eugenics into policy assumed a variety of forms. In America, one example was the policy of sterilizing a wide variety of individuals who were felt to have "heredity problems." Criminals, the mentally retarded, mentally ill, and others were at the top of their list. The first sterilization law passed in the United States was in Indiana. This law required mandatory sterilization of "confirmed criminals, idiots, imbeciles, and rapists in state institutions when recommended by a board of experts" (Haller 1984, 50).

The second eugenics movement achievement was the passage of a variety of laws restricting immigration of "inferior races" — a group on whose identity few agreed on, but in America often included the so-called darker races — Blacks, Slovaks, Jews, Greeks, Turks, Magyars, Russians, Poles, and even Italians.

Although the American courts challenged many of the eugenics laws, only one case, *Bell versus Buck*, 274 U.S. 200 (1927), reached the Supreme Court of the United States. In an eight to one vote, the high court *upheld* sterilization for eugenics reasons, concluding that "feeblemindedness" was caused by heredity, and therefore the state had the responsibility to control it by eugenic means. The court's opinion was penned by none other than Justice Oliver Wendell Holmes, who used his science knowledge in writing his erudite opinion. He forged a link between eugenics and patriotism, concluding that eugenics was a fact derived from empirical science. Numerous sterilization laws soon were passed in half of the states, many of which were more punitive than humanitarian (Hofstadter 1955).

The case that triggered this court ruling involved the daughter of Kerry Buck, who was proclaimed mentally deficient. The Supreme Court upheld Kerry's sterilization so that she would not produce any more "deficient children" like Vivian, a child that appeared to be mentally slow. Ironically, by the time Vivian started school, her teachers reportedly considered her very bright but, unfortunately, she died of an intestinal disorder in the second grade (Kevles 1985, 112).

After the U.S. Supreme Court ruling, many nations, including Finland, Denmark, Sweden, Germany, and others followed suit with their own eugenics laws (Proctor 1988). Soon, millions of people who did not have a heredity disorder, mental or otherwise, were sterilized. Numerous sterilization cases involved the town's "undesirable folk," such as "hillbillies."

Many eugenicists even believed that negative traits a person picked up during one's lifetime could be genetically passed on. The theory of the heritability of acquired characteristics was widely accepted and was not conclusively refuted until the work of August Weismann. Weismann cut off the tails of 901 mice for five successive generations and found that the mean tail length of each new generation was always within the normal curve of the previous generation.

Another evidence was a study that measured the foreskin length of Jewish and noncircumcised Gentile babies and found no difference, in spite of 4,000 years of its removal by Jews. The new view, called neo-Darwinian, taught that acquired characteristics could *not* be inherited. Thus the only hope for the permanent improvement of humans was through exercising an influence on the selective process of who could and could not breed (Warner 1894, 120–121). As a result, the disproof of the inheritance of acquired characteristics theory became "a major episode on the road to the acceptance of eugenics" because it opened up the door to the acceptance of strict Darwinism and eugenics (Haller 1984, 61).

Those in eugenics movements repeatedly ignored clear evidence against their theory, or endeavored to explain away the evidence that opposed their hypothesis. One evidence eugenicists used was the infamous Jukes study completed by prison reformer Richard L. Dugdale, who was generally supportive of the eugenics movement. This longitudinal study followed a so-called "degenerate clan" and found that it produced many criminal paupers and social misfits.

Many eugenicists were of the "heredity is destiny" school and, although hereditarians used the Jukes research to support their case, Dugdale himself was careful to stress that both heredity and environment were important. He repeatedly pointed out that "while children might inherit *tendencies* to crime, sensuality, and pauperism, the environment in which they were reared almost invariably reinforced the trials" (as quoted in Haller 1984, 22). Interestingly, his major recommendation was not a eugenics solution, but to remove children of poor and criminal parents from their surroundings and give them vocational training and assistance to overcome the negative effects of their initial environment. These recommendations were ignored by most eugenicists who put more faith in Darwinism than sociological studies.

Many people involved in the eugenics movement can best be summarized as true believers devoted to the cause, and blissfully ignored the evidence that did not support their theories. Yet many knew that the basic premise of eugenics was unsound, but often tried to rationalize its many problems. The founder of eugenics, Galton, "seems never to have been entirely at peace. He was continually plagued by varying degrees of nervous breakdown" (Kevles 1985, 9).

When the data did not conform to the eugenicists' expectations, they created ingenious ways of explaining the facts away. Professor Harry H.

Laughlin, who had a doctorate in biology from Princeton, reported to Congress in November 1922 that, although immigrants might be very healthy of mind and body, they carried bad recessive genes, which would cause problems in *future* generations. This claim was in response to the data that Laughlin himself had meticulously collected that found many problems among immigrants, such as feeblemindedness and criminal involvement, were often in many cases actually *lower* than in native-born Americans.

In the late 19th century, "when so many thought in evolutionary terms, it was only natural to divide man into the fit and the unfit." Even the unfortunates who failed in business and ended in poverty, or those who survived by petty thievery, were judged "unfit" and evolutionarily inferior by the eugenicists (Haller 1984, 35–36).

Because criminals and noncriminals are more alike than different, criminal identification based on physical traits is extremely difficult. The eugenicists also usually ignored upper class and white collar crime and the many offenses committed by high-ranking military officers and government officials, all of whose crimes were often well known by the people. They correctly identified some hereditary concerns but mislabeled many that are not (such as pauperism) and ignored the enormous influence of the environment in molding all that heredity gives us. They wrongly believed that since most social problems and conditions are genetic, they cannot be changed but can only be controlled by sterilization (Keith 1946).

Eugenics Falls Out of Favor

Among the large amount of research that discredited some of the eugenics ideas, probably the foremost was the realization that resulted from the ongoing research into genetics that the relationship between the genotype and the phenotype was *far more complex* than previously imagined. Much of this research was on so-called simple creatures such as the fruit fly (*Drosophila melanogaster*). In addition, it was realized that humans are produced from around 23,000 genes and that it was extremely difficult to determine if any one gene is "superior" to another as many eugenists taught for decades. We now realize most traits are produced by a set of genes.

At best, one could try to make judgments relative to the superiority of *one* specific trait compared to another trait. This is most easily achieved in the case of a mutation. A person who had a mutation that caused hemophilia could be considered inferior compared to the person who had a normal factor 8 gene. This method considers only one gene, and a person without the genetic defect for hemophilia will be genetically inferior in some other way because mutations or genes that produce inferior traits exist in all humans. A person may have a mutation for baldness, for example, and become bald later in life.

Even a person who has certain traits, such as below-average intellect, may in some other way be genetically superior — a determination that we cannot make until *all* of the estimated 23,000 genes are mapped and compared to the entire population. And *even then,* comparative judgments cannot be made except on very simplistic grounds, such as counting the total number of genes judged "inferior" and "superior." Even this approach falls short because certain single genes can cause far more problems than others and, conversely, can confer on the person more advantages than most other genes, such as genes that result in the production of above-average levels of glutathione S-transferase. This trait would reduce the likelihood of disease from cancer to heart disease to strokes. It then would be necessary to rate each individual gene and gene interaction — something that so far has not been done.

In addition, many so-called inferior genes are actually mutations that were caused somewhere in the human genetic past and were subsequently passed on to the victim's offspring. Of the identified diseases, over 5,000 are a result of heritable mutations — and none of these 5,000 existed in our past before the mutation causing it was introduced into the human gene pool. As these mutations accumulate, a deterioration of the genome called "devolution" results, an event that is the opposite of the eugenics goal of trying to create the most flawless race and then limit reproduction to members of this race. This goal is flawed because the accumulation of mutations tends to result in *all* "*races*" becoming less perfect (Sahlins,1977).

Although the validity of many of the eugenics studies and the extent of their applicability to humans were both serious concerns, the demise of the eugenics movement had more to do with social factors than new scientific discoveries. These social factors included "the rise of Nazism, the Holocaust, and America's struggle in World War II to defeat Hitler's Germany . . . the civil rights movement of the 1950s and 1960s, as well as the wars on poverty in the 1930s and 1960s" (Haller 1984, xi).

In addition, Haller notes that, although the American and European academic life was once "virtually a WASP preserve," it was increasingly joined by various racial minorities, including Asians, Indians, Orientals, and African-Americans. Many members of these groups either rejected a movement that labeled them inferior, or influenced the movement to accept them as equal to Aryans.

Furthermore, the eugenic caused atrocities and injustices committed both at home and in Europe made the once-respectable eugenics beliefs repugnant, even though the basic theory of evolution was still widely accepted by the scientific community. Another factor was a reevaluation of the research that supported eugenics, such as the work of Cyril Burt, one of the leading researchers in the genetic basis of human inferiorities such as IQ. The examination found serious flaws in his work, and eventually the evidence pointed to open fraud. The exposure of Burt for falsifying his twin study data that he claimed proved his eugenics ideas was a major blow to extreme biological determinism (Gould 1996).

Even though the movement was discredited, remnants still existed well into the 20th century. As late as 1955, a Canadian biology professor noted that "possibly the most significant fact is that he [Darwin] finally freed humanity from a great measure of church bigotry and church proscription and won his fellow men a measure of freedom of thought that had been unknown for centuries" (Rowan 1955, 12). Rowan then argued that reducing the Church's influence in society allowed the discovery of not only the *means* of evolution but also the knowledge that mankind had the means either to direct evolution or let it occur on its own, or worse, stop it by counteracting the forces that propel it, such as allowing the genetic inferior to reproduce, thereby causing devolution.

Rowan argued that humankind has, tragically, chosen the latter: "Selection is still as vital to human progress as it has ever been. The great Darwinian principle remains." He then added, "When man acquired intellect, he started on an entirely new path without precedent in the animal world, the course of which now depends, not on further physical changes, but on *intellectual* evolution and equally intellectual selection" (1955, 13). Unfortunately, he concludes, humans are "saving" the intellectually inferior and have "failed to order his affairs" according to the laws of biology (1955, 13). This discussion, although tactful, is clear: those whom evolutionists judged as less fit should be eliminated, or at the least, we should limit our efforts in saving them and let nature do its work. The eugenicists taught that not to do so will result in the eventual doom of humanity.

The importance of studying the eugenics movement today is not only to help us understand history but also to ensure that it is not repeated. A field growing in influence and prestige, *social biology*, in some ways is very similar to the eugenics movement. This school also claims that both biological and social traits have a genetic basis that exist as a result of the survival-of-the-fittest process. Although many social biologists take pains to disavow any connections, ideologically or otherwise, with the eugenics movement, the similarity is striking. This fact is a point that its many critics, such as Harvard's Stephen J. Gould and others, have often noted (Sahlins 1977; Montagu 1999).

Eugenics Contrasted with Christian Teaching

In contrast, Christian teaching presented very different conclusions than eugenics. Christianity declared that *anyone* who accepted Christ's message could be changed. The Scriptures and history give numerous examples of individuals who were liars, thieves, and moral degenerates whose lives radically turned around after their conversion. The regeneration of reprobates has always been an important attraction of Christianity. From its earliest days, one of the proofs of its validity was its effect on the lives of those who embraced the faith. Helping the poor, the weak, the downtrodden, the unfortunate, the crippled, and the lame was no minor part of Christianity. Indeed, aside from faith in Jesus Christ by God's grace, it was the *essence* of the religion — the outward evidence of the faith within.

Those who did not visit the sick and the poor, help those in prison, or give drink and food to the needy were "cursed," and were to be consigned to the fate "prepared for the devil and his angels" (Matt. 25:35–45, NKJV). And as to those who have "this world's goods, and sees his brother in need, and shuts up his heart from him, how does the love of God abide in him" (1 John 3:17). Nor was this attitude exclusive among the Christians, but it was also required of Jews:

> If there be among you a poor man . . . within any of the gates in thy land . . . thou should not harden thine heart, nor shut thine hand from [them]. . . . But thou shall open thy hand wide unto him, and shalt surely lend him sufficient for his need ... For the poor shall never cease out of the land: therefore I command thee, saying, thou shalt open thine hand wide unto thy brother, to thy poor, and to thy needy in thy land" (Deut. 15:7–15, 18 and Lev. 25:35–43... paraphrase).

Another conflict was over the fact that the Church stressed helping the weak and afflicted. Almost all denominations concluded from Scripture and history that many who seem to be without hope can be "reformed" and then assume responsible positions in society. The churches easily could point to many well-documented examples of this claim. Furthermore, in contrast to eugenics, religious leaders often attributed the cause of physical and mental degeneracy to individual and societal sins. The behavioral sciences often argued that what was needed to improve society was not genetic, but social changes. In a summary of the history of mental illness treatment, Sarason and Sarason conclude that

> during the Middle Ages the importance of the Christian spirit of charity, particularly towards stigmatized groups such as the severely mentally disturbed, cannot be over estimated. For example, in Gheel, Belgium, the church established a special institution for the care of retarded and psychotic children. As they improved, these children were often placed with sympathetic families in the neighborhood of the institution (1989, 33–34).

Not surprisingly, much of the opposition to the eugenics programs came from the religious community. Conditions such as feeblemindedness (a general term for those who would today be termed mentally slow due to genetics or, more often, environment) and mental illness, they reasoned, could not have been solely inherited traits because these people were part of God's creation, and Genesis states that when God created Adam and Eve they were "very good." The cause of these conditions must be something other than humankind's innate inherited genetic program.

Many Catholics were especially critical of eugenics because they believed that the human spirit, not the human body, is paramount, and God does not judge persons according to IQ tests or skull shapes but according to his or her spiritual attributes. Many genuinely retarded persons were likable, friendly, outgoing, and nonaggressive; a good example is many of those diagnosed with Down's Syndrome (Gould 1996). Much of the Church's criticism was against evolution itself; most eugenicists believed that humans came from lower "beasts," and if this idea was wrong, then the very foundation of the eugenics movement was flawed.

The conflict between Christianity and eugenics was also due to the latter's conflicts with the major doctrine of Christianity — that is, that humans through sin had fallen from their once-high state. In contrast, the eugenics doctrine teaches that humans have risen from a lower state. The fact that the eugenics movement was directly at odds with both Christian and Jewish teachings was not lost on those in the movement: many eugenicists were openly critical of Christianity, and large numbers, including Erasmus, Robert, Charles, and Leonard Darwin, plus Galton, Huxley, Davenport, Wells, and Pearson, were all open agnostics or atheists.

The founder of eugenics, Francis Galton, was not only an agnostic, but also openly hostile toward religion: "While he tolerated Louise's (his wife) practice of religion in the home, he rarely missed an opportunity to jibe at the clerical outlook" (Kevles 1985, 11). Advocates of the eugenics approach called their opposers "sentimentalists," and the eugenicists claimed the "natural ally" of the sentimentalists was "the preacher" (Haller 1984, 46).

Other Opposition

The Darwinian view that the biological progress of humans results from the selection of the most fit and the elimination of the unfit was prone to provoke conflicts in not only the "unfit" but also those close to them such as parents. The value of superior humans was such that Darwin was critical of all Christian attempts at helping the weak. In his *Descent of Man, and Selection in Relation to Sex*, Darwin stated that we

> build asylums for the imbecile, the maimed, and the sick; we institute poor-laws; and our medical men exert their utmost skill to save the life of every one to the last moment. There is reason to believe that vaccination has preserved thousands, who from a weak constitution would formerly have succumbed to small-pox. Thus the weak members of civilized societies propagate their kind. No one who has attended to the breeding of domestic animals will doubt that this must be highly injurious to the race of man. It is surprising how soon a want of care, or care wrongly directed, leads to the degeneration of a domestic race; but excepting in the case of man himself, hardly any one is so ignorant as to allow his worst animals to breed. . . . We must therefore bear the undoubtedly bad effects of the weak surviving and propagating their kind (1896, 133–134).

A photograph of Havelock Ellis from 1913.

Nor was the eugenics world united on many of the fundamental eugenic questions. They criticized each other's methodology, statistical techniques, and, of course, each other's conclusions. Innumerable personality wars occurred between the most prominent eugenicists about implementing policy, and much jealousy existed over the role each one was taking.

Conflicts existed among the numerous eugenics advocates on major topics, including the level of influence of the genotype on the phenotype and, especially, how to go about applying this information for the betterment of society. Havelock Ellis concluded that compulsory sterilization should be applied *only* as a last resort. He felt that education, helping inferior individuals understand that it was their civic duty and responsibility to their race not to bear more of their kind, should be the primary method. Compulsion was to be applied *only* against the small number of people for whom such methods were unsuccessful. The education approach obviously never worked.

The Final Downfall of the American Eugenics Movement

As more and more empirical research by the scientists connected with universities was completed, it became apparent that the major conclusions of the eugenics movement were invalid. Many of the major conclusions that the various eugenics researchers used to support their position were from correlational studies that do not prove causation. Thus, their cause and effect conclusions were far more a result of belief than empirical evidence. Circular reasoning was especially pronounced: those who were immoral were obviously feebleminded, and feeblemindedness clearly produced immoral behavior.

Another problem was that very little was known about genetics at the turn of the century. Scientists slowly turned against the movement, or at least against some of the major aspects of the mainline movement. Included were Herman J. Muller, J.B.S. Haldane, Herbert Jennings, and even Julian Huxley. Not only advances in science, but also political changes — most notably the abuses in Nazi Germany but also in America — once they became known, caused many to realize that the basic eugenics conclusions were not just wrong, but inconsistent with basic human rights.

Ideas very close to Nazism were openly advocated by many eugenicists such as Albert Edward Wiggam. Wiggam (1922, 1924, 1925, 1927) wrote many books and articles defending extreme eugenics that sold many thousands of copies. After the defeat of Nazism and the general awareness of the results of eugenics in Europe, many influential persons were alienated from the eugenics movement, an important factor in its downfall (Mosse 1966).

Many also saw its horrendous potential for abuses. One of the major conflicts was determining just who was inferior. Under German influence, many eugenicists included Jews as an inferior race — a problem because many prominent biologists and anthropologists were also Jewish. One, Franz

Boaz of Columbia University, a German-Jewish immigrant, had become an eminent anthropologist. As a well-respected scientist, he wrote many popular books for both professionals and the lay public. When he attacked the eugenics movement, many listened. When eugenic science turned on Jewish scientists, the latter rallied their colleagues against the movement as a whole.

A serious problem with the theory was that it ascribed traits such as shyness to genes — and later research found that many shy youngsters grow out of their shells to become confident, assertive adults. Such traits were obviously not biologically fixed. These observations caused researchers to seriously question the validity of performance evaluations as a whole, forcing a damaging peg in the wholesale conclusion that certain groups were intellectually inferior in all areas. These research studies showed that the effective intelligence of a person is *highly influenced* by the interaction of heredity and environment. Furthermore, they found that more differences existed *within* a race than *between* the races.

It soon became apparent to almost everyone in the field that many of the eugenicists' hodgepodge claims were tenuous or openly wrong. Research by anthropologists showed how incredibly important culture and learning were, even in shaping minor behavioral nuances. As the supposedly biologically inferior groups reached the second and third generation in America, many did extremely well, documenting the fact that such groups were *not* biologically defective. Another problem was that not only Blacks and Jews were singled out as racially inferior, but also Irish, Welsh, and numerous other groups.

Other researchers proved that diet and sanitary conditions were extremely important, both pre- and postnatal, especially in the so-called feeblemindedness trait. The irony of the assumption that feeblemindedness was always inherited became apparent when it was determined by research that many clearly mentally deficient persons produced fully normal offspring, partly due to the regression toward the average phenomena. This was especially true of children who were reared by normal relatives, and who had decent food and positive environments. The government's past practice of sterilizing feebleminded people due to their poor environmental conditions was now recognized as inhumane.

Even the theory of natural selection came under attack. It was increasingly realized that the many supposed sources of natural selection, especially war, plagues, and disease, often did not kill off primarily the weaker members; rather, a major factor that influenced who died was *chance*. In the case of war, those who failed the army physical are not drafted, thus war is more likely to kill the *more fit* — the reverse of natural selection. And those who may have an innate disposition to resist a certain disease quite often had an innate weakness to succumbing to other diseases.

As J.B.S. Haldane proclaimed in 1932, a society of men that was uniformly perfect would still produce an imperfect society. The enormous genetic variety among humans — and among plants and animals, as well — was important because it will always allow some individuals to survive different environmental changes. When the Pilgrims came over to America, a few had the genetic predispositions that enabled them to survive the alien environment in America with its foreign germs and new living requirements. Those that survived may not have been the strongest in the land from which they came but were stronger in the new environment. If all those that came over were genetically identical, likely *none* of them would have survived (Jacquard 1984).

Although many prominent American biologists remained committed to the basic eugenics program and the idea that the human race could be drastically improved by eugenics methods, many others quietly dropped eugenic race ideas. Unfortunately, most scientists did not admit the errors of their past, even when the public tide turned strongly against the blatant racism of the movement as a whole. For most researchers, it became more and more apparent that many of the wholesale conclusions of the eugenicists not only were wrong, but tragically wrong, and caused enormous suffering in the world, even in America (Gallagher 1999).

References

Barzun, Jacques. 1958. *Darwin, Marx, Wagner.* Garden City, New York: Doubleday Anchor Books.

Chase, Allan. 1980. *The Legacy of Malthus; The Social Costs of the New Scientific Racism.* New York: Alfred Knopf.

Cravens, Hamilton. 1978. *The Triumph of Evolution; American Scientists and the Heredity-Environment Controversy 1900–1941.* Philadelphia, PA: University of Pennsylvania Press.

Darwin, Charles. 1896. *The Descent of Man, and Selection in Relation to Sex; The Works of Charles Darwin.* New York, NY: D. Appleton and Company (1st ed. by AMS Press, 1972).

Gallagher, Nancy. 1999. *Breeding Better Vermonters.* Hanover, NH: University Press of New England.

Galton, Francis. 1869. *Hereditary Genius.* London: Watts.

———. 1880. *Inquiries Into Human Faculty and Its Development.* 2nd ed. New York, NY: E.P. Dutton.

Goertzel, Victor, and Mildred Goertzel. 1962. *Cradles of Eminence.* Boston, MA: Little, Brown and Company.

Gould, Stephen Jay. 1996. *The Mismeasure of Man.* 2nd ed. New York: W.W. Norton.

Grant, George. 1988. *Grand Illusions; The Legacy of Planned Parenthood*. Brentwood, TN: Wolgemut & Hyatt.

Green, John C. 1981. *Science, Ideology, and World View*. Berkeley, CA: University of California Press.

Haller, John S. Jr. 1971. *Outcasts From Evolution: Scientific Attitudes to Racial Inferiority, 1859–1900*. Urbana, IL: University of Illinois Press.

Haller, Mark H. 1984. *Eugenics; Hereditarian Attitudes in American Thought*. New Brunswick, NJ: Rutgers University Press.

Himmelfarb, Gertrude. 1959. *Darwin and the Darwinian Revolution*. New York: Doubleday.

Hofstadter, Richard. 1955. *Social Darwinism in American Thought*. Boston, MA: Bacon.

Jacquard, Albert. 1984. *In Praise of Differences*. New York: Columbia University Press.

Jones, Greta. 1980. *Social Darwinism and English Thought; The Interaction Between Biological and Social Theory*. New Jersey: The Humanities Press.

Keith, Arthur. 1946. *Evolution and Ethics*. New York: G.P. Putnam's Sons.

Kevles, Daniel J. 1985. *In the Name of Eugenics; Genetics and the Uses of Human Heredity*. New York, NY: Alfred A Knopf.

Montagu, Ashley. 1999. *Race and IQ*. New York: Oxford.

Mosse, George L. 1966. *Nazi Culture; Intellectual, Cultural, and Social Life in the Third Reich*. New York, NY: Schocken.

Ordover, Nancy. 2003. *American Eugenics: Race, Queer Anatomy, and the Science of Nationalism*. Minneapolis, MN: University of Minnesota Press.

Proctor, Robert N. 1988. *Racial Hygiene: Medicine Under the Nazis*. Cambridge, MA: Harvard University Press.

Rowan, W. 1955. "Charles Darwin" in *Architects of Modern Thought*. Toronto: Canadian Broadcasting Corps.

Sahlins, Marshall. 1977. *The Use and Abuse of Biology; An Anthropological Critique of Sociobiology*. Ann Arbor, MI: University of Michigan Press.

Sarason, Irwin, and Barbara Sarason. 1989. *Abnormal Psychology*. 6th ed., New York, NY: Prentice-Hall.

Shannon, T.W. 1920. *Eugenics*. Topeka, KS: Standard Publishing Company, Inc.

Stanton, William. 1960. *The Leopard's Spots; Scientific Attitudes Towards Race in America, 1815–1859*. Chicago, IL: University of Chicago Press.

Warner, Amos. 1894. *American Charities*. New York, NY: Thomas W. Crowell.

Wiggam, Albert Edward. 1922. *The New Dialogue of Science*. Garden City, NY: Garden City Publishing Co.

———. 1924. *The Fruit of the Family Tree*. Indianapolis, IN: Bobs Merrill.

———. 1925. *The Marks of an Educated Man*. Indianapolis, IN: Bobs Merrill.

——— 1927. *The Next Age of Man*. Indianapolis, IN: Bobs Merrill.

Witkowski, Jan A., and John R. Inglis (editors). 2008. *Davenport's Dream: 21st Century Reflections on Heredity and Eugenics*. Cold Spring Harbor, NY: Cold Spring Harbor Laboratory Press.

Chapter 8

Darwinism's Important Influence on the Ku Klux Klan

Introduction

Racism is a major social problem in many nations today, including America. The most active American racist hate group is the Ku Klux Klan (KKK). In the last century the KKK had millions of members (Fry 1922). In the past, doctors, judges, lawyers, and even some congressmen were actively involved in the KKK (Gitlin 2009). Although the KKK has lost much of its support, especially after 1980, it is still active today. For this reason, the motives behind this group are of much concern in reducing this social problem (Lee 2003). In short, the Klan was guided by the view that they

> would protect the noble virtues that every white Southerner knew to be eternal. In short, Klansmen viewed blacks as an inferior race that must be subjugated to protect whites from lawlessness, crime, and the despoliation of the white race (Martin 2007, 18).

President Andrew Johnson, vetoed the Civil Rights Bill of 1866.

This goal even was accepted by President Andrew Johnson, who vetoed the 1866 Civil Rights Bill. U.S. President Johnson explained the reason for his veto was because

the federal government could not . . . protect any group, much less Negroes, from discrimination. In no uncertain terms, he voiced his opinion that "the distinction of race and color is by the bill made to operate in favor of the colored and against the white race." Citing fears of racial intermarriage and expressing his belief that blacks lack an adequate understanding of "the nature and character of our institutions," he echoed a widespread feeling in all sections of the country that Negroes simply were inherently inferior to whites. Johnson served notice that, unlike his predecessor, he was unable or unwilling to compromise or consider opinions aside from his own (Martinez 2007, 37).

The KKK Use Darwinism to Justify Their View of Black Inferiority

The Darwinian comparison of Blacks with monkeys and "savages" was a common theme in KKK speeches and literature. As the *Klan Watch* wrote, the "formal theories of racial superiority and inferiority did not appear until the early 1800s, and they came . . . from the laboratories and universities of Europe, from men of science" (Turner 1982, 34). Turner adds that in the early 1800s

the science of anthropology was embroiled in a controversy of whether all races of men were descended from a common ancestor or whether different races had different origins. This intellectual debate was frequently matched in America by the belief of many whites that blacks and Indians were not even human. . . . Charles Darwin's theory of evolution convinced most scientists that all men had common origins, but some continued to think that there were important differences between the races and that the white race was superior to all others (Turner 1982, 34).

Harvard Professor Stephen Jay Gould concluded that "biological arguments for racism may have been common before 1859, but they increased by orders of magnitude following the acceptance of evolutionary theory" after Darwin published his epic work on evolution in 1859 (1977, 127). In spite of the widespread acceptance of racist evolution, scientists could not deny the fact that

> interfertility was an accepted criterion for determining common species, and evidence abounded that mixed-race couples could produce fertile offspring. The diversity of physical appearances among peoples from different parts of the world was usually credited to the effects of environment; climate, diet, even civilization could, it was thought, alter skin color, skeletal structure, and physiological processes. Over time a population would adapt to a new environment. For example, the intensity of the Sun in the tropics darkened the skin of Africans, which made them better able to endure the torrid climate. Thus the biblical story of humankind's descent from Adam and Eve was largely supported by scientific thinking. Unity of species implied a common origin, and the human ability to adapt to environments accounted for racial diversity (Nelson 2003, 165).

When Darwinian ideas became widely accepted, this

> union of science and Christianity grew strained. By the eighteenth century, Europeans . . . were hard pressed to fit into the Bible's account of things, and some thinkers began to entertain the idea that possibly humans are not all part of the same family. . . . Not surprisingly, most Christians rejected polygenism, arguing that the Creation stories of Genesis and the Christian doctrines of the universality of sin and the offer of redemption through Christ's sacrifice presumed a *monogenesis (mono,* single *+ genesis),* a single origin for the human race (Nelson 2003, 165–166).

By 1871, the rapidly growing acceptance of Darwin began to change this and, as a result, pre-Adamism became more popular until the civil rights movement. Most of the references used by the KKK to support racism were from scientists that lived and worked from the late 1800s to around 1950. A 1934 KKK flyer reviewed the Darwinism racist case for white supremacy, adding that after the Whites lifted Negroes

A Ku Klux Klan parade in 1926.

out of savagery, we are under no obligation to bear him over our shoulders. . . . [R]eading, writing and arithmetic . . . is [*sic*] as much as they can absorb to advantage. . . . [N]o matter how many books you rub into his head, Nature created him Inferior . . . and if ever the white man lowers his level to that of the Negro . . . The Crime Against Civilization Will Be Punished. . . . Negroes with a suggestion of intellect are usually . . . mongrels in whose veins flow the blood of some depraved white man. The pure blood blacks who have exhibited intellectual and moral qualities superior to those of the monkey are few and far between (quoted in Newton 2010, 96).

Conversely, the Bible declares in no uncertain terms the solidarity of the human family, such as "[God] made of *one blood* all nations of men" (Acts 17:26, KJV, emphasis added), and Adam was "the first man" the father of all men (1 Corinthians 15:45, 47). Furthermore:

Most American Christians in the early nineteenth century read the biblical Creation stories as literal history. God, they believed, created Adam and Eve about six thousand years ago, shortly after getting the rest of the cosmos started. Descendants of the first couple multiplied rapidly, perhaps because of their extraordinary longevity, and quickly occupied the earth. . . . This information drawn from the Bible did not stand alone in Christian thinking. Science supported and embellished it (Nelson 2003, 162).

Although many Klansmen believed that the Bible was God's Word, they often attempted to combine evolution and Christianity into some form of theistic evolution, producing the following contradiction:

> Many hard-core racists are sickened by the mere sight of a black walking down the street and thoroughly disgusted at displays of race mixing, particularly mixed marriages. And some even claim that they extracted proof of black inferiority and the dangers of integration from the Bible (Gitlin 2009, 47).

Those who relied on the Bible for their evolutionary racist views often had to enormously pervert its clear teaching. For example, Rev. Reuben Sawyer introduced the British-Israelism creed, today often called "Christian identity," to Oregon Klansmen. Their racist doctrine proclaimed the ancient Europeans, and not modern-day Jews, were actually the "lost tribes of Israel" and for this reason were the

> rightful heirs to God's Old Testament covenant. Jews posing as Jehovah's "chosen people" are therefore impostors — and worse, since some Identity sects believe the first Jews sprang from Eve's sexual coupling with Satan in the Garden of Eden (which produced the first murderer, Cain). They, in turn, performed various prehistoric experiments resulting in creation of the nonwhite "mud races" that populated Africa, Asia and the pre-Columbian Americas (Newton 2007, 42).

Another popular attempt to combine evolution with Christianity was a form of polygenism (the idea that the races had separate origins) called the Pre-Adamite theory, which taught that

> God created inferior races — dubbed "beasts of the field" in *Genesis* 2:20 — before the creation of Adam and Eve. Adam's divinely-sanctioned "dominion" over those "beasts" thus justified slavery, segregation, or even genocide. Klan allies William Dudley Pelley and Gerald L.K. Smith embraced Christian Identity in the 1930s, while Klansman Wesley Swift emerged as the sect's leading spokesman after World War II (Newton 2007, 42).

The Pre-Adamite theory was long rejected by the Christian Church and those who "held to the Pre-Adamite view were . . . roundly condemned" (Browne 2003, 122–123). This Pre-Adamite view was extensively detailed by lawyer and KKK leader Ross Barnett, who wrote:

> I believe that the Good Lord was the original segregationist. . . .
> Mixing the races leads inevitably to the production of an inferior
> mongrel. . . . The Negro is different because God made him dif-
> ferent. His forehead slants back. His nose is different. His lips are
> different, and his color surely is different (quoted in Newton 2010,
> 117).

This view is a variety of the pre-Adamite theory, and some pre-Adamite
theories go far beyond it.

One active White power advocate, Adam White (pseudonym for Lee
Holloway), wrote that the Negro "is a beast of the field and was the tempter
of Eve." White's theory illustrates why "many African Americans continued
to view polygenism as a greater threat than Darwinism" to their civil rights
(Nelson 2003, 176). White's more extreme theory was held by some KKK
supporters and other racists. It taught that "no other animal, except the
negro, fits the description of the animal called 'the serpent' in the garden of
Eden." The evidence for this claim is

> (1) . . . the serpent's power of speech . . . Satan having spoken
> through the serpent. . . . The negro . . . fits the description as a
> "beast of the field" able to speak, because the negro has always pos-
> sessed the power of speech. (2) The negro possesses a high degree of
> intelligence in comparison with other animals. The description of
> "the serpent" as "more subtle" or wiser is most appropriate in con-
> ceiving of him as a negro. (3) According to the record, Eve showed
> no surprise at the ability of the serpent to speak. If the tempter were
> a familiarly known negro, obviously no surprise would have been
> felt by Eve. (4) The curse pronounced on the serpent to go on his
> belly has real meaning when applied to a negro.

He added that the Negro

> was cursed above all other beasts of the field . . . in being forced
> to crawl. . . . (5) The beast of the field . . . was a man eater and
> vegetable eater. . . . Such eating habits fit the negro exactly, particu-
> larly in his wild or natural state. The negro is well known for his
> cannibalism. . . . (6) If the serpent were a negro, we have a creature
> given over to the dominion of Adam which explains how Adam was
> to keep the garden of Eden in a proper condition. . . . Only a few

animals can be used for work, but the negro is the only animal able to do small hand work requiring tools. The negro is better able to follow spoken orders than other animals. . . . The "beast of the field" (negro) is specifically described in Jeremiah 27:6 as given to King Nebuchadnezzar "to serve him." The negro was clearly a servant to man from the beginning (White 1966, 5–6).

White reasoned that eating the forbidden fruit was rebellion against the authority of God because Adam accepted

the counsel of an animal, the negro . . . Eve and Adam . . . were to have dominion over the animals and not the opposite. Hardly anything could be more revolting than to think of men, created in the image of Almighty God, stooping to allow a lower form of life to advise them. . . . That, however, is exactly what Adam and Eve did. The sin of Adam and Eve in taking the counsel of a mere animal above the direct commands of God was soon followed by the sin of amalgamation (interbreeding between men and negroes). Apparently, this sin was first committed by Cain, the first murderer . . . to prove this point [w]e simply point to the fact that Cain had a wife before Adam and Eve had any daughters. The only possibility left was for the wife of Cain to have been a negress (White 1966, 6).

White then documents his conclusions by quoting several well-known evolutionary scientists and professors, such as Ernst Haeckel, who wrote in his book *The History of Creation* that

the excellent paleontologist, Quenstedt, was right in maintaining that "if negroes and Caucasians were snails, zoologists would universally agree that they represented two very distinct species which could never have originated from one pair by gradual divergence" (quoted in White 1966, 7).

White adds, quoting evolutionists Charles Morris (1888) and Ernst Haeckel:

"It may be remarked that all the savage tribes of the earth belong to the negro or Mongolian races. . . . On the other hand, the Caucasian is pre-eminently the man of civilization. . . . No traveler or historian records a savage tribe of Caucasian stock." (*The Aryan Race* 1888, 23) . . . On the opposite, and far distant shore of the great gulf, stands the ignorant savage negro, whose mental indolence and

incapacity accomplish nothing. History records no achievements of
his. His thousands of years lived out upon the earth, are as barren
of results as those of the gorilla. Throughout his whole existence he
figures only as a savage or a servant. No "woolly-haired nation has
ever had an important history" (White 1966, 7).

White then quoted other leading evolutionists, such as Professor Wyman,
to support his theory:

> "It cannot be denied, however wide the separation, that the negro
> and orang do afford the points where man and brute, when the
> totality of their organization is considered, most nearly approach
> each other." Prof. Haeckel quotes [an authority who] says: "I con-
> sider the negro as a lower species of man, and cannot . . . look upon
> him as a man and a brother, for the gorilla would then also have to
> be admitted into the family." . . . "In explaining the true cause of
> the differences in complexion, observable among the so-called 'races
> of men,' Topinard says: . . . "It is thus shown by the highest scien-
> tific authorities, that the black, colorless complexion of the negro
> . . . results solely from the black pigment intervening between the
> dermis and the epidermis . . . [the] difference between the blood of
> the white man and that of the negro . . . [is] proved by experimental
> test. The skin of the white man inserted in the flesh of the negro
> becomes black, and the skin of the negro grafted on the white man
> turns white. Nothing but the blood could produce this change"
> (quoted from *Anthropology for the People*) (White 1966, 7).

White adds that the long, fine straight hair of the white race "is in absolute
contrast to the short, course, wooly hair of the negro" and furthermore the
"comparatively short, broad skull of the white is in striking contrast to the
long, narrow skull of the negro." He concluded that the "length and narrow-
ness of the negro skull is a character of the ape" (White 1966, 7).

Quoting University of Michigan Anthropology Professor Alexander
Winchell (1978), who tried to meld Christianity and evolution together,
White adds that

> Prof. Winchell says: "a certain relative width of skull appears to be
> connected with energy, force and executive ability." This explains
> the negro's lack of executive ability — God made him so. The sig-
> nificance of this is easily seen when we pause to reflect that the task

to which man was assigned in the Creation required the highest executive ability. . . . The average weight of the European brain, males and females, is 1,340 grams; that of the negro is 1,178; of the Hottentot, 974; and of the Australian, 907.

White concluded that the significance of these comparisons is clear when we read that

> Broca, the most eminent of French anthropologists, states that, when the European brain falls below 978 grams (mean of males and females), the result is idiocy. . . . The color of the negro brain is darker than that of the white, and its density and the texture are inferior. The convolutions are fewer and more simple, and approximate those of the quadruma (primates not including man) (quoted from Winchell in *Preadamites*).

> "The relatively short, narrow jaw of the whites is in striking contrast to the long, broad jaw of the negro. The length and breadth of the negro's jaw is a character of the ape. The jaws of the negro, like those of the other apes, 'extend forward at the expense of the symmetry of the face, and backward at the expense of the brain cavity.' Quatrefages says: 'It is well known that in the negro the entire face, and especially the lower portion projects forward' " (quoted in *The Human Species*).

White then quotes distinguished French anthropologist Paul Topinard who wrote, "The space between the eyes of the negro is larger and flatter than in the white" (Topinard 1894, 489) (White 1966, 8–9). This view obviously requires a rejection of the clear biblical teachings about the origins of all humans. A review of the writings of prominent modern racists, such as David Duke, also finds that Darwinist ideas were critically important in developing and maintaining their racist ideas. Duke, the most prominent racist in America today, headed the largest White Supremacist organization in the world. His influence can be gauged by the fact that he was elected to serve in the congress of the state of Louisiana. His extensive writings about the central influence of Darwinist ideas on the development of his racist views are reviewed below.

Pre-Adamite theories began in the middle 1600s but were always regarded as heretical by mainline Christians. For example, Isaac de La Peyrere tried to explain not only early evolutionary teaching of primitive man but also the teaching of certain problematic Bible verses. He

> argued that the Bible really taught that Adam and Eve were not
> the first human beings, but merely parents of the Jewish people.
> All other races had been created earlier than Adam and Eve and
> belonged outside the Old Testament stories, which concerned only
> the Jewish people. The existence of preadamites, people before
> Adam, explained a number of awkward problems with certain bib-
> lical stories, such as how Cain had found a wife when he and his
> brother were Adam and Eve's only offspring, and who had peopled
> the biblical land of Nod. La Peyrere's theological work was roundly
> condemned as heretical throughout the seventeenth and eighteenth
> centuries. . . . Refutations of preadamism flowed from European
> pens for more than a century after La Peyrere . . . La Peyrere himself
> was forced to recant, but his ideas were not forgotten (Nelson 2003,
> 164).

Nonetheless, the scientists prevailed because early evolutionists and
ethnologists

> were far more impressed with the differences among various peoples
> than their similarities. Sensational stories of Hottentots mating with
> gorillas or orangutans persisted in Europe and America, testifying to
> the "otherness" that such distant people represented to them. They
> also suggested a gradation of human types from those closest to
> animals to those most removed (Nelson 2003, 165).

The conversion of David Duke from Christian creationist to theistic evolutionist is somewhat typical of the influence of Darwin on racism in the KKK
and other racist groups.

The David Duke Story

David Duke, a leader of several racist groups including the Ku Klux Klan
and the American Nazi party, has "become a political rock star of sorts" —
and one of the most well-known Americans of the past decade (Zatarain
1990, 10). Furthermore, Duke has worked with virtually every prominent
American racist of the last 30 years (Bridges 1994, 41, 115). Duke's popularity can be gauged by the fact that he received 680,000 votes in the 1991
Louisiana gubernatorial runoff and was elected to serve in congress for the
state of Louisiana (Bridges 1994, 2).

His Religious Background

Duke was reared a Methodist (his father was a Sunday school teacher) and later attended the Church of Christ (Duke 1998, 256). In his autobiography, Duke details his early religious upbringing and why he rejected Genesis and creationism and the "single origin of the races from Adam" teaching. To learn "how racial differences originated" he had to study evolutionary theory in detail (Duke 1998, 89). In short, when he accepted Darwinism he rejected the Bible and his church teaching, but, instead, relied on science, which he concluded was fact.

Once he understood the Darwinist teaching on "the realities of racial difference," he realized that "by learning about the evolutionary forces that created the different races, we can understand the character and conduct of the various races, our own included" (1998, 90). He noted that many Darwinists used the terms "race" and "breed" interchangeably, and so applied research on the evolution of animal "breeds" to humans.

The conflicts Duke had with the Church were not only with Darwinism, but also, especially, with the Church's opposition to racism. He bemoaned the fact that, when he graduated from college in the mid-1970s, an increasing number of churches were teaching that racism was a sin (257).

His Religious Battle

Duke's father, a geologist, tried to reconcile evolution with Christianity by concluding that evolution was the means that God used to create life. This background set the groundwork for Duke's later acceptance of Darwinism. As he read more and more on "the scientific issue of race," he became torn between his religion and science (Zatarain 1990, 80). As a youngster, Duke regularly read about science in *Science Digest, National Geographic,* and other science magazines (Duke 1998, 21).

Duke was involved in researching Darwinism while he was still attending a Church of Christ school in New Orleans. As a result of his study of evolution, Duke openly challenged his Sunday school teachers by discussing his evolving ideas about the origin of humans and their implication for racism. When endeavoring to combine his Darwinist racist beliefs with Christianity, Duke used many of the same rationalizations used by theistic evolutionists today to rationalize the plain statements of the Genesis creation account.

Duke eventually sided with Darwinism and rejected creationism. He concluded that with "each passing day more evidence emerges of the dynamic, genetically-born, physical and physiological differences between the races" (1998, 103). So ended his "fleeting commitment" to orthodox Christianity (Bridges 1994, 7), even though he still peppers his writings with religious phrases, such as if "I can move our people one inch toward . . . God . . . my life will have been worthwhile" (p. 273).

His life tells a very different story. In short, after his acceptance of Darwinism, Duke unabashedly classified both the European and Asian races at a "higher level of human evolution than the African race" (1998, 103). He concluded that "the evolution of man from his primitive to his modern state came from Nature" (1998, 104). Duke now firmly believes that "all life on Earth had evolved and is still undergoing change" (1998, 101).

Especially important in Duke's conversion to Darwinism was the "hard evidence of the great age of the Earth — such as the eras of geological time it took to raise Mount Everest from the bottom of the sea" (1998, 103). This evidence caused Duke to reject the biblical account of creation (even broadly interpreted) and accept the Darwinist interpretation. Long ages also figure prominently in Duke's racist arguments. He concluded that the amount of time Darwinists believe that blacks and whites have been separated by evolution is more than enough time to produce what he views as the profound differences that exist in human races (Duke 1998, 90–91).

Duke also argued that "denying the reality of race is a good example of how egalitarians are grasping for straws. A mass of scientific evidence proves the existence of traits and features that identify the genetically differentiated breeds of mankind, just as there are genetically differentiated breeds of dogs or cats" (1998, 87). Stressing gradualistic Darwinian theory, Duke argued that an increase in the average IQ to produce what he concludes is the approximate standard deviation difference existing today between the IQ of blacks and whites, controlling for the environment would require an increase of only a tiny fraction of one percent (.003) IQ each generation of whites. This conclusion relied on works such as Pendell (1951), which reviewed the research on IQ and race, and concluded that heredity plays "a leading role in intellectual ability" (p. 188).

Duke derisively called the "creationist belief that God instantaneously created mankind and all of Nature . . . egalitarianism," and bemoaned the fact that egalitarianism became the "dogma of our times." He was especially critical of creationism because creationists were egalitarians who teach "God made us all the same." He said he was amazed how the mass media helped to convert "both the scientific community — which espoused evolution and the fundamentally opposed creationist community — into spouting almost an identical egalitarian dogma (1998, 102–103). Duke claimed "anyone in the religious community who dared to tell the truth of race [negro inferiority] was accused of being against God Himself (Duke 1998, 103).

Duke used not only Darwinist arguments to justify racism, but also quotes Scripture, illustrating how important belief is in reaching conclusions. For example, he quoted the Scriptures that stated slaves should be obedient to their earthly masters (Ephesians 6:5, Timothy 6:2, and Titus, 2:9–11). This argument cannot be used to justify American racism because slavery in biblical days was very different than that practiced in the American south before the Civil War. In biblical days, a slave in Rome could become free by merit and work (some even became kings or high government officials).

Integral to Duke's racism is the conclusion that genetics is central to determining a large variety of traits, including even sexual deviance, male/female differences, homosexuality, and other traits. His conclusions in this area are similar to those of the early eugenics leaders who played an important role in American history at the turn of the last century, and also in Germany during Nazi rule. Duke discussed in some detail both positive and negative eugenics, implying support for both.

A concern repeatedly discussed by Duke is dysgenics — race degeneration that he concluded is caused by, among other factors, Caucasians interbreeding with "inferior" races. Duke makes clear in his autobiography that his racism is clearly a result of his acceptance, not only of Darwinism, but of the eugenics that logically results from Darwinism. Duke also repeats all of the arguments commonly published in the standard biological literature until the American civil rights movement — such as claiming that differences between the major races include not only skin color and hair texture, but also brain size, cranial structure, intelligence, musculature, hormonal levels, sexual behavior, temperament, dentition, and even personality (1998, 86).

Duke Confronts the Critics of Racism

Duke also reviewed the various scientific arguments *against* racism, such as Ashley Montagu's *Man's Most Dangerous Myth: The Fallacy of Race*. He concluded that Montagu's "myth of race" argument is analogous to saying that dog breeds are a myth because one can find specific traits that exist in various breeds: "I thought about the question long and hard, and I asked myself, 'because some similar traits are found in different breeds of dogs, does that mean there are no St. Bernards or Chihuahuas?' " (Duke 1998, 85).

Duke also reviewed Jared Diamond's arguments against racism, which he tried to refute by noting that the "closest relatives to man are the recent primates who are also relatively close in DNA. Chimpanzees, for instance, share 98.5 percent of the DNA with people" (Duke 1998, 103–104). He then argued that this claim is invalidated by the claim that Black and White DNA differ by less than one percent. Duke reasoned that, since only a 1.5 percent difference in DNA between humans and chimpanzees produced humans with brains about twice as large as chimps, small differences in DNA could produce large differences in the human races (1998, 85–86). Duke concludes, "If one follows Diamond's rationale, there is no difference between humans and chimpanzees because we can find sets of arbitrary selected genetic traits we share" (1998, 85).

The 98 percent idea often is used as an argument in favor of Darwinism and is repeated uncritically by Duke, even though the exact difference between humans and chimpanzees cannot be determined until much more is known about both the human and chimpanzee genome, especially the function and structure of chimpanzee genes. Estimates now range from below 80 percent similarity (Bergman and Tomkins 2012; Tomkins and Bergman 2012). Duke concludes that "the vast majority of the basic genes that make up the races are not only shared by them, but also by all mammals and even all other orders of life. What makes the important distinctions are the small percentage of genes that affect the structure and composition of those life forms" (1998, 86).

Darwinists Who Influenced Duke

Duke admits that his interest in "the effects of evolution on race" was originally stirred by professor Carleton Coon who was still an active professor when Duke was doing his research. Coon's racist ideas were then mainline, and influenced hundreds of his students, who themselves became professors of anthropology at many of America's leading universities. He was then the leading physical anthropologist and the president of the American Association of Physical Anthropologists. Coon published his many books with major publishers and, at the time of his death, was a research associate at the Peabody Museum of Harvard University.

Duke read all of Coon's books he could find, including the *Living Races of Man*, *Story of Man*, *Origin of the Races*, and *The Races of Europe*. Zatarain claimed that it was Coon who "introduced Duke to the view that race was a key factor in the development of modern man" (1990, 79). Duke was also heavily influenced by many other Darwinists, especially Harvard Professor of Anthropology Earnest Hooton. Although Duke relied upon many pre-1960 evolutionist writings in which racism was a dominant topic, he also quoted modern Darwinists.

After studying anthropological theories about the origin of races, Duke summarized the two dominant theories of evolution — the *single-origin hypothesis*, and the *multi-regional hypothesis* (advocated by University of Michigan Anthropology Professor Milford Wolpoff). The single-origin theory argued that the different races crossed the *Homo sapiens* threshold separately during evolution. Duke was especially impressed with the research that postulated *Homo sapiens* first evolved in Africa and then "evolved separately into two distinct genetic groups, the African and the non-African, about 120,000 years ago" (1998, 90–91).

Duke's belief that the major races have been in existence for tens of thousands of years meant there was "more than enough time for geography and climate to have created [by evolution] the profound differences that exist" today between the races (Duke 1998, 91). The Darwinist conclusion that the Caucasian and Negroid groups have been divided for at least a 110,000-year period convinced Duke that significant differences existed between them (1998, 91). In contrast, Caucasians and Asians have been separated by only 40,000 years.

For this reason, far fewer differences exist between Asians and Caucasians than exist between Negroids and Caucasians, who were separated long before this in the past. Duke repeatedly stressed that his conclusions on race were based on scientific research completed by leading modern scientists, and that this research forced him to reject the biblical creation account he was reared to believe (Maginnis 1992).

Professor Elmer Pendell's Influence

Another major influence on Duke was Professor Elmer Pendell's works, including *Why Civilizations Self-Destruct* (1977) and *Sex Versus Civilization* (1967). Both books concluded that more focus needs to be on the issue of human *quality*, as opposed to an almost exclusive focus on the concern of human *quantity* (1998, 109). Dr. Pendell, the editor/author of a major textbook (1942), taught at Cornell, Penn State, and Baldwin-Wallace College. He holds degrees from Cornell and the University of Chicago.

From Pendell, Duke obtained the idea that the less intelligent and less fit, as a whole, reproduce faster than the most intelligent and most fit (Duke 1998, 109). Pendell's solution was to have the state regulate reproduction according to eugenics principles, which translates into sterilization of "inferior" humans (Burch and Pendell 1945; Burch and Pendell 1947). Pendell reinforced Duke's view that "cultural superiority is the product of biology" (Bridges 1994, 123). Duke's racist views even touched on the abortion issue:

> Clearly, Duke's belief that many humans were "scum" and not worth nurturing was miles removed from the Christian underpinning of the right-to-life movement. But Duke's belief in eugenics caused him to oppose abortion. He was prolife not because he believed in the sanctity of the human being, as do Evangelical Christians, but because he thought banning abortions would produce more white babies and fewer minority ones (Bridges 1994, 125).

Professor Pendell stressed that "the only source of brains is heredity," and the key to evolution is "the elimination" of the less fit (1960, 20, 23). As a result, "As below average individuals were wiped out, the average moved up the scale . . . the weeding-out aspect of biological evolution has worked in the human species as well as in other species" and that "the culling of human flocks was basic to the development of mentality" (1960, 23, 28, 116–117). Pendell concluded that he was only "following through" on Darwin (1960, 208).

Race Mixing

It is clear that Darwinism was at the heart of Duke's racist argument — many of his arguments come from leading mainline Darwin theorists — some from the pre–civil rights era, but many from widely respected contemporary scientists. Duke actively supports eugenics — and for this reason he opposes all attempts to "pollute the races" by interbreeding, which he believes produces "dysgenic selection." He opposes "racial intermixture," because he believes that "race suicide" could be hastened if we allow "massive immigration of an alien race" into our society and "the loss of genetic survival through racial intermixture" (Duke 1998, 106).

Race mixing is especially anathema to Duke, and is the reason why he is so concerned about segregation. Preserving the Caucasian genotype is critical, and interracial marriage, which can be prevented only by separating the races, is required to prevent degeneration of the human genome. Duke even claims that interracial marriage is genocide and is no less terrible than what the Germans attempted against Jews — and the ultimate result, he stresses, will be identical (1998, 108–109). Preserving the Caucasian race is but a precondition for continuing its evolution to a higher level (1998, 110).

For all of these reasons, Duke is very concerned about what he concludes is the negative effects of all egalitarian efforts, especially integration and the push for equal schooling for the races. He concludes that the great challenge today is the "equality of the races" question — and that in order to move up the evolutionary ladder, humans have to become smarter and healthier, and cross genetic thresholds that will someday make traveling to the moon and other feats routine (1998, 110). Duke believes that Darwinism and racism are both clearly essential to the future of Western society and, thus, Duke is highly motivated to oppose all egalitarian efforts, and to support both segregation and the "advancement" of Caucasians.

Duke stresses that many of the contrasting traits of Caucasians and Negroids is a result of evolution. For example, Duke noted that, when researching evolution, he compared the behavior of "Negroids" and Caucasians. An example he gives is a fight between Muhammad Ali and Chuck Wepner (a Caucasian). He concluded that Ali had an "evolutionary advantage" in the fight, adding, "I was probably the only one in the neighborhood who thought about the evolutionary racial differences between Ali and Wepner as the replay of the fight came on TV" (Duke 1998, 97).

Those involved in racist movements are soon introduced to the idea that, not only are "Negroids" inferior, but Jews are as well. Duke, likewise, encountered this issue and dealt with it by studying the "applications of evolutionary biology to the development of the Jewish people" (1998, 450). He concluded that Jews are inferior for many of the same reasons that Hitler did. This belief partly accounts for his active involvement in the American Nazi party.

Duke argues that "Charles Darwin, in his study of the changing and evolving character of all life forms, demonstrated that principles of heredity combined with what he called, *Natural Selection*, had developed the exceptional abilities of mankind itself. His masterpiece, *The Origin of Species* has a subtitle that expresses his whole idea in a nutshell: *The Preservation of Favoured Races in the Struggle for Life*" (p. 640). Duke also noted that Darwin's *Preservation of Favoured Races in the Struggle for Life* concept dealt with natural selection not only at the individual level, but "even more importantly, on the selection process involving species and sub-species (races)" as the subtitle of his "masterpiece" demonstrates (1998, 450–451).

H.G. Wells's Influence on Duke

Duke's introduction to Darwinism occurred early in his life. He stated that one of the first books his father gave him to read in grade school was H.G.

Wells's classic, *The Outline of History* (1922). Wells was a lifelong crusader for Darwinism ever since he was introduced to the theory in college by his famous mentor, Darwin's bulldog, T.H. Huxley. *The Outline of History*, as Duke correctly notes, attempts to defend not only Darwinism, but also state-supported use of eugenics to breed superior humans (1998, 118–119).

Wells argues that evolution is an essential element in the rise and fall of nations: absorbing their conquered foes leads to dysgenics, and begins the process that leads to a nation's fall because the superior victors intermarry with the inferior losers, producing an inferior progeny — as a result, the conquerors are themselves conquered. Duke notes the theme of Wells's book is "great people arise having intelligence, strength, and ambition," and create a powerful society and conquer their less-fit neighbors. Soon the "process of absorbing the conquered in their nation-state" occurs and the

> traits that originally led them to victory and dominance are lost as they gradually absorb the defeated population. Invariably the process begins again, and another people come on the scene and conquer, only to once more be absorbed by those they had vanquished . . . it became obvious to me that the race factor is present in the rise and fall of every civilization. In fact, in every fallen civilization there had been a racial change from the original founding population. The only real justification for the survival of a nation is a racial one — the survival of that specific population as a distinct genetic entity, as a source for the next generation (1998, 118).

Wells's writing convinced Duke when he was still young that race was *central* to evolutionary advancement. From reading Wells's and Pendell's books, Duke came to conclude that his crusade against the black race is a matter of the very survival of America, a nation that he repeatedly states he loves (1998, 118–119). Although a disciple of Wells, Duke is actually working for much more moderate goals than his master. Wells had no qualms about admitting his solution to the world's problems — a radical eugenics program that openly involved killing inferior beings. Wells's attitude can best be summarized in his statement that, "there is only one sane and logical thing to be done with a really inferior race, and that is to exterminate it" (quoted in Trombley 1988, 32).

Duke was also influenced by Count Arthur DeGobineau's *Inequality of the Races* — a classic work that is still in print and that often is utilized by racists (1998, 119–120). Although DeGobineau wrote his infamous classic before Darwin published his *Origin of Species*, many of the ideas are the same. DeGobineau argued that civilization was ultimately the product of biology, specifically the racial characteristics of its founders. Civilization declined because of the inherent makeup of its founders changed, that is, their racial quality declined because of "racial mixing." Duke interpreted these concerns, especially those relating to the situation in America, as a result of Afro-Americans and Caucasians mixing.

Duke also used the idea advocated by DeGobineau (1966) and many other Darwinists that civilizations collapse because, after winning a war, the victor brought the conquered as slaves into their population — and they were eventually absorbed in the conqueror's gene pool. The result was the collapse of the conqueror's civilization due to being genetically weakened by interbreeding with the subjects who lost the war. Duke here assumes the common (but false) eugenic idea that those who win wars are genetically superior, and those who lose wars are genetically inferior.

Sociobiology, as advocated by Harvard's Edward Wilson and other biologists, was also critically important in the devolvement of Duke's thinking. Especially was "the landmark work of Dr. Edward Wilson in his seminal *Sociobiology; a Synthesis*" critical. Duke read this work a few months after it came out and "found it magnificent" (1998, 451). He concluded that Wilson

> offered powerful evidence that behavior in the most elementary creatures such as ants . . . to the complexities of mankind itself, had a biological basis driven by the urge to preserve the genotype. Genetic kinship turned out to be a powerful factor in evolution and behavior. In such a context, group loyalty and altruism became understandable from the evolutionary perspective in that the individual may sacrifice his life and his individual reproduction to ensure the survival to those who are genetically similar to him (1998, 451).

Dawkins's "selfish-gene" idea, as shown in this statement by Duke, was also critically important.

Other Evolutionists Who Influenced Duke

Of the many persons whom Duke lists that influenced his racist views, most were professional Darwinists, including Julian Huxley and George Bernard Shaw (p. 640). He also studied the books of Henry Garrett, former chair of the psychology department at Columbia University and head of the APA, and *African Genesis* by Robert Audry (Zatarain 1990; 79, 88). Duke also relied on Sir Arthur Keith's "dynamic" book, *A New Theory of Human Evolution* (1949), which stressed that not only individuals, but also groups (such as racial groups) are subjected to evolutionary pressures.

Duke even relied upon Frances Galton's writings, the man who coined the term "eugenics" and endeavored to control human reproduction to improve "the inborn qualities of a race" (1998, 640). Duke notes that Darwin wrote to Galton, openly giving complete support to Galton's eugenic views — and Duke concluded that relying on great men such as Darwin and Galton (as well as Harvard professors Wilson, Hooten, Coon, and others, including "many of the leading lights of Western Civilization") lent scientific support to his ideas, empowering him to carry on his campaign with confidence and vigor (1998, 640).

Many biological works completed by well-known scientists whom Duke had read have been reprinted by various modern racist groups. One example is University of Texas at Austin Professor Roger J. Williams's book, *Free and Unequal; The Biological Basis of Individual Liberty*, originally published in 1953 by the University of Texas Press and reprinted by Liberty Press, a racist organization. The book stresses that races, whether in mice, rats, horses, insects, or humans, all have developed by evolution — and that "if human beings failed to develop races they would constitute the only exception in the whole biological kingdom" (1953, 210).

Williams also notes that, although Caucasians and other races can interbreed, this does not prove equality. Furthermore, he stresses that the whole basis of evolution is variability and that some human variations are superior to others. In Williams's words, "Variability is at the very basis of human life and of all life. The concept of evolution as we have it today is one in which variation is absolutely indispensable. Without genetic variability, evolution could not possibly have happened, and in line with currently accepted thought, biology itself would not exist!" (1953, 56).

This variability is what evolution selects from — and while this work is mildly racist compared to many, the racist implications are clear — which is why it was reprinted by Liberty Press. Professor Williams makes clear that the writings of Darwin and his nephew, Galton, were the basis of eugenics. Williams admits that their ideas on improving the race did not have the advantage of knowing "how complicated heredity is," and they "not only flew in the face of religious teaching but were so over simplified that they came to be regarded as unsound scientifically" (1953, 314–315). Williams implies that a more sophisticated analysis of the problem may lead us to a practical, workable eugenics program.

The books that Duke cited as being critical in the development of his ideas also relied heavily upon Darwinism. For example, one of the most notorious racist books in the last century, Putnam's *Race and Reason: A Yankee View* (1961), published by the prestigious Public Affairs Press of Washington DC, has a laudatory introduction by Ruggles Gates, PhD, Henry Garrett, PhD, DSc, Robert Gayre, DSc, and Wesley C. George, PhD, all eminent Darwinist scientists. The foreword by T.R. Waring states that Dr. Gates is "generally acknowledged to be one of the world's leading human geneticists" (Putnam 1961, iv). Gates was a zoology professor at the University of California for many years, and ended his career as an honorary research fellow of biology at Harvard. Gayre was editor of *Mankind Quarterly*, professor of anthropology, and head of the post-graduate department of anthropogeography at the University of Sugaor in India. His many publications include a three-volume set titled *Ethnology*.

Wesley George was professor of anatomy at the University of North Carolina, where he was department head for a decade. He also was the author of many articles on the evolution of humans and other vertebrates. Waring concludes: "There can be no doubt that the endorsement of these men, taken together with the evidence of other scientists called as witnesses by the author in his text, guarantee the scientific integrity of *Race and Reason* and confirm the soundness of its premises" (Putnam 1961, v). It was this book that "began Duke's intellectual journey" as the most infamous living racist (Putnam 1961, 256).

Aside from quoting anthropologists and Darwinists who agreed with his racist position, Putnam also attacked scientists who disagreed with him. Foremost among them was Franz Boas and his students, especially Ashley Montagu and Gene Weltfish. Boas was one of the first anthropologists to openly and actively oppose the eugenics movement and the attempts to base racism on science. Putnam notes that Boas and his disciples are "the father of equalitarian anthropology in America" (Putnam 1961, 23).

Boas, a Jew, trained many anthropologists, including Margaret Mead (who also had a profound influence on anthropology). Boas began teaching at Columbia University in 1896 and was originally also a racist (what Putnam calls a "non equalitarian") until his "change of heart in the late 1920s" (Putnam 1961, 18) with the rise of anti-Semitism based on Darwin. After Boas died, Putnam notes that Columbia hired "non-equalitarian" Ralph Lintona — who dismissed all of Boas's untenured appointees and fired Weltfish on a charge of "too-long" tenure (Putnam 1961, 18).

Putnam's efforts to dismiss Boas's ideas amount to name-calling, such as that his ideas were "clever and insidious propaganda posing in the name of science, fruitless efforts at proof of unprovable theories" (Putnam 1961, 18). Putnam's concern was, how was it "possible that a whole generation of Americans were taken in . . . by Boas' writings?" (Putnam 1961, 18–19).

Although Putnam never even tried to refute Boas's conclusions (and history has proven many of them correct), he did state that he found "professional scientists aplenty who saw what I saw" — that is, that Boas's writings arguing for civil rights for African-Americans were scientifically invalid. Putnam concludes that Boas's argument rests on "the assumption of present day culture differences between the Negro and other races are due, not to any natural limitations, but to isolation and historic accident" (Putnam 1961, 24).

The reason Putnam opposed integration, both in schools and elsewhere, is, according to a letter from a physiology professor at a leading medical school: "School integration is social integration and social integration means an ever increasing rate of interbreeding. [This is true regardless of whether the sexes are separated in schools. The little brother would still bring his new Negro friend home after school.] As a biologist, I see the process as a mixing of Negro genes in our white germ plasma, a process from which there can be no unmixing" (Putnam 1961, 37, bracket material in Putnam).

A prime argument against intermarriage is the conclusion that Negroes have genetically lower intelligence — 10 to 20 points or more — and that mixing will lower the overall human IQ. As evidence, Putnam cites mainline journals, such as an article by Frank C.J. McGurk published in the winter 1959 issue of *Harvard Educational Review*. He also quotes such experts as McGill University's Wilder Pennfield, who stated, "There is no question that the frontal lobes of the typical Negro are smaller and the cerebral cortex less wrinkled than the typical white's" (Putnam 1961, 41). Several similar quotes left the impression that biologists and anthropologists agreed on this issue. To further emphasize his point, Putnam quotes half a dozen books by professors published by major publishers.

Putnam constantly appeals to science, claiming that his racial mixing view has "scientific validity" (Putnam 1961, 84). The many scientists and major scientific journals that support his views include Dr. Redzinski, who argued that the conglomeration "of racial and ethnic elements" in America now "renders a serious cultural decline inevitable" (Putnam 1961, 85). Putnam even argues that racism benefits those discriminated against — an approach that, no doubt, convinced many people at the time this book was written.

Putnam claims that the few examples of Afro-Americans who have done well had white genes. For example, he states, "George Washington Carver is held up as the ideal Negro scientist, but his white genes showed in his blue eyes" (Putnam 1961, 92). Intelligence and other similar attributes, he concludes, are white traits, and he adds that "the Negro's limitations are in the realms of character and intelligence" (Putnam 1961, 94).

Putnam concludes that the *Brown versus the Board of Education* court decision was based on "Boas anthropology," which is contrary to the testimony of (so he implies) almost the entire scientific world. Furthermore, Boas's "equalitarian anthropology has never been properly examined, the rotten core of this rosy apple, which is the apple upon which integration feeds, has never been laid bare to the judicial eye."

Putnam also quotes Harvard Professor Clyde Kluckhohn, who stated, "In the light of accumulating information as to significantly varying incidents of mapped genes among different people, it seems unwise to assume flatly that 'man's innate capacity does not vary from one population to another,' " which Putnam concluded meant that "racial equality in intellect could no longer be assumed" (Putnam 1961, 51).

Putnam then concludes, after quoting numerous other eminent professors (mostly anthropologists and Darwinists), that he would be "prepared to concede the possibility that the Negro may, through normal processes of mutation and natural selection . . . eventually overtake and even surpass the white race." This process, though, he estimates will take five hundred billion years! (Putnam 1961, 53). Evolution made "Whites" superior and the law of evolution cannot be broken, but must be obeyed.

Duke's Influence on Modern Racism Today

It would appear that Duke's writings on race, which quote many prominent scientists (his autobiography alone lists 45 pages of references, mostly academic) would be very convincing to many non-creationists who are conversant with evolutionary arguments. And, according to the Amazon.com reviews of Duke's 1998 autobiography, which is more an apologist for scientific racism, evolutionary racists arguments are very convincing to many people today. As of 2014, out of 146 reviews (the vast majority of books have far fewer reviews), the average customer review was exceptionally high (4.4 stars out of 5).

Most reviewers gave Duke's book five stars, and a handful gave it one star under such headings as "inaccurate and bigoted" or "propaganda at its shiniest." Several reviewers condemned Duke's "science," not realizing that many of his ideas were taken straight from the writings of highly respected scientists — although many, but not all, were pre–civil rights generation scientists. After Duke's "retirement" in 1980, no Klan leader has been able to achieve his effectiveness and, as a result, the Klan has lost much of its influence (Newton 2007, 39).

Summary of the Influence of Darwinism on the Klan

Professor Martin Gitlin, in an extensive historical research study of the Klan, concluded that:

> Most Klansmen and other white supremacists believe not only in the biological inferiority of blacks, but also in a modern-day Darwinism once embraced by Hitler and the Nazis. This view asserts . . . the Aryan white race is superior to all others and that blacks are the most inferior with various other races falling somewhere in between. They feel the natural order of the human race is no different than that of an animal world in which only the strongest survive. Hard-core racists with a political bent feel a race war will either cleanse America of what they perceive to be the inferior black race or at least provide separation [of the races] (Gitlin 2009, 49).

Furthermore, even though the Klan's loss of much of its influence in the late 1920s spelled the end of extensive female Klan involvement, many scholars "believed it to be absurd that Klansmen or Klanswomen would honestly support or fight for the Constitutional rights of a black race they have always considered inferior" (Gitlin 2009, 58). One example of the fact that the evolutionary belief of the Black inferiority doctrine had an enormous impact on the Klan's history is as follows:

> In light of the widespread power of the Ku Klux Klan in the Southern states, the impartiality of any white juror, no matter where he resided, would be suspect. . . . Historically, the testimony of black men against white men in Southern courts had been problematic. In some cases blacks were not allowed to testify against whites. Even when their testimony was permitted, juries tended to view blacks as inherently inferior to whites. Consequently, white jurors seldom believed testimony offered by blacks, or if they believed it, they afforded it little weight in their deliberations (Martinez 2007, 166).

The result was the long history of injustice against Blacks in America. As

Newton notes:

> The original Klan prescripts of 1867 and 1868 made no mention of white supremacy, simply because none was necessary. Reconstruction-era Klansmen were born and raised in a society which enslaved blacks . . . they took for granted [the view] that blacks were sub-humans unfit for any semblance of parity with whites — much less complete equality with its ever-present specter of miscegenation and "amalgamation." Even in its "innocent" fraternal days, between spring 1866 and April 1867, the KKK maintained racist tradition by dressing as ghosts to frighten ex-slaves. . . . The fact that those "undesirables" were nearly always black speaks volumes in regard to KKK mentality (2007, 38).

Thus it was widely believed "that blacks were inferior to whites and therefore deserving of lesser legal protections" (Martinez 2007, 169). This Darwinian view was reinforced by books such as *The Clansman,* a work that was

> saturated with racism on virtually every page, *The Clansman* was Dixon's most popular work. His view of blacks was hostile and insulting; he wrote of "a thick-lipped, flat nosed, spindle-shanked Negro, exuding his nauseous animal odor." This sentence was but one of many such descriptions. For his loyal readers, Dixon's views on race were far from extraordinary; he described what many whites already believed. What captivated the audience was not the denigration of the Negro. Instead, the mawkishly histrionic, ridiculously contrived plot lines appealed to whites (Martinez 2007, 242).

A review of KKK websites done in 2011 finds they still quote from evolutionists to justify their beliefs, such as Volume 19, page 344 of the well-respected 11th edition of the *Encyclopedia Britannica*: "The Negro would appear to stand on a lower evolutionary plane than the white man, and is more closely related to the highest anthropoids. . . . Mentally the Negro is inferior" to whites. They also use the standard reference book *Popular Science,* Volume 11, page 515 that stated: "The verdict [of science] is that the Negro does belong to an inferior race. His brain capacity is poorer, its construction simpler." They often neglected to note that this quote is from the 1931 edition of *Popular Science.*[1]

---

1. See http://kkk.org and http://www.thebirdman.org/Index/Others/Others-Doc-Blacks/+Doc-Blacks-Intelligence&Competence/ScientificFactsOfBlackIntelligence.htm. For an example that uses the pre-Adamite theory in an attempt to harmonize evolution with Darwinism see http://kkk.bz/shocking_story_of_real_slavery_i.htm.

Conclusions

It is clear from a review of the writings of many of the most prominent racists today that a major support for their beliefs was the writings of pre-1950 mainline evolutionary scientists. The "facts" of science and the acceptance of their racist conclusions by leading scientists, especially those from Ivy-league schools such as Harvard, convinced many racists that the key to America's salvation was reducing the harm caused by inferior races, especially Afro-Americans and Jews (Wise 2003; Rose 1992). Armed with this knowledge, Duke and others were determined to aggressively carry their message of Darwinism and eugenics — and where it led them, namely to racism — to the world.

David Duke concluded his autobiography with the following words: "I truly believe that the future of this country, civilization, and planet is inseparably bound up with the destiny of our White race" (1998, 273). He and others have dedicated their lives to this goal in spite of the fact that the racist Darwinian arguments Duke relied on have all been both carefully refuted, and documented to be harmful, by both creationists and evolutionists (Bergman 1993).

References

Bergman, Jerry. 1993. "Evolution and the Origins of the Biological Race Theory." *CEN Tech Journal* 7(2):155–168.

———— and Jeffery Tomkins. 2012. "Is the Human Genome Nearly Identical to Chimpanzee? — A Reassessment of the Literature." *Journal of Creation* 25(4):54–60.

Bridges, Tyler. 1994. *The Rise of David Duke*. Jackson, MS: University of Mississippi.

Brown, Harwood. 2000 (reprint edition). *Papers Read at the Meeting of Grand Dragons Knights of the Ku Klux Klan At their First Annual Meeting held at Asheville, North Carolina, July 1923*. North Stratford, NH: Ayer Company Publishers.

Browne, Janet. 2003. "The Flood, the Ark, and the Shaping of Natural History," chapter 5 in Lindberg and Numbers 2003.

Burch, Guy Irving, and Elmer Pendell. 1945. *Population Roads to Peace or War*. Washington, DC: Population Reference Bureau.

————. 1947. *Human Breeding and Survival: Population Roads to Peace or War*. New York: Penguin Books.

DeGobineau, Arthur. 1966. *The Inequality of Human Races: The Pioneering Study of the Science of Human Races*. Los Angeles, CA: The Noontide Press.

Duke, David. 1998. *My Awakening: A Path to Racial Understanding*. Covington, LA: Free Speech Press.

Fry, Henry P. 1922. *The Modern Ku Klux Klan*. Boston, MA: Small, Maynard & Company.

Gitlin, Marty. 2009. *The Ku Klux Klan: A Guide to an American Subculture*. Santa Barbara, CA: Greenwood.

Gould, Stephen Jay. 1977. *Ontogeny and Phylogeny.* Cambridge, MA: Harvard University Press.

Keith, Sir Arthur. 1949. *A New Theory of Human Evolution.* New York: Philosophical Library.

Lee, Martin A. 2003 "Detailing David Duke." Southern Poverty Law Center. http://www.splcenter.org/get-informed/intelligence-report/browse-all-issues/2003/spring/detailing-david-duke.

Lindberg, David, and Ronald Numbers. 2003. *When Science and Christianity Meet.* Chicago, IL: University of Chicago Press.

Maginnis, John. 1992. *Cross to Bear.* Baton Rouge, LA: Darkhorse Press.

Martinez, J. Michael. 2007. *Carpetbaggers, Cavalry, and the Ku Klux Klan: Exposing the Invisible Empire During Reconstruction.* New York: Rowman & Littlefield.

Morris, Charles. 1888. *The Aryan Race: Its Origins and Its Achievements.* Chicago, IL: S.C. Griggs and Company.

Nelson, G. Blair. 2003. "Men Before Adam! American Debates Over the Unity and Antiquity of Humanity." chapter 7, p. 161–181, in Lindberg and Numbers 2003.

Newton, Michael. 2007. *The Ku Klux Klan: History, Organization, Language, Influence and Activities of America's Most Notorious Secret Society.* Jefferson, NC: McFarland & Company, Inc., Publishers.

———. 2010. *The Ku Klux Klan in Mississippi: A History.* Jefferson, NC: McFarland.

Pendell, Elmer (editor). 1942. *Society Under Analysis, an Introduction to Sociology.* Lancaster, PA: Cattell.

———.1951. *Population on the Loose.* New York: Wilfred Funk.

———. 1960. *The Next Civilization.* Dallas, TX: Royal Publishing Company.

———. 1967. *Sex Versus Civilization.* Los Angeles, CA: Noontide Press.

———. 1977. *Why Civilizations Self-Destruct.* Cape Canaveral, FL: Howard Allen Enterprises.

Putnam, Carleton. 1961. *Race and Reason: A Yankee View.* Washington, DC: Public Affairs Press.

Quatrefages, A. De. *The Human Species,.* New York: D. Appleton and Company, 1879.

Rose, Douglas D. (editor). 1992. *The Emergence of David Duke and the Politics of Race.* Chapel Hill, NC: University of North Carolina Press.

Tomkins, Jeffery, and Jerry Bergman. 2012. "Genomic Monkey Business — Estimates of Nearly Identical Human-Chimp DNA Similarity Re-evaluated Using Omitted Data." *Journal of Creation* 25(4):94–100.

Topinard, Paul. 1894. *Anthropology.* London: Chapman & Hall.

Trombley, Stephen. 1988. *The Right to Reproduce: A History of Coercive Sterilization.* London: Weidenfeld and Nicholson.

Turner, John. 1982. *The Ku Klux Klan: A History of Racism and Violence.* Montgomery, AL: The Southern Poverty Law Center.

Wells, H.G. 1922. *The Outline of History.* New York: Collier.

White, Adam. 1966. *The Negro . . . Animal or Human?* Alexandria, VA: Adam White.

Williams, Roger J. 1953. *Free & Unequal: The Biological Basis of Individual Liberty.* Indianapolis, IN: Liberty Press.

Winchell, Alexander. 1978. *Proof of Negro Inferiority.* Metairie, LA: Sons of Liberty.

Winchell, Alexander, and Robert Bernasconi. *Preadamites*. Bristol, England: Thoemmes Press, 2002.

Wise, Tim. 2003. *Great White Hoax: Responding to David Duke and the Politics of White Nationalism*. Seattle, WA: Northwest Coalition for Human Dignity.

Zatarain, Michael. 1990. *David Duke: Evolution of a Klansman*. Gretna, LA: Pelican Publishing.

Chapter 9

Exploiting Non-Westerners for Evolutionary Evidence

Introduction

Africans and other non-Westerners were exploited in circuses and freak shows for decades as evidence of evolutionism. For over a century, these displays were a major attraction at many fairs and sideshows. They likely influenced millions of persons to accept the belief that humans evolved from some lower, less evolved, primate. Although money was usually the primary motive, the promoters of these shows deceptively tried to pass off various non-Western peoples as missing links, or at least as primitive humans who were evolutionarily less developed than Westerners. These displays had a significant influence on racism and were important support for movements such as the Ku Klux Klan. Today, we see this history as a major example of unethical exploitation of minorities.

For decades, major fairs, amusement parks, or carnival attractions displayed African, Asian, South American, or Australian natives who were billed and widely advertised as a "scientific presentation" of "primitive" or barbaric subhuman "men-monkeys," "ape men" and "ape women," or "missing links" (Bogdan 1988, 177). These non-Westerners typically were "elaborately embellished" and sold to the public by making up "a profusion of creative tales" all packaged "within a pseudo-anthropological framework" (Bogdan 1988, 178). These attractions "popularized Darwinian notions of racial progress from 'savagery' to 'civilization' " (Rydell 1999, 140).

Partly as a result, from the late 1800s to the early 1900s the general public was "fascinated by, or addicted to, the spectacle of primitive man" (Bradford and Blume 1992). Historically, these popular shows were, at least for the masses, one of the more convincing evidences for Darwinism (Gordon 1999; Parsons 1999). From the early 1800s until today, hundreds of millions of people the world over have visited fairs and circuses. Fairs were a leading form of entertainment for over a century and were popular even for some time after the introduction of motion pictures (Durant and Durant 1957; Bradna and Spence 1952). Consequently, millions were exposed to these Darwinian propaganda shows during a time "sometimes called the Age of Darwin" (Lindfors 1999, vii).

These shows used Africans and other ethnic minorities who were made up to appear to be convincing primitive men — ape-human links between humans and monkeys as Darwin's theory required (Lindfors 1999). Although the classic example is the display of a Pygmy named Ota Benga in a Bronx zoo, this practice had been going on for decades before this (Bradford and Blume 1992; Bergman 1993). It now is known that all of these claimed "Darwin's missing links" were normal humans from non-Western nations and cultures, usually Africans, but also Asians, Australians, and South Sea islanders.

One of the most famous circuses, Barnum and Bailey, regularly featured displays of humans that they claimed, or at least implied, proved Darwin's theory of human evolution or, more often, dishonestly led visitors to conclude they were valid evidence for Darwinism (Bergman 2002).

Many of the advertisements for these exhibits were specifically tailored to satisfy the public's curiosity about Darwin. One researcher concluded that Barnum was an expert in coming up with fake intermediate species, and "missing links were his specialty, and he kept his museum stocked with them, whether to flesh out the Great Chain of Being, or after 1859, when Darwin's *Origin of Species* appeared, to buttress the theory of evolution" (Blume 1999, 190). The importance of these shows was noted by Kunhardt et al. in their history of P.T. Barnum.

Barnum and Bailey's Greatest Show on Earth, here with the smallest man alive and the "Congo giant."

Barnum brought forth perhaps the most important spectacle of his entire career, a "Grand Ethnological Congress of Nations" made up of native "tribespersons" from all corners of the globe. He had been planning such an assemblage since at least 1860 and possibly since 1851 . . . in the 1880s, he wanted to show forth "the uncivilized." "I desire . . . a collection, in pairs or otherwise," he had written in August 1882, "of all the uncivilized races in existence." . . . Employing agents on every continent, eventually the project began to yield the longed-for "specimens" — Zulus and Polynesians, Nubians and Hindus, Todas Indians and Afghans, Australian aborigines and Sioux Indians and Laplanders. . . . Nothing of its kind had ever been seen before in America or elsewhere. . . . Public fascination with Barnum's "Congress" was intense; mostly white audiences howled with laughter at the "inferior" beings on display. The Chicago *Tribune* summed up Americans' attitudes by describing the Australian aborigines' "almost jet black skin" and "gorillaish features" (1995, 296).

Many of the "scientific" displays added to the problem. For example, displays of "native villages" at the 1893 Columbian Exposition in Chicago "inspired circuses to enlarge their own displays of tribal people" (Bogdan 1988, 185). One indication of the high level of popularity of "primitive people" displays was at the 1917 World's Fair. At this fair, the anthropology displays of "primitive" humans received fully 40 percent of all press notices. The "animality" of Africans was one trait thought to set them "apart from more rational varieties of the human species" (Lindfors 1983, viii). This fair, as did many, "displayed" a group of Pygmies — and "the historical record shows that Pygmies had been heavily in demand since time immemorial" (Bradford and Blume 1992, 18).

It was believed for decades, even by some "experts," that "the Pygmian race was a race of apes" (Bradford and Blume 1992, 20). The Pygmies "seemed scarcely human . . . not more intelligent than the trained baboon on a bicycle" (Green 1999, 172) and "were the subject of ethnological inquiry and debate by scientists in learned societies" (Bogdan 1988, 188). Many of these primitive people, the showman incorrectly claimed, had no recognized language, no marriage state, and lived like animals. In fact, the Pygmies were "in many ways . . . better men than the average European" — they respected property and "murder, theft, and sex before marriage were virtually unknown" (Marchand 2003, 300).

Likewise, other persons from Africa (such as from the Zulu tribe) were marketed as "apelike creatures" and "bestial Africans" (Bogdan 1988, 187). The Hottentots also were commonly displayed, often billed as "examples of the most primitive people in the world" (Bogdan 1988, 187). Advertisements of the day frequently claimed that, from an evolutionary viewpoint, the Africans were as near to the ape as they were to humans. Often, they would not openly claim that Negroes were a missing link, but rather use expressions similar to "we cannot help but wonder if" the Africans were "Darwin's missing link" (Bogdan 1988, 192).

Many other races also were considered less evolved than whites — living "links" to the human evolutionary past. People flocked to see these "ape men" at shows until scientists completely discredited the eugenic idea of human racial inferiority and also the whole eugenics movement. Green estimated that in one week "well over ten thousand Britons were entertained by the Congo Pygmies" (1999, 174). It was only with Turnbull's 1950s work that the Pygmies as a people were somewhat accurately understood and the conclusion that they were "ape-humans" was finally and fully discredited (Turnbull 1968).

Darwinism's Influence

Darwin's writings were critical in popularizing the view that humans evolved from some apelike ancestors. His work also was a critically important impetus to the exploitation of non-Westerners in freak shows. For example, Darwin's writings directly supported the conclusion "that some forms of humans were closer to their primitive ancestors than others" (Bogdan 1988, 249). Darwin devoted a whole chapter in his 1839 book, *Journal of Researchers*, to the "primitive" people. In it, he claimed they were so primitive that "when pressed in winter by hunger, they kill and devour their old women before the people kill their dogs" (1839, 214).

Soon after evolution became a widely discussed subject (and later widely accepted) because of the work of Darwin, both the frequency and diversity of "exotic people" shows grew steadily (Rothfels 1996, 164). Under the subheading "The Search for Man's Ancestors," Smith, et al. noted that after Darwin "the interest of anthropologists and of the intelligent lay public has been keenly alive to the possibility of finding, dead or alive, other links in man's ancestry" (1931, 20).

It was during these displays that people could see humans who, so it was claimed, looked similar to how humans looked not long after they had "left the ape behind" (Rothfels 1996, 164). Ape-looking tribes were used as evidence of evolution before Darwin published his classic work *The Origin of Species*, but many people, at least until the middle of the 19th century, believed that African inferiority was due to environment (Erlmann 1999, 112; Fiedler 1978, 240). Certain ethnic groups especially were exploited prior to Darwin's time, but after evolution was popularized by scientists (such as Erasmus Darwin in the early 1800s) and writers (such as Robert Chambers in the 1840s), the problem became much worse.

Although it was widely known in pre-Darwin times that many humans lived in primitive conditions or an uncivilized state, they still were considered noble beings created by a loving God (Snigurowicz 1999). When Darwinism was embraced by the masses, all this changed. Once the idea that humans evolved from lower primates was widely accepted, these savages became, not people living in primitive conditions, but biologically primitive creatures that were less evolved than Westerners.

Certain races (such as the Hottentots) widely were believed to be the "missing link" between humans and animals (Strother 1999, 10). When humans became "only transformed monkeys," as a result of Darwinism, we could expect to find some men who still were transforming, still evolving

(Snigurowicz 1999). Some Darwinists even claimed that "Negroes were a result of cross breeding between humans and Simians" (Fiedler 1978, 240). The impetus behind the display of non-Westerners in fairs was once explained as follows:

> With such sensational discoveries as the Neanderthal Man — one of the most important freaks of all time — in a cave outside Düsseldorf in 1856, and even more importantly, the publication in 1859 of Charles Darwin's *Origin of Species*, which was eagerly received by German scientists, the idea of evolution gained a scientific and popular currency in Germany that contrasts with reactions in other Western countries. Broad sectors of the public and scientific community became fascinated with what the theory of natural selection suggested about the development of man from nonhumanoid species, as well as with what it implied about the origins of races and cultures. Recalling the acceleration of interest in evolutionary theory in Germany, anthropologist Carl Stratz noted in 1904 that "the various more primitive human races were examined for their resemblance to apes . . . a list of pithecoid (ape-like) characteristics of man was compiled, and the missing link — the last connecting link between human and ape — was sought after with enthusiasm" (Rothfels 1996, 162).

Trained to Act Like Darwin's Missing Link

The men and women selected for these displays not only *looked* the part but also often were trained to *act* the part as well — for example, they were told how to act and often were given props such as sticks to hold, implying that they did not normally walk on two legs but rather locomoted like a monkey. Some were dressed in only loincloths, and were taught "jungle language" — mostly hideous grunts — to help them act out their Darwinian ape-man charade. Many were good actors and convinced millions to believe that they were in fact ape-men (Cook 1996).

Although most were nonwhites of normal intelligence, they learned how to act stupid and primitive (and had to be good actors to draw the crowds needed to make money). Common distortions of their culture included claims that they were cannibals who practiced polygamy, head hunting, or human sacrifices, and ate rodents, insects, and dirt. Other "lies and extravagant, overstated claims" were common (Bogdan 1988, 107). These "phony Zulus" were "easy to hire, cheap, and cooperative" (Bogdan 1988, 176). Not unexpectedly, after the widespread acceptance of Darwinism, a rapid rise of exploiting foreign races occurred:

> Darwin's evolutionary theorizing gave impetus to ever more fantastic speculation about the nature of the intermediary between "man" and monkey in the French social imaginary. Exhibits such as *hommes-* and *femmes-singes* (monkey-men and -women) and various other types of "primitive" intermediaries and *savages* proliferated in fairs and carnivals and other venues of popular entertainment, such as music halls and cafés-concerts. Press reports and articles, and dramatic and literary works satirized, lampooned, and otherwise conjectured about a possible intermediary between "man" and monkey (Snigurowicz 1999, 57).

The "Aztec Children" and other displays in the early 1850s preceded the great surge of excitement in evolution, but Darwinism soon became a major component in the enfreakment of a wide range of individuals (Rothfels 1996, 162). An example Rothfels mentions (which Darwin also discussed in his classic writings) is the "Tierra del Fuego" people. Rothfels concluded that:

> "Terra del Fuego" exhibit presents a classic case. . . . the "Fuegians" simply sat quietly, walked around the grounds, and prepared their food on an open fire without the use of pots. The public, despite the apparent mundaneness of these activities, was staggeringly enthusiastic. In Paris more than 50,000 people visited the show on one Sunday, and at the Berlin Zoological Gardens, "in order to avert the earlier wild scenes of the rush of the public, a large stage some four feet in height had to be erected upon which the Fuegians were situated." Most of the public was clearly more than satisfied with simply gazing upon these apparently "primitive people" (1996, 164).

Some Americans — who were fakes posing as African natives in the exhibits — later were "exposed for the 'civilized' humans that they were" (Snigurowicz 1999, 59; Killingray and Henderson 1999). Lindfors claims that "many" of the Zulu "performers" at one time were frauds (1983, 11). These "fake savages" were, though, just as fake as the real savages faking to be Darwinian ape-men links. Bogdan cited several cases of native-born Americans who were misrepresented as foreigners, such as Ohio-raised dwarfs who claimed to be from Borneo; a tall, black North Carolinian who, it was claimed, was from Dahomey, and "African natives" who actually were Blacks recruited from Chicago pool halls (1988, 107, 196).

Another example is, when in front of the public, the Aztecs' bushy hair always was tied up on topknots to emphasize their small heads, and they often were photographed in profile to display their "ape-like sloping foreheads" and noses (Snigurowicz 1999, 58). The people in many exhibits wore leopard-skin shorts or similar attire to look more primitive and more animal-like (Peacock 1999, 97). The makeup department did such a good job that some Africans "seemed scarcely human at all" (Green 1999, 172).

The Belgian Congo Ape-Like Ubangis

A good example of the exploitation of Africans was the Ubangis tribe. The Ubangis were a group of women imported from the Belgian Congo to play the role of Darwin's missing link in Barnum's circus. To emphasize their putative primitive human attributes, Africans often were displayed almost nude, often with monkeys and the sound of drums in the background (Bogdan 1988, 195). The Ubangi show advertisements claimed that they lived "like animals" and "smelled like hogs." When tossed bananas "as though they were so many chimpanzees," they ate the bananas "like apes" (Bradna 1952, 245). They were "easy to feed" — their diet consisted of only two meals a day "bananas with skins, peeled oranges, and raw fish" (Bradna and Spence 1952, 245). Bradna and Spence report that the "Ubangis had a hypnotic fascination, and the public could not get enough of them. Men and women gaped at them for five minutes steadily in the sideshow, then returned at the next performance for another look" (1952, 246). They claimed the Ubangi ape-women drew a greater crowd than any sideshow the circus ever presented (1952, 318). The Ubangis were displayed until at least 1932 (Lindfors 1983). The popularity of such shows was so great that

> by the nineteenth century, most cities of Europe had hosted regular exhibits of "strange" peoples, including the almost traditional appearances of Sub-Saharan Africans, Moors, Sami, and other Old World peoples, as well as such new arrivals as Native Americans, Inuit peoples, and South Sea Islanders. In the second half of the nineteenth century, both the frequency and diversity of the shows of "exotic" peoples grew steadily. . . . [and] among the most consistently popular exhibitions in the latter half of the century in Germany were those that focused on "primitive" peoples, who could, like "Krao," somehow be freaked as evolutionary ancestors of modern Europeans (Rothfels 1996, 164).

The Influence of Ape-Men Exhibits on the Common People

An important myth derived from Darwinism was the belief that creatures intermediate between humanoids and anthropoids must exist. Related to this idea is that of devolution, that is, that our children (or our children's children) may revert to the subhuman creatures that we once were in the distant past (Fiedler 1978, 241).

In the words of Odell, "The world was gradually preparing for Darwin and checking him up in terms of Barnum" (1931, 413). These ape-human exhibits were no doubt both highly impressive and very convincing to the large, naive, and often uneducated audiences who regularly viewed them. Otherwise, why would millions flock to see the shows for a price that was not cheap in their day? How many hundreds of millions of people visited these "ape-human" exhibits and as a result became convinced that Darwinism was true is unknown. It *is* known that the shows "made a lasting impression" on a large number of people (Bondeson 1997, 217).

These exhibits were not only blatantly dehumanizing, but also dishonest, because the exhibitors in virtually all cases deceptively pawned off their exhibits to the public either as proof of Darwin's theory of evolution, or occasionally as evolutionary throwbacks called atavisms. That most of these ape-humans were normal humans was well recognized even in the 1800s (Gould and Pyle 1896).

The circuses and exhibitors usually were not motivated primarily to prove evolution and, indeed, in many (if not most) cases, they knew that their exhibits were fully human. The primary motive in most cases was largely financial and was "big business" that enabled many people to become rich (Bogdan 1988, 198). Nonetheless, the end effect was to help convince the common people of the truth of Darwinism, which was one more factor that was influential in causing the rapid conversion of large segments of the population to belief in Darwinian evolution.

Common Objections to the Exhibits

One of the most common objections to the exhibits was the concern, especially by the clergy, that they could cause people to question the divine origin of life. Specific objections included the belief that they could cause some of the public to doubt that "life was the result of the Creator's 'divine spark,' and, moreover, that human life was endowed with special God-given qualities such as reason, creativity, and speech" (Snigurowicz 1999, 62).

Of course, this objection was fully valid because the shows probably did help to convince large numbers of people of Darwinism, and to accept (or reinforce) racism as well. The freak shows were "accompanied by the rise of the eugenics movement, a vicious use of social Darwinism which cautioned the nation that because modern societies protected their weak, the principle of survival of the fittest was not working" (Bogdan 1988, 62).

Many people also objected to these shows because the exhibits often were misleading and deliberately tried to give the impression that those individuals on display were less than human and were to be observed like animals in a zoo. Many persons recognized that the shows contributed not only to racism but also to acts of violence as well, especially against Blacks.

Most Scientists Were Silent

In general, scientists "limited their commentary to specific exhibits, describing them and reflecting on their scientific importance" (Bogdan 1988, 64). Some scientists recognized that many of the shows were, at best, misleading. Although Darwin concluded that the Fuegians were "the lowest of human forms yet discovered," other scientists, such as German anthropologist Rudolf Virchow, recognized that this ethnic group did *not* represent "some form of transitional stage between ape and man" (Rothfels 1996, 165). The latter view did not tend to help the ape-men business, nor did it support Darwinism, and so was ignored as much as possible.

The "popular perception . . . a perception rooted in the way the 'savages' were displayed and enfreaked — tended to focus on the deep differences between them and Europeans"

Undated photograph of German anthropologist Rudolf Virchow.

(Rothfels 1996, 165). Consequently, the views of scientists like Virchow usually were silent (or silenced). Carlyon, in a history about showman Dan Rice, said that the "racism of the day included confused racial categories, with the 'darkey' neither white, black, nor colored," and museums of the day did not do much to help the situation.

An important element of the Museum was the lecture room, which made the claim of education manifest. . . . Though the jumble of attractions at the Museum seems unscientific, it was not frivolous. Louis Agassiz, the famous naturalist and Harvard professor, came to New Orleans the same season for the same reasons as Rice's Dr. Koch, to lecture on natural history to inquisitive citizens. The Wild Men of Borneo may have been slaves, as many such exhibited "natives" were, and the Zeugladon might have been a fake, but, as people turned their gaze to the Pacific seas or into prehistory, the ground was being prepared for the work of anthropologists, and for the ideas of Darwin (2001, 154–155).

The problem of exploitation of non-Westerners also was usually ignored in the academic press, and the "ape-men" shows rarely or never were criticized or exposed for the harm they caused. All too often, non-Westerners were exploited by Darwinists themselves to document their case, even into the 1960s (for example, see Coon 1962). Steinitz even quoted Darwin's words from his *Journal of Researches* (1839) that the "Fuegians hardly seem to be fellow creatures and inhabitants of the same world" as we Westerners are. Rather, they "were crude, wretched creatures" that "smeared their ugly faces with paint" (quoted in Rothfels 1996, 165). No doubt, Darwin's writings and those of other persons with similar ideas (including his cousin Francis Galton) contributed to the later "genocide launched from the barrel of a gun" when the "Fuegians were mercilessly hunted down by European settlers" (Hazlewood 2000, 12, and illustration facing p. 273). Hazlewood adds that the story of Tierra del Fuego has been told many times by many writers including Darwin, but in all of these stories the

> Fuegians are absent, save as freaks and novelties or nuisances and obstacles to the advance of the white man and his civilization. To most of the Europeans and North Americans who ventured into these parts, they were a primitive and wretched group of savages, lawless atheists who lived in squalor — as Darwin was to say, they were "the most abject and miserable creatures I anywhere beheld" — and thus undeserving of a history. Eventually, when they began to be heard, as in the accounts of the Ushuaia mission station, established in the 1870s, it was. . . . too late. . . . Most tragically, by the time historians, anthropologists, archaeologists and ethnographers with a different, more sympathetic approach to the native population arrived on the scene, there was virtually no one left to study.

Wiped out in a genocide launched from the barrel of a gun and the
spread of alien diseases, much of the history of the Fuegian peoples
died with them (2000, 12).

Darwin's (and his followers') eugenics ideas were included in major textbooks as late as 1962 (Coon 1962). The civil rights movement had a major
impact in ending the exploitation of nonwhite races, especially those from
Africa. Such displays would be unthinkable in the Western world today.
This new enlightenment cannot change the fact that for decades "evolutionary theory propelled the search for individuals such as 'Krao,' and even
whole peoples such as the 'Fuegians,' who could somehow be construed as
representing links in human evolution" (Rothfels 1996, 165). Interestingly,
Darwin at first represented the Fuegians as primitive humans, but later
changed his view of them after he recognized the changes in their lives that
occurred after they converted to Christianity. As a result of this experience,
Charles Darwin personally contributed to the mission society working in
Tierra del Fuego (Hazlewood 2000).

Human-Animals Claimed to be Darwin's Missing Links

Some exhibits presented creatures that were allegedly a result of "crossbreed-
ing between man with beast [which] . . . also implied a biological link"
(Bogdan 1988, 106). Another popular explanation was that the humans
on display were atavistic or evolutionary throwbacks to earlier evolutionary
stages of humans (Bogdan 1988, 106). Animals, especially trained primates
including apes, chimps, and orangutans, also were touted by many circuses
and shows as "missing links" between animals and humans. For example,
in the 1840s, Barnum displayed — in a wildly popular exhibit — a normal
orangutan as "the connecting link between man and brute" (Saxon 1989,
98). Kunhardt et al., relate the story of one primate that became a famous
"missing link":

> In 1846, Barnum purchased, for $3,000, "the only living orang-
> outang in either England or North America." Calling her Made-
> moiselle Fanny, after the great ballerina Fanny Elssler, Barnum
> promoted the animal as a possible missing link. "Its actions, the
> sound of its voice while laughing and crying, approach as closely
> as possible to the human species," one paper reported. "Its hands,
> face and feet are pure white, and possess as soft a skin as any child
> living" (1995, 110).

Summary

For decades, charlatans have exploited non-Westerners as Darwin's "missing links" for profit and entertainment. The promoters of these shows not uncommonly, and quite often deceptively, passed off various non-Western peoples as missing links, or at least as primitive and less-developed peoples compared to Westerners. Africans and other non-Westerners were exploited in sideshows for over a century as evidence of Darwinism. These displays were a major attraction at many fairs and shows, and likely they influenced millions of persons to accept the theory of human evolution from the lower primates.

The contribution of these displays to racism and racist movements such as the Ku Klux Klan was also significant. Many of these non-Westerners "lived miserable lives," were exploited, and, in general, poorly treated. But this "did not seem to concern pre-1940s American audiences or the exhibitors — after all, the people being exhibited really were cannibals, savages, and barbarians" (Bogdan 1988, 198–199).

References

Bergman, Jerry. 1993. "Ota Benga: The Story of the Pygmy on Display in a Zoo." *Creation Research Society Journal* 30(3):140–149.

———. 2002. "Darwin's Ape-Men and the Exploitation of Deformed Humans." *T.J. Technical Journal* 16(3):116–122.

Blume, Harvey. 1999. (Bernth Lindfors, editor). "Ota Benga and the Barnum Perplex." *Africans on Stage: Studies in Ethnological Show Business.* Bloomington, IN: Indiana University Press.

Bogdan, Robert. 1988. *Freak Show; Presenting Human Oddities for Amusement and Profit.* Chicago, IL: The University of Chicago Press.

Bondeson, Jan. 1997. *A Cabinet of Medical Curiosities.* "The Strange Story of Julia Pastrana." Ithaca, NY: Cornell University Press. p. 216–244.

Bradford, Phillips Verner, and Harvey Blume. 1992. *Ota Benga: The Pygmy in the Zoo.* New York: St. Martin's Press.

Bradna, Fred, and Hartzell Spence. 1952. *The Big Top: My Forty Years with The Greatest Show on Earth by Fred Bradna as told to Hartzell Spence including A Circus Hall of Fame.* New York: Simon and Schuster.

Carlyon, David. 2001. *Dan Rice: The Most Famous Man You've Never Heard Of.* New York: Public Affairs Press.

Cook, James W. Jr. 1996. "Of Men, Missing Links, and Nondescripts: The Strange Career of P.T. Barnum's 'What Is It' Exhibition," p. 138–157, in Rosemarie Garland Thomson. 1996. *Freakery: Cultural Spectacles of the Extraordinary Body.* New York: New York University Press.

Coon, Carleton. 1962. *The Origin of Races.* New York: Alfred Knopf.

Darwin, Charles. 1839. *Journal of Researchers Into the Geology and Natural History of the Various Countries Visited by H.M.S. Beagle.* London: Henry Colburn.

Durant, John, and Alice Durant. 1957. *Pictorial History of the American Circus.* New York: A.S. Barnes.

Erlmann, Veit. 1999. Edited by Bernth Lindfors. "Spectatorial Lust": The African Choir in England, 1891–1893." *Africans on Stage: Studies in Ethnological Show Business.* Bloomington, IN: Indiana University Press.

Fiedler, Leslie. 1978. *Freaks: Myths and Images of the Secret Self.* New York: Simon and Schuster.

Gordon, Robert J. 1999. Edited by Bernth Lindfors. " 'Bain's Bushmen': Scenes at the Empire Exhibition, 1936." *Africans on Stage: Studies in Ethnological Show Business.* Bloomington, IN: Indiana University Press.

Gould, George M., and Walter L. Pyle. 1896. *Anomalies and Curiosities of Medicine.* Philadelphia, PA: W.B. Saunders.

Green, Jeffrey P. 1999. Edited by Bernth Lindfors. "A Revelation in Strange Humanity: Six Congo Pygmies in Britain, 1905–1907," in *Africans on Stage: Studies in Ethnological Show Business.* Bloomington, IN: Indiana University Press.

Hazlewood, Nick. 2000. *The Life and Times of Jemmy Button.* New York: St. Martins.

Killingray, David, and Willie Henderson. 1999. Edited by Bernth Lindfors. "Bata Kindai Amgoza Ibn LoBagola and the Making of An African Savage's Own Story," in *Africans on Stage: Studies in Ethnological Show Business.* Bloomington, IN: Indiana University Press.

Kunhardt, Philip B. Jr., Philip B. Kunhardt III, and Peter W. Kunhardt. 1995. *P.T. Barnum; America's Greatest Showman.* New York: Alfred A. Knopf.

Lindfors, Bernth. 1983. "Circus Africans." *Journal of American Culture* 6(2):9–14.

———— (editor). 1999. *Africans on Stage: Studies in Ethnological Show Business.* Bloomington, IN: Indiana University Press. Author of "Charles Dickens and the Zulus."

Marchand, S. 2003. "Priests among the Pygmies: Wilhelm Schmidt and the Counter-Reformation in Austrian Ethnology" in *Worldly Provincialism: German Anthropology in the Age of Empire.* Ann Arbor, MI: University of Michigan Press.

Odell, George. 1931. *Annals of the New York Stage. Vol. VI [1850–1857].* New York: Columbia University Press.

Parsons, Neil. 1999. Edited by Bernth Lindfors. " 'Clicko': Franz Taaibosch, South African Bushman Entertainer in England, France, Cuba, and the United States, 1908–1940," in *Africans on Stage: Studies in Ethnological Show Business.* Bloomington, IN: Indiana University Press.

Peacock, Shane. 1999. Edited by Bernth Lindfors. "Africa Meets the Great Farini." *Africans on Stage: Studies in Ethnological Show Business.* Bloomington, IN: Indiana University Press.

Rothfels, Nigel. 1996. "Aztecs, Aborigines, and the Ape-People: Science and Freaks in Germany 1850-1900," in Thomson 1996.

Rydell, Jeffrey P. 1999. Edited by Bernth Lindfors. " 'Darkest Africa': African Shows at America's World Fairs, 1893–1940." *Africans on Stage: Studies in Ethnological Show Business.* Bloomington, IN: Indiana University Press.

Saxon, A.H. 1989. *P.T. Barnum: The Legend and the Man.* New York: Columbia University Press.

Smith, G. Elliot, Sir Arthur Keith, F.G. Parsons, M.C. Burkitt, Harold J.E. Peake, and J.L. Myres. 1931. *Early Man: His Origin, Development and Culture.* London: Ernest Benn Limited.

Snigurowicz, Diana. 1999. "Sex, Simians, and Spectacle in Nineteenth-Century France; Or, How to tell a 'Man' from a Monkey." *Canadian Journal of History* 34:51–81.

Strother, Z.S. 1999. Edited by Bernth Lindfors. "Display of the Body Hottentot." *Africans on Stage: Studies in Ethnological Show Business.* Bloomington, IN: Indiana University Press.

Thomson, Rosemarie Garland. 1996. *Freakery: Cultural Spectacles of the Extraordinary Body.* New York: New York University Press.

Turnbull, Colin. 1968. *The Forest People.* New York: Simon and Schuster.

Chapter 10

Ota Benga: The Pygmy Displayed in a Zoo

One of the most fascinating historical accounts about the effects of Darwinism is the story of Ota Benga, a Pygmy who was put on display in an American zoo as an example of an evolutionarily inferior race in Africa (Verner 1901). The incident clearly reveals the racism Darwinism inspired and the extent that the theory gripped the hearts and minds of scientists and journalists in the early 1900s. As humans move away from this time in history, we can more objectively look back at some of the horrors that Darwinism caused society. The Ota Benga account is a poignant example that today has produced academic conferences to study the case (Rymer 1992).

The existence of genetic differences is imperative to Darwinism because they are the only ultimate source of innovation required for evolution to occur. History and tradition has, often with tragic consequences, grouped human variations together into categories now called races. Races function as evolutionary selection units of such importance that, as noted in a previous chapter, the subtitle of Darwin's classic 1859 book, *The Origin* of Species, was *The Preservation of Favoured Races in the Struggle for Life*. This work was critical in establishing the importance of the race fitness belief, and especially the "survival of the fittest" concept. A question asked in the early 1900s was, "Who was, and who was not human?" This question was a major concern

Ota Benga on display at the Bronx Zoo, 1906.

in turn-of-the-century Europe and America. . . . The Europeans . . . were asking and answering it about Pygmies. . . . often influenced by the current interpretations of Darwinism, so it was not simply who was *human*, but who was *more* human, and finally, who was the *most* human, that concerned them (Bradford and Blume 1992, 29).

Darwinism gave scientific support to the belief that some races were physically closer to the lower primates and were thus also inferior. The polyphyletic view was that Blacks evolved from the strong but less intelligent gorillas, the Orientals evolved from orangutans, and Whites from the most intelligent of all primates, the chimpanzees (Crookshank 1924). Many early evolutionists concluded that Blacks were less evolved than Whites and would eventually become extinct. The nefarious fruits of evolutionism, from the Nazis' conception of racial superiority to its utilization in developing governmental policy, are all well documented (Weikart 2004).

Some scientists felt that the solution to the problem of racism in early 20th-century America was to allow Darwinian natural selection to operate without interference. Bradford and Blume noted that Darwin taught that "when left to itself, natural selection would accomplish extinction" of the inferior races. Without

slavery to embrace and protect them, or so it was thought, blacks would have to compete with Caucasians for survival. Whites' greater fitness for this contest was [then believed] beyond dispute.

The disappearance of blacks as a race, then, would only be a matter of time (1992, 40).

1900 photo of William J. McGee, former president of the American Anthropological Association.

Each new American census showed that this prediction of Darwin was wrong because "the Black population showed no signs of failing, and might even be on the rise." Not content "to wait for natural selection to grind out the answer," one senator even tried to establish programs to convince — or even force — Afro-Americans to return back to Africa (Bradford and Blume 1992, 41).

One of the more poignant incidences in the history of Darwinism and racism is the story of the man put on display in a zoo (Birx 1992). Brought from the Belgian Congo in 1904 by noted African explorer Samuel Verner, he was eventually "presented by Verner to the Bronx Zoo director, William Hornaday" (Verner 1904; 1904b; 1904c; 1904d; 1905; Sifakis 1984, 253). The man, a Pygmy named Ota Benga, nicknamed "Bi" which means "friend" in Benga's native tongue, was born in 1881 in central Africa (Verner 1904a). When placed in the zoo, the 23-year-old 4 foot 11 inches tall Ota weighed a mere 103 pounds. Often referred to as a boy, he was actually a twice-married father — his first wife and two children were murdered by white colonists, and his second spouse died from a poisonous snake bite (Bridges 1974).

Ota was first displayed with other Pygmies as part of the "emblematic savage" exhibit in the anthropology wing at the 1904 St. Louis World's Fair. The exhibit was under the direction of William J. McGee of the Fair's Anthropology Department. McGee's ambition for his exhibit was to "be exhaustively scientific in his demonstration of the stages of human evolution." Therefore, he required for his anthropological display to have the darkest Blacks to contrast with Whites and "members of the 'lowest known culture' to contrast with 'its highest culmination' " (Bradford and Blume 1992, 94–95).

Ironically, Professor Franz Boas of Columbia University "lent his name" to the anthropological exhibit. This was ironic because Boas, a Jew who was one of the first anthropologists who opposed Darwinian racism, spent his life fighting the now infamous eugenics movement (Bradford and Blume 1992, 113). Pygmies were selected because they had attracted much attention as a perfect example of a "primitive" race (Verner 1906, 471). One *Scientific American* article specifically said that the Congo Pygmies were "small, ape-like, elfish creatures, furtive and mischievous" who

> live in the dense tangled forests in absolute savagery, and while they exhibit many ape-like features in their bodies, they possess a certain alertness, which appears to make them more intelligent than other negroes. . . . The existence of the Pygmies is of the rudest; they do not practice agriculture, and keep no domestic animals. They live by means of hunting and snaring, eking this out by means of thieving from the big negroes, on the outskirts of whose tribes they usually establish their little colonies, though they are as unstable as water, and range far and wide through the forests. They have seemingly become acquainted with metal only through contact with superior beings (Keane 1907, 107–108).

During the Pygmies' stay in America, they were studied by scientists to learn how the "barbaric races" compared with "intellectually defective" Caucasians on intelligence tests and how they responded to things such as pain (Bradford and Blume 1992, 113–114). The anthropometricists and psychometricists concluded that intelligence tests proved the Pygmies were similar to "mentally deficient persons, making many stupid errors and taking an enormous amount of time" (Bradford and Blume 1992, 121). Many Darwinists put the Pygmies evolution origins firmly in the Paleolithic period and concluded that they have the "cruelty of the primitive man" (Gatti 1937, 122). They did poorly even in sports: "The disgraceful record set by the ignoble savages" was so poor that "never before in the history of sport . . . were such poor performances recorded" (Bradford and Blume 1992, 122).

The anthropologists then measured not only live humans, but in one case a "primitive's" head was "severed from the body and boiled down to the skull." Assuming skull size was an "index of intelligence, scientists were amazed" to discover the "primitive's" skull was "larger than that which had belonged to the statesman Daniel Webster" (Bradford and Blume 1992, 16).

A *Scientific American* editor concluded, "Of the native tribes to be seen in the exposition, the most primitive are the Negritos . . . nothing makes them so happy as to show their skill, by knocking a five-cent piece out of a twig of a tree at a distance of fifteen paces. Then there is the village of the Head-Hunting Igorotes, a race that is . . . a fine type of agricultural barbarians" (Munn and Company 1904, 64). After referring to Pygmies as "ape-like little black people," Munn theorized that the evolution of the anthropoid apes was soon followed by "the earliest type of humanity which entered the Dark Continent, and these too, urged on by the pressure of superior tribes, were gradually forced into the great forests" (Munn 1905, 107). He added that modern humans

> in all probability, first emerged from the ape in southeastern Asia, possibly in India. . . . Even today, ape-like negroes are found in the gloomy forests, who are doubtless direct descendants of these early types of man, who probably closely resembled their simian ancestors. . . . Their faces are fairly hairy, with great prognathism, and retreating chins, while in general they are unintelligent and timid, having little tribal cohesion and usually living upon the fringes of higher tribes. Among the latter, individual types of the lower order crop out now and then, indicating that the two were, to a certain extent merged in past ages (Munn 1905, 107).

While on display, the Pygmies were treated very differently from how they first treated the Whites who came to Africa to see them. When Verner visited the African king, "He was met with songs and presents, food and palm wine, drums and was carried in a hammock." In contrast, when the Batwa were in St. Louis they were treated

> With laughter. Stares. People came to take their picture and run away . . . [and] came to fight with them. . . . Verner had contracted to bring the Pygmies safely back to Africa. It was often a struggle just to keep them from being torn to pieces at the fair. Repeatedly . . . the crowds became agitated and ugly; the pushing and grabbing took on a frenzied quality. Each time, Ota and the Batwa were "extracted only with difficulty." Frequently, the police were summoned (Bradford and Blume 1992, 118–119).

Why Ota Came to the United States

While Ota Benga was on a hunt away from his tribe, his people were massacred by the Force Publique. The Force Publique was a group of thugs working for the Belgian government endeavoring to extract tribute (in other words, steal labor and raw materials) from the native Africans living in the Belgian Congo. After Ota successfully killed an elephant on the hunt, he returned to his people with the good news. He then learned of the loss of his people and his wife and children. Their bodies were mutilated in a campaign of terror undertaken by the Belgian government against the "evolutionarily inferior natives" (Bradford and Blume 1992, 104). Ota was later captured and sold into slavery.

At this time, Verner was looking for several Pygmies to display at the Louisiana Purchase exposition and spotted Ota at a slave market. Verner bent down "and pulled the Pygmies' lips apart to examine his teeth. He was elated; the filed [to sharp points] teeth proved the little man was one of those he was commissioned to bring back. . . . With salt and cloth he was buying him for freedom, Darwinism, and the West" (Bradford and Blume 1992, 106).

Ota's world was shattered by the Whites and, although he did not know if the White man who was now his master had the same intention, he knew he had little choice but to go with him. Besides this, the events of the slave market were only one more event in Ota's life that pushed him further into the nightmare that began with his discovery of the slaughter and gross mutilation of his family. Verner managed to coerce only four Pygmies to go back with him, a number that "fell far short of McGee's . . . shopping list" of 18 Africans (Bradford and Blume 1992, 110).

After the fair, Verner took Ota and the other Pygmies back to Africa — Ota almost immediately remarried, but his second wife soon died. He now no longer belonged to any clan or family since they were all killed or sold into slavery. His other people also ostracized him, calling him a warlock, and claiming that he had chosen to stand in the White man's world and outside of their world.

The White men were both admired and feared, and were regarded both with awe and concern: they could do things like record human voices on Edison cylinder phonographs which the Pygmies saw as an object that stole the "soul" from the body, allowing the body to sit and listen to its soul talking (Verner 1906a).

After Verner collected his artifacts for museums, he decided to take Ota back to America (although Verner claims that it was Ota's idea) for a visit — Verner promised he would return him back to Africa on his next trip. Once back in America, Verner endeavored to sell his animals to zoos, and his crates of items he brought back from Africa to museums. Verner did not make the money he expected, so could no longer afford to take care of Ota — so was forced to find a place for him.

When Ota was presented to Director Hornaday of the Bronx Zoological Gardens, Hornaday's intention was clearly to "display" Ota. Hornaday "maintained the hierarchical view of races . . . large-brained animals were to him . . . the best evolution had to offer" (Bradford and Blume 1992, 176). A "believer in the Darwinian theory," he also concluded that there existed "a close analogy of the African savage to the apes" (*New York Times*, Sept. 11, 1906, p. 2). At first Ota was free to wander around the zoo, helping out with the animals, but this was soon to drastically change.

> Hornaday and other zoo officials had long been subject to a recurring dream in which a man like Ota Benga played a leading role . . . a trap was being prepared, made of Darwinism, Barnumism, pure and simple racism . . . so seamlessly did these elements come together that later those responsible could deny, with some plausibility, that there had ever been a trap or plan at all. There was no one to blame, they argued, unless it was a capricious Pygmy or a self-serving press (Bradford and Blume 1992, 174).

Ota was next forced to spend more time inside the monkey house. He was given a bow and arrow and encouraged to shoot it as part of "an exhibit." Ota was soon locked in his enclosure — and when he was let out of the monkey house, "the crowd stayed glued to him, and a keeper stayed close by" (Bradford and Blume 1992, 180). In the meantime, the publicity began — on September 9, a *New York Times* headline screamed "Bushman Shares a Cage with the Bronx Park Apes."

Although Director Dr. Hornaday insisted that he was merely offering an "intriguing exhibit" for the public's edification, he "apparently saw no difference between a wild beast and the little Black man; [and] for the first time in any American zoo, a human being was displayed in a cage. Benga was given cage-mates to keep him company in his captivity — a parrot and an orangutan named Dohong" (Sifakis 1984, 253). Hornaday believed that "it is a far cry from the highest to the lowest of the human race . . . the highest animals intellectually are higher than the lowest men" (Hornaday 1922, 67).

A contemporary account stated that Ota was "not much taller than the orangutan . . . their heads are much alike, and both grin in the same way when pleased" (Bradford and Blume 1992, 181). Verner also brought from Africa a "fine young chimpanzee" that was also deposited "in the ape collection at the Primates House" (Hornaday 1906, 302). Hornaday's enthusiasm for his new primate exhibit was reflected in an article that he wrote for the zoological society's bulletin, which began as follows:

On September 9, a *genuine* African Pygmy, belonging to the sub-
race commonly miscalled "the dwarfs". . . . Ota Benga is a well-
developed little man, with a good head, bright eyes and a pleasing
countenance. He is not hairy, and is not covered by the "downy fell"
described by some explorers. . . . He is happiest when . . . making
something with his hands (italics in original, 1906, 301).

Hornaday then tells about how he obtained the Pygmy from Verner who

was specially interested in the Pygmies, having recently returned to
their homes on the Kasai River the half dozen men and women of
that race who were brought to this country by him for exhibition
in the Department of Anthropology at the St. Louis [World's Fair]
Exposition (Hornaday 1906, 302; see also Verner 1916).

The Influence of Evolution

The many factors motivating Verner to bring Ota to the United States were
complex, but he evidently was "much influenced by the theories of Charles
Darwin" a theory of evolution which, as it developed historically, increasingly divided humankind into arbitrarily contrived races (Rymer 1992, 3).
Verner also believed that the Africans were an "inferior race" (Verner 1908a;
10, 717). Hallet shows that Darwin also felt Pygmies were inferior humans:

The Darwinian dogma of slow and gradual evolution from brutish
ancestors . . . contributed to the pseudo-history of mankind. On
the last page of his book *The Descent of Man*, Darwin expressed the
opinion that he would rather be descended from a monkey than
from a "savage." He used the words savage, low and degraded to
describe the American Indians, the Andaman Island Pygmies and
the representatives of almost every ethnic group whose physical
appearance and culture differed from his own. . . . Charles Darwin
labeled "the low and degraded inhabitants of the Andaman Islands"
in this book *The Descent of Man*. The Ituri Forest Pygmies have been
compared to "lower organisms" (Hallet 1973, 358–359, 292).

Although biological racism did not begin with Darwinism, Darwin did
more than any other person to popularize it. As early as 1699, English physician Edward Tyson studied a skeleton that he believed belonged to a Pygmy,
concluding that they were apes. It later turned out that the skeleton on
which this conclusion was based was actually a chimpanzee (Bradford and

Blume 1992, 20).

The conclusion accepted by most scientists in Verner's day was that Darwin "showed that all humans descended from apes," proving "that some races had descended further than others . . . [and that] some races, namely the white ones, had left the ape far behind, while other races, Pygmies especially, had hardly matured at all" (Bradford and Blume 1992, 20). Many scientists agreed with Pygmy scholar Sir Harry Johnson who concluded that the Pygmies were "very apelike in appearance [and] their hairy skins, the length of their arms, the strength of their thickset frames, their furtive ways, their arboreal habits all point to these people as representing man in one of his earlier forms" (Keane 1907, 99).

One of the most extensive early studies of the Pygmies concluded that they were "queer little freaks" and that the "low state of their mental development is shown by the" fact that they "have no regard for time, nor have they any records or traditions of the past; no religion is known among them, nor have they any fetish rights; they do not seek to know the future by occult means . . . in short, they are . . . the closest link with the original Darwinian anthropoid ape extant" (Burrows 1905; 172, 182).

The Pygmies were in fact a talented lot — experts at mimicry, physically agile, quick, nimble, and superior hunters, but the Darwinists did not look for these traits because they were blinded by their evolution glasses (Johnston 1902; 1902a; Lloyd 1899). Modern study has shown the Pygmies in a far more accurate light that demonstrates the absurdity of the 1900s evolution worldview (Turnbull 1968).

Ota Benga was "a bright little man" who taught one artist how to make a set of "string figures," material that she included in one chapter in her book on the subject (Jayne 1962, 276). Construction of string figures is a lost folk art at which Ota excelled. Hallet, in defense of Pygmies wrote:

> Darwin theorized that primitive people — or "savages," as he called them — do not and cannot envision a universal and benevolent creator. Schebesta's excellent study . . . correctly explains that the religion of the Ituri Forest Pygmies is founded on the belief that "God possesses the totality of vital force, of which he distributes a part to his creatures, an act by which he brings them into existence or perfects them" (1973, 14–15).

Hallet concluded:

> Scientists still accept or endorse the theory of religious evolution

propounded by Darwin and his nineteenth-century colleagues. They maintained that religion evolved from primitive animism to fetishism to polytheism to the heights of civilized Judeo-Christian monotheism. The Ituri Forest Pygmies are the most primitive living members of our species, yet far from being animistic, they pooh-pooh the local Negro tribes' fears of evil spirits. "If darkness is, darkness is good," according to a favorite Pygmy saying. "He who made the light also made the darkness" (1973, 14–15).

The Pygmies also deplored as

> superstitious nonsense the Negroes' magico-religious figurines and other so-called fetishes. They would take an equally dim view of churchly huts adorned with doll-like statues of Jesus and Mary. This would be regarded as idol worship by the Ituri Forest Pygmies, who believe that the divine power of the universe cannot be confined within material bounds. The authors of the Hebrew Old Testament would certainly agree, since they observed the well-known commandment forbidding "graven images" or idols (1973, 14–15).

Verner's Darwin Beliefs

Verner was no uninformed academic but "compiled an academic record unprecedented at the University of South Carolina," and in 1892 graduated first in his class at the young age of 19 (Bradford and Blume 1992, 69). In his studies, Verner studied the works of Charles Darwin, including *The Origin of Species* and *The Descent of Man,* which "engaged Verner on an intellectual level, as the theory of evolution promised to give scientific precision to racial questions that had long disturbed him. According to Darwin . . . it was 'more probable that our early progenitors lived on the African continent than elsewhere' " (Bradford and Blume 1992, 70).

His studies motivated him to answer some basic questions about Pygmies, such as:

> Are they men, or the highest apes? Who and what were their ancestors? What are their ethnic relations to the other races of men? Have they degenerated from larger men, or are the larger men a development of Pygmy forefathers? These questions arise naturally, and plunge the inquirer at once into the depths of the most heated scientific discussions of this generation (Verner 1902a, 192).

One hypothesis that he considered was that the Pygmies have not changed since they first evolved, a view that goes

> against both evolution and degeneracy. It is true that these little people have apparently preserved an unchanged physical entity for five thousand years. But that only carries the question back into the debated ground of the origin of species. The point at issue is distinct. Did the Pygmies come from a man who was a common ancestor to many races now as far removed from one another as my friend Teku of the Batwa village is from the late President McKinley? (Verner 1902a, 193).

Many people saw a clear conflict between evolution and Christianity, and "for most men, the moral resolve of an evangelist like Livingstone and the naturalism of a Darwin canceled each other out." To Verner, though, no contradiction existed: he was "equally drawn to evangelism and evolutionism, Livingstone and Darwin" (Bradford and Blume 1992, 70, 72). In short, the "huge gap between religion and science" did not concern Verner. He soon went to Africa to "satisfy his curiosity first hand about questions of natural history and human evolution" (Bradford and Blume 1992, 74). Verner concluded that the Pygmies were the "most primitive race of mankind" and were "almost as much at home in the trees as the monkeys" (1902a, 189–190).

He later wrote much about his African trips, even advocating that Whites take over Africa and run the country as "friendly directors" (Verner 1908a, 10718). He also argued that the Blacks in Africa should be put in reservations by "the White race" and that the social and legal conflicts between races should be solved by "local segregation" (1906a, 8235; 1907, 8736). Verner was not a mean person and cared deeply for other races, but this care was influenced in a major adverse way by his evolution beliefs (Verner 1902).

The Zoo Exhibit

Henry Fairfield Osborn, a staunch Darwin advocate, spent much of his life proselytizing his faith and attacking those who were critical of evolution, especially William Jennings Bryan, who made the opening-day remarks when the zoo exhibit of Ota first opened (Bradford and Blume 1992, 175). Osborn and other prominent zoo officials believed that, not only was Ota less evolved, but that this exhibit allowed the Nordic race to have "access to the wild in order to recharge itself. The great race, as he sometimes called it, needed a place to turn to now and then where, rifle in hand, it could hone its [primitive] instincts" (Bradford and Blume 1992, 175).

The Ota exhibit was described by contemporary accounts as a sensation — the crowds especially loved Ota's gestures and faces (Bradford and Blume 1992, 180). Some officials may have denied what the exhibit was trying to achieve, but the public knew full well its purpose: "There was always a crowd before the cage, most of the time roaring with laughter, and from almost every corner of the garden could be heard the question 'Where is the Pygmy?' and the answer was, 'in the monkey house'." (*New York Times*, Sept. 10, 1906, p. 1). The implications of the exhibit were also clear from the visitors' questions:

> Was he a man or monkey? Was he something in between? "Ist dass ein Mensch?" asked a German spectator." "Is it a man?" . . . No one really mistook apes or parrots for human beings. This — it — came so much closer. Was it a man? Was it monkey? Was it a forgotten stage of evolution? (Bradford and Blume 1992, 179).

One learned professor even suggested that the exhibit should be used to help indoctrinate the public in the truth of human evolution:

> It is a pity that Dr. Hornaday does not introduce the system of short lectures or talks in connection with such exhibitions. This would emphasize the scientific character of the service, enhance immeasurably the usefulness of the Zoological Park to our public in general, and help our clergymen to familiarize themselves with the scientific point of view so absolutely foreign to many of them (Gabriel 1906, 6).

That he was on display was indisputable: a sign was posted on the enclosure that said "The African Pygmy, 'Ota Benga.' Age, 23 years. Height, 4 feet 11 inches. Weight 103 pounds. Brought from the Kasai River, Congo Free State, South Central Africa by Dr. Samuel P. Verner. Exhibited each afternoon during September" (*New York Times*, Sept. 10, 1906, p. 1). And what an exhibit it was:

> The orangutan imitated the man. The man imitated the monkey. They hugged, let go, flopped into each other's arms. Dohong [the orangutan] snatched the woven straw off Ota's head and placed it on his own. . . . the crowd hooted and applauded. . . . children squealed with delight. To adults there was a more serious side to the display. Something about the boundary condition of being human was

exemplified in that cage. Somewhere man shaded into non-human. Perhaps if they look hard enough the moment of transition might be seen. . . . to a generation raised on talk of that absentee star of evolution, the Missing Link, the point of Dohong and Ota disporting in the monkey house was obvious (Bradford and Blume 1992, 181).

The point of the exhibit was also obvious to a *New York Times* reporter who stated, "The Pygmy was not much taller than the orangutan, and one had a good opportunity to study their points of resemblance. Their heads are much alike, and both grin in the same way when pleased" (Sept. 10, 1906, p. 1). That he was mocked is also indisputable: he was once given a pair of shoes, and "over and over again the crowd laughed at him as he sat in mute admiration of them" (*New York Times*, Sept. 10, 1906, p. 1). In another *New York Times* article one of the editors, after studying Ota in his cage, penned the following:

> Ota Benga . . . is a normal specimen of his race or tribe, with a brain as much developed as are those of its other members. Whether they are held to be illustrations of arrested development, and really closer to the anthropoid apes than the other African savages, or whether they are viewed as the degenerate descendants of ordinary negroes, they are of equal interest to the student of ethnology, and can be studied with profit (Sept. 11, 1906, p. 6).

The reporter asserted that Ota Benga

> is probably enjoying himself as well as he could anywhere in this country, and it is absurd to make moan over the imagined humiliation and degradation he is suffering. The Pygmies are a fairly efficient people in their native forests. . . . but they are very low in the human scale, and the suggestion that Benga should be in a school instead of a cage ignores the high probability that school would be a place . . . from which he could draw no advantage whatever. The idea that men are all much alike except as they have had or lacked opportunities for getting an education out of books is now far out of date. With training carefully adapted to his mental limitations, this Pygmy could doubtless be taught many things . . . but there is no chance that he could learn anything in an ordinary school (Sept. 11, 1906, p. 6).

That the display was extremely successful was never in doubt. Bradford and Blume claimed that on September 16, "40,000 visitors roamed the New York Zoological Park . . . the sudden surge of interest . . . was entirely attributable to Ota Benga" (1992, 185). The crowds were so enormous that a police officer was assigned to guard Ota full time (the zoo claimed this was to protect him) because he was "always in danger of being grabbed, yanked, poked, and pulled to pieces by the mob" (Bradford and Blume 1992, 187).

Although it was widely believed at the time, even by eminent scientists, that Blacks were evolutionarily inferior to Caucasians, caging one in a zoo produced much publicity and controversy, especially from ministers and Afro-American community leaders who were at the forefront of the protest against Ota's confinement (Adams 2001, 40). Putting a Black man in a cage was the "springboard for a story that worked up a storm of protest among Negro ministers in the city" (Bridges 1974, 224). Their indignation was conveyed to Mayor George B. McClellan, who refused to do anything. Adams wrote that:

> The outrage of prominent African Americans is not surprising, for zoo visitors found Ota Benga sharing a cage with Dohong, an orangutan. . . . In an era when Darwinian theory regularly provided scientific justification for racial prejudice, the exhibit suggested an evolutionary proximity between Africans and apes. Moreover, a conjunction of props and performance associated Ota Benga with the primitive savagery of the freak show wild man: bones were scattered around the floor of the cage, and he was encouraged to charge at the crowds while baring his teeth, which were filed to sharp points as is customary for the Batwa (Adams 2001, 32).

When the storm of protests rose, Hornaday "saw no reason to apologize," stating that he "had the full support of the Zoological Society in what he was doing" (Bradford and Blume 1992, 182). Evidently not many persons were very concerned about doing anything until the Afro-American community entered the foray. Although some Blacks at the time accepted the notion that the Pygmies were "defective specimens of mankind," several Black ministers were determined to stop the exhibit (*New York Times*, Sept. 10, 1906, p. 1). The use of the display to argue that Blacks were an inferior race especially made them angry.

The ministers had "heard Blacks compared with apes often enough before; now the comparison was being played flagrantly at the largest zoo on earth." In Reverend Gordon's words, "our race . . . is depressed enough without exhibiting one of us with the apes. We think we are worthy of being considered human beings, with souls" (*New York Times*, Sept. 11, 1906, p. 2). Furthermore, many of the ministers opposed Darwinism, concluding that "the exhibition evidently aims to be a demonstration of the Darwinian theory of evolution. The Darwinian theory is absolutely opposed to Christianity, and a public demonstration in its favor should not be permitted" (*New York Times*, quoted in Bradford and Blume 1992, 183).

A *Times* article responded to the criticism that the display lent credibility to Darwinism by mocking the ministers with the following words: "One reverend colored brother objects to the curious exhibition on the grounds that it is an impious effort to lend credibility to Darwin's dreadful theories . . . the reverend colored brother should be told that evolution . . . is now taught in the textbooks of all the schools, and that it is no more debatable than the multiplication table" (Sept. 12, 1906, p. 8). Yet, *Publishers Weekly* commented that the creationist ministers were the only ones that "truly cared" about Ota (1992, 56).

Some reporters, instead of ridiculing the zoo, criticized those who objected to the exhibit because they did not accept evolution. In Bradford and Blume's words, "New York scientists and preachers" wrangled over Ota, and those who believed that "humans were not descended from the apes and that Darwinism was an anti-Christian fraud . . . were subject to ridicule on the editorial pages of the *New York Times*" (Bradford and Blume 1992, 191, 196).

Soon some Whites also became concerned about the "caged Negro," and, in Sifakis's words, part of the concern was because "men of the cloth feared . . . that the Benga exhibition might be used to prove the Darwinian theory of evolution" (1984, 253). The objections were often vague, as in the words of a *New York Times* article:

> The exhibition was that of a human being in a monkey cage. The human being happened to be a Bushman, one of a race that scientists do not rate high in the human scale, but to the average non-scientific person in the crowd of sightseers there was something about the display that was unpleasant. . . . It is probably a good thing that Benga doesn't think very deeply. If he did it isn't likely that he was very proud of himself when he woke in the morning and found himself under the same roof with the orangutans and monkeys, for that is where he really is (September 9, 1906, p. 9).

Although opinions about the incident varied, they did result in many formal protests and threats of legal action to which the zoo director eventually acquiesced, and "finally . . . allowed the Pygmy out of his cage" (Sifakis 1984, 253). Once freed, Ota spent most of his time walking around the zoo grounds in a white suit, often with huge crowds following him. He returned to the monkey house only to sleep at night. Being treated as a curiosity, mocked, and made fun of by the visitors eventually caused him to "hate being mobbed by curious tourists and mean children" (Milner 1990, 42). In a letter to Verner, Hornaday revealed some of the many problems that the situation had caused, claiming they had not exhibited Ota Benga

> in the cage since the trouble began. Since dictating the above . . . Ota Benga . . . procured a carving knife from the feeding room of the Monkey House, and went around the Park flourishing it in a most alarming manner, and for a long time refused to give it up. Eventually it was taken away from him. Shortly after that he went to the soda fountain near the Bird House, to get some soda, and because he was refused the soda he got into a great rage. . . . This led to a great fracas. He fought like a tiger, and it took three men to get him back to the monkey house. He has struck a number of visitors, and has "raised Cain" generally (Bridges 1974, 227–228).

He later "fashioned a little bow and a set of arrows and began shooting at zoo visitors he found particularly obnoxious!" (Milner 1990, 42) *The New York Times* described the problem as follows:

> There were 40,000 visitors to the park on Sunday. Nearly every man, woman and child of this crowd made for the monkey house to see the star attraction in the park — the wild man from Africa. They chased him about the grounds all day, howling, jeering, and yelling. Some of them poked him in the ribs, others tripped him up, all laughed at him (Sept. 18, 1906, p. 9).

After Ota "wounded a few gawkers, he had to leave the Zoological Park for good" (Milner 1990, 42). The resolution of the controversy resulted from the fact that "Hornaday decided his prize exhibit had become more trouble than he was worth and turned him over to the Reverend Gordon, who also headed the Howard Colored Orphan Asylum in Brooklyn" (Ward 1992, 14).

Although Hornaday claimed that he was "merely offering an interesting exhibit and that Benga was happy," Milner (1990, 42) noted that this "statement could not be confirmed" since we have no record of Benga's feelings, but many of his actions reveal that he adjusted poorly to zoo life. Unfortunately, Ota Benga did not leave any written records of his thoughts about this or anything else, thus the only side of the story that we have is Verner's voluminous records, the writings by Hornaday, the many newspaper accounts, and a 281-page book titled *The Pygmy in the Zoo* by Philip Verner Bradford, Verner's grandson. Bradford, in doing his research, had the good fortune that Verner saved virtually every letter that he had ever received, many which discuss the Ota Benga situation, and all which he had access to when doing his research. Interestingly, Verner related what he feels is the Pygmy view of evolution:

> After my acquaintance with the Pygmies had ripened into complete mutual confidence, I once made bold to tell them that some of the wise men of my country asserted that they had descended from the apes of the forest. This statement, far from provoking mirth, met with a storm of indignant protestation, and furnished the theme for many a heated discussion around the Batwa firesides (Verner 1902a, 190).

After Benga left the zoo, he found homes at a succession of institutions and with several sympathetic individuals but was never able to shed his freak label history. First sent to a "colored" orphanage, Ota learned English and took an interest in a certain young lady there, a woman named Creola. Unfortunately, even Ota's supporters believed some of the stories about him, and an "incident" soon took place that ignited a controversy. As a result, Ota was soon forever shuffled miles away from both Brooklyn and Creola. In January 1910, he arrived at a Black community in Lynchburg, Virginia, and there seemed to shine. Some Black families

> entrusted their young to Ota's care. They felt their boys were secure with him. He taught them to hunt, fish, gather wild honey. . . . The children felt safe when they were in the woods with him. If anything, they found him over-protective, except in regard to gathering wild honey — there was no such thing as too much protection when it came to raiding hives. . . . A bee sting can feel catastrophic to a child, but Ota couldn't help himself, he thought bee stings were hilarious (Bradford and Blume 1992, 206–207).

Ota soon became a baptized Christian and his English vocabulary rapidly improved. He also learned how to read — and occasionally attended classes at a Lynchburg seminary. He was popular among the boys and learned several sports such as baseball (at which he did quite well). Every effort was made to help him blend in (even his teeth were capped to help him look more normal), and, although he seemingly had adjusted, inwardly he had not. Several events that occurred caused him to become despondent.

Ota later ceased attending classes and, at ten dollars a month plus room and board, became a laborer on the Obery farm (Bradford and Blume 1992, 204). The school concluded that his lack of education progress was because of his African "attitude," but actually probably "his age was against his development. It was simply impossible to put him in a class to receive instructions . . . that would be of any advantage to him" (Ward 1992, 14). He had enormous curiosity and a drive to learn but preferred performance tests as opposed to the multiple-choice type.

Later employed as a tobacco factory laborer in Lynchburg, Virginia, he grew increasingly depressed, hostile, irrational, and forlorn. When people spoke to him, they noticed that he had tears in his eyes when he told them he wanted to go home. After checking on the price of steamship tickets to Africa, he concluded that he would never have enough money to purchase one.

He had not heard from Verner in some time and did not know how to contact him.

Eventually, Ota "removed the caps from his teeth. When his small companions asked him to lead them into the woods again, he turned them away. Once they were safely out of sight, he shot himself" (Bradford and Blume 1992, 14). Concluding that he would never be able to return to his native land, Ota Benga committed suicide with a revolver on March 20, 1916 (Sanborn 1916).

To the end, Hornaday was inhumane, seriously distorting the situation, even slanderously stating that Ota "would rather die than work for a living" (Bradford and Blume 1992, 220). In an account of his suicide published by Hornaday in the 1916 *Zoological Bulletin*, his evolution-inspired racist feelings again clearly showed through:

> The young negro was brought to Lynchburg about six years ago, by some kindly disposed person, and was placed in the Virginia Theological Seminary and College here, where for several years he *labored to demonstrate to his benefactors that he did not possess the power of learning*; and some two or three years ago he quit the school and went to work as a laborer (1916, 1356, emphasis mine).

In Hornaday's words, Ota committed suicide because "the burden became so heavy that the young negro secured a revolver belonging to the woman with whom he lived, went to the cow stable and there sent a bullet through his heart, ending his life."

Verner's grandson, a Darwinist himself, wrote "the forest dwellers of Africa still arouse the interest of science. Biologists seek them out to test their blood and to bring samples of their DNA. They are drawn by new forms of the same questions that once vexed S.P. Verner and Chief McGee; What role do Pygmies play in human evolution? What relationship do they have to the original human type . . ." (Bradford and Blume 1992, 230–231).

He added, "Today's evolutionists do not, like yesterday's anthropometricists, include demeaning comments and rough treatments in their studies" (Bradford and Blume 1992, 231). They now openly admit that the "triumph of Darwinism" was "soon after its inception [used] to reinforce every possible division by race, gender, and nationality" (Bradford and Blume 1992, xx). Part of the problem also was "the press, like the public, was fascinated by, or addicted to, the spectacle of primitive man" (Bradford and Blume 1992, 7). The tragedy, as Buhler expressed in a poem, is:

> From his native land of darkness, to the country of the free, in the interest of science . . . brought wee little Ota Benga . . . scarcely more than ape or monkey, yet a man the while! . . . Teach the freedom we have here in this land of foremost progress — in this Wisdom's ripest age — we have placed him, in high honor, in a monkey's cage! Mid companions we provide him, apes, gorillas, chimpanzees (1906, 8).

Summary

Ota Benga was a "Pygmy" brought to America by anthropologist Samuel Verner and eventually found his way (or more accurately was forced) into a zoo, specifically in the monkey house of the Bronx New York Zoological Park. The people who visited the zoo knew the purpose of the exhibit and some objected to it on the grounds that it was a deliberate attempt to prove evolution. The blatant racism, though, is nowhere as clear as the statements of the contemporary Darwinists, many of whom made it very clear that they believe the "Negro race" is less evolved than Caucasians, and less worthy as humans. The existence of Pygmies, evolutionists felt, made a lie of the Genesis teaching that all men are brothers, all descendants of Adam and Eve. What further proof did they need than a living, breathing, evolutionary link who was clearly not the equal of white men but was more than just a monkey?

This account illustrates the results of Darwinism and its impact in American society, especially American science. It also provided an appreciation of Ota and his incredible skill in surviving in this world, and how without him and other Pygmies, many Whites, including Verner himself, would likely have died in the African jungles. Once in America, Ota assimilated Western living skills to help him survive in a world hostile to him.

Although Whites were intrigued with Pygmies, the Pygmies were likewise intrigued with Whites — and many could flawlessly imitate their behavior, such as their folding or unfolding of maps, cursing at mosquitoes, or writing notes in their journals. Interestingly, Ota's view of evolution was like that of the Pygmies of Africa, who were "very partial about how they apply the theory of evolution. When it comes to white men descending from the apes, they say they knew it all along" (Bradford and Blume 1992, 157).

The account also makes Ota a real, living person with thoughts, feelings, and fully human emotions. This background shows the irony of both displaying him in a zoo and the words of his contemporaries about evolution. Unfortunately, the "primitive race" concept is still very much with us, and reviewing the life of Ota shows that, although he was culturally different, he was a very intelligent person in his own world, a world in which the Whites were stupid and bumbling.

The story ended not long after Ota was released from the zoo when, on March of 1916 he tragically committed suicide with a gun where he was then living in Lynchburg, Virginia. His body was discovered on Monday, March 20, 1916. Thus ended Ota's forced isolation from his family and people, most of which were murdered by the "evolutionarily superior" race bent on exploiting their land and property. The irony of ironies is that the location of his grave is unknown although official records indicate he was buried in Methodist Cemetery, and all efforts to locate it so far have failed (Delaney 2007). The story of Ota tells much about the racism of Darwinism at the time.

Note: The spelling in some of the quotes has been modernized.

References

Adams, Rachel. 2001. *Sideshow USA: Freaks and the American Cultural Imagination.* Chicago, IL: University of Chicago Press.

Birx, H. James. 1992. "Ota Benga: The Pygmy in the Zoo." *Library Journal,* Aug., 117(13): 134.

Bradford, Phillips Verner, and Harvey Blume. 1992. *Ota Benga: The Pygmy in the Zoo.* New York: St. Martins.

Bridges, William. 1974. *Gathering of Animals: An Unconventional History of the New York Zoological Society.* New York: Harper and Row.

Buhler, M.E. 1906. "Ota Benga." *New York Times,* Sept. 19, p. 8.

Burrows, Guy. 1905. *The Land of the Pygmies.* New York: Thomas Y. Crowell & Co.

Crookshank, T.G. 1924. *The Mongol in Our Midst.* New York: E.F. Dutton.

Delaney, Ted. 2007. *Life After Death: The Mystery of Ota Benga's Burial.* Paper presented at the Ota Benga Conference held at Lynchburg College.

Gabriel, M.S. 1906. "Ota Benga Having a Fine Time: A Visitor at the Zoo Finds No Reason For Protests About the Pygmy." *New York Times,* Sept. 13, p. 6.

Gatti, Attilio. 1937. *Great Mother Forest.* New York: Charles Scribner's Sons.

Hallet, Jean-Pierre. 1973. *Pygmy Kitabu.* New York: Random House.

Hornaday, William T. 1906. "An African Pygmy." *Zoological Society Bulletin,* Oct., 23:301–302.

———. 1916. "Suicide of Ota Benga, The African Pygmy." *Zoological Society Bulletin,* May, 19(3):1356.

———. 1922. *The Minds and Manners of Wild Animals.* New York: Charles Scribner's Sons.

Jayne, Caroline Furness. 1962. *String Figures and How to Make Them.* New York: Dover, reprinted from the original published by Charles Scribner's Sons, 1906, under the title *String Figures.*

Johnston, H.H. 1902. "Pygmies of the Great Congo Forest." *Smithson Report,* p. 479–91.

———. 1902a. "Pygmies of the Great Congo Forest." *Current Literature* 32:294–5.

Keane, Arthur H.J. 1907. "Anthropological Curiosities; the Pygmies of the World." *Scientific American Supplement*, August 17, 64(1650):99.

Lloyd, A.B. 1899. "Through Dwarf Land and Cannibal Country." *Athenaeum* 2:894–5.

Milner, Richard. 1990. *The Encyclopedia of Evolution: Humanity's Search for Its Origins.* New York: Facts on File, Inc.

Munn and Company (editors). 1904. "The Government Philippine Exposition." *Scientific American,* July 23, p. 64–67.

———. 1905. "Pygmies of the Congo." *Scientific American,* August 5, 93:107–108.

Ota Benga: The Pygmy in the Zoo." 1992. Review in *Publishers Weekly,* July 27, 239(23):56.

Rymer, Russ. 1992. "Darwinism, Barnumism and Racism." A Review of "Ota Benga: The Pygmy in the Zoo." *The New York Times Book Review,* Sept. 6, p. 3.

Sanborn, Elwin R. (editor). 1916. "Suicide of Ota Benga, the African Pygmy." *Zoological Society Bulletin*, May, 19(3):1356.

Sifakis, Carl. 1984. "Benga, Ota: The Zoo Man," in *American Eccentrics,* New York: Facts on File, p. 252–253.

Turnbull, Colin. 1968. *The Forest People.* New York: Simon and Schuster.

Verner, Samuel P. 1901. "Development of Africa." *Forum* 32:366–382.

———. 1902. "An Education Experiment with Cannibals." *World's Work* 4:2289–2295.

———. 1902a. "The African Pygmies." *Atlantic* 90:184–95.

———. 1904. "Affairs of the Congo State." *Forum* 36:150–9.

———. 1904a. "Bringing the Pygmies to America." *Independent* 57:485–9.

———. 1904b. "How the Batwa Pygmies Were Brought to the St. Louis Fair." *Harpers Weekly* 48:1618–20.

———. 1904c. "Pioneering in Central Africa." Review. *Nation* 78:357–8; H.A. Coblentz, *Dial* 36:363–4; *Independent* 57:739.

———. 1904d. "The Adventures of an Explorer in Africa; How the Pygmies Were Brought to the St. Louis Fair." *Harper's Weekly,* Oct. 22, p. 1618–1620.

———. 1905. "African Pygmies." *Scientific American,* supplement 59:24,567–24,568.

————. 1906. "The African Pygmies." *Popular Science* 69:471–3.

————. 1906a. "The White Man's Zone in Africa." *World's Work* 13:8227–36.

————. 1907. "Africa Fifty Years Hence." *World's Work* 13:8727–37.

————. 1907a. "American Invasion of the Congo." *Harper's Weekly* 51:644.

————. 1907b. "Belgian Rule on the Congo." *World's Work* 13:8568–75.

————. 1908. "A Trip Through Africa." *World's Work* 16:10768–73.

————. 1908a. "The White Race in the Tropics." *World's Work* 16:10715–20.

————. 1916. "The Story of Ota Benga, the Pygmy." *Zoological Society Bulletin,* July, 19(4):1377–1379.

Ward, Geoffrey C. 1992. "Ota Benga: The Pygmy in the Zoo." *American Heritage,* Oct., 43:12–14.

Weikart, Richard. 2004. *From Darwin to Hitler: Evolutionary Ethics, Eugenics, and Racism in Germany.* New York: Palgrave Macmillan.

Newspaper Articles about Ota Benga in St. Louis

"African Pygmies for the World's Fair; Amazing Dwarfs of the Congo Valley to be Seen in St. Louis. Some Red, Some Black. They Antedate the Negro in Equatorial Africa. Fearless Midgets Who Boldly Attack Elephants with Tiny Lances, Bows and Arrows." *St. Louis Post-Dispatch,* June 26, 1904.

"An Untold Chapter of My Adventures While Hunting Pygmies in Africa [by] Samuel P. Verner." *St. Louis Post-Dispatch,* Sept. 4, 1904.

"Barbarians Meet in Athletic Games; Pygmies in Mud Fight, Pelted Each Other Until One Side Was Put to Rout. Crow Indian Won Mile Run; Negritos Captured Pole-Climbing Event and Patagonians Beat Syrians in Tug-of-War." *St. Louis Post-Dispatch,* August 6, 1904.

"Cannibals Will Sing and Dance." *St. Louis Post-Dispatch,* August 6, 1904.

"Driven From Huts by Rainstorm; Pygmies and Ainus Seek Shelter for Night in Indian School; Resembles Noah's Ark; Savages Insist on Taking Pets from Jungle Homes with Them to Escape Terrors of Lightning." *St. Louis Republic,* August 20, 1904.

"Enraged Pygmies Attack Visitor; H.S. Gibbons of Durango Colo., Photographed Them, But Gave No Tips. He Was Pursued and Beaten; Money Would Have Been an Effective Weapon, But He Wouldn't Use It." *St. Louis Post-Dispatch,* July 19, 1904.

"Exposition Envoy Pygmies' Victim? Fair Officials Have Not heard for Two Months From Explorer Sent to African Wilds. Tribe Uses Deadly Arrows; Perilous Undertaking of Anthropological Department Approved by Belgian Colonial Government." *St. Louis Post-Dispatch,* Monday, April 18, 1904.

"Gifts to Royal Pair Cost $2.50; President Francis Makes Happy the Hearts of World's Fair Pygmies for $8.35. Barrel of Salt for King; and Other Presents of Similar Value Are Given Little Africans Before Departure." *St. Louis Post-Dispatch,* Dec. 4, 1904.

"Pygmies Demand a Monkey Diet; Gentlemen from South Africa at the Fair Likely to Prove Troublesome in Matter of Food." *St. Louis Post-Dispatch,* July 2, 1904.

Pygmies Shiver Over Camp Fire; "Give Us Blankets," Is Their Greeting to Missionary Who Brought Them out of Africa. Say It's Cold in St. Louis; Discard Palm Leaf Suits for Warmer

Clothing — Declare Americans Treat Them as They Would Monkeys." *St. Louis Republic,* Saturday, August 6, 1904.

"Pygmy Dance Starts Panic in Fair Plaza; Seeing Unclad Africans Advancing Toward Her, Brandishing Their Spears, Woman Screams and Crowd Follows Her in Terror." *St. Louis Post-Dispatch,* July 1904.

"10,000 Strange People for Fair; The World's Fair Pike Will Soon be the Most Cosmopolitan Spot on Face of the Earth. Whole Shiploads en Route; Furthermost Corners of the Earth are to be Represented by Natives in their Characteristic Splendor." *St. Louis Post-Dispatch,* Friday, April 1, 1904.

"To Exhibit Man at the St. Louis Fair; Dr. McGee Gathering Types and Freaks From Every Land. He Explains the Plans of the Department of Anthropology, of Which He Is the Head." *New York Times,* Nov. 16, 1904.

"Trying Ordeal for Savages; Scientists Will Begin a Special Study of World's Fair Tribes September 1." *St. Louis Republic,* Aug. 14, 1904.

"Verner Escapes Being Eaten by Cannibals; Man Who Went in Quest of African Pygmies Cables Exposition Company." *St. Louis Republic,* Thursday, May 5, 1904.

"World's Fair Department of Anthropology: Portions of Ancient Cities Are to be Represented and Unwritten History Revealed. Treasures of Antiquity Will be So Arranged As to Show the Bearing Man's Past Achievements Have Upon Contemporary Progress." *St. Louis Republic,* Sunday, March 6, 1904.

Newspaper Articles about Ota Benga in New York

"African Pygmy's Fate Is Still Undecided; Director Hornaday of the Bronx Park Throws Up His Hands. Asylum Doesn't Take Him; Benga Meanwhile Laughs and Plays with a Ball and Mouth Organ at the Same Time." *New York Times,* Sept. 18, 1906, p. 9.

"A Pygmy Among the Primates; One of the 'Bantams' of the African Race at the Zoological Park — His Diversions — Twenty-Three, and Twice married — To Return to Africa Later." [New York] *Evening Post,* Sept. 10, 1906.

"A Word For Benga; Mr. Verner Asks New York Not to Spoil His Friend, the Bushman." *New York Daily Tribune,* Oct. 3, 1906.

"Benga." *New York Times,* Sept. 23, 1906: Editorial, p. 8.

"Bushman Shares a Cage With Bronx Park Apes; Some Laugh Over His Antics, But Many Are Not Pleased; Keeper Frees Him at Times; Then, With Bow and Arrow, the Pygmy From the Congo Takes to the Woods." *New York Times,* Sept. 9, 1906, p. 9.

"Benga Tries to Kill; Pygmy Slashes at Keeper Who Objected to His Garb." *New York Daily Tribune,* Sept. 26, 1906.

"Colored Orphan Home Gets the Pygmy; He Has a Room to Himself and May Smoke if He Likes. To Be Educated If Possible; When He Returns to the Congo He May Then Help to Civilize His People." *New York Times,* Sept. 29, 1906, p. 7.

"Escaped the Gridiron; Pygmy Man Saved From Cannibals Visits New York." *New York Daily Tribune,* Sept. 16, 1906.

"Hope for Ota Benga; If Little, He's No Fool; and Has Good Reason for Staying in the White Man's Land. Won't Be an Entree Here; But His Chief in Africa May Die Soon and the Custom Is to Have a Cannibal Feast." *New York Times,* Sept. 30, 1906, p. 9.

"Lively Row Over Pygmy." *New York Times,* Sept. 10, 1906.

"Man and Monkey Show Disapproved by Clergy; The Rev. Dr. MacArthur Thinks the Exhibition Degrading. Colored Ministers to Act; The Pygmy Has an Orang-outang as a Companion Now and Their Antics Delight the Bronx Crowds." *New York Times,* Sept. 10, 1906, p. 1.

"M'Clellan Snubs Colored Ministers; Curtly Refuses to Receive Protest Against Exhibition of Man in Ape Cage." *New York American,* Sept. 12, 1906.

"Negro Clergy Protest; Displeased at Exhibition of Bushman in Monkey House." *New York Daily Tribune,* Sept. 11, 1906, p. 6.

"Negro Ministers Act to Free the Pygmy; Will Ask the Mayor to Have Him Taken from Monkey Cage. Committee Visits the Zoo; Public Exhibitions of the Dwarf Discontinued, But Will Be Resumed, Mr. Hornaday Says." *New York Times,* Sept. 11, 1906, p. 2.

"No Aid From M'Clellen; Mayor "Too Busy" to See Committee of Colored Men; They Visited to Protest Against the Public Exhibition of a Negro Dwarf in the Monkey House at the Zoological Park — The Delegation Told by a Subordinate to Complain to the New York Zoological Society." *The [New York] Evening Post,* Sept. 11, 1906.

"Ota Benga at Hippodrome; Pygmy Meets His Old Friend, the Baby Elephant, Giving Out Programs." *New York Daily Tribune,* Oct. 3, 1906.

"Ota Benga New a Real Colored Gentleman; Little African Pygmy Being Taught Ways of Civilization at Howard Colored Orphan Asylum." *New York Daily Globe,* Oct. 16, 1906.

"Ota Benga, Pygmy Tired of America; The Strange Little African Finally Ended Life at Lynchburg, VA. Once at the Bronx Zoo; His American Sponsor Found Him Shrewd and Courageous — Wanted to be Educated." *New York Times,* July 16, 1916, p. 12.

"Ota Benga Says Civilization Is All Witchcraft; On Exhibition at the New York Zoological Park, in Bronx, He Rules Monkey House by Jungle Dread. Wants to Go Home to Buy Him a Wife; African Pygmy Asserts New York Is Not Wonderful and That We Are All Madmen." *New York World,* Sept. 16, 1906.

"Pygmy to Be Kept Here; Colored Ministers Want to Take Him When Guardian Comes." *New York Times,* Sept. 19, 1906, p. 1.

"Still Stirred About Benga." *New York Times,* Sept. 23, 1906, p. 9.

"The Black Pygmy in the Monkey Cage; An Exhibition in Bad Taste, Offensive to Honest Men, and Unworthy of New York City's Government." *New York Journal,* Sept. 17, 1906.

"The Mayor Won't Help to Free Caged Pygmy; He Refers Negro Ministers to the Zoological Society. Crowd Annoys the Dwarf; Failing to Get Action from Other Sources the Committee Will Ask the Courts to Interfere." *New York Times,* Sept. 12, 1906, p. 9.

"Topics of the Times; Send Him Back to the Woods." *New York Times,* Sept. 11, 1906, p. 6.

"Topics of the Times; The Pygmy Is Not the Point." *New York Times,* Sept. 12, 1906, p. 8.

"Zoo Has a Pygmy Too Many; Does Anybody Want This Orphan Boarder? He Does Not Bite, He Does Not Vote, His Manners, Though Various, are Mild — Prof. Verner, African Traveler, Why Don't You Come and Get Him?" *New York Sun,* Sept. 17, 1906.

Chapter 11

Darwinism and the Exploitation of Deformed Humans

Introduction

From the early 1800s until today, hundreds of millions of people the world over have visited amusement parks and circuses (Milner 2002; Lindfors 1983). Until the introduction of motion pictures, circuses were the leading form of commercial entertainment for over a century (Bradna and Spence 1952). A major circus attraction for decades was sideshow displays of deformed humans who were widely advertised as "Darwin's missing links," "man-monkeys," "ape-men," or "ape-women."

These circus displays were usually deceitfully made to appear to be convincing ape-human links as required by Darwin's theory. The shows were historically one of the most convincing evidences of Darwinism for the general populace. These "shows, which often presented individuals as monstrous intermediaries between humans and animals, relied on a new interest in biological aspects of human nature generally and Darwinism in particular"

199

(Zimmerman 2001, 4).

It now is known that all of these claimed "missing link" cases were normal humans afflicted with various genetic deformities or diseases which in most cases have been accurately identified by medical researchers (Thomson 1996). An example is "Schlitzie, the missing link" a microcephalic, as were many of the sideshow missing links (Hartzman 2005, 210). The "missing link" idea existed before Darwin, but

> came to a crux with publication of Darwin's *On the Origin of Species* in 1859. While many of the ideas and themes addressed by Darwin were not new, the *Origin of Species* was clearly a major publishing event that dramatically changed the nature of discussion on the question of origins (Browne and Messenger 2003, 155).

This chapter covers a few of the more well-known examples.

The Story of Zip

One of the most famous circuses, Barnum and Bailey, regularly featured displays of diseased or deformed humans that they claimed proved Darwin's theory of human evolution or, more often, dishonestly misled visitors to conclude they were valid scientific evidence for Darwinism. Many of the advertisements for these exhibits were specifically designed to satisfy the public's curiosity about Darwinism. Kunhardt et al. even stated that Barnum's missing link "was strengthened by an unwitting Barnum ally, the English scientist Charles Darwin" (1995, 149). Many "missing links" were microcephalics. A disciple of Darwin, Carl Vogt, even published a set of articles arguing that microcephalics were atavistic recollections of "a missing link between apes and humans" (Rothfels 1996, 75).

Giant Paul Herold pictured with Zip, considered the "missing link," though actually an African American named William Henry Johnson.

This example, one of the first of many such "missing links," was introduced in the early 1860s just months after "the earth-shattering appearance of Darwin's *Origin of Species*" (Kunhardt et al. 1995, 149). Furthermore, "Barnum knew the world was ready to believe in the possibility of a 'missing link,' a living, breathing bridge between man and ape, and would likely pay a lot of money to see it with their own eyes" (Homberger 2005, 122). In what Kunhardt et al. called one of Barnum's all-time great human presentations, Barnum's "Man-Monkey" was depicted on advertising posters as "nothing less than the 'missing link' " (1995, 149).

This "savage creature" called "Zip" was even immortalized by a Currier and Ives engraving. Zip was claimed to have the anatomy of an orangutan and the countenance of a human. The circus claimed his ape anatomy included "the perfect head and skull of the Orang Outang, while the lower part of the face is that of the native African" (Cook 1996, 148). To support his ape status, it was also claimed that his ears were set back too far to be a human, his teeth were "double nearly all around," and as a result, he could not close his mouth entirely (Saxon 1989, 99). The circus claimed he was examined "by some of the most scientific men we have," who declared he was "a CONNECTING LINK BETWEEN THE WILD NATIVE AFRICAN AND THE BRUTE CREATION" (Saxon 1989, 99, emphasis in original).

This "great fact for Darwin" not only looked the part but also was instructed to play the part — he was given a long staff to hold to imply that he did not normally stand on two legs but rather walked like a monkey (Saxon 1989, 99). Dressed in only a loincloth, he was taught "jungle language" — mostly hideous grunts — to help him act out his ape-man charade. When given a cigar, he would grunt and grin, then eat the cigar (Wallace 1959, 117). A good actor, he convinced millions to believe that he was, in fact, an ape-man. The publicity described "it" as the fusion of an African Negro and an orangutan, implying how close humans and apes were biologically (Adams 2001, 36).

In truth, he was an African American male dwarf named William Henry Johnson (circa 1842–1926) who suffered from a brain disorder now known as microcephalicism. Then called "pin-head" or "cone-head" disease, microcephalics have abnormally small brains, are mentally retarded, and have many superficial ape-like features. Johnson's friends claimed that he was "a good-natured imbecile who enjoyed being exhibited" (Durant and Durant 1957, 114).

According to Kunhardt, et al., Johnson was enlisted into a lifetime of conspiracy to fool the public into believing he was Darwin's missing link (1995, 149). During the 1925 Scopes trial, "Zip, the Missing Link" even offered himself as an exhibit to prove evolution (Hartzman 2005, 50). Billed as "a man-monkey captured while swinging from trees in an African jungle," he was "unlike other ape men" in that he "was not so wild or brutish that he had to be chained, handcuffed, or confined behind bars" (Lindfors 1999, ix).

He convincingly played this charade for over half a century — from the 1860s until his death in 1926 (Bradna and Spence 1952, 242). Shortly before he died from pneumonia at the age of 81, now a very wealthy man, he reportedly said to his sister, "Well, we fooled 'em for a long time" (Bradna and Spence 1952, 242). Some have concluded that Zip's comment "may have been referring only to being the 'missing link' " (Homberger 2005, 124). Bradna and Spence concluded that Zip was "the greatest freak" of all time (1952; 242, 318).

Julia Pastrana: Darwin's Missing Link

Probably one of the most convincing — and also the most famous — Darwinian missing links was Julia Pastrana (1834–1860). She had an overdeveloped ape-like jaw, a long beard and mustache, and her entire face and body (with the exception of the palms of her hands and the soles of her feet) were covered with thick, black, curly hair (Anonymous 1855). She also had a broad, flat nose, thick lips, large ears, and in other ways was remarkably ape-like (Miles 1974). These traits, plus her thick, short neck, and her four-foot-six-inch height, only served to support her billing as an "ape-woman," a "semi-human . . . between a human being and an ourang-outang [sic]," and Darwin's missing link (Odell, 1931, 413; Laurence 1857).

Miß Julia Pastrana.

Julia Pastrana, who suffered from several genetic diseases, was considered a missing link.

In fact, Julia suffered from several genetic diseases,

including a form of hirsutism (a deformity that produces an enormous level of abnormal hair growth) properly called *genetic hypertrichosis terminalis* or *polytrichosis,* and she also was afflicted with *gingival hyperplasia,* which produced an ape-like protruding jaw (Bondeson and Miles 1993; Anavi et al. 1989; Horning et al. 1985). Pastrana was only 1 of over 50 verified sufferers of hirsutism, many of whom were "entirely covered with long hair and who were taken to be specimens of Darwin's missing link" (Drimmer 1973, 126). Many of them worked in circuses as "ape-men or human werewolves" (Maugh 1997, 335).

The hirsutism condition can be caused by several factors, including endocrine gland abnormalities. A damaged or abnormal adrenal cortex can produce excessive amounts of androgens (male hormones), causing a woman to lose female traits, cease menstruating, and develop many male traits, especially a beard and a deep voice. In a normal female fetus, the cistome (the area between the medulla and adrenal gland cortex) disappears entirely. When the cistome persists or enlarges due to a tumor, an abundance of facial and body hair can result in females. Another cause of hirsutism is a rare inheritable disease called *congenital hypertrichosis universalis* (Suskind and Esterly 1971).

If a tumor develops in the adrenal glands as an adult, the same hirsutism condition can occur. Known as adrenal virilism, it typically is corrected by excising the tumor. A mild form of this condition can also be brought on by menopause. Julia also may have had defective ovaries and possibly a tumor or other abnormalities that caused her ovaries to produce too many male hormones. This conclusion is supported by the evidence that her parents were both normal (Cockayne 1933, 249). Treatments for all of these conditions were unknown when Julia was young.

What most convincingly supported the ape-woman claim was her face: "Nothing about her was more apelike than her head" (Drimmer 1991, 73). Her jaw pushed forward like a gorilla, exaggerating her already large lips. Her flat nose and heavy brow ridges gave her a strong Neanderthal appearance (Adams 1990, 59–60). Julia's defective dentition included what looked like an irregular tooth arrangement, likely due to severe *gingival hyperplasia* (overdevelopment of the gum).

Some even claimed that she had a complete extra set of normal teeth. The incorrect conclusion that she had a double set of teeth resulted from the fact that her thickened alveolar processes could be confused with teeth (Bondeson 1997, 242). Charles Darwin, who "certainly took an interest in her," according to Bondeson (1997, 223), perpetuated this misinformation. Darwin concluded that Julia had a thick masculine beard and a hairy forehead; she was photographed, and her stuffed skin was exhibited as a show; but what concerns us is, that she had in both the upper and lower jaw an irregular double set of teeth, one row being placed within the other, of which Dr. Purland took a cast. From the redundancy of teeth her mouth projected, and her face had a gorilla-like appearance (1896, 321).

Darwin did not state if he believed she was a missing link, but did not seem too concerned about her being "stuffed" like an animal and displayed to the public as one after she died. Gylseth and Toverud noted:

Charles Darwin may have been correct about Julia's character but scientifically he was wrong because, if anyone had bothered to ask her, she could have immediately responded that she certainly did not have any extra rows of teeth in her mouth (though she did have gum problems) (2003, 39).

The cause of her dental abnormalities could have been linked to her hirsutism or could have been caused by scurvy due to a diet lacking in vitamin C when she was young (Vogel 1977; Miles 1974). Her teeth, her pronounced alveolar process, her prognathism, and her thick and heavy gums (gingival hyperplasia) all served to push her lips outward, giving her a very "apelike appearance" (Gould and Pyle 1896, 229; Drimmer 1991, 80). Julia Pastrana usually wore costumes that exposed her legs, arms, and shoulders so people could see her thick body hair that supported the ape-human intermediate impression (Drimmer 1991, 75).

Publicity pamphlets of the time described Julia as "semi-human" and a "hybrid of a human being and an ape" (Adams 1990, 59). Pastrana and her ape-like cohorts were sometimes billed as a "cross between a human being and an ape," which gave the equally misleading impression that apes and humans were so close that they could interbreed. This idea further strengthened the belief that humans evolved from apes. Reode even described her as a type of ape that was "extinct ten thousand years before Adam" (quoted in Bondeson 1997, 223).

Julia was so successful that she did not need to tour with a circus, but could work on her own. When she was on stage, the audience voiced "loud gasps. One woman screamed. Another slumped fainting in her seat" (Drimmer 1991, 73). Because it was not sufficient for her to simply parade past the audience to display her ape-like body, she put on a talent show. Some nations, such as Germany, all but prohibited "freak" shows that degraded such people.

To get around this problem, she danced, sang, and otherwise entertained her audiences. After she had danced, "the applause was stormy, wave upon wave of it. Ape-woman she may be, the audience seemed to be saying, but she can dance!" (Drimmer 1991, 74). She also sang, often in Spanish or English, and her mezzo-soprano voice was said to be tender and sweet, emphasizing her human-ape traits.

Pastrana's success was so great that "today, more than a hundred years after her death, people still know her name" (Drimmer 1991, 75). The famous Italian director Carlo Ponti in 1994 even produced a stage play of her life titled *The Ape Woman* (Ponti 1996). In the play, originally released in Italian as *La Donna Scimmia*, a man discovers a shy, sensitive girl whose body is covered in hair and realizes she can make him rich on the freak-show circuit. Another play by Shaun Prendergast, based on Julia's life, emphasized her tragic exploitation (Mather 1999).

Another film about her that has a budget of 40 million dollars, directed by Taylor Hackford, and starring Richard Gere as her manager, is planned. At least one doctoral dissertation and one book were written about her (Fuchs 1918; Gylseth and Toverud 2003). Even poetry has been penned about Julia — one poem is titled "The Litanies of Julia Pastrana" (Shapcott 1998, 325–329).

Her Early Life

Pastrana's early life is clouded with uncertainty. One of her managers once claimed that she was discovered as an infant abandoned in a remote region in Central America (Miles 1974; Drimmer 1973, 201). More likely, she was born to a tribe of Sierra Madre Indians in the State of Sinaloa on the west coast of Mexico (Bondeson 1997, 218; Drimmer 1991, 76). Pamphlets advertising her show claimed that her relatives "lived in caves, in a naked state" and that "their features have a close resemblance to those of a . . . Orang Outang [sic] . . . [although] they have intellect and are endowed with speech . . . they have always been looked upon by travelers as a kind of link between the man and the brute creation" (quoted in Drimmer 1991, 76).

This apocryphal explanation was fabricated to support the illusion that Julia was Darwin's missing link. In fact, she had a job working in the governor's house where she learned how to read Spanish and converse intelligently. She had this position until shortly before she left for America in April of 1854 (Bondeson and Miles 1993). She was "discovered" when she was only 20 by a man named Retes who persuaded her to come to the United States to be exhibited.

Retes convinced Julia to leave Mexico by promising her a better life. She arrived in New Orleans in October of 1854 and then headed directly to New York. Some historical accounts state that she eventually learned how to read in English and indulged in romantic novels — a dream world that allowed her to forget who and what she was and to become a beautiful and adored young woman like the heroines she read about (Drimmer 1991, 83; Mather 1999). She gave many interviews to leading journalists and was commonly described by them as a good natured, gentle, affable, sociable, warmhearted, "intelligent and quick," woman in control of herself — all evidence that blatantly contradicted allegations of her ape-human status (Bondeson 1997, 225; Miles 1974; Laurence 1857, 48). She soon was put on display in London at the Regent, Burlington, and other Galleries (Laurence 1857, 48; Van Hare 1888, 46; Altick 1978).

The allegation made by some contemporaries that she was a "Negro" implied that she was not an ape-woman but a fraud. Obviously, this allegation was not good for business, so her manager had her examined by a physician named Alexander B. Mott, who concluded that she was an ape-human hybrid where the woman nature predominated over the orangutan brute (Bondeson 1997, 219; Drimmer 1991, 79).

To further bolster her promoters' claims, Julia was also examined by Cleveland physician Dr. S. Brainerd. The doctor compared Julia's hair to that of an African under a microscope and concluded from this "test" that Julia contained "no trace of Negro blood" (Bondeson 1997, 219; Drimmer 1991, 80). He also concluded that she was part of a "distinct species." These outrageous conclusions can be explained by the fact that physicians in the 1800s often were poorly trained, especially about genetic issues.

Other people were less inclined to accept the evolutionary explanation. Dr. Kneeland, a comparative anatomist, was asked to judge Julia's place in the animal kingdom. According to his opinion "she was entirely human" and was not a Negro (Bondeson 1997, 220). British naturalist Francis T. Buckland concluded that she was "simply hideous," but only a deformed Mexican Indian woman (Buckland 1865, 44–51). Obviously, only the claims that supported the Darwinian ape-woman explanation were used for publicity, and the ape-woman claims worked — she toured both the United States and Europe for almost half a decade until she died after giving birth to her first child at age 26.

When her last manager, Mr. Theodore Lent, learned that his star was going to leave him for another manager (as had happened in the past), he convinced her that he loved her, and they soon married (Bondeson 1997,

226). She eventually became pregnant and delivered a boy. It was said that when Julia saw her son, she was so distraught because the child had many of her ape-like traits that she died on March 25, 1860, only a few days after his birth (Miles 1974; Fiedler 1978, 145). The official account states that she died in Moscow of complications following childbirth. Her last words reportedly were, "I die happy; I know I have been loved for myself" (Miles 1974, 10). The cause of death was listed as *metro-peritonitis puerperalis,* which is infection of the peritoneum, the membrane that forms the lining of the abdominal cavity, likely caused by the unsanitary hospital conditions common then (Bondeson 1997, 229).

Any doubts about her husband's true motives were dispelled when he allowed her body and that of their son to be embalmed by a Professor Suka-loff in Moscow. Mr. Lent then displayed them for anyone willing to pay the price of admission, which was not cheap. The embalming was carried out at Moscow's Anatomical Institute, where the professor achieved excellent results. Browne and Messenger note that when she died

> it was far easier now for medical men to examine and discuss her body parts, and to speak freely about her possible ancestry and to locate her in the evolutionary scheme of nature. From bear-woman to gorilla-woman, she spanned the Darwinian movement (2003, 159).

Mr. Lent soon found another "ape-woman" named "Zenora," and within a few years became a wealthy man from his ape-women exhibitions. In 1884 he went insane, was committed to a Russian asylum, and died soon thereafter. After his death, the exhibition of Julia and her son continued in Europe for decades. Their corpses were briefly returned to America, then recrossed the Atlantic and placed in the Institute of Forensic Medicine in Norway (Bondeson 1997, 241; Adams 1990, 60). At this time, some people wanted the bodies of Julia and her son buried in Julia's homeland, Mexico, and others wanted them to be preserved so they could be studied by science.

As late as the 1970s, Julia was displayed as an "ape-woman" and her body was then stored in the University of Oslo, Norway (Browne and Messenger 2003, 155). Her body was finally returned to Sinaloa, de Layva, a city in Mexico, in 2013. She was then given last rites by a Catholic priest and buried in a local cemetery. Some feel her interment here amounts to burying this tragic part of history, both literally and figuratively, so this crime of evolutionism will be forgotten. In contrast, the Jews want to make sure the world knows what happened during the Holocaust and to keep the memory alive in whatever way they can.

Other Missing Links

Even *before* Darwin published his classic work, circuses in Barnum's day were displaying alleged ape-men based on the belief, much discussed by scientists then, that life

> might not be immutable, but subject to a process of gradual change. It was left to Wallace and Darwin to formulate the theory of natural selection, but even before the publication of the latter's controversial *Origin of Species* in 1859 sufficient evidence had accumulated to convince many scientists that evolution occurred, although its mechanism was then but dimly perceived (Saxon 1989, 97).

Another exhibit was of a "deformed but talented man-monkey" named Hervey Leach, whom Barnum attempted to pass off as "The Wild Man of the Prairies" (Saxon 1989, 98). Barnum wrote the following in the advertisements announcing his show at London's Egyptian Hall in 1846:

> Is it an animal? Is it human? . . . Or is it the long sought for link between man and the Ourang-Outang, which naturalists have for years decided does exist, but which has hitherto been undiscovered? . . . Its features, hands, and the upper portion of its body are to all appearances human, the lower part of its body, the hind legs, and haunches are decidedly animal. It is entirely covered, except the face and hands, with long flowing hair of various shades. It is larger than an ordinary sized man, but not quite so tall. . . . its food is chiefly nuts and fruit, though it occasionally indulges in a meal of raw meat; it drinks milk, water, and tea, and is partial to wine, ale, and porter (Saxon 1989, 98).

"The Wild Man of the Prairies" was later proven to be a fraud, and Barnum even tried to deny his involvement with the charade. Apes were also commonly displayed as proof of evolution, and shows could usually get away with it because few

> Westerners had seen a gorilla in the 1860s. London Zoo displayed a young orangutan called Jenny from the mid-1830s, whose endearingly human-like behaviour captured the public's imagination and also made several important appearances in Charles Darwin's earliest evolutionary notebooks (Browne and Messenger 2003, 158–159).

Advertising an African American as a missing link contributed to the racism of the last two centuries (Adams 2001, 164). Some presenters were more honest and avoided the "missing link" claim, but rather claimed the freaks were evolutionary throwbacks called atavisms:

> Anthropologists encountered Darwinism most directly in freak shows, which often occurred in the same venues as ethnographic spectacles. These shows employed Darwinism to bill various deformed humans as atavisms, individuals whose development had somehow been arrested and thus who shared characteristics with their animal ancestors (Zimmerman 2001, 73).

Other so-called missing links include Lionel, the lion-faced man born in Poland in 1890 to normal parents. He was a featured attraction in Barnum and Bailey's Circus for years. A female "missing-link" named Grace Gilbert (billed as "the woolly child") and another woman called the "female Esau" (born in Michigan in 1880) both toured for years. Yet another example was "Jo-Jo, the dog-faced boy" who was born in Russia, as was Fedor Jeftichew. He was described in advertisements as a "savage" that could not be civilized. In fact, he was very civilized and spoke Russian, German, and English.

One of the best examples of an advertised Darwinian missing link was Percilla Bejano, "the monkey girl," also a victim of hirsutism. She was displayed from the age of 3 in shows, and died in her sleep on February 5, 2001, at age 89 (Huffines 2001). She often appeared on stage with a trained chimpanzee to emphasize her missing-link status. Another "monkey girl" was Priscilla, who looked a lot like Julia Pastrana, and it was claimed that she was "inspected by many, many specialists, and they all claim that she had features that were those 'of a monkey' (Levenson 1982, 59). Yet another example, this one called the "Gorilla Girl" and "the Goddess of terror," toured as recently as 1974 in Maumee, Ohio, under a sign that asked, "Was Darwin right? Did man evolve from Ape?" (Levenson 1982, 23).

Krao: The Perfect Missing Link

Another "Darwin's missing link," a girl named Krao Farini (1876–1926), was first exhibited in Europe in the early 1880s when she was only about six or seven years old, and soon thereafter was exhibited in the United States (Hartzman 2005, 54). Krao, evidently a native of Indochina, an area that is now known as Laos, was covered with thick, black hair, lacked nose cartilage, and had cheek pouches that she could project forward almost to the same degree as a chimp, all of which made her look very ape-like (Snigurowicz 1999). First, she was called an "ape-child," then, as she grew, an "ape-girl," and, last, an "ape-woman" (Rothfels 1996, 126–163). Krao's face was described as the "prognathic type, and with her extraordinary prehensile powers of feet and lips, [that] gave her the title of 'Darwin's missing link' " (Gould and Pile 1896, 231). To better convince the public of her ape-human status, she was "fraudulently presented as having pouches in her mouth, prehensile toes, cartilage in her nose, and other simian features" (Bogdan 1988, 115).

As a young girl, she was photographed in a jungle setting in poses that deliberately reinforced the public perception of her as an ape-human hybrid (Durant and Durant 1957, 105). She was even claimed to have been part of a whole race of "ape-people," but her keeper claimed the "King" of Laos gave only Krao permission to leave the country (Rothfels 1996, 163). In fact, she was a "typical Siamese" suffering from a "pathological condition" (Rothfels 1996, 163). The deception worked: the "hairy girl from Thailand" was "a Ringling Brothers star for years" (Drimmer 1973, 219). The exhibit, displayed first by a well-known London showman named Farini, was described as follows:

> It was the heyday of the controversy over Charles Darwin's theory that man was descended from ape-like creatures (Darwin never said that man was descended from apes themselves) and his followers were constantly hoping to turn up a creature intermediate between man and the apes. To some, Krao appeared to be just what they were looking for (Drimmer 1991, 162–163).

The fact was

> Darwin's *Origin of Species*, though published about fifteen years before Krao was introduced to Europe and America, was still very much on the minds of people. The pull toward believing in evolution was becoming stronger, and scientists and naturalists alike were intrigued and widely fooled by the little specimen in their raw desire to prove the connection [of apes and humans] (Homberger 2005, 116).

Farini also claimed that Krao belonged to a tribe of extraordinary "ape people" who lived "high up in the trees," and subsisted on

> raw meat and rice. Farini said that he had personally received permission from the Burmese royal family to take the girl to England and adopt her as his own daughter. And he topped this by claiming that

she was an example of Darwin's missing link (Gylseth and Toverud 2003, 95–96).

Hartzman concluded "Krao was marketed as Darwin's missing link" and promoters "capitalized on the debate, offering Krao as proof of Darwin's ideas — a middle ground between man and ape. . . . Some scientists took this 'missing link' claim seriously and actually focused papers on Krao" (2005, 54).

She was even displayed in some of the leading academic institutions of her day as a Darwinian "missing link" (Rothfels 1996, 163). Homberger noted that

> Dr. A.H. Keane led the supporters of the group who believed that Krao was, indeed, the missing link they had been searching for. His theory suggested that there existed in the jungles of Laos a race of hirsute people and these people were the bridge between man and beast. That Krao was Laotion was all he needed to know. His examination of her confirmed, beyond a shadow of a doubt, exactly what they had been looking for [to prove ape-human evolution] (Homberger 2005, 116).

To support the circus' and scientists' claims, Mr. Kaulitz-Jarlow, a corresponding member of the Institution Ethnographique, did a "scientific" study of Krao when she was about six years old. He described her as particularly ape-like, having thick, jet-black smooth hair that covered her head and formed a virtual mane on her neck. He then "went on to point out in detail how closely her facial structure resembled that of the gorilla" (Drimmer 1973, 163; see also Drimmer 1991, 74).

The researchers turned out in force to see the fantastic "ape person" (Gylseth and Toverud 2003, 96). One example shows the police were smarter then the ape-man theory of some scientists. This "ape-like" status and "missing-link" conclusion was "widely entertained," but it is now known that it was a "mistaken view" that Hutchinson claimed "the newspapers helped to spread" (1902, ii).

> In 1884, Krao was exhibited at the Berlin Aquarium. Here, some unscrupulous show promoters thought it would be a fantastic idea to put her in a cage with "other" apes — the German police did not think so and they were probably right. That anyone could think putting a small human child into a gorilla cage was less an

act of stupidity, though, than an act of pure faith. Reportedly, a huge debate raged regarding Krao and whether or not she was fully human. Thus, a case can be made that the promoters truly believed she was one with the gorillas and that the gorillas would see it that way too (Homberger 2005, 116).

Not all scientists went along with the missing link idea, and

> the nonbelievers were led by a Dr. Fauvelle. He, like Keane, was quite anxious to *want* to accept Krao as a missing link, but he possessed a more scientific skepticism about the whole thing. Although he could see that Krao had physical characteristics that were very simian, her grasp of language, acute reflexes, and quick intelligence made him certain that Krao was pure human, afflicted with a condition of severe hirsuteness, and nothing more. She was not a half-ape after all. But despite the proof, Keane refused to accept any other explanation than the one onto which he had glommed (Homberger 2005, 116).

The expert concluded that, although of normal intelligence, fluent in several languages, well-read, and of cheerful disposition, if Krao was annoyed, "her wild nature at once comes to the fore; she throws herself on the ground, screams, kicks, and gives vent to her anger by pulling her hair in a very particular way" (quoted in Drimmer 1973, 163). Hartzman wrote, "In truth, the supposed tree dweller was well-read, multilingual, and probably more intelligent than many of the gawkers who paid to see her" (2005, 54).

Krao's supposed "ape-like characteristics" were probably due to hirsutism, and she likely suffered from the same or similar deformities as Julia Pastrana. Possibly, as with Julia, she had a vitamin C deficiency as a child, and that may have produced some of her ape-like features such as her protruding lips. Krao continued to be a star of the Ringling Brothers, Barnum and Bailey Circus until she died on April 16, 1926, at the age of 49.

The Motivations for the Exploitation of Deformed People

The circuses and exhibitors often were not motivated primarily to prove evolution to the public. In fact, in many, if not most cases, they knew that their exhibits were merely diseased or deformed humans. The primary motive no doubt was often financial. Nonetheless, the end result was to help convince the common people of the validity of Darwinism and was one more factor that was influential in causing the rapid conversion of large segments of the population to Darwinian evolution.

Even some trained anthropologists and biologists were fooled. Milner, in a study of this period, concluded that "early evolutionists thought . . . Julia Pastrana was a 'throwback' to an ape-like stage of humanity" (1990, 354). Although most anthropologists and textbook authors did not use these examples as proof of Darwinism, Darwin, Haeckel, and Wallace all discussed these examples as evidence for macroevolution.

One "standard anthropological text," *The Living Races of Mankind* (Hutchinson 1902, v), contained a photograph of Julia Pastrana that has been used in some American racist publications that claimed she was a hybrid "between a black person and an ape" (Bondeson 1997, 243). Darwin even described Julia Pastrana's appearance as "gorilla-like" and as evidence of the great extent of genetic variation found in humans that would allow natural selection to select from (1896, 321). We now know that this uniqueness was not due to normal genetic variation but instead was a result of rare diseases.

Haeckel described Miss Pastrana as an ape-like human that was more highly developed than the long-nosed apes (1905, 372). Author Audrey Topping claimed that for years the Chinese "thought these hairy people were a reversion to an ancestral prototype such as the ape-men" (1981, 113). Evolutionists rarely openly exposed these cases in print as fraudulent and, therefore, as invalid support for Darwinism, even though some medical doctors examined these "missing links" and verified that they were merely diseased humans.

Some scientists did examine individual claims, and one such study by English anthropologist Professor Keane concluded that Krao was clearly genus *Homo sapiens* (Snigurowicz 1999; see also Harrison 1883). Rothfels noted that, as a whole, the

> scientific community and the "educated" tended to frown on claims by the exhibitors of "savages" and "ape-men" that the freaks were in fact the much-theorized missing links. . . . Despite educated skepticism, however, the popular *and* scientific interest in "missing links" rarely abated (1996, 162, emphasis in original).

By their silence, they allowed the dishonesty and outright frauds to continue for decades. Some scientists even lent their prestige and authority to the "missing link" fraud. The showmen

> asked scientists to authenticate the origin and credibility, and the scientists' commentary appeared in newspapers and publicity pamphlets. Some exhibits were presented to scientific societies for dis-

cussion and speculation. Showmen played up the science affiliation. They used the word "museum" in the title of many freak shows and referred to freak show lecturers as "professor" or "doctor." Linking freak exhibits with science made the attractions more interesting, more believable, and less frivolous to Puritanical anti-entertainment sentiments (Thomson 1996, 29).

The Influence of Circus Ape-Men on the Common People

An important myth that resulted from Darwinism was that there must exist, somewhere in the present or past, creatures that were intermediate between humanoids and anthropoids. Related to this idea is that of devolution — that our children or our children's children may revert to the subhuman creatures that we were at one time in the past (Fiedler 1978, 241). Both of these ideas were exploited by circuses.

How many millions of people saw these various "ape-human" exhibits and, as a result, became convinced that Darwinism was true is unknown. Interviews reveal that those exhibits "made a lasting impression" on some people, influencing many to accept evolution (Bondeson 1997, 217). This was true even though most all of these ape-human deformities were caused by recognizable medical defects (often genetic) and was well recognized even in the 1800s (Gould and Pyle 1896).

These exhibits were not only blatantly dehumanizing, but the exhibitors in virtually all cases deceptively pawned the "freaks" off to the public either as proof of Darwin's theory of evolution or, occasionally, atavisms. In the words of Odell, "The world was gradually preparing for Darwin and checking him up in terms of Barnum" (1931, 413). To the untrained audiences who viewed them, these ape-human exhibits were no doubt highly impressive and very convincing. Otherwise, as mentioned earlier, why would millions flock to see them for a price that was not cheap in its day?

The Influence of Circus Ape-men on Racism

Bearded ladies and ape-like looking people were known long before Darwin published his *Origin of the Species* and were also used as evidence of macroevolution prior to Darwin. Biological evolution ideas extend far back in history. Voltaire even claimed, "The white man is to the Black as the Black is to the monkey" (quoted in Fiedler 1978, 240). Others had claimed that the "Negroes were a result of cross breeding between humans and Simians." Racist ideas existed before Darwin, but things changed drastically after his writings were published. Fielder wrote that the "racist mythology did not play a determining role in the perception of non-Europeans by Europeans until the triumph of the theory of organic evolution in Darwin's" *Origin of the Species* published in 1859. Then "its extension by analogy into early developmental anthropology" became common because almost all of Darwin's

> early readers took him to be saying that beyond *Homo sapiens* organic evolution is neither possible nor desirable — and the struggle to survive, therefore, though it does not cease at that point, moves from the biological to the social or cultural plane. This second "ascent of man," the new anthropology taught, has raised men from "primitivism" or "savagery" to "civilization," from a culture without the alphabet or the wheel to one with a printing press and an advanced technology, from, in short, the "nasty, brutish and short" life eked out in most of the world to the kind enjoyed in Europe — and after a while, the United States (Fiedler 1978, 240–241).

The racism in Darwinism, Fiedler argues, was also important in influencing, for example, the rise of racist ideas and movements such as the Ku Klux Klan. Furthermore, convincing many people of the reality of evolution also had many unintended racist side effects that, no doubt, helped to legitimize movements such as the Ku Klux Klan. An example is found in the 1915 film titled *The Birth of a Nation*, when a White father says to a Harvard-educated "mulatto" who had asked for his daughter's hand in marriage, "I happen to know the important fact that a man or woman of Negro ancestry, though a century removed, will suddenly breed back to a pure Negro child, thick-lipped, kinky-headed, flat-nosed, black-skinned. One drop of your blood in my family could push it backward three thousand years in history" (quoted in Fiedler 1978, 241–242).

The effect of attempts to pass off diseased and genetically deformed persons as Darwin's missing link also had negative, if not tragic, effects on the victims themselves. Instead of helping them to deal with their condition, it no doubt perpetuated their maladjustment to society, producing the derogatory label "freak" that made it even more difficult for them to establish reasonable normal relationships with others (Drimmer 1991; Fiedler 1978). Most of "Darwin's Ape-Men" suffered from congenital hypertrichosis lanuginosa (long non-pigmented hair over the entire body) or congenital hypertrichosis terminalis (long pigmented hair over the entire body) and/or gingival hyperplasia.

The realization that these people were not missing links but medically or genetically diseased, plus the compassion of those who learned of their plight, contributed to the legislation and local sentiment that opposed displaying these people in side shows as was once common. Various church leaders have protested the display of Julia Pastrana many times during the last century, because they viewed such not only as sordid but also as degrading to humanity (Bondeson 1997, 239). If someone attempted a similar show today, no doubt public outrage would rapidly shut the show down as racist and fraudulent. Unfortunately, the harm they caused is now done and cannot easily be undone.

Summary

Diseased and deformed humans were exploited as sideshow "freaks" for decades to "prove" Darwinism. These displays were a major attraction in many leading circuses and shows for over a century and likely influenced millions of people to accept the theory of human evolution. One of the latest examples was in 1974, and no doubt more recent ones exist. Even Darwin, Haeckel, and Wallace all discussed these examples as potential evidence for macroevolution. Medical doctors examined these putative Darwinian missing links and verified that they were diseased but otherwise normal humans. Although most anthropologists and textbook authors do not use circus "freaks" today to prove Darwinism, rarely do they expose their use as fraudulent support for Darwinism. By their silence, they have allowed the dishonesty to continue for over a century.

References

Adams, Rachel. 2001. *Sideshow U.S.A.: Freaks and the American Cultural Imagination.* Chicago, IL: University of Chicago Press.

Adams, Russell (editor). 1990. "The Exploited Apewomen" in *Mysteries of the Human Body.* New York: Time-Life Publishers.

Altick, Richard. 1978. *Shows of London.* Cambridge, MA: Harvard University Press.

Anavi, Y., P. Lerman, S. Mintz, S. Kiviti. 1989. "Idiopathic Familial Gingival Fibromatosis Associated with Mental Retardation, Epilepsy and Hypertrichosis." *Developmental Medical Child Neurology* 31(4):538–542.

Anonymous. 1855. *Hybrid Indian! The Misnomered Bear Woman, Julia Pastrana.* Boston, MA. (A copy is in the Yale University Library.)

Bogdan, Robert. 1988. *Freak Show: Presenting Human Oddities for Amusement and Profit.* Chicago, IL: University of Chicago Press.

Bondeson, J., and A.E. Miles. 1993. "Julia Pastrana, the Nondescript: An Example of Congenital, Generalized Hypertrichosis Terminalis with Gingival Hyperplasia." *American Journal of*

Medical Genetics 47(2):198–212.

Bondeson, Jan. 1997. "The Strange Story of Julia Pastrana." *A Cabinet of Medical Curiosities.* Ithaca, NY: Cornell University Press, p. 216–244.

Bradna, Fred, and Hartzell Spence. 1952. *The Big Top: My Forty Years with The Greatest Show on Earth by Fred Bradna as told to Hartzell Spence including A Circus Hall of Fame.* New York: Simon and Schuster.

Browne, Janet, and Sharon Messenger. 2003. "Victorian Spectacle: Julia Pastrana, the Bearded and Hairy Female." *Endeavor* 27(4):155–159.

Buckland, Francis T. 1865. *Curiosities of Natural History. Vol. 2.* London: Bentley.

Cockayne, E.A. 1933. *Inherited Abnormalities of the Skin and its Appendages.* London: Oxford University Press.

Cook, James W. Jr. 1996. (Rosemarie Garland Thomson, editor). "Of Men, Missing Links, and Nondescripts: The Strange Career of P.T. Barnum's 'What Is It' Exhibition." *Freakery: Cultural Spectacles of the Extraordinary Body.* New York: New York University Press, p. 139–157.

Darwin, Charles. 1896. *The Variation of Animals and Plants Under Domestication.* New York: D. Appleton.

Drimmer, Frederick. 1973. *Very Special People; The Struggles, Loves, and Triumphs of Human Oddities.* New York: Amjon Publishers.

———. 1991. "Apewomen." *Born Different.* New York: Bantam, p. 72–91.

Durant, John, and Alice Durant. 1957. *Pictorial History of the American Circus.* New York: A.S. Barnes.

Fiedler, Leslie. 1978. *Freaks: Myths and Images of the Secret Self.* New York: Simon and Schuster.

Fuchs, Josef. 1917. *Über Trichoson, besonders die der Julia Pastrana.* Bonn, Germany: Universität Bonn. Doctoral Dissertation.

Gould, George M., and Walter L. Pyle. 1896. *Anomalies and Curiosities of Medicine.* Philadelphia, PA: W.B. Saunders.

Gylseth, Christopher Hals, and Lars O. Toverud. 2003. Translated by Donald Tumasonis. *Julia Pastrana: The Tragic Story of the Victorian Ape Woman.* England: Sutton Publishing.

Haeckel, Ernst. 1905. *The Evolution of Man.* New York: G.P. Putnam's Sons.

Harrison, J.P. 1883. "Krao, the So-called Missing Link," *Report of the British Association for the Advancement of Science,* p. 575.

Hartzman, Marc. 2005. *American Sideshow: An Encyclopedia of History's Most Wondrous and Curiously Strange Performers.* New York: Jeremy Tarcher/Penguin.

Homberger, Francine. 2005. *Carny Folk: The World's Weirdest Sideshow Acts.* New York: Kensington Publishing Company.

Horning, G.M., J.G. Fisher, B.F. Barker, W.J. Killoy, and J.W. Lowe. 1985. "Gingival Fibromatosis with Hypertrichosis. A Case Report." *Journal of Periodontology* 56(6):344–347.

Huffines, Scott. 2001. *On the Sawdust Trail.* June. www.atomicbooks.com/shocked/0601/sawdust062001.html.

Hutchinson, H.N. 1902. *The Living Races of Mankind.* New York: Appleton.

Kunhardt, Philip B. Jr., Philip B. Kunhardt III, and Peter W. Kunhardt. 1995. *P.T. Barnum; America's Greatest Showman.* New York: Alfred A. Knopf.

Laurence, J.Z. 1857. "A Short Account of the Bearded and Hairy Female." *Lancet* 2(48).

Levenson, Randal. 1982. *In Search of the Monkey Girl.* Millerton, NY: Aperture.

Lindfors, Bernth. 1999. *Africans on Stage.* Bloomington, IN: Indiana University Press.

———. 1983. "Circus Africans." *Journal of American Culture* 6(2):9–14.

Mather, Christine. 1999. Review of "The True History of the Tragic Life and Triumphant Death of Julia Pastrana, the Ugliest Woman in the World" by Shaun Prendergast. *Theater Journal.* 51(2):215–216.

Maugh, Thomas H. 1997. "Werewolf Gene" in *Science Supplement.* New York: Grolier.

Miles, A.E.W. 1974. "Julia Pastrana: The Bearded Lady." *Proceedings of the Royal Society of Medicine* 67(2):160–164.

Milner, Richard. 2002. *Savages and Beasts: The Birth of the Modern Zoo.* Baltimore, MD: The Johns Hopkins University Press. p. 38–39, 74–75, 110–11, 116–121.

———. 1990. *The Encyclopedia of Evolution.* New York: Facts on File. "Julia Pastrana," p. 354.

Odell, George. 1931. *Annals of the New York Stage. Vol. VI [1850–1857].* New York: Columbia University Press.

Ponti, Carlo. Producer. 1996. *The Ape Woman.* English Subtitles. Seattle, WA: Something Weird Video. Original title *La Donna Scimmia.*

Rothfels, Nigel. 1996. "Aztecs, Aborigines, and the Ape-People: Science and Freaks in Germany 1850–1900," p. 158–172, in Thomson 1996.

Saxon, A.H. 1989. *P.T. Barnum: The Legend and the Man.* New York: Columbia University Press.

Shapcott, Thomas, editor. 1998. *The Moment Made Marvelous.* Queensland, Australia: University of Queensland Press.

Snigurowicz, Diana. 1999. "Sex, Simians, and Spectacle in Nineteenth-Century France; Or, How to tell a 'Man' from a Monkey." *Canadian Journal of History* 34:51–81.

Suskind, R. and N.B. Esterly. 1971. "Congenital Hypertrichosis Universalis." *Birth Defects Original Article Series,* 7(8):103–106.

Thomson, Rosemarie Garland. 1996. *Freakery: Cultural Spectacles of the Extraordinary Body.* New York: New York University Press.

Topping, Audrey. 1981. "Wild Men." *Science Digest* August, p. 66–113.

Van Hare, G. 1888. *Fifty Years of a Showman's Life.* London: W.H. Allen.

Vogel, R.I. 1977. "Gingival Hyperplasia and Folic Acid Deficiency from Anticonvulsive Drug Therapy: A Theoretical Relationship." *Journal of Theoretical Biology* 67(2):269–278.

Wallace, Irving. 1959. *The Fabulous Showman; The Life and Times of P.T. Barnum.* New York. Knopf.

Zimmerman, Andrew. 2001. *Anthropology and Antihumanism in Imperial Germany.* Chicago, IL: University of Chicago Press.

Chapter 12

Darwinists Taught Human Females Are Inferior to Males

Introduction

A review of the prominent late-19th-century writings reveals that a major plank of early evolution theory was the belief that women were intellectually and physically inferior to men. Female inferiority was a logical conclusion of the Darwinian worldview, because males were believed to be exposed to far greater selective pressures than females, especially in war, competition for mates, food, and clothing. Conversely, women were protected from selection by norms that required adult males to provide for and protect women and children (Sherfey 1973).

Darwinists taught that, as a result of this protection, natural selection operated far more actively on males than on females. As a result, males became "more evolved" than women and more superior in virtually all intellectual and skill areas. The women inferiority doctrine is an excellent example of the fact that armchair logic often has been more important in building

Darwinian theory than fossil and other empirical evidence.

Evidence for the Theory

Darwinists once widely taught that women were at a "lower level of development" than men because an "earlier arrest of individual evolution" had occurred in human females (Gilmore 2001, 124). Furthermore, women had smaller, less-developed brains, and were believed to be "eternally primitive" and childlike. Otto Weininger even argued that women were "social parasites," who "must be repressed for the good of the race." Women not only were considered less evolved than men, but also were regarded by many sociologists as less spiritual, more materialistic, less normal, and "a real danger to contemporary civilization and had to be repressed for the good of all humankind" (Gilmore 2001, 125). Emile Durkheim, a founder of the modern field of sociology, concluded that women were not equal to men, an inequality that grows proportionately with civilization.

These views were not those of a small minority of intellectuals, but were "a majority view in the formative sociology of the late Victorian period" (Gilmore 2001, 124; Gamble 1849). Charles Darwin's writings played a major role in the development of this attitude. This chapter details how these misogynist views developed and the evidence used to support them.

The Importance of Darwinism

The central mechanism of Darwinism is survival of the fittest, requiring biological differences from which nature can select. As a result of natural selection, inferior animals were more likely to become extinct, and, conversely, superior ones were likely to thrive and leave more offspring (Darwin 1871). The biological racism of late-19th-century Darwinism has now been both well documented and widely publicized. Especially influential in the development of biological racism was the eugenics theory, developed by Charles Darwin's cousin, Sir Francis Galton (Bergman 1992; Stein, 1988). Less widely known is that many evolutionists, including Darwin, taught that women were both biologically and intellectually inferior to men.

The intelligence gap that many leading Darwinists believed existed between males and females was so great that some classified the sexes as two distinct species — males as *Homo frontalis* and females as *Homo parietalis* (Love 1983). The inference is clear from the genus-species binomial nomenclature used: *Homo parietalis* for women, *Homo frontalis* for men, is comparable to *Homo sapiens*, *Homo erectus*, *Homo ergaster*, *Homo heidelbergensis*, and *Homo neanderthalensis.*

Darwin himself argued that the differences between human males and females were so great that he was amazed "such different beings belong to the same species" and was surprised that "even greater differences" had not evolved (Rosser 1992, 59). Eminent science historian Professor Sue Rosser, PhD, is a leading academic with a BA, MS, and PhD in zoology from the University of Wisconsin-Madison. Her professorships include anthropology, zoology, and women's studies. Her 52-page summary of her academic work includes 13 books, 73 book chapters, and 67 peer-reviewed journal articles, including several on women in science. She wrote that

> writing in the nineteenth century, but echoed by sociobiologists (Barash 1977; Wilson 1978) in this century, Charles Darwin (1867) remarks specifically on the vast differences between males and females. What amazed him was the fact that such different beings belong to the same species. . . . In order to make the differentiation between males and females as strong as possible, the theory of sexual selection is needed. It is the agent of differentiation, that which assures an ever-increasing separation between the sexes, their operation in two quite distinct realms that touch only for the purpose of procreation. At one point Darwin even suggests that it is as preposterous to suggest that a human male should be born of a female as it is that "a perfect kangaroo were seen to come out of the womb a bear" (Darwin 1967, 425; quoted in Rosser 1992, 155).

She elaborated this further, writing that

> Darwin's suggestion that human females and males differ as much as separate species has stuck in my mind ever since I first studied the passage some 14 years ago. Early this year while reading in an introductory biology text the standard definitions of interactions between species, this passage from Darwin again came to mind. It occurred to me that the metaphor of woman as a separate species . . . has served as a useful construct for evolution of some Marxist-feminist theory (Rosser 1992, 155).

Furthermore, she concluded from her decades of research on this topic that what

> struck Darwin most when he observed males and females of species throughout the natural world was the tremendous difference

between them: "How enormously these sometimes differ in the most important characters is known to every naturalist" (Darwin 1859, 424). What amazed him was the fact that such different beings belong to the same species. When viewing the human world in the light of other natural realms, he was even surprised to note that even greater differences still had not been evolved. "It is, indeed, fortunate that the law of the equal transmission of characters to both sexes prevails with mammals; otherwise it is probable that man would have become as superior in mental endowment to woman, as the peacock is in ornamental plumage to the peahen" (Darwin 1871, 565). At first view it may seem strange that Darwin stresses the differences between the sexes. In the *Origin* he depicts the struggle for existence as a mainly intraspectific conflict, claiming that competition is fiercest among those closest in the scale of nature (Darwin 1859, 76; Rosser 1992, 59).

In short, natural and sexual selection were at the core of Darwinism, and human female inferiority was both a major proof and a chief witness.

Darwin argued that men shaped women's evolution to the male's liking by sexual selection, just as animal breeders shaped animals (Richards 1983a, 78). Conversely, war tended to prune the weaker men, allowing only the more fit to return home and reproduce. Men also were the hunters, another activity that pruned weaker men. Women, in contrast, were not subject to these selection pressures because they "specialized in the 'gathering' part of the primitive economy" (Dyer 1985, 122).

Male superiority was so critical for evolution that George claimed the "male rivalry component of sexual selection was *the key*, Darwin believed, to the evolution of man: of all the causes which have led to the differences . . . between the races of man . . . sexual selection has been the most efficient" (1982, 136, emphasis added). Although selection struggles existed between groups, they were "more intense among members of the same species" because they "have similar needs and rely upon the same territory to provide them with food and mates" (Reed 1975, 45). Until recently, Darwinists taught that the intense struggle for mates within the same species was a major factor in producing male superiority for all sexual species.

The reasons for belief in the biological inferiority of women are complex, but Darwin's natural and sexual selection ideas were a major factor. Darwin's views about women logically followed from evolutionary theory, "thereby nourishing several generations of scientific sexism" (Richards 1983,

887). Importantly, Darwin's ideas, as elucidated in his writings, had a major impact on both science and society. As a result, scientists were inspired to use biology, ethnology, and primatology to build support for the position that women had a "manifestly inferior and irreversibly subordinate" status to men (Morgan 1972, 1).

The extent of the doctrine's adverse effects can be gauged from the fact that the "biological inferiority of women" concept heavily influenced many theorists that have had a major role in shaping our generation — from Sigmund Freud to Havelock Ellis (Shields 1975). As eloquently argued by Durant, both racism and sexism were central to Darwinism:

> Darwin introduced his discussion of psychology in the *Descent* by reasserting his commitment to the principle of continuity . . . [and] . . . Darwin rested his case upon a judicious blend of zoomorphic and anthropomorphic arguments. Savages, who were said to possess smaller brains and more prehensile limbs than the higher races, and whose lives were said to be dominated more by instinct and less by reason . . . were placed in an intermediate position between nature and man; and Darwin extended this placement by analogy to include not only children and congenital idiots but also women, some of whose powers of intuition, of rapid perception, and perhaps of imitation were "characteristic of the lower races, and therefore of a past and lower state of civilization" (Durant 1985, 295, referencing *Descent* 1871:326–327).

Darwin's Personal Beliefs

Darwin's theory of origins may have reflected his personal attitudes about women. For example, when Darwin was concerned that his brother, Erasmus, might marry author and reformer Harriet Martineau (1802–1876), he wrote to his brother, noting that if he marries her he will not be ". . . much better than her 'nigger.' — Imagine poor Erasmus a nigger to so philosophical & energetic a lady." Darwin added, "Perfect equality of rights is part of her doctrine. I much doubt whether it will be equality in practice. We must pray for our poor 'nigger' " (Darwin 1985, 518–519). According to Desmond and Moore (1991, 201), part of the problem was that Ms. Martineau had just returned from a visit to America and "was full of married women's property rights." Harriet Martineau was a prominent women's liberation advocate (see her 1877 autobiography).

Among the more telling indications of Darwin's attitude toward women are statements he penned as a young man when listing what he viewed as the advantages of marriage, including children and a constant companion "who will feel interested in one object to be beloved and played with — *better than a dog anyhow* — Home, and someone to take care of house — Charms of music and female chit-chat. These things good for one's health" (1958, 232–233, emphasis added). Darwin's arguments against marriage included his conclusion that if he had remained single, he would have had more freedom to travel, less anxiety and responsibility, and more time and money. He adds that having many children would force him to earn a living, adding that his wife may not like London; "then the sentence is banishment and degradation" (1958, 232–233).

Darwin perceived that, as a married man, he would be a "poor slave . . . worse than a negro," but then reminisces that, "One cannot live this solitary life, with groggy old age, friendless and cold and childless staring one in one's face." Darwin summarized his evaluation on the philosophical note that "There is many a happy slave" and shortly thereafter, in 1839, married his cousin, Emma Wedgewood (1958, 234).

On the basis of such statements, many Darwin biographers concluded that he had a very low opinion of women: "It would be hard to conceive of a more self-indulgent, almost contemptuous, view of the subservience of women to men" (Brent 1981, 247). Richards argued that Darwin had

> clearly defined opinions on woman's intellectual inferiority and her subservient status. A wife did not aspire to be her husband's intellectual companion, but rather to amuse his leisure hours . . . and look after his person and his house, freeing and refreshing him for more important things. These views are encapsulated in the notes the then young and ambitious naturalist jotted not long before he found his "nice soft wife on a sofa" . . . (although throughout their life together it was Charles who monopolized the sofa, not Emma) (1983, 886).

Darwin supporters often claimed "time and time again, that the reason Darwin's theory was so . . . sexist, and racist is that Darwin's society exhibited these same characteristics." Obviously, his society and social class were influential, but as Hull notes, Darwin was not "so callow that he simply read the characteristics of his society into nature" (1999).

A reading of Darwin's works and those of his disciples reveals that the women's inferiority doctrine was *central* to early evolution theory. The major justifications Darwin gave for his female inferiority conclusions are summarized in his classic work, *The Descent of Man*. In this book, Darwin argued that *adult females* of most species resembled the *young* of both sexes and that "males are more evolutionarily advanced than females" (Kelves 1986, 8). He concluded that, since female evolution progressed at a slower rate than male evolution, a woman was "in essence, a stunted man" (Shields 1975, 749). This degrading view of women rapidly spread to Darwin's scientific and academic contemporaries.

For example, Darwin's contemporary and disciple, anthropologist Allan McGrigor, argued that women were less evolved than men and "physically, mentally and morally, woman is a kind of adult child . . . it is doubtful if women have contributed one profound original idea of the slightest permanent value to the world" (1869, 210). Carl Vogt, professor of natural history at the University of Geneva, also accepted many of "the conclusions of England's great modern naturalist, Charles Darwin." Vogt argued, "The child, the female, and the senile White" all had both the intellectual features and personality of the "grown up Negro" and that in the female, intellect and personality are similar to both infants and members of the "lower" races (1864, 192). Vogt argued from his study that human females are closer to the lower animals than males and likewise have "a greater" resemblance to apes than men (Lewin 1987, 305).

Vogt even concluded that the gap between males and females becomes greater as civilizations progress and is greatest in the advanced European societies (Richards 1983, 75). Darwin was "impressed by Vogt's work and proud to number him among his advocates" (Richards 1983, 74). The many other Darwinists who accepted the conclusion that sexual selection had enormous creative power included eminent physiologist George John Romanes. Shortly before Romanes' death, Darwin handed over to him

> a great deal of data he had not had time to sort out. . . . [and] according to Romanes, [these data showed] as the sexes moved toward more divergent roles . . . *females became increasingly less cerebral and more emotional. Romanes . . . shared Darwin's view that females were less highly evolved than males — ideas which he articulated in several books and many articles that influenced a generation of biologists.* . . . At the University of Pennsylvania, the influential American paleontologist Edward Drinker Cope wrote that male animals play a "more active part in the struggle for existence" . . . both Romanes and Cope . . . included human beings in their generalizations (Kelves 1986, 8–9, emphasis mine).

Romanes used this data to continue his work.

Sexual Selection

Darwin reasoned that many of the differences between males and females were due partly, or even largely, to sexual selection. He argued that in order to pass on his genes, a male must prove himself both physically and intellectually superior to other males in the competition for females. Conversely, a woman must be superior only in sexual attraction. Darwin also argued that "sexual selection depended on two different intraspecific activities: the male struggle with males for possession of females; and female choice of a mate" (George 1982, 69). In his words, evolution resulted from a "struggle between the males for possession of the females " (Darwin 1959, 88).

In support of his conclusion, Darwin wrote, "With barbarous nations, for instance with the Australians, the women are the constant cause of war both between the individuals of the same tribe and between distant tribes," resulting in sexual selection from sexual competition (1871, Vol. 2, 323). To support his conclusion, he quotes Hearne who wrote that in war "of course, the strongest party always carries off the prize" namely women (1871, Vol. 2, 324). Darwin also cited the North American Indian custom that required males to fight against male competitors to gain wives. The result was that a weaker man seldom could "keep a wife that a stronger man thinks worth his notice" (Darwin 1871, Vol. 2, 324).

Darwin used many similar examples to illustrate the evolutionary forces that he believed produced men of superior physical and intellectual strength and sexually coy, docile women. He reasoned that, since humans evolved from lower animals, "No one will dispute that the bull differs in disposition from the cow, the wild-boar from the sow, the stallion from the mare, and, as is well known to the keepers of menageries, the males of the larger apes from the females" (1871, Vol. 2, 326). Darwin argued that similar differences existed among humans. The result of this selection was that men are not only "more courageous, pugnacious and energetic than woman" but have a "more inventive genius" (Darwin 1871, Vol. 2, 316).

A major problem in applying these observations from the animal kingdom to humans is that scientists then debated the "most complex problems of economic reforms not in terms of the will of God," as once was common, "but in terms of the sexual behavioral patterns of the cichlid fish" (Morgan 1972, 1). Darwin and his disciples convinced a generation of evolutionists that science proved what was widely assumed then — namely, that women differed considerably from men in both mental disposition and intelligence. The differences resulted in white women that were so inferior to white men that many of their traits were seen as "characteristic of the lower races, and therefore of a past and lower state of civilization" (Darwin 1871, Vol. 2, 327). In summary, Darwin concluded that the intellectual superiority of males is proved by the fact that men achieve

> a higher eminence, in whatever he takes up, than women can attain — whether requiring deep thought, reason, or imagination, or merely the use of the senses and hands. If two lists were made of the most eminent men and women in poetry, painting, sculpture, music . . . history, science, and philosophy . . . the two lists would not bear comparison. We may also infer, from the law of the deviation from averages, so well illustrated by Mr. Galton, in his work on "Hereditary Genius," that if men are capable of a decided preeminence over women in many subjects, the average standard of mental power in man must be above that of woman (1871, Vol. 2, 327).

Darwin held these "male supremacy" views, which he believed were a central prediction of evolution, throughout his life (Richards 1983, 885). Shortly before his death, Darwin stated that he agreed with Galton's conclusion that "education and environment produce only a small effect" on the mind of most women because "most of our qualities are innate and not learned" (1958, 43).

In short, Darwin believed, as do many sociobiologists today, that biology rather than the environment was the primary source of mental qualities, including behavior and morals (Richards 1983, 67–68). Obviously, Darwin almost totally ignored the influence of the more critical factors, including culture, family environment, social conditioning, and the fact that relatively few occupational and intellectual opportunities existed in Darwin's day for women (Williams 1977).

Furthermore, although Darwin attributed most female traits to male sexual selection, he concluded that only a few male traits were caused by female selection. One reason was because he believed most females were not choosy about their mate's physical or mental traits (Richards 1983, 65). Consequently, men not only were "more powerful in body and mind than woman," but had even had "gained the power of selection" — evolution was in the males' hands, and females were often largely passive in this area (Darwin 1871, Vol. 2, 371). This is why many Darwinists believed that instinct and emotions dominated women, a trait that was their "greatest weakness" (Shields 1975, 742).

Major problems with the sexual selection hypothesis included the fact that marriages in many societies are arranged by relatives mostly for prag-matic considerations, such as to unite certain families, to obtain a dowry, or to release the parents from the need to support female offspring. Darwin also argued that the intellectual powers in males were

> normally developed before the reproductive age and their heritable component would not be affected by the environment. Intellectual superiority of the human male was innate but how had it come about? By sexual selection, said Darwin, not by female choice. Man's beard might be the result of female choice . . . but, considering the condition of women in barbarous tribes — where men kept women "in a far more abject state of bondage than does the male of any animal" — it was probably the male that chose. Different standards of beauty selected by the male might, thus, account for some of the differentiation of tribes (George 1982, 74).

Traits that Darwin reasoned were due to sexual selection include the numer-ous secondary sexual characteristics that differentiate humans from all other animals, including the human torso shape and limb hairlessness. What remains unanswered is why males or females would select certain traits in a male when they had been successfully mating with hair-covered mates for eons, and no nonhuman primate preferred these "human" traits.

Darwin's conclusion that a single cause explains a wide variety of sexual differences is problematic (George 1982, 71). If sexual selection caused the development of the male beard and its lack in females, why do women often prefer clean-shaven males? Obviously, cultural norms are critical in deter-mining what is considered sexually attractive, and these standards change, precluding the long-term sexual selection required to biologically evolve them (Millman 1980; Beller 1977).

Males were also believed by many Darwinists to be the superior sex because they varied to a greater degree than females in most *all* traits (Darwin 1871). This was important because variations from the norm were accepted by most Darwinists to be a result of evolutionary mechanisms and for the reason that

> the male was the more variable sex, it soon was universally con-cluded that the male is the progressive element in the species. . . . Once deviation from the norm became legitimized by evolutionary theory, the hypothesis of greater male variability became a conve-nient explanation for a number of observed sex differences, among

them the greater frequency with which men achieved "eminence" (Shields 1975, 743).

Proponents of this women's inferiority argument used evidence such as the fact that a higher percent of *both* the mentally deficient *and* the mentally gifted were males. They reasoned that since selection operates to a greater degree on men, the weaker males would be more rigorously eliminated than the weaker females, raising the evolutionary level of males as a whole.

Darwin's critics argued that sex-linked diseases (as well as social factors) were a major influence in producing the higher number of males that were born feebleminded. Furthermore, the weaker females would be preserved by the almost universal norms that protected them. Few women were defined as eminent because their social roles often confined them to housekeeping and child rearing. Furthermore, constraints on the education and employment of women by both law and custom rendered comparisons between males and females useless in determining innate abilities.

Consequently, differences of intelligence, feeblemindedness, eminence, and occupational success between males and females cannot be attributed to biology without considering these critical factors. Most arguments for women's inferiority that once seemed well supported (and consequently were accepted by most biologists) were later shown to be invalid, as illustrated by the changes in Western society that occurred in the last generation (Shields 1975). The belief was that the female role as homemaker enabled feebleminded women to survive better outside institutional settings, and this is why institutional surveys located fewer female inmates.

Darwin's Influence on Society

The theory of the natural and sexual selection origin of both the body and the mind had major consequences on society soon after Darwin completed his first major work on evolution in 1859. The "innate inferiority of females" was strongly supported by biological determinism and the primacy of "nature over nurture" doctrine. In Shields's words, the leitmotif of "evolutionary theory as it came to be applied to the social sciences was the evolutionary supremacy of the Caucasian male" (Shields 1975, 739).

One of the leading late 1800s evolutionists, Joseph Le Conte, even concluded that male and female differences resulting from organic evolution also must limit female societal roles (Stephens 1976, 241). Consequently, Le Conte opposed women's suffrage, because evolution made women "incapable of dealing rationally with political and other problems which required emotional detachment and clear logic" (Stephens 1976, 247).

After reviewing the once widely accepted *tabula rasa* theory which taught that the environment was responsible for personality, Fisher noted that Darwinism resulted in a radical change in society, and

> the year in which Darwin finished the first unpublished version of his theory of natural selection [1842], Herbert Spencer began to publish essays on human nature. Spencer was a British political philosopher and social scientist who believed that human social order was the result of evolution. The mechanism by which social order arose was "survival of the fittest" a term he, not Darwin, introduced. In 1850, Spencer wrote *Social Statics*, a treatise in which he . . . opposed welfare systems, compulsory sanitation, free public schools, mandatory vaccinations, and any form of "poor law." Why? Because social order had evolved by survival of the fittest. The rich were rich because they were more fit; certain nations dominated others because these peoples were naturally superior; certain racial types subjugated others because they were smarter. Evolution, another word he popularized, had produced superior classes, nations, and races (1982, 115–116).

Fisher noted that the early evolutionists' teachings included not only superior race ideas, but also "superior sex" conclusions and that males were destined to dominate females as a result of evolution.

Males were also believed to be more evolved because they were historically subjected to many more selection pressures than women: the stronger and quicker males were more apt to survive a hunt and bring back food; consequently, natural selection would impact them to a greater degree than the females. Hunting can be a dangerous activity: one could become lost or injured, and the hunter sometimes became the hunted.

Darwin taught that another major reason for male superiority was that males had to fight and die to protect themselves, their children, and females. Nineteenth-century Darwinist Topinard argued that males have "all the responsibility and the cares of tomorrow" and constantly are "active in combating the environment and human rivals"; thus, they need more brains "than the woman whom he must protect and nourish . . . the sedentary woman, lacking any interior occupations, whose [sole] role is to raise children, love, and be passive" (Gould 1996, 136).

In short, Darwinists taught that male superiority was due to the "inheritance from his half-human male ancestors . . . the long ages of man's savagery, by the success of the strongest and boldest men, both in the general struggle for life and in their contests for wives; a success which would have ensured their leaving a more numerous progeny than their less favored brethren" (Darwin 1896, 563). Conversely, women, instead of hunting or fighting wars, have historically taken care of domestic, often menial, repetitive tasks, and as a result were far less affected by selection pressures.

The long tradition for males to protect females was especially reflected in war behavior: only men went to battle, and war norms generally forbade soldiers from deliberately killing females and young males. Women were sometimes killed, kidnapped, or raped, but they were rarely formally involved in war as combat troops. Dyer concluded that combat was exclusively a male occupation, because men were better suited to fighting due to their

> greater physical strength and their freedom from the burden of childbearing . . . almost every living male for thousands of generations has imbibed some of the warrior mystique . . . and men were specialized in the hunting and warrior functions for the same physical reasons long before civilized war was invented (1985, 122).

Since long-term selection prunes out the weak, all those factors that facilitate saving the weak allow them to pass their inferior genes to their offspring, which works against evolution. Females were inferior as a result of the greater Darwinian selection of males compared to females, and for males the

> possible winnings, either in immediate reproduction or in an ultimate empire of wives and kin, are greater. So are its possibilities for immediate bankruptcy (death) or permanent insolvency from an involuntary but unavoidable celibacy . . . a male's developmental program must gamble against odds in an effort to obtain the upper tail of the fitness distribution. . . . Female mortality will be found to exceed male, not in species with female heterogamety, but in those with female masculinity (Williams 1977, 138–139).

Darwinists also argued that skill plays a far greater role in hunting and fighting than in domestic tasks completed by women. Consequently, because women's lives typically required "less skill than men's activities . . . [and] available evidence suggests that men vary much more in hunting abilities than women do in gathering abilities, hence, as with violence, *selection acts far more intensely among males than among females*" (Symons 1980, 162, emphasis mine). In Williams's words, at every moment in life, "the masculine sex is playing for higher stakes" (1977, 138).

The Importance of Female Inferiority in Darwinism

Female inferiority was considered by most Darwinists to be a core aspect of, and unassailable evidence for macroevolution. It was especially important evidence of Darwin's major contributions to evolution theory, natural and sexual selection. Just how critical the women's inferiority conclusion was for evolution was noted by George:

> The chief difference between men and women, however, lay in their intellectual power, "man attaining to a higher eminence, in whatever he takes up, than can woman — whether requiring deep thought, reason or imagination or merely the uses of the senses and hands." Those striking differences, Darwin argued, could not have been the result of use and disuse, of the inheritance of acquired characters; for hard work and the development of muscles was not the prerogative of man: "in barbarian societies women work as hard or harder." . . . Intellectual superiority of the human male was innate but how had it come about? By sexual selection, said Darwin, not by female choice (1982, 74).

The female inferiority doctrine was considered a major proof of evolution by natural selection and was taken for granted by most scientists in the late 1800s. Gould claims that *almost all scientists* then believed that Blacks, women, and other groups were intellectually inferior and biologically closer to the lower animals than white males (Gould 1996, 57). Nor were these scientists simply repeating their cultural prejudices; their beliefs were based on extensive research and evolution theory, some of which will now be reviewed.

Nor was Darwin simply providing biological reasons to support a view that was widely held in his day. Tavris noted that it had been widely believed among scientists for centuries "that most of men's and women's body parts were perfectly interchangeable, and that the parts that were not — those interesting reproductive organs — were nevertheless analogous: women's organs were the same as men's, 'turned outside in' " (1992, 97). Darwinism caused a drastic change in this once-common view and resulted in scientists in all fields attacking this premise. Instead, many Darwinists emphasize what they saw as a chasm between masculine and feminine natures, physical and mental. They concluded that differences between male and female bodies were correspondingly vast, because female development had been arrested at a lower stage of evolution. Women, they said, could be placed on the evolutionary ladder along with children, apes, and "primitive" people. Even illustrations of female skeletons reflected this belief in female inferiority. Female skeletons were drawn with tiny skulls and ample pelvises, to emphasize the idea that women were intellectually weak and suited mainly for reproductive functions (Tavris 1992, 97).

To scientifically *prove* this major plank in Darwinism required producing reams of empirical research that supported the position that women were inferior. Even today, some evolutionary scientists still accept many of these conclusions (Rushton and Ankney 1996; Shields 1975). Gibbons notes that many evolutionists ignore the critical importance of social factors and conclude that sexual differences in mental activity have their "roots in strong evolutionary pressures on the sexes during prehistory when the brain was rapidly expanding" (1991, 958).

Female Brain Capacity Inferior

One approach seized upon scientifically to demonstrate that females were inferior to males was to "prove" that their average brain capacity was smaller. Researchers first endeavored to demonstrate smaller female cranial capacity by skull measurements and then tried to prove the more difficult task that brain capacity had a direct causal relationship to intelligence (Van Valen 1974). The justification for this approach toward proving inferiority was explained by Darwin:

> As the various mental faculties gradually developed themselves the brain would almost certainly become larger. . . . the large proportion which the size of man's brain bears to his body, compared to the same proportion in the gorilla or orang, is closely connected with his higher mental powers. . . . that there exists in man some close relation between the size of the brain and the development of the intellectual faculties is supported by the comparison of the skulls of savage and civilized races, of ancient and modern people, and by the analogy of the whole vertebrate series (1896, 54).

One of the more eminent of the numerous early researchers who used craniology to prove the intellectual inferiority of women was Darwinist Paul Broca (1824–1880). Professor Broca was a surgeon on the Paris faculty of medicine, one of Europe's most esteemed physical anthropologists, and founder of the prestigious Anthropological Society (Fee 1979, 415). A major preoccupation of this society was measuring various human traits, including skulls, in order to "delineate human groups and assess their relative worth" (Gould 1996, 115).

Broca concluded that in healthy humans, the brain is, on average, larger in "men than in women," larger in "eminent men than in men of mediocre talent," and larger "in superior races than in inferior races" (Gould 1996, 115). He added, other things being equal, that "there is a remarkable relationship between the development of intelligence and the volume of the brain" (Gould 1996, 115).

In view of his conclusions, Broca's research was not superficial as we may expect, but was so extensive and thorough that one cannot read his writings "without gaining enormous respect for his care in generating data" (Gould 1996, 117). Broca focused on intellectual and cranial comparisons, and of all the comparisons he collected, the greatest amount of information was on the brains of women vs. men (Gould 1996, 135). He concluded that "the relatively small size of the female brain" was due to her physical and intellectual inferiority (Gould 1996, 136). Broca added that the disparity between men's and women's brains was still increasing in modern society as a result of "differing evolutionary pressures" (Gould 1996, 136).

The measurement of brain size was critical in proving women's inferiority, because it was assumed that brain size correlated with intelligence. This correlation was considered critical

> from a biological and evolutionary standpoint . . . there has been a direct causal effect, through natural selection in the course of human evolution, between intelligence and brain size. The evolutionary selective advantage of greater brain size was the greater capacity for more complex intellectual functioning. "Natural selection on intelligence at a current estimated intensity suffices to explain the rapid rate of increase of brain size in human evolution" (Jensen 1980, 361).

Darwinist Gustave Le Bon (1841–1931), a founder of the social psychology field and a pioneer in the collective behavior field whose classic study of mob behavior, *The Crowd* (1895), is familiar to every social science student, taught that even in the most intelligent races, a large number of women have brains that

> are closer in size to those of gorillas than to the most developed male brains. This inferiority is so obvious that no one can contest it for a moment; only its degree is worth discussion. . . . Women . . . represent the most inferior forms of human evolution and . . . they are closer to children and savages than to an adult, civilized man. They excel in fickleness, inconsistency, absence of thought and logic, and incapacity to reason. Without a doubt there exist some distinguished women . . . but they are as exceptional as the birth of any monstrosity, as, for example, of a gorilla with two heads; consequently, we may neglect them entirely (Gould 1996, 136–137).

Other evolutionists were convinced that the many differences between male and female brains included less-developed frontal lobes and softer, more slender cerebral fibers in females. Male frontal lobes were in every way more extensively developed than those of females, a sex difference that even existed in the unborn fetus (Shields 1975). Other putative differences that indicated males were superior included the complexity and conformation of the gyri, the sulci, the corpus callosum, and the fetus cortex development rate (Shields 1975, 740–742).

A modern study by Van Valen (which University of California–Berkeley psychologist Arthur Jensen concluded was the "most thorough and methodologically sophisticated recent review of all the evidence relative to human brain size and intelligence") found that the best estimate of the within-sex correlation between brain size and IQ "may be as high as 0.3" (Jensen 1980, 361; Van Valen 1974, 417). Unfortunately for Darwinists, a correlation of 0.3 accounts for only 9 percent of the variance between the sexes, a difference that may be more evidence of test and cultural bias than of biological inferiority.

Schluter even argues that comparing brain size and intelligence (controlling for height and weight) can be interpreted to conclude that "women have larger brains than men" (Schluter 1992, 181). He then explains why it is naive to use statistical analysis, such as multiple regression, to make comparisons between the brain sizes of women and men, even when one attempts to control for body size and weight differences. Prior conclusions can allow one to argue convincingly for comparatively larger brains for either men or women, even if one has collected large amounts of accurate data. Many Darwinists in the past misused or misunderstood statistical analysis and, therefore, made the same type of mistake Schluter illustrated.

In his extensive review of Professor Broca's work, Gould concluded that Broca's conclusions only reflected "the shared assumptions of most successful white males during his time — themselves on top . . . and women, Blacks, and poor people below" (1996, 117). How did Broca arrive at these conclusions? Gould responds that "his facts were reliable . . . but they were gathered selectively and then manipulated unconsciously in the service of prior conclusions," namely the conclusion that women were intellectually and otherwise demonstratively inferior to men, just as evolution predicted.

Broca's own further research and the changing social climate later caused him to modify his views, concluding that culture was more important than he and other Darwinists first assumed (Ellis 1934).

Overturning the Female Inferiority Doctrine

Although inequality was long believed, "the subordinate position of women had for too long rested on easy assumptions about female inferiority," and these inferiority assumptions have been scientifically investigated since the 1970s (Rosser 1992; Fee 1979, 415). Modern critics of Darwinism often were motivated by the women's movement to challenge Darwin's conclusion that evolution has produced men who "were superior to women both physically and mentally" (Rosser 1992, 58). These critiques have demonstrated major flaws in the evidence used to prove female inferiority and, as a result, have identified fallacies in major aspects of Darwinism (Alaya 1977). For example, Elizabeth Fisher argues that the theory of natural selection as applied to humans by Darwin is questionable. Fisher quotes Chomsky, who noted that the process by which the human mind achieved its present state of complexity is

> a total mystery. . . . It is perfectly safe to attribute this development to "natural selection," so long as we realize that there is no substance to this assertion, that it amounts to nothing more than a belief that there is some naturalistic explanation for these phenomena (Chomsky 1972, 97).

Fisher also argued that modern genetic research has seriously undermined several major aspects of Darwin's hypothesis — especially his sexual selection theory. In contrast to the requirement for Darwinism, even if natural selection were to operate differentially on males and females, males would pass on many of their superior genes to *both* their sons *and* daughters, because most all "genes are not inherited along sexual lines." Aside from the genes that are on the Y chromosome, "a male offspring receives genes from both mother and father" (Fisher 1979, 112).

Darwin and his contemporaries had little knowledge of genetics, but this did not prevent them from making sweeping conclusions about inheritance. Darwin even made the false claim that the characteristics acquired by sexual selection are usually confined to one sex (Crook 1972). Yet Darwin elsewhere recognized that women can transmit most of their characteristics to their offspring of both sexes, a fact he ignored in much of his writing (1871, Vol. 2, 236, 298, 308, 329). As an example, Darwin claimed that many traits, including genius and the higher powers of imagination and reason, were "transmitted more fully to the male than to the female offspring. The man has ultimately become superior to woman" (1871, Vol. 2, 328). The scientific basis on which this conclusion was made was not stated.

The inheritance of acquired characteristics was an important part of Darwinism. Two major reasons why Darwin accepted the male superiority view were his pangenesis theory and his view that certain acquired characteristics could be inherited. Among the major blows to both pangenesis (and all other forms of Lamarckism) was the work of August Weismann, who proved that reproductive cells of animals were "distinct, identifiable and differentiated at an early stage in development in both males and females [and] there was no way in which the body cells could affect the germ cells" (George 1982, 63). Although most scientists still supported Lamarckism long after Weismann's work was published, as new work increasingly supported Weismann's conclusions, Lamarckism slowly died (although it has been resurrected several times in history).

Later, the Mendelian and De Vriesian inheritance models proved that the mother and father contributed equal amounts of somatic chromosome genetic information to both their male and female offspring. Ironically, this major blow to the male superiority theory — which rendered it largely untenable — did not result in any major widespread repudiation of the theory. Only the civil rights movement forced a reevaluation of attitudes that were highly ingrained in both scientific theory and the cultural norms of society.

Modern genetics does not totally negate the reasons used to conclude that females were evolutionarily inferior, because some sex-linked traits would still normally be inherited only by males on the Y chromosome. The Y chromosome is much shorter and has far fewer genes than the X chromosome. Because normal women inherit two X chromosomes, many deleterious recessive genes on their one X chromosome are masked by the dominant non-deleterious genes on her other X chromosome. Males do not have this advantage. Many traits that are masked in females are expressed in males, because the male Y chromosome lacks many X alleles. This fact argues for woman's genetic superiority and is the reason why many genetic diseases such as color blindness and hemophilia are far higher in males than females. These genetic traits, though, often are inherited through the mother and expressed only by sons (Hardy 1981).

Darwin's Contribution to Sexism

Even though Darwin's theory supported (and in many ways advanced) biologically based racism and sexism, some argue that he would not approve of, and could not be faulted for, the results of his theory. Many of his disciples went far beyond him — Darwin's cousin Galton even concluded from his lifelong study on the topic that "women tend in *all* their capacities to be inferior to men" (Shields 1975, 743, emphasis mine).

Richards added that "recent scholarship has emphasized the central role played by economic and political factors in the reception of evolutionary theory" and that Darwinism provided "the intellectual underpinnings of imperialism, war, monopoly, capitalism, militant eugenics," racism, and sexism and that "Darwin's own part in this was not insignificant, as has been so often asserted" (1983a, 88). After noting Darwin believed that the now-infamous social-Darwinist Herbert Spencer was "by far the greatest living philosopher in England . . ." Fisher concluded that the evidence for the negative effects of evolutionary teaching in history are unassailable:

> Europeans were spreading out to Africa, Asia, and America, gobbling up land, subduing the natives and even massacring them. But any guilt they harbored now vanished. Spencer's evolutionary theories vindicated them. . . . Darwin's *Origin of Species*, published in 1859, delivered the *coup de grace*. Not only racial, class, and national differences but every single human emotion was the adaptive end product of evolution, selection, and survival of the fittest (1982, 116).

These Darwinian conclusions about females agreed with "other mainstream scholarly conclusions of the day. From anthropology to neurology, science had demonstrated that the female Victorian virtues of passivity, domesticity, and greater morality (. . . less sexual activity) were rooted in female biology" (Steinem 1992, 133). Consequently, many persons concluded that "evolutionary history has endowed women with domestic and nurturing genes and men with professional ones" (Hubbard et al. 1979, 208). Steinem added that

> the passive, dependent, and childlike qualities of the "darker races" (then still called the "white man's burden") were [believed by evolutionists to be] part of their biological destiny. Evolutionists also chimed in with a reason for all this: men who were not Caucasians and women of all races were lower on the evolutionary scale. In the case of race, this was due to simple evolutionary time. . . . In the case of Caucasian women — who obviously had been evolving as long as their male counterparts — there was another rationale. The less complex nervous systems and lower intelligences of females were evolutionary adaptations to the pain of childbirth, repetitive domestic work, and other physical, nonintellectual tasks. Naturally, females of "lower" races were also assumed to be inferior to their male counterparts (1992, 133–134).

Many 19th-century biologists argued for women's inferiority because they believed that "unchecked female militancy threatened to produce a perturbance of the races and to divert the orderly process of evolution" (Fee 1979, 415). Other researchers adopted the approach that the collectivist's social organization of the last century and similar factors are slowly reducing the existing biological sex inequalities (Borgese 1963). The teaching also had clear social policy implications:

> For Darwin, the intellectual differences between the sexes, like their physical differences, were entirely predictable on the basis of a consideration of the long-continued action of natural and sexual selection. . . . Male intelligence would have been consistently sharpened through the struggle for possession of the females (that is, sexual selection) and through hunting and other male activities such as the defense of the females and young (that is, natural selection) (Richards 1983, 886–887).

She added, according to Darwin

> "man has ultimately become superior to woman." On this basis, he argued in *The Descent* that the higher education of women, which was being furiously contested in Victorian England, could have no long-term impact on this evolutionary trend to ever-increasing male

intelligence. . . . male intelligence would be constantly enhanced by the severe competitive struggle males necessarily underwent in order to maintain themselves and their families, and "this will tend to keep up or even increase their mental powers, and, as a consequence, the present inequality between the sexes (Richards 1983, 886–887).

The inferiority-of-women belief was so ingrained in evolutionary biology that Morgan concluded that researchers tended to avoid "the whole subject of biology and origins," hoping that this embarrassing history would be ignored and that scientists could "concentrate on ensuring that in the future things will be different" (1972, 2).

Even women scientists largely have ignored the Darwinian inferiority theory (Margulis and Sagan 1986; Tanner and Zihlman 1976). Morgan stresses that we simply cannot ignore evolutionary biology, though, because the belief that the "jungle heritage and the evolution of man as a hunting carnivore has taken root in man's mind as firmly as Genesis ever did" and that males have built a theory "with himself on top of it, buttressed with a formidable array of scientifically authenticated facts" (1972, 2–3). Morgan argues that these "facts" must be reevaluated, because scientists have at times "gone astray" due to prejudice and philosophical proscriptions. Morgan argues that, even though scores of researchers have adroitly overturned the theory that women are biologically inferior to males, the theory must be further challenged.

Cultural Influences on the Darwinist's View of Women

Culture was of major importance in shaping Darwin's theory (Rosser 1992, 56). Victorian middle-class views about men were blatant in *The Descent of Man* and other Darwinists writings. Richards stresses that Victorian assumptions of both the inevitability and rightness of

> woman's role of domestic moral preceptor and nurturer and man's role of free-ranging aggressive provider and jealous patriarch — [were] enshrined in Darwin's reconstruction of human evolution. Our female progenitors . . . were maternal, sexually shy, tender and altruistic, while our male ancestors were "naturally" competitive, ambitious and selfish, not unlike Darwin himself who . . . wrote in *The Descent:* "Man is the rival of other men; he delights in competition . . ." it was . . . the natural order of things, just as man was "nat-

urally" more intelligent than woman, as Darwin demonstrated to his satisfaction through the dearth of eminent women intellectuals and professionals: "The chief distinction in the intellectual powers of the two sexes is shown by man's attaining to a higher eminence in whatever he takes up, than can women — whether requiring deep thought, reason, or imagination, or merely the use of the senses or hands" (1983, 885).

Although Darwinism did much to impede human rights, other forces also influenced the acceptance of the inferiority of women doctrine:

> Long before Darwin, earlier "evolutionists" had likewise relegated women to a role of subjugation and inferiority in both atheistic and pantheistic religious cultures (consider the common image of the "caveman" dragging his mate by the hair, as well as the subservient role of women in practically all pagan and ethnic religions) (Morris 1989, 135}.

The Darwinian concept of male superiority also served to increase the secularization of society, and made the evolutionary naturalism view that humans were created by natural law rather than by divine direction more palatable (George 1982). Naturalism was critically important in developing the women inferiority doctrine.

> Darwin's consideration of human sexual differences in *The Descent* was not motivated by the contemporary wave of anti-feminism . . . but was central to his naturalistic explanation of human evolution. It was his theoretically directed contention that human mental and moral characteristics had arisen by natural evolutionary processes which predisposed him to ground these characteristics in nature rather than nurture — to insist on the biological basis of mental and moral differences (Richards 1983a, 97).

A major method used to attack the evolutionary conclusion of female inferiority was to critique the evidence for Darwinism itself. Fisher, for example, noted that it is difficult to postulate theories about human origins on the actual brain organization "of our presumed fossil ancestors, with only a few limestone impregnated skulls — most of them bashed, shattered, and otherwise altered by the passage of millions of years [and to arrive at any valid conclusions on the basis of this] . . . evidence, would seem to be astronomical" (1979, 113).

Hubbard adds, "Darwin's sexual stereotypes" still are commonly found "in the contemporary literature on human evolution. This is a field in which facts are few and specimens are separated by hundreds of thousands of years, so that maximum leeway exists for investigator bias" (1979, 26). Hubbard then discusses our "overwhelming ignorance" about human evolution and the fact that much currently accepted theory is pure speculation.

Many attempts to disprove the view that women are intellectually inferior similarly attack the core of evolutionary theory itself, because this belief is inexorably bound up with human group inferiority (which must first exist for natural selection to occur). Evaluations of the female inferiority theory have produced many incisive, well-reasoned critiques of both sexual and natural selection, as well as other aspects of Darwinism.

Evolution can be used to argue for male superiority, but it also can be used to build a case for the opposite. The evidence contains so many areas open to "individual interpretation" that some feminist authors and others have used "the same evolutionary story to draw precisely the opposite conclusion," namely supposedly proving the evolutionary superiority of *women* (Love 1983, 124). One notable early example is Montagu's classic 1952 book, *The Natural Superiority of Women*. Some female biologists even have argued for a gynacocentric theory of evolution, concluding that women are the trunk of evolution history, and men are only a branch, a grafted scion (Hill 1980). Others have tried to integrate reformed "Darwinist evolutionary 'knowledge' with contemporary feminist ideals" (Hill 1980, 263).

Hapgood even concludes that evolution demonstrates that males exist to serve females, arguing that "masculinity did not evolve in a vacuum" but because it was selected by females. He notes that many animal species are parthenogenetic and can reproduce without males, and the fact that they do not need the male gender proves that "males are unnecessary" in certain environments (Hapgood 1979, 23–24). It is the female that reproduces, and evolution teaches that survival is important only to the degree that it promotes reproduction. Consequently, Hapgood argues, Darwinists would conclude that males evolved only to serve females in all aspects of child bearing and nurturing, which would include both ensuring that the female becomes pregnant and protecting her progeny.

Another revisionist theory is that women were not only superior, but that most societies were once primarily matriarchal. These revisionists also argue that patriarchal domination was caused by factors that occurred relatively recently (Reed 1975). Of course, the theories that postulate the evolutionary inferiority of males suffer from many of the same problems as those that postulate women's inferiority.

Darwinism's Influence on Society

Some scientists, including certain sociobiologists, argue that Darwinism should be used to produce our moral system (Goldberg 1973). For example, Ford argued the idea that we have to eliminate sexism as erroneous and that "the much-attacked gender differentiation we see in our societies is actually . . . a necessary consequence of the constraints exerted by our evolution. There are clear factors which really do make men the more aggressive sex" (Ford 1980, 8).

After concluding that female inferiority is a result of natural selection, it often is implied that what natural selection produces is natural, thus proper, or at least gives a "certain dignity" to behaviors that we might "otherwise consider aberrant or animalistic" (Symons 1980, 61). For example, evolutionary success is defined as leaving more offspring; consequently, promiscuity in human males would be selected. This explanation is used to justify both male promiscuity and irresponsibility and argues that trying to change "nature's grand design" is futile (Symons 1980, 61).

Fox even argues that the high pregnancy rate among unmarried teenage girls today is due to our "evolutionary legacy," which "drives" young girls to get pregnant (1980). Consequently, Fox concludes, cultural and religious prohibitions against unmarried teen pregnancy are doomed to fail. In response to these ideas, Tang-Martinez shows that the application of evolution to behavior, a field called sociobiology, is

flawed and unscientific, and there is little credible evidence to support sociobiological claims about male-female differences [and] . . . human sociobiology is biologically deterministic and serves only to justify and promote the oppression of women by perpetuating the notion that male dominance and female oppression are natural outcomes of human evolutionary history. Furthermore, they argue that reliance on questionable evolutionary scenarios can be used to rationalize and exonerate obnoxious male behavior. For example, the middle-aged man who leaves his middle-aged wife for a younger woman can be excused because he is acting in accordance with sociobiological theory by behaving so as to maximize his genetic contribution to future generations by leaving an older spouse who has "low reproductive value" in favor of a younger female with higher reproductive value (1997, 117).

Eberhard argues that male physical aggressiveness is justified by sexual selection and that "males are more aggressive than females in the sexual activities proceeding mating (discussed at length by Darwin in 1871 and confirmed many times since . . .)" (Eberhard 1985, 67). Furthermore, the conclusion "now widely accepted . . . that males of most species are less selective and coy in courtship because they make smaller investments in off-spring" is used to justify male sexual promiscuity (Eberhard 1985, 69). Male promiscuity, in other words, is determined genetically and thus is "natural" or normal because "males profit, evolutionarily speaking, from frequent mating, and females do not" (Tavris 1992, 214).

The reason is, the more females with whom a male mates, the more offspring he will produce — whereas a female need mate only with one male to become pregnant. Evolution can progress only if females select the most-fit male, as predicted by Darwin's sexual selection theory. For this reason, males have "an undiscriminating eagerness" to mate, whereas females have "a discriminating passivity" (Tavris 1992, 214). Some theorists even argue that sexual coercion (and even rape) by males is predicted by evolution:

> Psychological adaptation underlies all human behavior. Thus, sexual coercion by men could either arise from a rape — specific psychological adaptation — or it could be a side effect of a more general psychological adaptation not directly related to rape. Determining the specific environmental cues that men's brains have been designed by selection to process may help us decide which of these rival explanations is correct. . . . Current data support all six predictions and are hence consistent with the rape-specific hypothesis, but this does not eliminate the side-effect hypothesis, which is likewise compatible with the findings, as well as with the further evidence that forced matings increased the fitness of ancestral males during human evolution (Thornhill and Thornhill 1992, 363).

Some Darwinists also conclude that because many sexual behavioral differences (such as sexual aggression by males) are a result of evolution, they are, therefore, an unalterable part of our biology (Ghiselin 1974). Endeavoring to alter the "natural order" of female inferiority is also contrary to "nature's grand design" (Ghiselin 1974). Symons argues that many attitude and behavior differences between the sexes are innate and cannot be eliminated by identical rearing of males and females (1980, 162).

The reason is because females evolved to be loyal and males to be disloyal, males to be just and females to lack a sense of justice — and changing these biological differences is impossible, or at least rife with difficulties (Ghiselin 1974, 13). In response to these conclusions, Richards argued that scholars concerned with disputing evolutionary arguments such as these must explore the "social dimensions of Darwin's writings on the biological and social evolution of women." When they do, they

> are unanimous in their categorization of them as . . . supporting a prejudiced and discriminatory view of women's abilities and potential. . . . The small section of the appropriately named *Descent of Man*, where Darwin deduced the natural and innate inferiority of women from his theory of evolution by natural and sexual selection, is fast becoming notorious in feminist literature (Richards 1983a, 59–60).

Conclusions and Implications

The Darwinian conclusion that women are inferior has had many major unfortunate historical social consequences. Sexual selection is believed to be critical in evolution, and among the data Darwin and his followers gathered to support the inferiority of women view, those supporting natural selection were critical (Mosedale 1978). Disproof of women's inferiority theory resulted from the fact that a major mechanism originally hypothesized to account for evolutionary advancement turned out to be erroneous. The data, although much more complete today, is similar to that that Darwin utilized to develop his theory, yet support radically different conclusions. This vividly demonstrates how important both preconceived ideas and theory are in interpreting data. The idea of women's evolutionary inferiority developed partly because measurement was then and now

> glorified as the essential basis of science: both anatomists and psychologists wanted above everything else to be "scientific." . . . Earlier psychological theory had been concerned with those mental operations common to the human race: the men of the nineteenth century were more concerned to describe human differences (Fee 1979, 419).

These human differences were not researched to understand (and help society overcome) them, but rather to justify a theory postulated to support a specific set of social beliefs. The implications of Darwinism cannot be ignored today, because the results of this belief have been tragic, especially in the area of racism, making for poor history of science to ignore the role of such baggage in Darwin's science. The time-worn image of the detached and objective observer and theoretician of Down House, remote from the social and political concerns of his fellow Victorians who misappropriated his scientific concepts to rationalize *their* imperialism, *laissez-faire* economics, racism and sexism, must now give way before the emerging historical man, whose writings were in many ways so congruent with his social and cultural milieu (Richards 1983, 887, emphasis added).

Hubbard et al., (1979) go even further and call Darwinism "blatant sexism" and place major responsibility for scientific sexism and its mate, social Darwinism, squarely at Darwin's door. Advancing knowledge has shown that social Darwinism is not only wrong, but tragically harmful and still adversely affects society today, such as in the modern form called sociobiology. Hubbard concluded that Darwin "provided the theoretical framework within which anthropologists and biologists have ever since been able to endorse the social inequality of the sexes" (Richards 1982a, 60). Consequently, "it is important to expose Darwin's androcentrocism," not only for historical reasons, but also because it "remains an integral and unquestioned part of contemporary biological theories" (Hubbard et al. 1979, 16).

The importance of male superiority is so critical that George states, "The male rivalry component of sexual selection was the key, Darwin believed, to the evolution of man" because Darwin taught "of all the causes which have led to the differences in external appearance between the races of man, and to a certain extent between man and the lower animals, sexual selection has been the most efficient" (1982, 136). A critical reason for Darwin's conclusion

Watercolor painting of Emma Darwin, 1840.

was his rejection of the Western belief that man and woman were specific creations made to complement each other. In contrast, Darwin believed the human races "were the equivalent of the varieties of plants and animals which formed the materials of evolution in the organic world generally," and the struggles that animals underwent to both survive and mate were the same means that originally formed the sexes and races (Richards 1983a, 64).

Having disregarded the traditional view, Darwin needed to replace it with another one, and the one he selected, the struggle for possession of females and food, resulted in males competing against other males. The idea that evolution favors the most vigorous and sexually aggressive males leads to the conclusion that these traits were selected because those males with them usually leave more progeny (Hubbard et al. 1979). Because Darwin used animals as models, Darwinists came to many clearly erroneous conclusions about humans (Rosser 1997, 22). Researchers now realize this approach is invalid for many reasons, including the fact that the degree of sexual dimorphism in modern *Homo sapiens* is less than in most animals and even less than in most primates (Zihlman 1997).

The modern equality of the sexes policy in both the United States and Europe, and the lack of support for the position of female biological inferiority, is a goal in considerable contrast to the conclusions derived from evolutionary biology in the middle and late 1800s (Montagu 1999). In the author's judgment, the history of these teachings is a clear illustration of the excesses to which Darwinism can lead (Phillips 1984).

References

Alaya, Flavia. 1977. "Victorian Science and the "Genius" of Women." *Journal of the History of Ideas* 38:261–280.

Beller, Anne Scott. 1977. *Fat & Thin; A Natural History of Obesity.* New York: McGraw Hill.

Bergman, Jerry. 1992. "Eugenics and the Development of Nazi Race Policy." *Perspectives on Science and Christian Faith,* June, 44(2):109–123.

Borgese, Elizabeth Mann. 1963. *Ascent of Women.* New York: Braziller.

Brent, Peter. 1981. *Charles Darwin: A Man of Enlarged Curiosity.* New York: Harper and Row.

Campbell, Bernard, editor. 1972. *Sexual Selection and the Descent of Man 1871–1971.* Chicago, IL: Aldine Publishing Company.

Chomsky, Noam. 1972. *Language and Mind.* New York: Harcourt, Brace and World.

Crook, John Hurrell. 1972. *Sexual Selection, Dimorphism, and Social Organization in the Primates,* in Campbell, editor.

Darwin, Charles. 1958. Nora Barlow, editor. *The Autobiography of Charles Darwin 1809–1882.* New York: W.W. Norton & Company, Inc.

————. 1959. *The Origin of Species by Means of Natural Selection.* London: John Murray.

————. 1871. *The Descent of Man, and Selection in Relation to Sex.* London: John Murray. 2 volumes.

————. 1896. *The Descent of Man, and Selection in Relation to Sex.* New York: D. Appleton and Company. Revised edition.

————. 1897. *The Origin of Species by Means of Natural Selection.* New York: D. Appleton and Company, 1897 edition.

————. 1985. (Frederick Burkhardt and Sydney Smith, editors). *The Correspondence of Charles Darwin. Volume 1: 1821–1836.* New York: Cambridge University Press.

Desmond, Adrian, and James Moore. 1991. *Darwin.* New York: Warner Books.

Durant, John R. 1985. "The Ascent of Nature in Darwin's *Descent of Man*" in *The Darwinian Heritage,* David Kohn, editor. Princeton, NJ: Princeton University Press.

Dyer, Gwynne. 1985. *War.* New York: Crown Publishers, Inc.

Eberhard, William G. 1985. *Sexual Selection and Animal Genitalia.* Cambridge, MA: Harvard University Press.

Ellis, Havelock. 1934. *Man and Women. A Study of Secondary and Tertiary Sexual Characteristics.* London: Heinemann.

Fee, Elizabeth. 1979. "Nineteenth-Century Craniology: The Study of the Female Skull." *Bulletin of the History of Medicine* 53:415–433.

Fisher, Elizabeth. 1979. *Woman's Creation; Sexual Evolution and the Shaping of Society.* Garden City, NY: Anchor Press/Doubleday.

Fisher, Helen E. 1982. *The Sex Contract; The Evolution of Human Behavior.* New York: William Morrow and Company, Inc.

Ford, Brian J. 1980. *Patterns of Sex; The Mating Urge and our Sexual Future.* New York: St. Martin's Press.

Fox, Robin. 1980. *The Red Lamp of Incest.* New York: E.P. Dutton.

Gamble, Eliza Burt. 1849. *Evolution of Women: An Inquiry Into the Dogma of Her Inferiority to Man.* London: Samuel French.

George, Wilma. 1982. *Darwin.* London: Fantana Paperbacks.

Ghiselin, Michael T. 1974. *The Economy of Nature and the Evolution of Sex.* Berkeley, CA: University of California Press.

Gibbons, Ann. 1991. "The Brain as 'Sexual Organ.' " *Science,* Aug. 30, 253:957–958.

Gilmore, David D. 2001. *Misogyny: The Male Malady.* Philadelphia, PA: University of Pennsylvania Press.

Goldberg, Steven. 1973. *The Inevitability of Patriarchy; Why the Biological Difference Between Men and Women Always Produces Male Domination.* New York: William Morrow & Company, Inc.

Gould, Stephen Jay. 1996. *The Mismeasure of Man.* New York: W.W. Norton & Company.

Hapgood, Fred. 1979. *Why Males Exist; An Inquiry Into the Evolution of Sex.* New York: William Morrow and Company, Inc.

Hardy, Sarah Blaffer. 1981. *The Woman That Never Evolved.* Cambridge, MA: Harvard University Press.

Hill, Mary A. 1980. *Charlotte Perkins Gilman. The Making of a Radical Feminist 1860–1896.* Philadelphia, PA: Temple University Press.

Hollingworth, L.S. 1914. "Variability as Related to Sex Differences in Achievement." *American Journal of Sociology* 19:510–530.

Hubbard, Ruth. 1979. "Have Only Men Evolved?" in *Women Look at Biology Looking at Women,* R. Hubbard et al. editors. p. 7–35, Intro, p. XV.

———, Mary Sue Henifin and Barbara Fried. 1979. *Women Look at Biology Looking at Women; A Collection of Feminist Critiques.* Cambridge, MA: Schenkman Publishing Co.

Hull, David. 1999. "Uncle Sam Wants You." A review of the book *Mystery of Mysteries: Is Evolution a Social Construction?* by Michael Ruse. *Science* 284:1131-1132.

Jensen, Arthur. 1980. *Bias in Mental Testing.* New York: Free Press.

Kevles, Bettyann. 1986. *Females of the Species; Sex and Survival in the Animal Kingdom.* Cambridge, MA: Harvard University Press.

Lewin, Roger. 1987. *Bones of Contention.* New York: Simon and Schuster.

Love, Rosaleen. 1983. *Darwinism and Feminism: The 'Women Question' in the Life and Work of Olive Schreiner and Charlotte Perkins Gilman,* p. 113–131.

Margulis, Lynn, and Dorion Sagan. 1986. *Origins of Sex; Three Billion Years of Genetic Recombination.* New Haven, CT: Yale University Press.

Martineau, Harriet. 1877. *Harriet Martineau's Autobiography.* Boston, MA: James R. Osgood and Co.; Reprinted in 1983. New York: Virago.

McGrigor, Allan J. 1869. "On the Real Differences in the Minds of Men and Women." *Journal of the Anthropological Society* 7:210.

Millman, Marcia. 1980. *Such a Pretty Face; Being Fat in America.* New York: W.W. Norton and Company.

Montagu, Ashley. 1952. *The Natural Superiority of Women.* New York: Lancer Books.

———. 1999. *The Natural Superiority of Women.* 5th edition. Walnut Creek, CA: Rowman and Littlefield.

Morgan, Elaine. 1972. *The Descent of Woman.* New York: Stein and Day.

Morris, Henry. 1989. *The Long War Against God.* Grand Rapids, MI: Baker Book House.

Mosedale, S. Sleeth. 1978. "Corrupted — Victorian Biologists Consider 'The Women Question.' " *Journal of the History of Biology* 9:1–55.

Phillips, John A. 1984. *Eve; The History of an Idea.* San Francisco, CA: Harper & Row Publishers.

Reed, Evelyn. 1975. *Woman's Evolution; From Matriarchal Clan to Patriarchal Family.* New York: Pathfinder Press.

Richards, Evelleen. 1983. "Will the Real Charles Darwin Please Stand Up?" *New Scientist,* Dec. 22/29, 100:884–887.

———. 1983a. "Darwin and the Descent of Women, in David Oldroyd and Ian Langham, editors. *The Wider Domain of Evolutionary Thought.* Holland: D. Reidel, p. 57–111.

Rosser, Sue V. 1992. *Biology and Feminism; A Dynamic Interaction.* New York: Twayne.

———. 1997. "Possible Implications of Feminists Theories for the Study of Evolution." *Feminism and Evolutionary Biology.* Edited by Patricia Adair Gowaty. New York: Chapman &Hall, p. 21–41.

Rushton, J.P., and C.O. Ankney. 1996. "Brain Size and Cognitive Ability; Correlations with Age, Sex, Social Class, and Race." *Psychonomic Bulletin Review,* 3(1):21–36.

Schluter, Dolph. 1992. "Brain Size Differences." *Nature* Sept. 17, 359:181.

Sherfey, Mary Jane. 1973. *The Nature & Evolution of Female Sexuality.* New York: Vintage Books.

Shields, Stephanie A. 1975. "Functionalism, Darwinism, and the Psychology of Women; A Study in Social Myth." *American Psychologist* 30(1):739–754.

Stein, George J. 1988. "Biological Science and the Roots of Nazism." *American Scientists,* Jan–Feb, 76:50–58.

Steinem, Gloria. 1992. *Revolution from Within; A Book of Self-Esteem.* Boston, MA: Little, Brown and Company.

Stephens, Lester D. 1976. "Evolution and Women's Rights in the 1890s: The views of Joseph LeConte." *The Historian* 38(2):239–252.

Symons, Donald. 1980. *The Evolution of Human Sexuality.* New York: Oxford University Press.

Tang-Martinez, Z. 1997. "The Curious Courtship of Sociobiology and Feminism: A Case of Irreconcilable Differences," in *Feminism and Evolutionary Biology; Boundaries, Intersections and Frontiers.* Patricia Growaty, editor. New York: Chapman and Hall, p. 117.

Tanner, Nancy, and Adrienne Zihlman. 1976. "Women in Evolution. Part I: Innovation and Selection in Human Origins." *Signs: Journal of Women in Culture and Society* 1(3)585–608.

Tavris, Carol. 1992. *The Mismeasure of Women; Why Women Are Not the Better Sex, the Inferior Sex, or the Opposite Sex.* New York: Simon and Schuster.

Thornhill, R., and N.W. Thornhill. 1992. "The Evolutionary Psychology of Men's Coercive Sexuality." *Behavioral & Brain Sciences* 15(2):363.

Van Valen, Leigh. 1974. "Brain Size and Intelligence in Man." *American Journal of Physical Anthropology* 40:417–423.

Vogt, Carl. 1864. *Lectures on Man: His Place in Creation, and the History of Earth.* James Hunt, editor. London: Paternoster Row, Longman, Green, Longman, and Roberts.

Williams, George C. 1977. *Sex and Evolution.* Princeton, NJ: Princeton University Press.

Zihlman, A. 1997. "Women's Bodies, Women's Lives: An Evolutionary Perspective," in *The Evolving Female A Life-History Perspective,* M. Morbek, A. Gallaway, and A. Zihlman, editors. Princeton, NJ: Princeton University Press.

Chapter 13

Darwinism's Critical Influence on Ruthless Capitalism

Introduction

Darwinism was critically important, not only in supporting the development and rise of Nazism and communism (and in producing the Nazi and communist holocausts), but also in allowing the rise of the many ruthless robber baron capitalists that flourished in the late 1800s and early 1900s (Morris and Morris 1996). Furthermore, Darwin has influenced not only economics, but also political science and all social sciences (Hsü 1986a, 1986b). Consequently, "All social scientists in the twenty-first century somehow have to settle their accounts with both Darwin and Marx" (Hodgson 2006, vii).

A review of the writings of the leading so-called "robber baron" capitalists reveals that many of them were significantly influenced by the Darwinian conclusion that the strong eventually will destroy the weak. Their faith in Darwinism helped them to justify this view as morally right. As a result, they concluded that their ruthless, and often illegal and even lethal, business practices were justified by science. They also concluded that the Darwinian concept of survival of the fittest is an inevitable part of the "unfolding of history" and consequently, for this reason, practicing ruthless capitalism was not immoral but was both moral and natural.

As Julian Huxley and H.B.D. Kittlewell concluded, social Darwinism has led to many evils, including "the glorification of free enterprise, *laissez faire* economics and war, to an unscientific eugenics and racism, and eventually to Hitler and Nazi ideology " (1965, 81). A major contributor to this extreme form of capitalism was the Darwinian belief that it is natural and proper to exploit without limits both "weaker" persons and businesses: the weaker businesses deserve to die off, and it is only natural that the stronger businesses prosper. The fact is,

> Social Darwinism permeated many aspects of American life in the last decades of the nineteenth century, but none so clearly and quickly as the business community. When Spencer died in 1903, at a time when ten thousand copies constituted a best seller, over 238,000 copies of his works had been sold. Social Darwinism was a congenial justification for the fierce business competition that saw monopolistic practices carried to the utmost, competition eliminated, and a few industrialists rise to a peak of power that was far greater than that of government or labor (Zubilka 1992, 30).

Many of the robber baron capitalists often concluded that, because survival of the fittest was an inevitable outcome of history, their behavior was justified by "natural law" (Josephson 1934). The result was a level of ruthless business practices that rose to the extent of justifying homicide. The robber barons' lack of concern for the social welfare of the community, and even their companies' own workers, adversely affected millions of lives. Injuries on the job due to unsafe working conditions were a major cause of death and permanent injury in the West for decades. Around 1900, the annual total of mortality (deaths) and morbidity (injury and illness) from industrial accidents was estimated to be a million workers (Hunter 1965).

Common Working Conditions in the 1800s

Conditions such as unguarded motor belt drives and power shafts were the norm in the 1800s and much of the 1900s. The result was the loss of fingers, hands, and even entire limbs. For workers, loss of body parts and severe injury were often almost an inevitable result of a lifetime of factory or industrial employment. Worker surveys revealed that over half sustained serious injuries, ranging from appendage loss to loss of vision or hearing during their careers. In some vocations, virtually every worker suffered injury — almost all stiff-brim hat manufacturing workers suffered from mercury poisoning, and almost all radium dial painter workers sooner or later were stricken by cancer (Stellman and Daum 1973).

Even when the employers were fully aware of the dangers their workers faced, most did little or nothing to improve the conditions of the work environment. Steel mill foundry workers often worked 12-hour shifts in 117°F heat for $1.25 a day (Bettmann 1974, 68). President Harrison noted in 1892 that the average American worker was subject to danger every bit as great as soldiers in war (Bettmann 1974, 70). Upton Sinclair immortalized the atrocious conditions in the meat packing industry in his now classic book, *The Jungle*, first published in 1906. *The Jungle* was widely considered a major catalyst motivating changes of labor laws, and it eventually was translated into 17 languages and millions of copies were sold. This book so moved Theodore Roosevelt that he worked tirelessly to reform business avarice. The result included the passage of a stream of important laws including the Pure Food and Drug Act.

Human lives were considered so expendable by many capitalists that, to cite one example, hundreds needlessly died laying railroad track (Zinn 1999, 255). Causes including poor living conditions provided by the railroad, poor working conditions, including excessive heat and cold, disease such as malaria spread by mosquitoes, and even inadequate protection from Indian attacks. An excellent example of this exploitation occurred when J.P. Morgan purchased 5,000 defective rifles for $3.50 each and sold them to the army for $22.00 each. The defect caused the rifle to occasionally shoot off the thumbs of users (Zinn 1999, 255). The victims sued, and a federal judge upheld the sale as legal and appropriate. In this case, as was common then, the courts usually sided with the robber barons (Bettmann 1974, 71).

Many judges were schooled in Darwinism and, for this reason, often also accepted the survival of the fittest ideology, concluding that the lives of common men and women were worth little. As one employer noted when asked to build roof protection for his workers, "Men are cheaper than shingles" (Bettmann 1974, 71). The ruthlessness of the capitalists was so extreme that eventually governments the world over passed hundreds of laws against these common practices. Laws against monopolies are only one example of a result of the corruption common during this era of American history.

From Christianity to Darwinism

Many of the robber barons were reared as theists but either had abandoned that belief or modified it to include Darwin's and Spencer's ideas about survival of the fittest. Like Stalin, Marx, Lenin, and Hitler, Carnegie also once professed a belief in Christianity but abandoned it for Darwinism. Carnegie stated in his autobiography that when he and several of his friends came to doubt the teachings of the Bible, "including the supernatural element, and indeed the whole scheme of salvation" he discovered

> Darwin's and Spencer's works. . . . I remember that light came as in a flood and all was clear. Not only had I got rid of theology and the supernatural, but I had found the truth of evolution. "All is well since all grows better" became my motto, my true source of comfort. Man was not created with an instinct for his own degradation, but from the lower he had risen to the higher forms. Nor is there any conceivable end to his march to perfection (1920, 327).

Carnegie was evidently first introduced to Darwinism by a group of "free and enlightened thinkers . . . seeking a new 'religion of humanity' " that met in the home of a New York University professor (Wall 1970, 364). Carnegie's conclusions were best summarized when he stated, "The law of competition, be it benign or not, is here; we cannot evade it . . . and while the law may be sometimes hard for the individual, it is best for the race, because it ensures the survival of the fittest in every department" (quoted in Hsü 1986a, 10). He soon became a close friend of the famous social Darwinist Herbert Spencer. Although Carnegie proclaimed himself a "Darwinist," he actually drew most of his inspiration from Herbert Spencer

> Spencer had sought to apply evolutionary thinking across a broad spectrum of political and social questions. "Before Spencer," Carnegie said repeatedly, "all for me had been darkness, after him, all had become light — and right" (Milner 1990, 72).

Spencer, not Darwin, was actually the originator of the phrase "survival of the fittest" and many ideas referred to as Darwinian were taken from the writings of Spencer (Laurent and Nightingale 2001, 21; Milner 1990, 72). Professor Asma observed that, although "Spencer coined the phrase *survival of the fittest*," Darwin adopted the parlance "in later editions of his *Origin of Species*:"

According to Spencer and his American disciples — business entrepreneurs like John D. Rockefeller and Andrew Carnegie — social hierarchy reflects the unwavering, universal laws of nature. Nature unfolds in such a way that the strong survive and the weak perish. Thus, the economic and social structures that survive are "stronger" and better, and those structures that don't were obviously meant to founder. It is *better* that capitalism has survived the Cold War just as it was better that the mammals survived the Mesozoic Era when dinosaurs became extinct. "How do we know that capitalism is better than Communism and the mammal is better

Depiction of commercial might versus divine right.

than the dinosaur? Because they survived, of course" (Asma 1993, 11, emphasis in original).

Standiford concluded that Carnegie found in his

> travels nothing but support for his conviction that survival of the fittest was not only the operating principle upon which the world order depended, but that Darwinism justified every action he would take in his own business life. The measuring stick was calibrated in dollars, and every tick that Carnegie marked off was a sign of progress toward the greater good (Standiford 2005, 50).

Standiford then documented Carnegie's ruthless Darwinian survival-of-the-fittest philosophy in great detail, applying it not only to his competition but also to his own employees.

Carnegie's Social Darwinism

Herbert Spencer (1820–1903) was one of Darwin's most prominent disciples. Spencer, a radical eugenicist and social Darwinist, concluded certain races were inferior and eventually would be "selected into extinction." He felt that the same things would happen to weaker individuals. Many of

Spencer's books were best sellers and often were used as college texts. They also influenced many of our nation's top business leaders. Carnegie,

> who practically worshipped Spencer, replaced his disenchanted Christian theology with the laissez-faire motto All is well since all grows better. . . . These capitalist moguls eagerly embraced a metaphysics that provided the ultimate justification for their ruthless business tactics (Asma 1993, 11).

Spencer's books and articles

> made him world famous by 1870 and, in America, his star rose higher than that of his countryman Charles Darwin. A very successful American magazine, the *Popular Science Monthly*, was founded . . . as a forum for Spencer's ideas. Industrialist Andrew Carnegie gave a dinner in his honor, [that was] attended by everybody who was anybody during the Gilded Age. Yet today, Spencer's works are unread, his name greeted by yawns and he is no hero even to philosophers or evolutionists. . . . Spencer . . . became best known for providing an ethical rationale for *laissez-faire* industrial capitalism. Although the idea became known as Social Darwinism, it was really Social Spencerism (Milner 1990, 415).

The problem was, Spencer concluded, that social evolution would eliminate the less fit or weaker individuals and businesses, and "rational men" should not interfere

> with the inexorable "laws" of evolution. The result, he believed, would be an evolved society that functioned smoothly and for the general good of its (future) members. Perpetual progress was the rule of evolution, with individual and social happiness its eventual goal (Milner 1990, 415).

Carnegie, once the richest man in the world, was the undisputed leader of the steel industry. The importance of both Carnegie to capitalism, and of Darwinism to Carnegie, was explained by Milner as follows:

> Carnegie rose in business to become a powerful, ruthless tycoon who exploited man and Earth, crushed competition, and justified his actions by a philosophy of Social Darwinism. Entrepreneurial competition, he believed, does a service to society by eliminating the weaker elements. Those who survive in business are "fit," and

therefore deserve their positions and rewards. Carnegie elevated the capitalist ethic to a law of nature (Milner 1990, 72).

From about 1870 onward, Carnegie "loudly trumpeted to the world — in public speeches, books, articles, in private conversations, and even in personal letters — his intellectual and spiritual indebtedness to Herbert Spencer" (Wall 1970, 381). In his publications and personal correspondence

> Carnegie makes frequent and easy allusions to the Social Darwinist credo. Phrases like "survival of the fittest," "race improvement," and "struggle for existence" came easily from his pen and presumably from his lips. He did see business as a great competitive struggle and he was always painfully aware of the weak who did not survive (Wall 1970, 389).

The Darwinian idea was held mostly by successful business entrepreneurs *after* they achieved success. The victims of unjust competition no doubt did not attribute their failures to their personal weakness or lack of fitness in the struggle of life (Wall 1970, 377). Although many modern evolutionists deplored the excess of social Darwinism, it nonetheless "became very popular among the laissez-faire capitalists of the 19th century because it did, indeed, seem to give scientific sanction to ruthless competition in both business and politics" (Morris and Morris 1996, 83).

Picture of Andrew Carnegie, William Jennings Bryan, and other businessmen of the day.

Many capitalists did not totally discard their belief in God but instead tried to blend it with Darwinism. The result was a compromise somewhat like theistic evolution. Most American businessmen probably were not consciously social Darwinists but tended to attribute their success to more lofty personal traits such as their intelligence, skill, industry, and virtue, rather than as a result of ruthlessly

> trampling on their less successful competitors. After all, most of them saw themselves as Christians, adhering to the rules of "love thy neighbor" and "do as you would be done by." So, even though they sought to achieve the impossible by serving God and Mammon simultaneously, they found no difficulty in accommodating Christianity to the Darwinian ideas of struggle for existence and survival of the fittest, and by no means all of them consciously thought of themselves as being in a state of economic warfare with their fellow manufacturers (Oldroyd 1980, 216).

John D. Rockefeller reportedly stated that the "growth of a large business is merely a survival of the fittest . . . the working out of a law of nature" (Ghent 1902, 29). The Rockefellers, while maintaining a Christian front, fully embraced evolution and dismissed Genesis as mythology (Taylor 1991, 386). When a philanthropist pledged $10,000 to help found a university to be named after William Jennings Bryan, John D. Rockefeller Jr. retaliated the very same day with a $1,000,000 donation to the openly anti-creationist University of Chicago Divinity School (Larson 1997, 183).

The philosophy expressed by Carnegie was embraced not only by Rockefeller and railroad magnates such as James Hill, but also by most other capitalists of their day (Morris and Morris 1996, 87). Even "Henry Ford, America's preeminent capitalist . . . found in Darwinism the perfect rationale for the free-enterprise system" (Levine and Miller 1994, 161). The marriage of Darwinism and capitalism is best expressed by an incident that occurred on Spencer's way back to England from a trip to America:

> However imperfect the appreciation of the guests for the niceties of Spencer's thought, the banquet showed how popular he had become in the United States. When Spencer was on the dock, waiting for the ship to carry him back to England, he seized the hands of Carnegie and Youmans. "Here," he cried to reporters, "are my two best American friends." For Spencer it was a rare gesture of personal warmth; but more than this, it symbolized the harmony of the new

science [of social Darwinism] with the outlook of a business civilization (Hofstadter 1955, 49).

Spencer's ideas also had clear implications in other areas, as well. The late Isaac Asimov noted that Darwinism can be used to justify ignoring normal social responsibility to the unemployed or needy:

> This view seemed to be made "scientific" by the works of the English sociologist Herbert Spencer, who applied the views of evolution, first elaborated by the English naturalist Charles Robert Darwin, in 1859, to society. . . . Spencer coined the phrase "survival of the fittest" and in 1884 argued, for instance, that people who were unemployable or burdens on society should be allowed to die rather than be made objects of help and charity. To do this, apparently, would weed out unfit individuals and strengthen the race. It was a horrible philosophy that could be used to justify the worst impulses of human beings (1977, 94).

Darwinism Inspired Both Communism and Arch-capitalism

It is well documented that Darwinism inspired not only Hitler but also Stalin and Lenin. That evolution inspired both communists and arch-capitalists is not as surprising as it may first appear. Both openly opposed the core values of Christianity and were only on different sides of the so-called "class struggle" that was believed to be an inevitable part of history (Perloff 1999, 226). Both the left wing Marxist-Leninism and the right wing ruthless capitalists were anti-creationists and "even when they fight with each other, they remain united in opposition to creationism" (Morris and Morris 1996, 82).

Shortly after Darwin published his landmark *Origin of Species* in 1859, "the survival of the fittest" theory in biology was interpreted by capitalists as "an ethical precept that sanctioned cutthroat economic competition" (Rachels 1990, 63; see also Hsü 1986a, 10). Millionaire Houston oilman Michel Halbouty, who was typical of the robber barons, justified his ruthless exploits by reasoning, "As in nature, the principle of survival of the fittest will prevail" (quoted in Olien and Olien 1984, 113). Historian Gertrude Himmelfarb noted that Darwinism was rapidly accepted in England but was resisted for decades in France, in part because it justified the greed of the robber barons:

> The theory of natural selection, it is said, could only have originated in England, because only laissez-faire England provided the atomistic, egotistic mentality necessary to its conception. Only there could

Darwin have blandly assumed that the basic unit was the individual, the basic instinct self-interest, and the basic activity struggle. Spengler, describing the *Origin* as "the application of economics to biology," said that it reeked of the atmosphere of the English factory . . . natural selection arose . . . in England because it was a perfect expression of Victorian "greed-philosophy," of the capitalist ethic and Manchester economics (1962, 418).

Furthermore, many recognized that Darwinian ideas, although based "more on the writings of Herbert Spencer than of Charles Darwin," implied approval for cutthroat business practices and "its proponents urged *laissez-faire* economic policies to weed out the unfit, inefficient and incompetent" (Milner 1990, 412).

Americans associated Darwinian natural selection, as it applied to people, with a survival-of-the-fittest mentality that justified laissez-fair capitalism, imperialism, and militarism. Decades before . . . [Bryan's] crusade [against the teaching of Darwinism in the schools], for example, Andrew Carnegie and John D. Rockefeller Sr., claimed this as justification for their cutthroat business practices (Larson 1997, 27).

As Colson and Pearcey note, "Today we are appalled at such a crass attitude, and rightly so" (1994, 106).

Use of Darwinism to Justify Ruthless Capitalism

One of social Darwinism's leading spokesmen was Princeton University Professor William Graham Sumner, who concluded that millionaires were the "fittest" individuals in society, and therefore

deserved their privileges. They were "naturally selected in the crucible of competition." Andrew Carnegie and John D. Rockefeller agreed and espoused similar philosophies they thought gave a "scientific" justification for the excesses of industrial capitalism (Milner 1990, 412).

Many other prominent professors in addition to Herbert Spencer supported the application of the "survival of the fittest" philosophy to society. Leading sociologists including Cooley, Sorokin, Sumner, Ross, and even Park all adhered to biological racist doctrines that justified and even encouraged survival of the fittest social policy (Rosenthal 1977).

Historically, theories that behavior was largely genetic have had the effect of promoting an attitude of acceptance toward radical capitalism, racism, sexism, and even war (Rosenthal 1997). Rosenthal noted that this was true even though no scientific evidence exists that human social behavior at its basis is biogenetic or that business/social competition, male dominance, aggression, territoriality, xenophobia, and even patriotism, warfare, and genocide are genetically based human universals (Rosenthal 1977).

Nonetheless, biogenetic doctrines occupied a prominent place throughout most of American sociological academic history. The concept of "struggle for existence" meant for many capitalists ruthlessly destroying what they regarded as their weaker, less-worthy competition. Doing so was merely a result of the omnipresent "survival of the fittest" law that operated not only in nature, but also in every other sphere of life including business. In Carnegie's words: "While the [survival of the fittest] law may sometimes be hard for the individual, *it is best for the race*, because it ensures the survival of the fittest in every department" including business (1920, 327, emphasis mine). Many Darwinians concluded that to survive, a business *must* follow the laws of Darwinism. To ignore Darwin's laws could lead to extinction, just as occurs in the biological world.

Although many robber barons gave away large sums of money, their Darwinian ideas even affected them in this area. Carnegie gave away $125 million from 1887 to 1907 alone, but "none of it went for the direct relief of the unfortunate classes. As a good Darwinian, he saw no reason for trying to save the unfit. . . . Throwing money into the sea was more preferable" (Wyllie 1954, 92). The robber barons did not see Darwinism as necessarily a negative force, but in the words of the president of Clark University, G. Stanley Hall:

> Nothing so reinforces optimism as evolution. It is the best, or at any rate not the worst, that survive. Development is upward, creative, and not de-creative. From cosmic gas onward there is progress, advancement, and improvement (1928, 546).

An analysis of the Anthracite Coal Strike Commission (1902/03) hearings found "the coal trust preached a social Darwinist ideology, conflating 'survival of the fittest' with freedom and individual rights" (Doukas 1997, 367). This study concluded that "the popularity of social Darwinism in the U.S. national ideology should be comprehended as an innovation of corporate capitalism" (Doukas 1997, 367).

Darwinian Ideas Persist in Business Even Today

As the title of one book indicates, *Business Darwinism: Evolve or Dissolve*, the application of Darwinian concepts to business is still very much with us today (Marks 2002). The Enron case may be the most famous example but only touches the surface of this problem and the tendency to advocate this philosophy (for example see Catt 1971). One of many possible examples is the manner in which Robert Blake and his coauthors openly applied modern Darwinism in their best seller titled *Corporate Darwinism*. The authors concluded that business evolves, grows, and expands in very predictable ways, specifically in defined stages — very much like the stages of human evolution (1966).

In keeping with Darwinian principles, natural "business evolution" means either swallow the competition or you will be swallowed by them. The authors also argued that Darwinism applies best to corporations rather than individuals. An academic study by Hodgson also argues that the application of Darwinism is central to developing a viable modern economic theory (2006).

A study by Laurent and Nightingale concluded that Darwinian evolution "is the best model we have" to understand, not just the natural world, but also the social and economic worlds (2001, 5–6). Economics and Darwinian theory have had "close, if not always comfortable, association . . . since the very formation of Darwin's theory" (2001, 15).

Another popular book is Richard Koch's 2001 best seller *The Natural Laws of Business; How to Harness the Power of Evolution, Physics, and Economics to Achieve Business Success*. A whole branch of economics called "evolutionary economics" now exists. They published at least two books and the journal *Evolutionary Economics*. One of the most influential evolutionary economists was Alfred Marshal, and he and his most famous student, John Maynard Keynes, were both highly influenced by Darwin and also by eugenics (Groenewegen 2001; Laurent 2001).

In a history of the Texas oil industry, Olien and Olien noted that even after World War II, many independent oilmen still believed that their economic success depended on the Darwinian struggle of the fittest philosophy (1984, 113). Yale Professor David Gelernter quoted former Microsoft executive Rob Glaser, who concluded that the world's richest man, Bill Gates, is "relentless, Darwinian. Success is defined as flattening the competition, not creating excellence." (1998, 202).

A major response to the excess of capitalism justified by Darwinism is that Darwin's ideas were *misapplied* to economics. However, Darwin himself "believed that his biological theory lent support to individualist economic competition and laissez-faire economics" (Weikart 1995, 609).

Conclusions

Darwinism played a critical role in the development and growth not only of Nazism and communism, but also of the ruthless form of capitalism best illustrated by the 19th- and 20th-century robber barons. While it is difficult to confidently conclude that ruthless capitalism would not have blossomed as much as it did if Darwin had not developed his evolutionary theory, one thing is clear: if Carnegie, Rockefeller, and the many other ruthless capitalists had continued to embrace the unadulterated Judeo-Christian worldview of their youth rather than becoming Darwinians, capitalism would not have become as inhumane as it did in the late 1800s and early 1900s.

No doubt, other motivations, including greed and ambition, were also factors in the ruthlessness of the robber barons (Wyllie 1959). Many were inclined to claim that their successes were due to hard work, intelligence, thrift, and sobriety (Wall 1970, 379). Their lives, though, often told other stories. Darwinism, however, provided many capitalists with what appeared to be a scientific rationale that allowed capitalism to be carried to the extremes that were so common in the early parts of the last century (Morris and Morris 1996, 84; Hofstadtler 1955). In the words of Wall, the

> proto-tycoons of American industrialism apparently had no more need for a knowledge of Spencerian theory than did beasts of prey in the jungle, nevertheless it has been generally accepted that they, like their predatory counterparts, acted out in their daily lives the stern dicta of Darwinian evolution. The weaker were devoured, the fittest survived, and American industry and consequently American society benefited from this competitive struggle for existence (1977, 376).

The harm that resulted from the application of Darwinism to business was a major motivator of William Jennings Bryan in his campaign to counteract the spread of Darwinism. Larson noted that Bryan "built his political career on denouncing the excesses of capitalism and militarism" and "dismissed Darwinism in 1904 as 'the merciless law by which the strong crowd out and kill off the weak' " (1997, 27). History has shown Bryan's concern was fully justified. History also has shown that for many industrialists, Darwinism became their religion. Professor Wall provided an excellent example:

> Progress through evolution, both biological and technological,

bringing nature and man, "the machine and the garden," toward perfect harmony — this was to be the essence of Carnegie's faith in the ultimate perfectibility of the universe, and he would hold to that faith for the next thirty-five years (Wall 1977, 366).

For Carnegie, Spencer became a god. In Carnegie's own words, Spencer was "the greatest mind of his age or any other." And in Spencer's "ponderous volumes . . . lay the final essence of all truth and knowledge" (Wall 1970, 390). Christianity, on the other hand, advocated behavior quite in contrast to Darwinism. The Bible

> preached no warfare of each against all, but rather a warfare of each man against his baser self. The problem of success was not that of grinding down one's competitors, but of elevating one's self — and the two were not equivalent. Opportunities for success, like opportunities for salvations, were limitless; heaven could receive as many as were worthy. Such a conception of the economic heaven differed from the Malthusian notion that chances were so limited that one man's rise meant the fall of many others. It was this more optimistic view, that every triumph opened the way for more, which dominated the outlook of men who wrote handbooks of self-help (Wyllie 1954, 83–84).

If the robber barons had lived consistently by Wyllie's summary of Christianity, the abuses common in the 19th century likely never would have occurred. In the words of Colson and Pearcey, the "robber barons of industry didn't appeal to *Christianity* to justify their cutthroat tactics. They appealed to evolution" (1994, 106, emphasis added).

Summary

The writings of Darwinists helped to justify not only the murderous exploits of the Nazis and communists, but also the ruthless practices of capitalist monopolists such as Carnegie and Rockefeller.

> Darwinism was also used in a defense of competitive individualism and its economic corollary of laissez-faire capitalism in England and in America. Andrew Carnegie wrote that "the law of competition, be it benign or not, is here; we cannot evade it." Rockefeller went a step further . . . (Hsü 1986b, 534).

In short

> Gilded Age industrialists such as Andrew Carnegie, John D. Rocke-
> feller, and James J. Hill publicly and very bluntly justified their cut-
> throat business practices in social Darwinist terms. They said that
> what they were doing was right, and this [Darwinism survival of
> the fittest law] was why it was right. Sure, there were some losers in
> these business practices, and then there were the winners. . . . they
> happened to be the winners, and it was because they were the most
> fit. Ultimately, it was not to their benefit; ultimately, it was to the
> benefit of society (Larson 2002, 125).

The important contribution of Darwinism, especially as developed by Spencer to *laissez-faire* capitalism, is well documented.

References

Asimov, Isaac. 1977. *The Golden Door: The United States from 1876 to 1918.* Boston, MA: Houston Mifflin Company.

Asma, Stephen T. 1993. "The New Social Darwinism: Deserving Your Destitution." *The Humanist* 53(5):11.

Bettmann, Otto. 1974. *The Good Old Days — They Were Terrible!* New York: Random House.

Blake, Robert R., Warren Avis, and Jane Mouton. 1966. *Corporate Darwinism — An Evolutionary
Perspective on Organization Work in the Dynamic Corporation.* Houston, TX: Gulf Publishing.

Carnegie, Andrew. 1920. *Autobiography of Andrew Carnegie.* John C. Van Dyke, editor. 1986
reprint, Boston, MA: Northeastern University Press.

Catt, Ivor. 1971. *The Catt Concept: The New Industrial Darwinism.* New York: Putnam.

Colson, Charles, and Nancy Pearcey. 1994. *A Dangerous Grace.* Dallas, TX. Word

Doukas, Dimitra. 1997. "Corporate Capitalism on Trial: The Hearings of the Anthracite Coal Strike
Commission, 1902–1903." *Identities: Global Studies in Culture and Power* 3(3):367–398.

Gelernter, David. 1998. "Bill Gates." *Time Magazine* 152(23):201–205.

Ghent, William. 1902. *Our Benevolent Feudalism.* New York: Macmillan.

Groenewegen, Peter. 2001. "The Evolutionary Economics of Alfred Marshall: An Overview," in
Laurent and Nightingale, p. 49–61.

Hall, G. Stanley. 1928. *Adolescence and Its Psychology.* New York: D. Appleton.

Himmelfarb, Gertrude. 1962. *Darwin and the Darwinian Revolution.* New York: W.W. Norton.

Hodgson, Geoffrey. 2006. *Economics in the Shadows of Darwin and Marx.* Northhamton, MA:
Edward Elgar.

Hofstadter, Richard. 1955. *Social Darwinism in American Thought.* Boston, MA: Beacon.

Hunter, Robert. 1965. *Poverty.* New York: Torchbooks.

Hsü, Kenneth. 1986a. *The Great Dying; Cosmic Catastrophe, Dinosaurs and the Theory of Evolution.*
New York: Harcourt, Brace, Jovanovich.

————. 1986b. "Darwin's Three Mistakes." *Geology,* June, 14:532–534.

Huxley, Julian, and H.B.D. Kittlewell. 1965. *Charles Darwin and His World.* New York: Viking.

Josephson, Matthew. 1934. *The Robber Barons.* New York: Harcourt and Brace.

Koch, Richard. 2001.*The Natural Laws of Business; How to Harness the Power of Evolution, Physics, and Economics to Achieve Business Success.* New York, NY: Currency/Doubleday.

Larson, Edward J. 1997. *Summer for the Gods: The Scopes Trial and America's Continuing Debate Over Science and Religion.* New York: Basic Books.

————. 2002. *The Theory of Evolution: A History of Controversy.* Chantilly, VA: The Teaching Company.

Laurent, John. 2001. "Keynes and Darwinism." Chapter 5 in Laurent and Nightingale.

————, and John Nightingale. 2001. *Darwinism and Evolutionary Economics.* Northampton, MA: Edward Elgar.

Levine, Joseph, and Kenneth Miller. 1994. *Biology: Discovering Life.* Lexington, MA: D.C. Heath.

Marks, Eric A. 2002. *Business Darwinism: Evolve or Dissolve: Adaptive Strategies for the Information Age.* Chichester, England: John Wiley & Sons.

Milner, Richard. 1990. *The Encyclopedia of Evolution.* New York: Facts on File.

Morris, Henry, and John D. Morris. 1996. *The Modern Creation Trilogy. Vol. 3. Society and Creation.* Green Forrest, AR: Master Books.

Oldroyd, D.R. 1980. *Darwinian Impacts.* Atlantic Highlands, NJ: Humanities Press.

Olien, Roger M., and Diana Davids Olien. 1984. *Wildcatters: Texas Independent Oilmen.* Austin, TX: Texas Monthly Press.

Perloff, James. 1999. *Tornado in a Junkyard.* Arlington, MA: Refuge Books.

Rachels, James. 1990. *Created from Animals: The Moral Implications of Darwinism.* New York: Oxford University Press.

Rosenthal, Steven J. 1977. "Sociobiology: New Synthesis or Old Ideology?" Paper presented at the 1977 American Sociological Association Convention.

Sinclair, Upton. 1906. *The Jungle.* New York. Doubleday, Page & Company.

Standiford, Les. 2005. *Meet You in Hell.* New York: Three Rivers Press.

Stellman, Jeanne, and Susan Daum. 1973. *Work Is Dangerous to Your Health.* New York: Random House Vintage Books.

Taylor, Ian T. 1991. *In the Minds of Men: Darwin and the New World Order.* Minneapolis, MN: TFE Publishing.

Wall, Joseph F. 1970. *Andrew Carnegie.* New York: Oxford University Press.

Weikart, Richard. 1995. "A Recently Discovered Darwin Letter on Social Darwinism." *Isis* 86:609–611.

Wyllie, Irvin. 1954. *The Self-Made Man in America.* New Brunswick, NJ: Rutgers University Press.

————. 1959. "Social Darwinism and the Businessman." *Proceedings of the American Philosophical Society,* 103(5):629–640.

Zinn, Howard. 1999. *A People's History of the United States.* New York: Harper Collins.

Zubilka, Ivan L. 1992. *Scientific Malpractice: The Creation Evolution Debate.* Lexington, KY: Bristol Books.

Chapter 14

The Darwinian Foundation of the Communist Holocaust

Introduction

A review of the writings of communism's founders and leaders document that naturalistic evolution theory, especially as popularized by Darwin, was critically important in the development of modern communism. Many of the central architects of communism, including Stalin, Lenin, Marx, Mao, and Engels accepted the worldview portrayed in the book of Genesis until they were introduced to Darwin and other contemporary evolutionary thinkers, which ultimately resulted in their abandoning that worldview and becoming atheists and Darwinists (Engels 1876; Halstead 1980; Young 1982).

Darwinism also was critically important in their conversion to communism and to a worldview that led them to a philosophy based on atheism. The claim that the horrible events in the USSR were unrelated to the atheism of Marx and Lenin is false. An example is Article 124 of the USSR

Constitution that says, "In order to ensure citizen's freedom of conscience, the church in the USSR is separated from the state, and the school from the church. Freedom of religious worship and freedom of antireligious propaganda is recognized for all citizens." The phrase "freedom of antireligious propaganda" allows anyone to attack theism with abandon and that is what happened in Soviet schools and universities. They actually set up departments of atheism to make sure it was a significant part of the academic curriculum.

The phrase "separation of church and state" does not appear in the American Constitution, although the First Amendment says, "Congress shall make no law respecting an establishment of religion or prohibiting the free exercise thereof." The persecuted faiths in colonial America were very concerned about the civil government's favoritism concerning particular Christian denominations, as was the case in Europe. Many wanted to keep the state out of the Church. To reassure them that the Church would have full religious freedom, in 1802 President Thomas Jefferson wrote a letter to the Danbury Connecticut Baptist Association assuring them that the First Amendment protected the American people by erecting a "wall of separation between church and state" to keep the state from interfering with the church.

Darwinism also has had a profoundly adverse effect on the morals and behavior of these central architects of communism (Rachels 1990; Oldroyd 1980; Lenczowski 1996; Ruse 1986). An example is that a core communist idea is violent revolution in which the strong overthrow the weak. This worldview was a natural and inevitable part of the unfolding of history that came from Darwinistic concepts and conclusions.

Darwinism as a worldview was a critical factor not only in influencing the development of Nazism, but also in the rise of the communist Holocaust that, by one estimate, took the lives of almost 200 million persons (Courtois et al. 1999, 4; Azar 1990). As Morris notes:

> both Marx and Hitler, with all their respective forebears, associates and successors, were doctrinaire evolutionists, trying to build their respective societies on evolutionary premises. There is abundant documentation of this assessment and, in fact, few would even question it (1997, 419).

Evolution was not a minor aspect, but rather a "central plank in Marxist doctrine." The communists were convinced that evolution from molecules to man had taken place, that all biology had evolved spontaneously upward, and that in-between links (or less evolved types) should be actively eradicated. They believed that natural selection could and should be actively *aided*, and therefore instituted political measures to eradicate . . . [those] whom they considered as "underdeveloped" (Wilder-Smith 1982, 27, italics in original).

For very good reasons, "for nearly a century the names of Karl Marx and Charles Darwin have been linked in an apparently indissoluble union" (Ball 1979, 469). As John Spargo wrote in the late 1960s, Karl Marx said, "Nothing ever gives me greater pleasure than to have my name linked onto Darwin's. His wonderful work makes my own absolutely impregnable. Darwin may not know it, but he belongs to the Social [communist] Revolution" (quoted in Weikart 1999, 15).

Many communist leaders consider Marx and Darwin "the two most revolutionary and influential thinkers of the nineteenth century" (Wheen 1999, 362). Furthermore, Marx and Darwin lived "only twenty miles apart for most of their adult lives, and had several acquaintances in common" (Wheen 1999, 312). The "marriage of the evolutionists and the revolutionists" was not made in heaven but, it turned out, was made in hell. Stalin said that "neo-Darwinism . . . evolution prepares for [communist] revolution and creates the ground for it; revolution consummates the process of evolution and facilitates its further activity . . . Marxism rests on Darwinism and treats it uncritically" (1954, 1, 304, 310).

Many extremist reformers were active before Darwin published his seminal work, *The Origin of Species*, in 1859. However, since religious faith prevailed among both scientists and nonscientists before Darwin, it was very difficult for these radicals to persuade the masses to accept communistic or other radical leftist ideologies. Partly for this reason, Western nations blocked the development of most radical movements for centuries. Darwin, however, opened the door to Marxism by providing what Marx believed was a "scientific" rationale to deny creationism and, by extension, to deny God's existence (Perloff 1999, 244).

The Founder of Communism, Karl Marx, Discovers Darwin

Marx was baptized a Lutheran in 1824, attended a Lutheran elementary school, received praise for his "earnest" essays "on moral and religious topics," and was judged by his teachers to be "moderately proficient" in theology. His first written work, titled *The Union of the Faithful with Christ,* was a treatise on the "love of Christ" (Berlin 1959, 31; Wurmbrand 1986, 11). He remained a committed Christian until the time he encountered the materialist and atheistic writings and ideas at the University of Berlin as a student from 1836 to 1841 (Koster 1989, 163).

Marx's denial of God and his conversion to Darwinism were both critical in the development of his godless worldview now known as communism. And, like all Darwinists, Marx stressed that his communistic worldview was "scientific" and, as such, employed a "scientific methodology and scientific outlook" (Kolman 1931, 705). Marx admired Darwin's book,

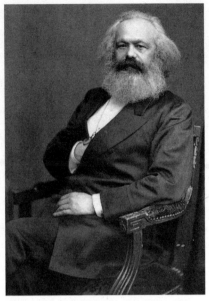

A portrait of Karl Marx, circa 1875.

> not for economic reasons but for the more fundamental one that Darwin's universe was purely materialistic, and the explication of it no longer involved any reference to unobservable, nonmaterial causes outside or "beyond" it. In that important respect, Darwin and Marx were truly comrades (Bethell 1978, 37).

Both Marx and Engels were convinced that Darwin had "delivered the mortal blow to teleology in natural science by providing a rational explanation of functional adaptation in living things and by proving his explanation empirically. On the most general level, they welcomed Darwin's [theory]" (Joravsky 1961, 12). Perloff, as a former leftist atheist, studied communism and concluded that "evolution and Marxism go hand in hand" (1999, 244). Marx's coauthor of his communism theory, Frederick Engels, also believed that Darwinian ideas were a critical part of the communist worldview. Engles wrote to Marx in 1859 informing him that he was then reading Darwin's 1959 book, writing it was "absolutely splendid. . . . Never before has so grandiose an attempt been made to demonstrate historical evolution in Nature, and certainly never to such good effect" in understanding humans (quoted in Patterson 2009, 87). Historian Chris Talbot remarked that "throughout their lives they [both Marx and Engles] insisted on the importance of Darwin's work" (2012, 1).

Karl Marx Comes Under the Spell of Darwinism

Karl Marx (1818–1883) wrote tirelessly until he died, producing hundreds of books, monographs, and articles. Marx historian Isaiah Berlin even claimed that no thinker "in the nineteenth century has had so direct, deliberate and powerful an influence upon mankind as Karl Marx" (1959, 1). Both Hitler and Marx saw the living world in terms of a Darwinian "survival of the fittest" struggle involving the triumph of the strong and the subjugation of the weak (Pannekoek 1912; Joravsky 1961). Darwin taught that the "struggle of the fittest" existed among all forms of life, including humans. Hitler concluded from this idea that the major "struggle for existence" among humans occurred primarily between the races, but Marx believed that the major struggle was between the social classes. Marx believed his own work to be the exact parallel of Darwin's, and

> like Darwin, Marx thought he had discovered the law of development. He saw history in stages, as the Darwinists saw geological strata and successive forms of life . . . both Marx and Darwin made struggle the means of development. Again, the measure of value in Darwin is survival with reproduction — an absolute fact occurring in time and which wholly disregards the moral or aesthetic quality of the product. In Marx the measure of value is expended labor — an absolute fact occurring in time, which also disregards the utility of the product. Both Darwin and Marx [also] tended to hedge and modify their mechanical absolution in the face of objections (Barzun 1958, 170).

Even though they applied Darwinism to different groups, both Hitler and Marx owed a major debt to Darwin for their central ideas. *The Origin* had impressed Marx more than most books and "perhaps as deeply as any book he read in his maturity" (Colp 1972, 332). In Marx's words: "Darwin's book is very important and serves me as a basis in natural selection for the class struggle in history . . . not only is it [Darwin's book] a death blow . . . to 'Teleology' in the natural sciences but their rational meaning is empirically explained" (Zirkle 1959, 86).

Marx first read Darwin's *The Origin of Species* a year after its publication. He was so enthusiastic about the book that he reread it two years later (Colp 1972, 329). Marx thought so much of Darwin that he sent a copy of *Das Kapital* (first published in 1867) to Darwin. In it, Marx describes himself as a "sincere admirer" of Darwin (Gould 1974, 70). Furthermore, "Marx himself viewed Darwin's work as confirmation by the natural sciences of his own views" (Stein 1988, 52).

Other lines of evidence support the conclusion that Darwin's ideas were very influential in Marx's overall conclusions and especially in the historical sections of *Das Kapital*. The evidence for this includes the fact that Marx cited Darwin twice in *Das Kapital*. In 1862, Marx attended a series of six lectures by Thomas Huxley on Darwin's ideas and spoke of "nothing else for months but Darwin and the enormous significance of his scientific discoveries" (Colp 1972, 329–330). Marxists, communists, and socialists today are proud of the role Marx played in propagating Darwinism. Biologist and Marxist J.D. Bernal noted that Marx was one of the first intellectuals

> to accept the evolutionary ideas which, although then suspect, were, thanks to Darwin, to become dominant in the latter part of the nineteenth century. His appreciation of Darwin's *Origin of Species* was immediate though not uncritical. . . . Since that time the idea of evolution, with changes more sudden than Darwin imagined, has spread beyond the world of organism to the earth and the whole universe. In the light of recent discoveries scientists are now more willing to accept the phenomena of nature as *processes* not things given or created. Intellectually, therefore, Marx who saw it all over a hundred years ago, stands revealed as a mind of the first calibre. Nevertheless if he had restricted himself to founding a materialist historical worldview, humanity would have missed something much greater than any intellectual construction (1952, 12–20).

According to a close associate of Marx, Marx was also one of the first major thinkers

> to grasp the significance of Darwin's research. Even before 1859, the year of the publication of *The Origin of the Species* — and, by a remarkable coincidence, of Marx's *Contribution to the Critique of Political Economy* — Marx realized Darwin's epoch-making importance. For Darwin . . . was preparing a revolution similar to the one which Marx himself was working for. . . . Marx kept up with every new appearance and noted every step forward, especially in the fields of natural sciences (Liebknecht 1968, 106).

After Marx became a Darwinist, he passionately detested any "belief in supernatural causes" (Berlin 1959, 30). He also openly denounced all religion as "the opiate of the people," and in nearly every nation where the communists assumed power the churches were either abolished outright, or neutralized.

Darwin and Marx were two of the four men most responsible for producing many of the most significant events of the 20th century (Hyman 1966). Marx was "infatuated" with Darwin, and Darwin's ideas had a major influence not only on him and Engels, but also on both Lenin and Stalin. Furthermore, these men's writings frequently discussed Darwin's ideas (Heyer 1975). Marx and Engels "enthusiastically embraced" Darwinism, kept up with Darwin's writings, and often corresponded with each other (and others) about their reactions to Darwin's conclusions (Conner 1980, 4; Heyer 1975; Marx and Engels 1936). The communists recognized the importance of Darwin

Russian revolutionary and politician, Vladimir Lenin, 1920.

to their movement and, therefore, vigorously defended Darwin:

> The socialist movement recognized Darwinism as an important element in its general world outlook right from the start. When Darwin published his *Origin of Species* in 1859, Karl Marx wrote a letter to Frederick Engels in which he said, ". . . this is the book which contains the basis in natural history for our view." . . . And of all those eminent researchers of the nineteenth century who have left us such a rich heritage of knowledge, we are especially grateful to Charles Darwin for opening our way to an evolutionary, dialectical understanding of nature (Conner 1980, 12, 18).

Did Marx send the Galley proofs of *Das Kapital* to Darwin?

It was widely believed that Marx sent the galley proofs of his magnum opus, *Das Kapital*, to Darwin and offered to dedicate it to him. It also was assumed that Darwin declined, fearing that such an act "might cause some members of my family [embarrassment] if in any way I lent my support to direct attacks on religion" (quoted in Keith 1955, 234; original quote in the Marx-Engels Institute, Moscow). Further research indicates that it actually was not Karl Marx that sent the letter to Darwin, but the husband of Eleanor Marx, Edward Aveling (Wheen 1999, 366–367). The book sent to Darwin was not *Das Kapital,* which was already published when the letter was sent, but *The Student's Darwin,* which was part of a series edited by "crusading atheists."

This finding helps us to understand Darwin's letter and why he felt endorsing an atheist book would embarrass his family. The mix-up was partly due to the fact that the "crusading atheist," Mr. Aveling, filed the letter in the folder that contained letters from his "two heroes," Marx and Darwin. This incident clearly reveals that a close association of Darwin and Marx was seen by many communists, and for this reason the account commonly is found in works about Marx. Marx did send a copy of *Das Kapital* to Darwin, and it is still in Darwin's Down House home (Colp 1972, 333). Darwin wrote back that he was "honoured" to receive a copy of Marx's "great work."

The Darwin-Marx association also was reflected when prominent communist Friedrich Lessner concluded that *Das Kapital* and Darwin's *The Origin of Species* were the "two greatest scientific creations of the century" (1968, 109). The importance of Darwinism in the estimated 140 million deaths caused by communism was partly because "for Marx man has no 'nature.' . . . For man is his own maker . . . in complete freedom from morality or from the laws of nature and of nature's God. . . . Here we see why Marxism justifies the ruthless sacrifice of men living today, men who, at this stage of history, are only partly human" (Eidelberg 1984, 10). Halstead adds that the theoretical foundation of communism

> is dialectical materialism which was expounded with great clarity by Frederick Engels in *Anti-Dühründ* and *The Dialectics of Nature.* He recognized the great value of the contributions made by geology in establishing that there was constant movement and change in nature and the significance of Darwin's demonstration that this applied also to the organic world. . . . The crux of the entire theoretical framework, however, is in the nature of qualitative changes. This is also spelt out by Engels in *The Dialectics of Nature,* "a development in which the qualitative changes occur not gradually but rapidly and abruptly, taking the form of a leap from one state to another." . . . Here then is the recipe for revolution (Halstead 1980a, 216–217).

Communism teaches that by "defending Darwinism, working people strengthen their defenses against the attacks of . . . reactionary outfits, and prepare the way for the transformation of the social order," i.e., a communist revolution (Conner 1980, 12).

Friedrich Engels Embraced Darwinism

Probably no one had a greater influence on Marx than Friedrich Engels. Marx's coworker and frequent coauthor, Engels, also was raised by a strict and "pietistic" Bible-believing father. Although reared in a devout Christian family, Engels started to seriously question his faith when he read liberal German theologians, such as Bruno Bauer, at the University of Berlin (Wurmbrand 1986, 36–37). Importantly, a major factor that influenced the theologies of these liberal theologians was the writings of Darwin. In time, Engels also became an active opposer of not only Christianity, but also theism itself, evidently as a result of his studies at the University of Berlin (Koster 1989, 164). The reason he opposed not only Christianity but also became an atheist was, in his own words, due to his acceptance of Darwinism. In his words, "Nowadays, in our evolutionary conception of the universe, there is absolutely no room for either a Creator or a Ruler" (Engels 1907, xv). He added that

> there is no creator and no Ruler of the universe . . . matter and energy can neither be created nor annihilated. . . . mind is a mode of energy, a function of the brain; all we know is that the material world is governed by immutable laws. . . . Thus . . . scientific man . . . is a materialist; outside his science, in spheres about which he knows nothing, he translates his ignorance into Greek and calls it agnosticism (Engels 1907, xviii).

As to the credit for this worldview, Engels stated that

> Darwin must be named before all others. He dealt the metaphysical conception of Nature the heaviest blow by his proof that all organic beings, plants, animals, and man himself, are the products of a process of evolution going on through millions of years (Engels 1907, 34–35).

At Marx's graveside during the burial, Engels declared, "Just as Darwin discovered the law of evolution in organic nature, so Marx discovered the law of evolution in human history" (Treadgold 1972, 50; Engels 1968). Historian

Gertrude Himmelfarb concluded from her study of Darwin that there was much truth in this eulogy to Marx:

> What they both celebrated was the internal rhythm and course of life, the one the life of nature, the other of society, that proceeded by fixed laws, undistracted by the will of God or men. There were no catastrophes in history as there were none in nature. There were no inexplicable acts, no violations of the natural order. God was as powerless as individual men to interfere with the internal, self-adjusting dialectic of change and development (Himmelfarb 1959, 422–423).

And Hofstadter noted that most of the early orthodox Marxists

> felt quite at home in Darwinian surroundings. . . . Reading *The Origin of Species* in 1860, he [Marx] reported to Friedrich Engels, and later declared to Ferdinand Lassalle, that "Darwin's book is very important, and serves me as a basis in natural science for the class struggle in history." On the shelves of the socialist bookstores in Germany the works of Darwin and Marx stood side by side (1959, 115).

In addition, the communist books that poured from the Kerr press in Chicago, the major U.S. publisher of communist books, were frequently adorned with glowing quotes from Darwin, Huxley, Spencer, and Haeckel (Hofstadter 1959, 115).

Marx, Engels, and Darwin

Marx and Engels coauthored an entire book on evolution (1955). In it was manifested evidence of a basic knowledge of Darwinism. For example, they wrote that the progress in paleontology, anatomy, and physiology in general, particularly since the discovery of the cell, had accumulated so much evidence that they concluded macroevolution was now a scientifically well-documented fact (Marx and Engels 1955, 162–163). They write that research comparing various homologous organs in different animals with each other was made

> not only in the adult condition but at all stages of their development. The more deeply . . . this research was carried on, the more did the rigid system of an immutable fixed organic nature crumble

away. . . . Not only did the separate species of plants and animals become more and more inextricably intermingled, but animals turned up, such as *Amphioxus* and *Lepidosiren*, that made a mockery of all previous classification, and finally organisms were encountered of which it was not possible to say whether they belonged to the plant or animal kingdom. More and more the gaps in the palaeontological record were filled up, compelling even the most reluctant to acknowledge the striking parallelism between the history of the development of the organic world as a whole (Marx and Engels, 1955, 162–163).

Furthermore: "With man we enter *history*. Animals also have a history, that of their descent and gradual evolution to their present position" (Marx and Engels 1955, 168). Darwin, Marx, and Engels all argued "that free competition, the struggle for existence . . . is *the normal state of the animal kingdom*" (Marx and Engels 1955, 169, emphasis added). And application of the laws of evolution to humans proves that evolution "can lift mankind above the rest of the animal world" (Marx and Engels 1955, 169). They add that the progress of science, including in the fields of geology, embryology, physiology, and organic chemistry, is important because "everywhere on the basis of these new sciences brilliant foreshadowings of the later theory of evolution were appearing (for instance, Goethe and Lamarck)" (Marx and Engels 1955, 233). They concluded that humans evolved from simple protoplasm, a belief that "Darwin first developed," namely that all life existing

today, including man, is the result of a long process of evolution from a few originally unicellular germs, and that these again have arisen from protoplasm or albumen, which came into existence by chemical means. Thanks to these . . . great discoveries and the other immense advances in natural science, we have now arrived at the point where we can demonstrate the interconnection between the process in nature . . . and so can present in an approximately systematic form a comprehensive view of the interconnection in nature by means of the facts provided by empirical natural science itself (Marx and Engels 1955, 252–253).

They added that the natural science were once in turmoil, but

during the last fifteen years had reached a clarifying, relative conclusion. New scientific data were acquired to a hitherto unheard of

extent, but the establishing of interrelations, and thereby the bringing of order into this chaos of discoveries following closely upon
each other's heels, has only quite recently become possible . . . three
of the decisive discoveries — that of the cell, the transformation of
energy and the theory of evolution named after Darwin (Marx and
Engels 1955, 234).

A monograph authored by Frederick Engels (1975) likewise illustrates
that both Marx and Engels had more than an average knowledge about
evolution.

Alexander Herzen Becomes a Convert

Another person who also was critically important in the development of the
communist movement included Alexander Herzen (1812–1870), the first
man to articulate the new radicalism in Russia. He was in full harmony with
Marx's ideas and a pioneer in calling for a mass revolt to achieve communist
power. His theory was a distinctively Russian version of socialism based on
the peasant commune, which furnished the primary ideological basis for
much of the revolutionary activity in Russia up to 1917. Herzen also was
heavily influenced by Darwinism:

> Herzen's university writings are concerned primarily with the theme
> of biological becoming. . . . Herzen displays a good knowledge of
> the serious scientific literature of the period . . . especially works
> which announced the idea of evolution . . . [including] the writings
> of Erasmus Darwin, the grandfather of Charles and to a point his
> ideological predecessor. . . . He was abreast of the debate between
> the followers of Cuvier, who held to the immutability of species,
> and Geoffroy-Saint-Hilaire, the tranformationist or evolutionist;
> and of course he took the side of the latter, since the idea of continu-
> ous evolution was necessary to illustrate the progressive unfolding
> of the Absolute. In short, Herzen's scientific training lay essentially
> in the raw materials for the biology of the *Naturphilosophie* (Malia
> 1961, 91).

Herzen was the "most vivid figure" in the movement that eventually over-
threw the Russian government and established a communist state (Shub
1951, 7). Many persons accepted Darwinism first, then they accepted communism, or as Pusey concluded: "Marxism converted intellectuals — but
[only] intellectuals who were already converted to Darwinism" (1983, 452).

Acceptance of Darwinism and rejection of religion were both critical for the new communism and Nazism movements for reasons that include the

> generation which made a fuller and seemingly final rejection of religion . . . were the Darwinian-minded "social scientists," who followed what they conceived to be the lead of the new biology, which made God dispensable. Darwinism itself did more. It postulated a theory of evolutionary change which the intellectuals eagerly embraced and applied not merely to the human species, as Darwin suggested, but also to human society and the state. Evolutionary doctrines did not begin with Darwin, but Darwinism in Western Europe and America gave them wide popularity. It was sometimes used by such men as Herbert Spencer, to justify certain existing institutions, but more often it was employed to attack them as obsolete. Nicholas Danilevsky and a few others turned Darwinism to conservative purposes, but in Russia Reform Darwinists were the rule (Treadgold 1972, 32).

Hitler's motivations in accepting and implementing Darwinism were in several ways different than the Darwinistic motivations involved in the communist revolutions. In harmony with many of the leading biologists in his day (including German, American, French, and English biologists), Hitler believed that the human races evolved separately and, consequently, were unequal. Interbreeding would mix the races that had superior traits with those that had inferior traits, resulting in mediocre (or worse) offspring. The solution to human problems was to prevent interbreeding of the superior and inferior races and to ensure that the superior races ruled the nation, industry, and all institutions (Macrone 1995).

The communists interpreted Darwin somewhat differently. They saw the Marxist theory of labor as critical in the "transition from ape to man" (Engels 1950, 1). A core concern of both, however, was to eradicate religion and "both Nazism and Communism insisted that atheistic evolution, as scientific, had replaced God" (Azar 1990, x). The critical importance of eradicating religion via communism is apparent from a review of the history of the development of communism, which goes back at least to Georg Wilhelm Friedrich Hegel (1770–1831).

Why Communism Is Atheistic and Produced Holocausts

Darwinism commonly leads to atheism in many scientists (Provine 1999,

S123. See also Lachs 1967; Kernig1972; and Bergman 2010). No doubt, it also influenced Marx to adopt atheism. Marx also was influenced considerably by Hegel's dialectic concept (Hull 1985). George Hegel held that religion, science, history, and "most everything else" evolves to a higher state as time progresses (Macrone 1995, 52). It does this by a process called the *dialectic*, in which a *thesis* (an idea) eventually confronts an *antithesis* (an opposing idea), producing a *synthesis* or a blend of the best of the old and new ideas (Macrone 1995, 51).

Marx argued that capitalism is the thesis, and the organized proletariat is the antithesis. Essentially, the central conflict in capitalism was between those who controlled the means of production (the *owners*, the wealthy class, or the bourgeoisie) and those who did the actual physical work (the *worker* or the *proletariat*). Marx's central idea was that the synthesis (i.e., communism) would emerge from the struggle between the proletariat and the bourgeoisie. This is illustrated by Marx's famous phrase, "Workers of the world unite and overthrow your oppressors."

Marx concluded that the masses (persons who worked in the factories and the farms) would struggle with the business owners, the wealthy, and the entrepreneurs. Since there were a lot more workers than owners, Marx believed that the workers would eventually overthrow the entrepreneurs by violent revolution, taking their factories and wealth. The result would be a dictatorship by the proletariat. Marx believed that private property then would be abolished, and the workers would collectively own the country, including the farms and the means of production. All the workers would then share equally in the fruits of their labor, producing a classless society in which everyone earned equal amounts of money.

This philosophy obviously appealed to millions of people, especially the poor, the downtrodden, and many middle class people who had a concern for the poor (del Rio 1976; Arlen 1984). Communist revolutions often resulted in forcibly taking the wealth from the land-owning classes, the wealthy, the industrialists, and others. Many of these people had built their wealth from hard work and astute business decisions and were not willing to give up what, in many cases, they had worked very hard for decades to achieve.

In general, appropriating the land and wealth from the property owners resulted in an enormous amount of widespread resistance. As a result, a bloodbath ensued that cost the lives of hundreds of millions of people. Those murdered often included the most talented entrepreneurs, the most skilled industrialists, and the intellectual backbone of the nation.

The workers were put in charge of the companies and factories once run by what Marx called the "bourgeoisie." Unfortunately, and not surprisingly, many of these workers lacked the skills, intelligence, and personal qualities necessary to run these businesses. Consequently, inferior products, low productivity, and an incredible amount of waste was the rule for generations in the communist world.

Marx's theory unified Darwinism and revolution and "an historian can hardly fail to agree that Marx's claim to give scientific guidance to those who would transform society has been one of the chief reasons for his doctrine's enormous influence" (Joravsky 1961, 4). As an example, a central tenet of Marxism was that humanity was "evolving toward Communism, and that this evolution could not be halted any more than an amoeba could have halted the evolutionary process in the organic domain" (Azar 1990, 219).

Marx's Uncompromising Opposition to Theism

Critical in the development of Marx's theorizing, as well as that of many of his followers, was his rejection of Christianity and its moral values and his acceptance of an agnostic/atheistic worldview. When Marx lost his Christian faith and became an atheist, he concluded that theistic religion was a tool of the rich to subjugate the poor, as summarized in his famous saying that religion is the "opiate of the people" (Marx 1844, 57). Opium is a pain-killing drug, and Marx characterized religion as having the same function, i.e., it was used to pacify the oppressed because it stressed peace, nonviolence, and loving one's neighbor. The result was that it made them *feel* better but did not solve their problem, which Marx concluded was the need to redistribute the wealth of the nation.

Marx felt that religion is not just an illusion: it had a deleterious social function, namely to distract the oppressed from the truth of their oppression and to prevent people from seeing the harsh realities of their existence. As long as the workers and the downtrodden believed their moral behavior and sufferings would earn them freedom and happiness in heaven, they would allow themselves to be oppressed. Marx concluded that workers would change their perception of reality only when they realized that there is no God, no afterlife, and no good reason not to have what they want now, even if they have to take it from others.

Marx concluded that the solution was to abolish religion, which then would allow the poor to openly revolt against their "oppressors" (the land owners, the wealthy, the entrepreneurs, et al.) and redistribute their wealth so the poor could enjoy the rich men's wealth in *this* world. Furthermore, since the rich and powerful are not just going to hand their wealth over without a struggle, the masses will have to seize it by force (Macrone 1995, 216). Eidelberg noted that "Marx's eschatology, his materialistic philosophy of history is, for all practical purposes, a doctrine of *permanent* revolution, a doctrine which cannot but result in periodic violence, terror, and tyranny" (1984, 10).

This is why Marx concluded that the "abolition of religion" is a prerequisite for the attainment of real happiness of the people (1844, 58). Consequently, an important cornerstone of communism was to take away the opium (religion) from the people and convince them that they should eat, drink, and be merry now, for tomorrow they may die. The only way to have the resources to do this was to take the property that belonged to the rich and successful. Marx stressed the Darwinist conclusion that, aside from personal pleasures in the here and now, life in the long run has no meaning or purpose because we were accidents of nature that, in all likelihood, would never again occur on the earth (Gould 1989, 233).

One important factor, however, was not appropriately accounted for in Marx's unrealistic (yet idealistic) worldview. The first was the fact that, as the Scriptures stress, workers are worthy of their wages. Starting a business usually entails an enormous amount of risk and requires extremely hard work and long hours by persons who often must have special skills to guide that business to success. Most new businesses fail — fewer than one out of five succeeds — and the success of the vast majority of these usually is only moderate.

On the other hand, enormous rewards can result if a business does succeed. The rewards include not only wealth and prestige, but also the satisfaction of achieving the building of a successful business. The rewards have to be great in order for people to assume the risks involved. Many people who fail in business lose everything they own. This was a major factor absent in communism that doomed it.

To ensure that communism maintains its power base, it is necessary to indoctrinate people against religion, especially the Jewish, Christian, and Muslim religions, all of which stress that depriving people of their property without due compensation is wrong and that killing people to take away their property is a grievous sin (Wurmbrand 1986). Furthermore, these same religions also stress that, while we should stand up for what is right, justice is not guaranteed in this world, but God has promised rewards in heaven for those who pursue righteousness.

The Scriptures teach that care, compassion, and concern should be expressed toward the poor, widows, orphans, deformed, social outcasts, and even criminals. However, they also stress that the worker is worthy of his wages, and condemn murder even if part of a social revolution — he who lives by the sword will perish by the sword (Revelation 13:10). Christianity generally has served as a conserving force that has resisted depriving people of the fruits of their labor. J. Edgar Hoover noted that communists

> believe that whatever man does, thinks, or feels can be explained in terms of dynamic matter alone, and that matter is the only thing that exists. . . . *Communists claim that matter is self-sufficient — self-developing and self-perpetuating — and that there is no Supreme Being, or God, responsible for either the creation or the preservation of the universe. . . . Communists concluded that all religions and all moral codes derived from spiritual concepts are based on fantasy.* In adopting their materialistic interpretation, Communists assert that there is no essential difference between man and other forms of life. Man is merely the product of chemistry and physics, differing from the other forms of life only in the degree of his development. Therefore, Communists argue, since there is no Supreme Being, any moral law or code based on spiritual concepts is invalid (1962, 31, italics in original).

Of course Marx did not abandon all religion but rejected the Judeo-Christian religion and developed his own religion, "the religion of Communism" (Berdyaev 1970, 243). His religion was both a "system of universal economic metaphysics" and a system of ontology (Berdyaev 1970, 243).

The results of Marx's atheistic ideal have now tragically become very clear. The communist ideal that "each takes according to his needs, and each gives according to his abilities" all too often became "take whatever you can, and give back as little as you can." The result has been economic bankruptcy for most communist countries. In the past decade, we have witnessed the collapse of most communist regimes and their replacement by either capitalist or socialist governments. Cuba and China now have socialist governments, China has instituted major broad capitalist reforms as it endeavors to coexist with capitalism, and North Korea is moving toward a socialist government.

The quality of the society is, in part, a result of the caliber of its leaders. The most qualified people should be running the schools, factories, and governments. The economic poverty of Russia and much of Eastern Europe, although due to complex interrelated factors, eloquently testifies to the failure of the communist system.

Russia too became infected with Darwinism — so much that Vladimir Solovyer said: "The Russian intelligentsia produced a faith based upon a strange syllogism: Man is descended from the apes, therefore we must love one another" (Payne 1964, 629). Even women's groups were active in producing "good reading for the younger generation . . . [and] included Darwin's *Origin of Species* at the top of their list" (Stites 1991, 69). This is all not surprising, considering what happened in Russia soon after communism took over. Furthermore:

> When the Bolsheviks came into power in 1917, they made this defiant and dogmatic atheism the basis of their action. There is evidence that it did not lack extensive popular support. Up and down the country there ensued, in the villages as well as in the factories, a great deal of what we can only describe as spontaneous mass conversions to atheism (Webb and Webb 1935, 1006–1007).

Lenin Converts to Darwinism

Vladimir Ulyanov, known to the world as Lenin (1870–1924), also was significantly influenced by Darwinism. Lenin was the founder of the first "socialists state" and the organizer and first leader of communist Russia. He ruled Russia with an iron hand until he died and Stalin took over (Obichkin 1969). Lenin ran Russia in accordance with the philosophy "fewer but better," a restatement of natural selection (Schwartz 1972, 30).

Lenin was raised by devout Bible-believing parents in a middle-class home (Miller et al. 1963, 33). Then, around 1892, he discovered Darwin's and Marx's writings, and his life (and the world) was changed forever (Miller et al. 1963, 36). Historian Alain Besançon noted that "Marx laid claim to Darwin as an influence. So did Lenin (and so, incidentally, did Hitler)" (1981, 8).

Lenin soon developed a "fascination with the ideas of Charles Darwin" to the degree that Marxism and Darwinism became his new religion (Service 2000). Bertrand Russell concluded that the materialist conception of history literally was Lenin's life-blood (Clark 1988). Lenin believed that "Darwin put an end to the view of animal and plant species being unconnected, fortuitous, 'created by God' and immutable, and was the first to put biology on an absolutely scientific basis by establishing the mutability and the succession of species" (Lenin 1978, 142).

A catalyst to Lenin's adopting Marxism and Darwinism was the fact that the unjust Russian educational system canceled his father's tenure with one year's grace, thus throwing his family into turmoil. Within a year of the loss of his job, Lenin's father died, leaving Lenin embittered at age 16 (Koster 1989, 174). Lenin greatly admired his father, who was a hard-working, religious, and intelligent man, and his loss was devastating. Lenin's conversion to Darwinism was so complete that the "only piece of art work in Lenin's office was a kitsch statue of an ape sitting on a heap of books — including *Origin of Species* — and contemplating a human skull." This symbol of

> Darwin's view of man, remained in Lenin's view as he worked at his desk, approving plans or signing death warrants. . . . The ape and the skull were a symbol of his faith, the Darwinian faith that man is a brute, the world is a jungle, and individual lives are irrelevant. Lenin was probably not an instinctively vicious man, though he certainly ordered a great many vicious measures. Perhaps the ape and the skull were invoked to remind him that, in the world according to Darwin, man's brutality to man is inevitable. In his struggle to bring about the "worker's paradise" through "scientific" means, he ordered a great many deaths. The ape and the skull may have helped him stifle whatever kindly or humane impulses were left over from a wholesome childhood (Koster 1989, 174).

This ten-inches tall bronze statue occupied a dominant position on his desk (Payne 1964, 629). Payne comments that there is

> nothing in the least amusing about the appearance of the ape, which is sordidly bestial, with its small head and great curving shoulders and long dangling arms; and the human skull, with gaping mouth and empty eye sockets, is even less amusing. The ape gazes ponderously at the skull, and the skull gazes back at the ape. We can only guess at the nature of the interminable dialogue which is being maintained between them (1964, 626).

Furthermore, Lenin was open about his "affection" for the statue, which was displayed in

> a prominent position for all to see. It was the only piece of sculpture on the desk, the first thing that met the eye; and whenever Lenin looked up from his desk to gaze at the very large photograph of Karl Marx and the plaque bearing the name of Stepan Khalturin in gold letters, he would inevitably see the ape. There is a sense in which its

vivid presence dominated the room (Payne 1964, 626–627).

After Lenin died and his study was converted to a museum, the statue remained because "Lenin was one of those men who knew exactly what he liked and disliked. There was no object in the room which did not have a precise meaning for him" (Payne 1964, 627). Such was his devotion to Darwinism and whatever else the statue may have represented to him; it represented the triumph of Darwinism over humankind.

As a "devotee" of Russian communism, Lenin was not only an atheist, but felt Marxism "absolutely had to involve atheism," because atheism was the "path of science and progress" (Service 2000; 85, 148). His behavior certainly would not agree with Christian ideals — he instructed his followers to rob banks, to use bombs as a means of terrorism, and to resort to violence if it furthered their objective of producing a communist revolution (Service 2000). Until communism fell, Russians regarded him as their greatest national hero.

How a person becomes a communist, and the importance of Darwinism in the process, was reviewed by Schwartz. He noted that in college, students were often taught that the idea of God is for second-rate minds and that, since they were intelligent, they had no need for God. Such students also typically accept the Darwinian hypothesis concerning the origin of humans, and the Marxist hypothesis concerning the origin of civilization, culture, morality, ethics, and religion (Schwartz 1972, 34). Thus, they saw their future in communism and, consequently, dedicated their lives to achieving Communist goals (which included violent revolution). The result was a reign of terror that cost millions of lives during the last century and still takes many lives, even today.

The Soviet War against Christianity

The Soviet communist's Darwinian science led to their brutal campaign against Christianity. Webb and Webb note that there were both "positive and creative aspects of the cult of science in the USSR" but there was "also a negative and destructive side: the violent denunciation and energetic uprooting, from one end of the Soviet Union to the other, of religion, and especially of the Christian religion" (Webb and Webb 1935, 1004). Lenin wanted to replace religion, especially Christianity, with science, specifically Darwinism, and was adamant about his opposition to Christianity. He

insisted, as the basis of all his teaching, on a resolute denial of there being any known manifestation of the supernatural. He steadfastly insisted that the universe known to mankind (including mind equally with matter) was the sphere of science; and that this steadily advancing knowledge, the result of human experience of the universe, was the only useful instrument and the only valid guide of human action (Webb and Webb 1935, 1006).

In short, Lenin believed that there existed

nowhere any miracle, nowhere any "immortality"; no "soul" other than the plainly temporary "mind" of man; and no survival or revival of personality after death. Lenin refused to admit any hesitation or dubiety in the matter. He would not consent to any veiling of these dogmatic conclusions by the use of such words as agnosticism or spiritualism. He wrote a whole volume to mark off, most resolutely, from his own following, anyone who presumed to treat religion as anything but superstition, leading to mere magic without scientific basis, and serving, as Marx had once said, as opium for the people (Webb and Webb 1935, 1006).

Hitchens added that Lenin actually attempted to destroy Christianity in Russia:

Vladimir Ilyich Lenin's secret Shuya Memorandum of March 22, 1922, launched the state-sponsored looting of Russia's churches in the hope of provoking the Orthodox hierarchy into resistance and so crushing them. "In order to get our hands on this fund of several hundred million gold rubles (and perhaps even several hundred billion), we must do whatever is necessary. . . . We must now give the most decisive and merciless battle to the Black Hundreds clergy and subdue its resistance with such brutality that they will not forget it for decades to come" (Hitchens 2010, 179).

It turned out that the "Bolshevik expectations of gold from this source were absurdly ambitious and probably a red herring. . . . The real motive was to goad Christians into defending themselves and then to smash them in pieces" (Hitchens 2010, 179–180). This goal succeeded. In 1922 alone, "2,691 priests, 1,962 monks, and 3,447 nuns were killed" (Courtous 1999, 126). William Chamberlin, during his 12 years as a Moscow correspondent wrote, "In Russia the world is witnessing the first effort to destroy completely any belief in supernatural interpretation of life" (quoted in Hitchens

2010, 179–180).

The churches that attempted to compromise and accommodate communism and their Christian beliefs also ended up betrayed. For example, the group known as the "Living Church"

> was composed of priests and bishops who were more than ready to place Orthodox Christianity at the disposal of the Council of People's Commissars. But after having served the Bolsheviks by splitting and weakening the Orthodox Church, the leaders of the Living Church were arrested (and presumably murdered in prison, since no more was heard of them) in the early 1930s. The same thing happened to their Jewish equivalents, the "Yevseksiy" (Jewish sections of the Communist Party). These were wound up in 1929, their functionaries purged in 1937. . . . their chairman, Semyon Dimanshtein, was shot in captivity (Hitchens 2010, 198).

The common pattern repeated here is Darwinism first led to atheism, and, in this case, to communism and, eventually, to the mass murder of Christians and others.

Leon Trotsky Becomes a Darwinist

The conversion to Darwinism also was important in Leon Trotsky's evolution from Orthodox Judaism to atheistic Marxism (Woolley 2001). Born Lev Davidovich Bronstein in 1879, Trotsky played a major role in developing the Russian Communist Party. As one of the founders and chief architects of Soviet communism (and the second most powerful man in Russia for years), he was also the primary organizer of the famous Soviet Red Army. His accomplishments in building the totalitarian Soviet State were so impressive that Trotsky was in line to succeed Lenin but lost to Stalin in a power struggle and eventually was assassinated, evidently on orders from Stalin.

While in prison for his revolutionary activities as a young man, Trotsky read Darwin, and so important was Darwin to his conversion, that his writings were the first book he listed when discussing what he read while in prison (Eastman 1970, 116). Trotsky's life and writings indicate that Darwin made a lasting impression on him when he was still a young man. Trotsky would later admit that he "argued about Darwinism" on his way to becoming a Marxist and that "Darwin destroyed the last of my ideological prejudices" (Trotsky 1931, 103). Trotsky claimed that his Odessa prison reading in science enabled him to develop a solid scientific world outlook, and, as a result, the

> idea of evolution and determinism — that is, the idea of a gradual development conditioned by the character of the material world — took possession of me completely. Darwin stood for me like a mighty doorkeeper at the entrance to the temple of the universe. I was intoxicated with his minute, precise, conscientious, and at the same time powerful, thought. I was the more astonished when I read in one of the books of Darwin, his autobiography, I think, that he had preserved his belief in God. I absolutely declined to understand how a theory of the origin of species by way of natural and sexual selection, and a belief in God, could find room in one and the same head (Eastman 1970, 117–118).

He "insatiably" studied Darwinism and "the best arguments against Catholicism, Protestantism" and other isms (Trotsky 1931, 117). He found the truth in Marx, Engels, and other atheistic thinkers and was especially interested in the relationship between Marxism and Darwinism (Trotsky 1931. 122, 127, 130).

Joseph Stalin Becomes a Darwinist

The second Soviet dictator, Joseph Stalin (1879–1953) was born Joseph Djugashvili (also spelled Dzhughashvilis). His father, an alcoholic with a volcanic temper, was jealous of the attention his wife gave to their son, Joseph, and treated both wife and son very poorly (Service 2005, 16). Joseph took the last name Stalin, which means "steel," during his days as a violent revolutionary. As the Soviet leader, Stalin had an estimated 60 million humans murdered (Antonov-Ovesyenko 1981). Like Darwin, he was once a theology student and, also like Darwin, evolution was a critical factor in transforming Stalin from a Bible believer to, for all practical purposes, a functional atheist (Koster 1989, 176; Service 2005, 30; Humber 1987). While still an ecclesiastical student, Stalin

> began to read Darwin and became an atheist. G. Glurdjidze, a boyhood friend of Stalin's, relates: "I began to speak of God. Joseph heard me out, and after a moment's silence said: "You know, they are fooling us, there is no God. . . ."
> "I was astonished at these words. . . . How can you say such things, Soso [Stalin]?" I exclaimed.

"I'll lend you a book to read; it will show you that the world and all living things are quite different from what you imagine, and all this talk about God is sheer nonsense," Joseph said.

"What book is that?" I inquired.

"Darwin. You must read it," Joseph impressed on me (Yaroslavsky 1940, 8–9).

Montefiore reported that when Stalin was around age thirteen, Lado Ketskhoveli took him [Stalin] to a little bookshop in Gori where he paid a five kopeck subscription and borrowed a book that was probably Darwin's *Origin of Species*. Stalin read it all night, forgetting to sleep, until Keke [his mother] found him. "Time to go to bed," she said. "Go to sleep — dawn is breaking." "I loved the book so much, Mummy, I couldn't stop reading. . . ." As his reading intensified, his piety wavered.

One day Soso [Stalin] and some friends, including Grisha Glurjidze, lay on the grass in town talking about the injustice of there being rich and poor when he amazed all of them by suddenly saying: "God's not unjust, he doesn't actually exist. We've been deceived. If God existed, he'd have made the world more just." "Soso! How can you say such things?" exclaimed Grisha. "I'll lend you a book and you'll see." He presented Glurjidze with a copy of Darwin (Montefiore 2007, 49).

Stalin read not only Darwin, but also Marx and Lenin (Service 2005, 40). These books impressed him greatly and he soon became an "avid Darwinian," abandoned his faith in God, and "began to tell his fellow seminarians that people were descended from apes and not from Adam" (Koster 1989, 176). He became a "militant atheist" even ungratefully disdaining the support and help he personally received from the Church (Service 2005, 13).

It "was not only with Darwin that the young Stalin became familiar in the Gori ecclesiastical school; it was while there that he got his first acquaintance with Marxist ideas" (Yaroslavsky 1940, 9). Miller adds that Stalin had an extraordinary memory, had the highest marks in almost every subject, and learned his lessons with so little effort that the monks who taught him concluded that he would become an outstanding priest. After

five years at the seminary he became interested in the nationalist movement in his native province, in Darwin's theories and in Victor

Hugo's writings on the French Revolution. As a nationalist he was anti-Tsarist and joined a secret socialist society (Miller et al. 1963, 77).

The result of this experience was that Stalin's

> brutal childhood and the worldview he acquired in that childhood, reinforced by reading Darwin, convinced him that mercy and forbearance were weak and stupid. He killed with a coldness that even Hitler might have envied — and in even greater numbers than Hitler did (Koster 1989, 177).

Stalin's writings attempted to justify his use of brutal power to achieve his Darwinian goals by means of Darwinism. In his words:

> Evolution prepares for revolution and creates the ground for it; revolution consummates the process of evolution and facilitates its further activity. Similar processes take place in nature. The history of science shows that the dialectical method is a truly scientific method: from astronomy to sociology, in every field we find confirmation of the idea that nothing is eternal in the universe, everything changes, everything develops. Consequently, everything in nature must be regarded from the point of view of movement, development. And this means that the spirit of dialectics permeates the whole of present-day science . . . minor, *quantitative* changes sooner or later lead to major, *qualitative* changes — this law applies with equal force to the history of nature. The same thing is shown in biology by the theory of neo-Lamarckism, to which neo-Darwinism is yielding place. . . . Lamarck and Darwin [were not] revolutionaries, but their evolutionary method put biological [Darwinian] science on its feet (Stalin 1906, Vol 1., 304–306 emphasis in original).

He adds, quoting a Soviet authority, that "Marxism rests on Darwinism and treats it uncritically" (Vol. 10, 310). The central role of Darwinism in his thought is also shown in his rejection of Cuvier's basic conclusion:

> Cuvier rejects Darwin's theory of evolution, he recognizes only cataclysms, and cataclysms are *unexpected* upheavals "due to *unknown* causes." The Anarchists say that the Marxists *adhere to Cuvier's view* and therefore *repudiate Darwinism*. Darwin rejects Cuvier's cataclysms, he recognizes gradual evolution. But the same Anarchists

say that "Marxism rests on Darwinism and treats it uncritically," i.e., the Marxists repudiate *Cuvier's cataclysms* (Vol. 10, 310–311, emphasis added).

Which view is correct? Stalin concludes that "in the opinion of Marx and Engels, revolution is engendered not by Cuvier's 'unknown causes,' but by very definite and vital social causes called 'the development of the productive forces' " [i.e., evolution] (p. 311).

Stalin, one of the "most notorious figures in history," as head of a "one-party, one-ideology dictatorship" ordered "the systematic killing of people on a massive scale" (Service 2005, 3).

Koster added that Stalin had people murdered for two major reasons, namely because they were personal threats to either him or the progress of his programs "which in Marxist-Darwinian terms meant some sort of evolution to an earthly paradise" (Koster 1989, 178). A third reason was his hatred of God and, by extension, Christians that he actively persecuted (Service 2005). The importance of Darwin's ideas to Stalin's evolution into a communist is stressed by Parkadze, a close childhood friend of Stalin, who wrote

> in order to disabuse the minds of our seminary students of the myth that the world was created in six days, we had to acquaint ourselves with the geological origin and age of the earth, and be able to prove them in argument; we had to familiarize ourselves with Darwin's teachings. We were aided in this by . . . Lyell's *Antiquity of Man* and Darwin's *Descent of Man*, the latter in a translation edited by Sechenov. Comrade Stalin read Sechenov's scientific works with great interest. We gradually proceeded to a study of the development of class society, which led us to the writings of Marx, Engels and Lenin (Yaroslavsky 1940, 12–13).

For reading Marxist literature at this time one could be punished because it was

> revolutionary propaganda. The effect of this was particularly felt in the seminary, where even the name of Darwin was always mentioned with scurrilous abuse. . . . Comrade Stalin brought these books to our notice. The first thing we had to do, he would say, was to become atheists. Many of us began to acquire a materialist outlook and to ignore theological subjects. Our reading in the most

diverse branches of science not only helped our young people to escape from the bigoted and narrow-minded spirit of the seminary, but also prepared their minds for the reception of Marxist ideas. Every book we read, whether on archaeology, geology, astronomy, or primitive civilization, helped to confirm to us the truth of Marxism (Yaroslavsky 1940, 12–13).

As a result of the influence of Lenin, Stalin, and other Soviet leaders, Darwin "became an intellectual hero in the Soviet Union. There is a splendid Darwin museum in Moscow, and the Soviet authorities struck a special Darwin medal in honor of the centenary of *The Origin*" (Huxley and H.B.D. Kittlewell 1965, 80). Stalin also justified his war against religion by Darwinism. He wrote that the Communist Party "cannot be neutral towards religion" but must attempt to destroy it, and for this reason

> it conducts anti-religious propaganda against all religious prejudices because it stands for science, whereas religious prejudices run counter to science, because all religion is the antithesis of science. Cases such as occur in America, where Darwinists were prosecuted recently, cannot occur here because the Party pursues a policy of defending science in every way (Stalin 1927, Vol. 10, 138).

The case Stalin cited is the 1925 Scopes Trial,

> a trial took place in the state of Tennessee, U.S.A., which attracted world-wide attention. A college teacher named John Scopes was tried for teaching Darwin's theory of evolution. The American reactionary obscurantists found him guilty of violating the laws of the state and fined him) (Stalin 1927, Vol. 10, 394–395).

Stalin adds that the communist "conduct, and will continue to conduct, propaganda against religious prejudices" because the

> Party cannot be neutral towards the disseminators of religious prejudices, towards the reactionary clergy, who poison the minds of the laboring masses. Have we repressed the reactionary clergy? Yes, we have. The only unfortunate thing is that they have not yet been completely eliminated. Anti-religious propaganda is the means by which the elimination of the reactionary clergy will be completely carried through. Cases occur sometimes when certain members of the Party hinder the full development of anti-religious propaganda.

If such members are expelled it is a very good thing, because there is no room for such "Communists" in the ranks of our Party (Stalin 1927, Vol. 10, 138–139).

Summary

A review of the history of communism shows that Darwin's ideas played a critically important role in the development and growth of this system (Howitt 1963). While it is difficult to conclude that communism would not have blossomed as it did if Darwin had not developed his evolution theory, it is clear that if Marx, Lenin, Engels, Stalin, and Mao had continued to embrace the Judeo-Christian worldview and had not become Darwinists, communist theory and the revolutions it inspired would never have spread to the many countries that it did.

It follows, then, that the Holocaust produced by communism (which caused over one-quarter of a billion deaths) likely never would have occurred. In Nobel Prize winner Alexander Solzhenitsyn's words, "If I were asked today to formulate as concisely as possible the main cause of the ruinous revolution that swallowed up some 60 million of our [Russian] people, I could not put it more accurately than to repeat: 'men have forgotten God; that's why all this has happened' (quoted in Ericson 1985, 24).

Darwinian materialism was critical in the development of Marx's principal theory of "dialectic materialism" because, until Darwin, most scientists were creationists. Only when a possible explanation for the existence of the creation without a Creator existed could atheism be based on an intellectual foundation. Some have argued that if evolutionism had not been developed by Charles Darwin, other theorists eventually would have developed and popularized a very similar theory. The Soviet policy is not unlike that existing now in America:

> Does that mean that the Party is neutral towards religion? No, it does not. We conduct, and will continue to conduct, propaganda against religious prejudices. The laws of our country recognize the right of every citizen to profess any religion. That is a matter for the conscience of each individual. That is precisely why we separated the church from the state. But in separating the church from the state and proclaiming freedom of conscience we at the same time preserved the right of every citizen to combat religion, all religion, by argument, by propaganda and agitation (Stalin 1927, Vol. 10, 138).

One problem with such a conclusion is that Charles Darwin was in a very unique position to develop and actively propagate the theory. He had the determination, time, money, intelligence, and likable personality to spend his entire life propagating what is now, for good reason, called a "Darwinian worldview" (Taylor 1991).

Furthermore, Darwin was a highly effective propagandist and spared neither resources nor time in order to sell his theory. His over 20 books and thousands of letters and articles focused primarily on one theme, i.e., selling his evolution worldview. No doubt other researchers would have developed similar ideas, as some already had before Darwin, but it is likely that without a skilled, dedicated, financially independent propagandist, their ideas never would have caught on to the extent that Darwinism did, or would not have become generally accepted until much later, if at all. It is clear that both Marx and Darwin have drastically altered history. Young, a Darwin and Marx admirer, even claims that Darwin's *The Origin of Species*, along with *Das Kapital*, are "one of the most significant works in the intellectual history of the nineteenth century" (1971, 440).

This review of the development of Marxist-Leninism indicates that without Darwinism the communist Holocaust likely never would have occurred or would have been very different and far less extensive in its effects. This conclusion supports Hsü's comment that Darwinism contains "wicked lies," and that it has produced a horrible fruit and is not a natural law formulated on the basis of evidence but rather "a dogma" (1986, 730). Preeminent historian Will Durant summed up the issue as follows:

> By offering evolution in place of God as a cause of history, Darwin removed the theological basis of the moral code of Christendom. And the moral code that has no fear of God is very shaky. That's the condition we are in (quoted in Morris 1997, 473).

The concern of many people is: "If evolution holds sway, any meaning to life, and with it the basis for morality, will fall as surely as the Tower of Babel" is supported by history (Steele 1999, 1484).

References

Antonov-Ovesyenko, Anton. 1981. *The Time of Stalin: Portrait of A Tyranny.* New York: Harper and Row.

Arlen, Michael. 1984. *Voyage Home.* New York: Farrar, Straus and Giroux.

Azar, Larry. 1990. *Twentieth Century in Crisis: Foundations of Totalitarianism.* Dubuque, IA: Kendall Hunt.

Ball, Terence. 1979. "Marx and Darwin: A Reconsideration." *Political Theory*, November 4, 7(4):469–483

Barzun, Jacques. 1958. *Darwin, Marx, Wagner: Critique of a Heritage.* 2nd ed. Garden City, NY: Doubleday.

Berdyaev, Nicholas. 1970. "The Religion of Communism," in Joseph K. Davis, *Man in Crisis.* Glenview, IL: Scott Foresman.

Bergman, Jerry. 2010. "Why Orthodox Darwinism Demands Atheism." *Answers Research Journal* 3:147–152.

Berlin, Isaiah. 1959. *Karl Marx: His Life and Environment.* New York: Oxford University Press.

Bernal, J.D. 1952. *Marx and Science.* London: Lawrence and Wishart Ltd.

Besançon, Alain. 1981. *The Rise of the Gulag: Intellectual Origins of Leninism.* New York: Continuum.

Bethell, Tom. 1978. "Burning Darwin to Save Marx." *Harper's Magazine*, December, 31–38, 91–92.

Clark, Ronald W. 1988. *Lenin.* New York, NY: Harper & Row.

Colp, Ralph Jr. 1972. "The Contracts Between Karl Marx and Charles Darwin." *Journal of the History of Ideas*, April–June, 35(2): 329–338.

Conner, Cliff. 1980. "Evolution vs. Creationism: In Defense of Scientific Thinking." *International Socialist Review* (Monthly Magazine Supplement to *The Militant*), Nov.

Courtois, Stephene, Nicolas Werth, Jean-Louis Panne, Andrzej Paczkowski, Karen Bartosek, and Jean-Louis Margolin. 1999. *The Black Book of Communism: Crimes, Terror, Repression.* Cambridge, MA. Harvard University Press.

del Rio, Eduardo. 1976. *Marx for Beginners.* New York: Pantheon Books.

Eastman, Max. 1970. *Leon Trotsky: The Portrait of a Youth.* New York: AMS Press.

Eidelberg, Paul. 1984. "Karl Marx and the Declaration of Independence: The Meaning of Marxism." *Intercollegiate Review* 20:3–11.

Engels, Frederick. 1876. *The Part Played by Labor in the Transition from Ape to Man.* New York: International Publishers.

———. 1907. *Socialism: Utopian and Scientific.* Chicago, IL: Charles H. Kerr & Company. Translated by Edward Aveling.

———. 1950. *The Part Played by Labor in the Transition from Ape to Man.* New York: International Publishers.

———. 1968. "Karl Marx's Funeral" in *A Worker's Reminiscences of Marx and Engels.* Moscow: Foreign Language Pub. House.

———. 1975. *The Part Played by Labor in the Transition from Ape to Man.* Peking: Foreign Languages Press.

Ericson, Edward. 1985. "Solzhenitsyn: Voice from the Gulag." *Eternity*, October, 21–24.

Gould, Stephen Jay. 1974. "Darwin's Delay." *Natural History* 83(10):68–70.

———. 1989. *Wonderful Life; Burgess Shale and the Nature of History.* New York: W.W. Norton.

Halstead, L. Beverly. 1980. "Museum of Errors." *Nature* 288:208.

———. 1980a. "Popper: Good Philosophy, Bad Science?" *New Scientist* 87:215–217.

Heyer, Paul. 1975. *Marx and Darwin: A Related Legacy on Man, Nature and Society.* PhD Dissertation, Rutgers University.

Hickey, David R. 1992. "Evolution, Environment, and the Collapse of Soviet Communism." *The Humanist* 52:33–35, 40.

Himmelfarb, Gertrude. 1959. *Darwin and the Darwinian Revolution.* New York: W.W. Norton.

Hitchens, Peter. 2010. *The Rage Against God: How Atheism Led Me to Faith.* Grand Rapids, MI: Zondervan.

Hofstadter, Richard. 1959. *Social Darwinism in American Thought.* New York: George Braziller, Inc.

Hoover, J. Edgar. 1962. *A Study of Communism.* New York: Holt, Rinehart and Winston.

Howitt, John. 1963. *Karl Mark as an Evolutionist.* Hants, England: EPM.

Hsü, Kenneth. 1986. *The Great Dying: Cosmic Catastrophe, Dinosaurs and the Theory of Evolution.* New York: Harcourt, Brace Jovanovich.

Hull, David L. 1985. "Darwinism and Dialectics," review of *The Dialectical Biologist,* by Richard Levins and Richard Lewontin, *Nature,* 320:23–24.

Humber, Paul G. 1987. "Stalin's Brutal Faith." *Impact,* October.

Huxley, Julian, and H.B.D. Kittlewell. 1965. *Charles Darwin and His World.* New York: Viking Press.

Hyman, Stanley Edgar. 1966. *The Tangled Bank: Darwin, Marx, Frazer & Freud as Imaginative Writers.* New York: Grosset and Dunlap.

Joravsky, David. 1961. *Soviet Marxism and Natural Science; 1917–1932.* London: Routledge and Kegan Paul.

Keith, Arthur. 1955. *Darwin Revalued.* London: Watts, p. 233–234.

Kernig, G.D. 1972. *Marxism, Communism, and Western Society: A Comparative Encyclopedia.* New York: Herder and Herder.

Kolman, E. 1931. "Marx and Darwin." *The Labour Monthly* 13(11):702–705.

Koster, John. 1989. *The Atheist Syndrome.* Brentwood, TN: Wolgemuth and Hyatt..

Lachs, John. 1967. *Marxist Philosophy: A Bibliographic Guide.* Chapel Hill, NC: University of North Carolina Press.

Lenczowski, John. 1996. "The Treason of the Intellectuals: Higher Education, the Culture War and the Threat to U.S. National Security." *Policy Counsel,* p. 35–52.

Lenin, V.I. 1978. *V.I. Lenin Collected Works. Volume 1: 1893–1894.* London: Lawrence Y Wishart.

Lessner, Friedrich. 1968. "A Workers Reminiscences of Karl Marx" in *Reminiscences of Marx and Engels.* Moscow: Foreign Languages Publishing House.

Liebknecht, Wilhelm. 1968. "Reminiscences of Marx" in *Reminiscences of Marx and Engels.* Moscow: Foreign Languages Publishing House.

Macrone, Michael. 1995. *Eureka! 81 Key Ideas Explained.* NY: Barnes and Noble.

Malia, Martin. 1961. *Alexander Herzen and the Birth of Russian Socialism.* Cambridge, MA: Harvard University Press. Reprinted 1971, New York: Grossett and Dunlap.

Marx, Karl. 1844. "A Contribution to the Critique of Hegel's Philosophy of Right." Reprinted in *Early Political Writings,* edited and translated by Joseph O'Malley. Cambridge, UK: Cambridge University Press, 1994.

Marx, Karl, and Frederick Engels. 1936. *Correspondence 1846–1895,* translated by Dona Torr. New York: International Publishers.

Marx, Karl, and Frederick Engels. 1955. *On Religion.* Moscow: Foreign Languages Publishing House.

Miller, William, Henry Roberts, and Marshall Shulman. 1963. *The Meaning of Communism.* Morristown NJ: Silver Burdett.

Montefiore, Simon Sebag. 2007. *Young Stalin.* New York: Knopf.

Morris, Henry. 1997. *That Their Words May Be Used Against Them.* Green Forrest, AR: Master Books.

Obichkin, G.D., editor. 1969. *V.I. Lenin: A Short Biography.* Moscow: Progress Publishers.

Oldroyd, D.R. 1980. *Darwinian Impacts: An Introduction to the Darwinian Revolution.* Atlantic Highlands, NJ: Humanities Press, p. 216.

Pannekoek, Anton. 1912. *Marxism and Darwinism.* Chicago, IL: Charles A Kerr.

Patterson, Thomas C. 2009. *Karl Marx, Anthropologist.* New York: Berg Publishers

Payne, Robert. 1964. *The Life and Death of Lenin.* New York: Simon and Schuster.

Perloff, James. 1999. *Tornado in a Junkyard.* Arlington, MA: Refuge Books.

Provine, Will. 1999. "No Free Will." *Isis* 90:S117–S132.

Pusey, James. 1983. *China and Charles Darwin.* Boston, MA: Harvard University Press.

Rachels, James. 1990. *Created from Animals: The Moral Implications of Darwinism.* New York: Oxford University Press, p. 64.

Ruse, Michael. 1986. "Biology and Values: A Fresh Look," in *Logic, Methodology, and Philosophy of Science,* by Marcus et al. Elsevier Science Publications B.V.

Schwartz, Fred. 1972. *The Three Faces of Revolution.* Falls Church, VA: The Capitol Hill Press.

Service, Robert. 2000. *Lenin: A Biography.* Cambridge, MA: Harvard University Press.

———. 2005. *Stalin: A Biography.* Cambridge, MA: Belknap Press of Harvard University Press.

Shub, David. 1951. *Lenin.* Garden City, NY: Doubleday & Company, Inc.

Stalin, Joseph. 1906. "Anarchism or Socialism." *Akhali Tskhovreba,* 21, 24, 28 Jun and 9 July 1906, reprinted in Stalin, *Works.* Moscow: Foreign Languages Publishing House, 1954, 1:304–6).

———. 1927. "Interview with the First American Labor Delegation." *Pravda,* September 15, 1927, reprinted in *J.V. Stalin, Works.* Moscow: Foreign Languages Publishing House, 1954, vol. 10:97–158.

———. 1954. *J.V. Stalin, Works.* Moscow: Foreign Languages Publishing House, Vol. 1.

Steele, Fintan. 1999. "Lingua Franca." *Science* 286:1484.

Stein, George J. 1988. "Biological Science and the Roots of Nazism." *American Scientist,* 76:50–58.

Stites, Richard. 1991. *The Women's Liberation Movement in Russia.* Princeton, NJ: Princeton University Press.

Talbot, Chris. 2012. "Mark and Darwin: Two Great Revolutionary Thinkers of the Nineteenth Century." *World Socialists Web Site.* Part 1.

Taylor, Ian T. 1991. *In the Minds of Men: Darwin and the New World Order.* Minneapolis, MN:

TFE Publishing.

Treadgold, Donald. 1972. *Twentieth Century Russia.* Chicago, IL: Rand McNally.

Trotsky, Leon. 1931. *My Life.* New York: Charles Scribner's Sons.

Webb, Sidney, and Beatrice Webb. 1935. *Soviet Communism: A New Civilisation?* New York: Longmans, Green and Co., Ltd.

Weikart, Richard. 1999. *Socialist Darwinism.* Lanham, MD: International Scholars Publications.

Wheen, Francis. 1999. *Karl Marx: A Life.* New York, NY: W.W. Norton & Company.

Wilder-Smith, Beate. 1982. *The Day Nazi Germany Died.* San Diego, CA: Master Books.

Woolley, Barry. 2001. "The Darwin/Trotsky Connection." *Creation,* 23(2):54–55.

Wurmbrand, Richard. 1986. *Marx and Satan.* Bartlesville, OK: Living Sacrifice Book Company.

Yaroslavsky, Emelian. 1940. *Landmarks in the Life of Stalin.* Moscow: Foreign Languages Publishing House.

Young, Robert. 1971. "Darwin's Metaphor: Does Nature Select?" *The Monist* 55(3):442–503.

Young, Robert M. 1982. "The Darwin Debate." *Marxism Today* 26:20–22.

Zirkle, Conway. 1959. *Evolution, Marxian Biology, and the Social Scene.* Philadelphia, PA: University of Philadelphia Press, p. 85–87.

Chapter 15

How Darwinism Inspired the Chinese Communist Holocaust

Introduction

Charles Darwin and his close disciples, especially Thomas Henry Huxley and Ernst Haeckel, had a profound influence on the Chinese communists' policies and the Holocaust that they inflicted on their own people. Professor Azar even concluded that Darwinism was the foundation of modern totalitarianism in China and elsewhere (1990). According to Chinese historian Hu Shih:

> When Thomas Huxley's *Evolution and Ethics* was published in 1898, it was immediately acclaimed and accepted by Chinese intellectuals. Rich men sponsored cheap Chinese editions so they could be widely distributed to the masses "because it was thought that the Darwinian hypothesis, especially in its social and political application, was a welcome stimulus to a nation suffering from age-long inertia and

stagnation" (Milner 2009, 79; quoted from *Living Philosophies*, 1931, published in Chinese).

Yan Fu's "late 1890s translations of Darwin and Herbert Spencer, while not the first introduction of Darwin's thought to China, fell on fertile soil at the turn of the century and soon swept the Chinese intellectual field" (Karl 1998, 1103). Many other major Darwinist's works, such as Huxley's *Evolution and Ethics,* also were translated into Chinese at this time (Boorman 1963, 5). Rankin stressed that China enthusiastically attempted to adopt "science" in their society and "Science in 1903 particularly meant Darwinism and especially Social Darwinism, which . . . promised a scientific explanation of the workings of politics and society" (1971, 20). Within only a few years, Darwinism became so widely accepted in China that "evolutionary phrases and slogans" were common Chinese proverbs. The Darwin personality cult became so radical that thousands of parents named their children after famous Darwinists or evolution ideas

> to "remind themselves of the perils of elimination in the struggle for existence, national as well as individual." A famous general called Chen Chiung-ming renamed himself "ching-tsun" or "Struggling for Existence." Author Shih himself adopted the name "Fitness" (Shih), from the phrase "survival of the fittest." He recalled that because of the great vogue of evolution in China . . . two of my schoolmates bore the names 'Natural Selection Yang' and 'Struggle for Existence Sun' " (Milner 2009, 79; quoted from *Living Philosophies*, 1931, published in Chinese).

Darwin's revolutionary theory was "first unfurled in China during the Reform Movement of 1895–98, in response to China's defeat in the Sino-Japanese War" (Pusey 2009, 162). The two major groups working to change China were the reformers, who were loyal to the Manchu Qing Dynasty, and the revolutionaries, who wanted a clean break with the past. Both used Darwinism to guide their different political philosophies.

Since "change" was anathema to conservative Chinese officials, the reformers turned to Darwin as an authority to promote change, presenting him not "as a natural scientist who had discovered an amazing fact of life but as a political scientist who had discovered a cosmic imperative for change" which they used to justify violent revolution (Pusey 2009, 162). The Chinese Evolution Society, quoting Thomas Huxley, wrote in 1919 that if education "cannot fundamentally alter the decadent condition in which the great majority of humankind lives, then . . . let us quickly call upon that merciful comet to wipe out this globe, and us with it" (Dirlik,1989, 80).

Mao Tse-tung Becomes a Darwinist

Darwinism also had an enormous influence on several of the highest level revolutionary Chinese Communist Party leaders, including Mao Tse-tung.

Chairman Mao was "indisputably one of the most important figures of the twentieth century" both in China and the rest of the world (Benton and Chun 2010, 15). As a youth, Mao Tse-tung (1893–1976), the cofounder of China's modern Communist Party and the first Chinese communist dictator, "devoured" many Western authors, especially Darwin, Huxley, Herbert Spencer, and other 19th-century Darwinists (Short 1999; Devillers 1967, 26; Pusey 1983). The first Chinese Communist Party was founded in July 1921 by Chen Duxiu and Li Dazhao. After the Communist Party suffered heavy

Portrait of Mao Zedong at Tiananmen Gate.

losses at the hands of the Kuomindang in 1926–27, a new party was built by Mao Zedong and Zhou Enlai that became the government existing today (Meisner 2007).

Reared by a religiously devout mother and a religiously skeptical father, as he read Charles Darwin, Herbert Spencer, John Stuart Mill, and Jean Jacques Rousseau, Mao became "more and more skeptical" of religion (Snow 1961, 128–129). Mao judged Darwinism as a "fragrant flower," not a "poisonous weed," writing

> Throughout history, at the outset new and correct things often failed to win recognition from the majority of people and had to develop by twists and turns through struggle. Often, correct and good things were first regarded not as fragrant flowers but as poisonous weeds. . . . Darwin's theory of evolution (was) once dismissed as erroneous and had to win out over bitter opposition (quoted in Sing 2000, 18).

Mao actually viewed "Darwin, as presented by the German Darwinists, as the foundation of Chinese scientific socialism" (Stein 1988, 52). Mao openly advocated achieving world communism by both violence and war — selection of the fittest — and the policies that Mao developed to achieve this goal resulted in the murder of as many as 80 million Chinese (Ruse 1986, 460). Others estimate the number was far lower, but clearly the "revolution he led . . . took the lives of many millions," up to "30 million excess deaths" (Benton and Chun 2010, 15).

The Results of Mao's Darwinian Rule

Mao's personal physician, who knew him better than almost all of Mao's close associates, wrote that he once revered Mao, but his respect dissipated as he got to know more about Mao through his intimate association with his patient. The reasons he came to despise Mao include:

> What lofty moral principles did he follow? He had cast aside Peng Dehuai, one of the country's great revolutionary leaders, a man loyal to the communist cause and devoted to the good of China, as if he were garbage, and he was gathering young women around him like the most degenerate of ancient emperors. And the Chinese people? The Communist party had taken "the people" and praised them to the sky while these very people were being oppressed and exploited, forced to endure every hardship, accept every insult, merely to survive. "The people" were nothing but a vast multitude of faceless, helpless slaves. This was the "new society," the communists' "new world." Jiang Qing was right that I was disgusted . . . "New China" had become corrupt (Zhisui 1994, 354–355).

Examples include Mao's poor

> personal hygiene, his imperial lifestyle in luxury villas and his licentious relationships with selected nurse/concubines. . . . His treatment of his wives was often callous or cruel and his children were certainly not lucky in their father. Some were left with peasants and disappeared during the revolutionary wars, others died, and two suffered mental breakdowns (Benton and Chun 2010, 16–17).

Darwin Applied to Daily Life in China

The extent that Darwinism was applied to daily life in China is illustrated by Kenneth Hsü when he was a student in China in the 1940s. He claimed that after their morning exercises, his class was harangued by the school's rector with Darwinian propaganda for the remainder of the hour: "We had to . . . fight in the struggle for existence, he told us. The weak would perish; only the strong would survive" (Hsü 1986, 1). Hsü added that they were taught that one acquires strength, not by hard work as his mother taught, but through constant struggle in which the Darwinian "fittest" were more likely to prevail. Hsü concluded that

> we were victims of a cruel social ideology that assumes that competition among individuals, classes, nations, or races is the natural condition of life, and that it is also natural for the superior to dispossess the inferior. For the last century and more this ideology has been thought to be a natural law of science, the mechanism of evolution which was formulated most powerfully by Charles Darwin in 1859 in his *On the Origin of Species by Means of Natural Selection, or the Preservation of Favored Races in the Struggle for Life.* Three decades have passed since I was marched into the schoolyard to hear the rector contradict my family's wisdom with his Darwinian claim to superiority (Hsü 1986, 1–2).

In view of what happened in the war and after (and what may happen in the future), Hsü was forced to question what sort of fitness was "demonstrated by the outcome of such struggles. As a scientist, I must especially examine the scientific validity of a notion that can do such damage" as Darwinism (1986, 2).

Hsü reports that the importance of Darwinism was indicated by Theo Sumner's experience on a trip to China with German Chancellor Helmit Schmit. Theo personally witnessed Mao acknowledge the debt he had to Darwinism, especially to the Darwinist who also inspired Hitler, Ernst Haeckel (Hsü 1986, 13).

Hsü concluded that Mao was convinced that "without the continual pressure of natural selection," humans would degenerate. This idea inspired Mao to, in Hsü's words, advocate "the ceaseless revolution that brought my homeland to the brink of ruin" (1986, 13). The role of college students in the Chinese Communist Holocaust also was important. Editorials and other articles openly expressed their favorable views on Darwin

> and contain the same general ideas found in all radical student publications in 1903. There are the familiar themes of the Darwinian

struggle for existence, the imperialist threat to national existence, the ignorance and barbarism of the Chinese people (Rankin 1971, 71).

Race Becomes Prominent in China

Race, due to Darwinism, was also a critical factor in bringing China "to the brink of ruin." The Chinese revolutionaries blended

> traditional xenophobia and Sinocentrism to their new concepts of nationalism and Darwinian struggle. Racial themes that pervaded the 1911 revolutionary literature . . . showed a genuine tendency to see the world in racial terms. Thus they foreshadowed the extreme, racially tinged nationalism often expressed by the Communists after 1949. The subject of race appeared critically important to the 1911 radicals because of its relation to the development of the nation-state. . . . They argued that the Chinese people under the Ch'ing dynasty were particularly removed from the government because the ruling house was of a different race (Rankin 1971, 26).

One example was the view called "bigenism," the belief that humans had two separate origins, the yellow race and the white race. Bigenism was developed further

> by Jiang Zhiyou, who collaborated with Liang Qichao. Jiang's inquiry into the origins of the Chinese race was dominated by the influence of Terrien de Lacouperie. Jiang established a continuity between the Sumero-Akkadians, from whom the Yellow Emperor was descended, and the Finno-Tartar group, linguistically associated with the Mongolians, or the yellow race (Dikötter 1992, 74).

The revolutionaries concluded that, of the many "factors linking the inhabitants of a country — language, culture, history, geography — race was the most important" (Rankin 1971, 26). He added that nations

> were formed through racial struggles and, as a corollary, if a race were to survive it had to establish a nation. If there were two races in a country the unity between people and state would be destroyed. One race might be or become slaves and, therefore, have no relation to the state. One race might be assimilated or destroyed. Or it might develop racial consciousness and break away to form a new nation

as occurred when the Austro-Hungarian empire split. Whatever happened, a racially divided country would lack internal strength and, at a time of rising, aggressive nationalism was risking destruction (Rankin 1971, 26).

Furthermore, the revolutionaries believed that this conclusion

was clearly illustrated by the effect of Manchu rule in China. Virtually all their publications enlarged upon the alleged inferiority of the Manchu race, the alleged viciousness of its conquest of China and exploitation of the Chinese people. Revolutionaries often felt compelled to draw up detailed racial classifications of the peoples of the world (Rankin 1971, 27).

As was also true in Nazi Germany, the specifics of their racist and political

schemes were not very important nor necessarily very accurate. Their main functions were to lend an aura of scientific authenticity to racial messages and to show that the Chinese and Manchus really were different peoples despite the embarrassing fact that the differences between them were considerably less than those between both of them and the white race (Rankin 1971, 26–27).

Karl concluded that "central to the precipitous rise in the use of Social Darwinian language and concepts to describe the world and China's precarious position in it was the concept of race" (Karl 1998, 1103).

Racism Evolved

The development of racism in China involved three steps. First was historic polygenism, then monogenism due to the influence of the Christian missionaries, and, last, back to polygenism because of the influence of Darwinism:

China believed in polygenism whereas the West was absorbed by the Judeo-Christian thesis of monogenism. The Bible depicted the sons of Noah as the ancestors of all the peoples of the three parts of the world: humanity descended from one (*mono*) kind (*genus*). In the nineteenth century, European thought had to eliminate Adam in order to reject the unity of mankind. The monogenist thesis was introduced to China by missionaries in the seventeenth century. The convert Li Zubai (died 1665) wrote a history of the Christian church in Chinese in 1663, in which his people were presented as a branch of Judea that migrated to China (Dikötter 1992, 70–71).

Chinese racial attitudes seemed to parallel the prejudices of White Euro-American; in its "scientific" formulations (Karl 1998, 1103). This was true even though

> Chinese intellectuals received the theory of evolution in a socio-political context very different from that of the West. They operated within a symbolic universe that led them to reinforce different aspects of the evolutionary paradigm (Dikötter 1992, 101).

Rankin noted, "Although the idea of struggle for survival could be used in almost any context, the 1911 revolutionaries tended to apply it particularly in racial terms" (1971, 30). This was because the

> predominant interpretation of the theory of natural selection was one of racial competition (*zhongzu jingzheng*) and racial survival (*boazhong*). The main external source of inspiration was the synthetic philosophy of Spencer and the linear model of Lamarck (Dikötter 1992, 101).

The Chinese used Darwinism to deal with their political situation by adopting "the principles of Social Darwinism to explain the workings of international affairs" which

> gave particular urgency to the problem of revitalizing China. . . . The law of the survival of the fittest condemned people ruled by foreigners to a decline. They would become slaves, be unable to develop their natural abilities, and be ground down under the tyranny which the revolutionaries believed was an inevitable ingredient of foreign rule. In China this process had already begun. For two hundred and sixty years the Chinese had been slaves of the Manchus, and now that the Manchus had sunk under Western domination, Chinese had become slaves of slaves (Rankin 1971, 29).

For example, Tsou Jung postulated what amounted to "a reverse form of evolution if the Chinese failed to reform themselves. They would sink still deeper into slavery, become apes . . . and finally become extinct" (Rankin 1971, 29). These fears of racial extinction, which appeared

> in the writings of many Chinese revolutionaries including Sun

Yat-sen, seem wildly exaggerated when viewed from an objective distance. Nonetheless, they were a basic element in the reaction against the imperialism of another race. The expressions were hyperbolic extensions of the radicals' preoccupation with the struggle for existence and their determination to fight for survival. The poignancy of the racial fears of radical intellectuals who view themselves struggling against a different people are suggested by certain similarities between statements of the 1911 Chinese revolutionaries and black militants in the United States in the 1960s (Rankin 1971, 29).

Portrait of Sun Yat-Sen.

Darwinian Ethics in China

In the minds of Hitler, Stalin, and Mao, *treating* people as animals was not wrong because they all believed that Darwin had "proved" humans were *not* God's creation, but instead were animals descended from a "simple" one-celled organism. All three of these men believed it was morally proper to eliminate the less fit or "herd them like cattle into boxcars bound for concentration camps and gulags" if it helped to achieve the goals that their Darwinist philosophy demanded (Perloff 1999, 225).

The extent that Darwinism was inculcated into the Chinese people is indicated by the fact that Mao was still using the Darwinian idiom "the triumph of the fittest" as late as 1957 (Pusey 1983, 452). Even in the post-Mao period, some of the most harmful "Darwinism myths" still influenced Chinese government policy (Pusey 1983, 452).

The Europeans also used Darwinism to help justify their imperialism against China. As the most fit race, they declared it was their right to rule the "unfit" races. Furthermore, although the Darwinian

> idea of struggle for survival could be used in almost any context, the 1911 revolutionaries tended to apply it particularly in racial terms. A crisis was now imminent; the white race had already subjugated the black, red, and brown races, leaving the current struggle between the white and yellow races. In this battle the white race was superior in industry, military might, government organization, and the

independent spirit of its people. Nonetheless, the example of Japan showed it was possible for the yellow race to rise (Rankin 1971, 30).

Some evolutionists even argued that "China's decline would result in extinction if unchecked," but the revolutionaries argued that the laws of evolution could be altered by human intervention and there was still

> time for the Chinese to adapt to the conditions of the modern world if they would arouse themselves quickly. To find a way out of the intolerable future that China faced from evolution the revolutionaries abandoned science in favor of the voluntary exercise of individual wills and sought a substitute for material strength in moral regeneration (Rankin 1971, 30).

She adds that the remedy to being destroyed as a result of "the laws of evolution" was revolution and violence and, furthermore, "China's desperate position justified and even demanded the use of violence" (1971, 30–31). At the same time the Chinese accepted the Darwin imperialism argument, one of the leading reformers, Liang Qichao, said in 1898: "If a country can strengthen itself and make itself one of the fittest, then, even if it annihilates the unfit and the weak, it can still not be said to be immoral. Why? Because it is a law of evolution" (Pusey 2009, 162).

Lu Xun (1881–1936), one of China's most important writers, tried to make practical sense of the Chinese Darwinism-inspired revolution (Pusey 1998; Fan 1998). Lu Xun relied heavily not only on Darwin, but also Haeckel whom he "accepted uncritically," especially Haeckel's "know-it-all-ism" idea that the "progressive evolution of mankind" has been proven "beyond the shadow of a doubt" and that there "was nothing that could not be explained by natural law" (Pusey 1998, 75).

As a result, he helped to "propagate a superstitious faith in science" (Pusey 1998, 75). Fortunately, Lu Xun "would not give in to the social Darwinian contention that his race was evolutionary low life" (Pusey 1998, 77). This, though, did not stop the Chinese from judging other races as evolutionarily inferior. The result was as follows:

> Although the idea of struggle for survival could be used in almost any context, the 1911 revolutionaries tended to apply it particularly in racial terms. A crisis was now imminent; the white race had already subjugated the black, red, and brown races, leaving the current struggle between the white and yellow race to rise. . . . China

was facing disaster; but the revolutionaries were proclaiming an urgent warning. . . . The natural laws of evolution were not impervious to human intervention (Rankin 1971, 30).

She adds: "The Remedy: Revolution and Violence" (Rankin 1971, 30).

Darwin Dominates Chinese Politics

Some of the early political reformers supported democracy but, realizing that the people in their country were totally unprepared for a democratic form of government, they emphasized Darwin's step-by-step gradualism that would give both direction and stability to their country. Thus, by appealing to Darwinian "natural law," they assumed that they could reach their goal. As a result, Darwinian belief impeded working directly toward democracy because of the conclusion that the step-by-step progress model was a fixed natural law *requiring* each stage to be achieved in order to achieve the end goal, democracy.

Conversely, as noted above, the revolutionaries also embraced Darwin, drawing inspiration from the idea that the "superior survive and the inferior are defeated." The man who introduced Darwinian evolution to the 1895 reformers was Yan Fu.

The reformers and the revolutionaries vigorously debated "with both sides wildly waving Darwin's banner" (Pusey 2009, 163). The leaders of these movements imbibed the scientific racism ideas coming from both America and Germany at that time, and saw themselves as most "fit" to rule. Pusey wrote that, unfortunately,

> both camps also accepted the pervasive Western view that Darwin had proven races unequal — that one race was "fitter" and therefore better than another. The reformers had originally done so to disassociate themselves from those who had fallen prey to the imperialists, such as the Africans and Indians. But in their exile in Japan, reformers and revolutionaries alike turned angrily on the Manchus as scapegoats, labeling them evolutionary low life, whose "unnatural" conquest of the Han Chinese was responsible for China's peril (Pusey 2009, 163).

The growth of Marxism in China after World War I was partly due to the fact that traditional Chinese pacifist philosophies were perceived as weak, and the Marxist worldview "seemed to them the fittest faith on Earth to help China to survive" (Pusey 2009, 163). This result was not totally due to

Darwin's ideas,

> but Darwin was involved in it all. To believe in Marxism, one had to
> believe in inexorable forces pushing mankind, or at least the elect,
> to inevitable progress, through set stages (which could, however, be
> skipped). One had to believe that history was a violent, hereditary
> class struggle (almost a "racial" struggle); that the individual must
> be severely subordinated to the group; that an enlightened group
> must lead the people for their own good; that the people must not
> be humane to their enemies; that the forces of history assured vic-
> tory to those who were right and who struggled (Pusey 2009, 163).

Pusey then asked, "Who taught Chinese these things? Marx? Mao? No.
Darwin" (Pusey 2009, 163). The end result was that the revolutionaries
"accepted terrorism as the best method for overthrowing the tyrannical
government" (Rankin 1971, 31). The result was a bloodbath greater than
any known in history, before or after. Some of the horrors committed by
the Chinese communists were documented by Yahya (2004). The Chinese
Holocaust was based on racial views and the conclusion that "racial differences irreconcilably divided peoples so that it was impossible for two races
to share equally and amicably in a government" (Rankin 1971, 56).

The Chinese Death Toll from Darwinian Marxism

Using primary documents, Chang and Halliday concluded that Mao was
"responsible for well over 70 million deaths in peacetime, more than any
other twentieth-century leader" (2005, 3). While some dispute this number,
the other figures provided are still in the multimillions (Benton and Chun
2010; Azar 1990). Schwartz (1972, 1985) claims that Mao Tse-tung's "Great
Cultural Revolution" Holocaust alone was responsible for some 29 million
deaths, as well as the disruption of the lives of over 600 million people.

Sonam Topgyal (1984, 7) calculated that the Chinese murdered
1,278,387 persons during their 33-year rule of Tibet. Specifically, 174,138
Tibetans, considered an inferior race and one that the Chinese government
was trying to control, died in prison and labor camps, 156,758 were executed, 432,607 died fighting, 413,151 died of starvation, 92,731 of torture,
and 9,002 of suicide.

Of the more than 7,000 active monasteries present in the Himalayas
before the 1950 Chinese takeover, only 6 remain today. During one three-
year period alone, the Chinese Red Army killed, or lost through desertion,

close to 150,000 of its own soldiers for disobeying orders, almost as many as were killed in action, captured, or discharged from the army for health reasons (Chang and Halliday 2005, 296).

The Mass Murderer Pol Pot

Mao Tse-tung modified Darwinism, changing the struggle for existence to a cultural revolution "struggle" in which his view of communism replaced his predecessors, such as Stalin. Mao Tse-tung's follower, Pol Pot, took yet a different view of the Darwinian struggle. Pol Pot was "introduced by his professor, Jean-Paul Sartre, to the idea of evolution to higher forms" of life which he translated in terms of an "urban-rural struggle in which one fourth of the population died" (Johnson 2012, 138).

As a result, Cambodia's Pol Pot soon became one of the world's worst mass murderers. He led the Khmer Rouge to genocide against his own people in a bloodthirsty regime that was inspired by the communism of China's notorious Mao Zedong. Race was a critical factor in Pot's extermination program, not the American or German racism, but racism based on physical features not usually associated with race in the Western sense (Kiernan 2008, 26). Estimates today are that the Pol Pot regime murdered or starved to death over a million and a half up to as many as three million of Cambodia's eight million inhabitants in a mere three short years, from 1975 to 1979.

The People's Republic of China was the main source of both financial and military support to the Pol Pot regime and, to some degree, is responsible for what happened in that country. Walter Moss writes:

> At the time of Mao's death in 1976 a Mao admirer in Cambodia, Pol Pot, was attempting to apply many of Mao's ideas in his own country. This Marxist and leader of the Khmer Rouge came to power in 1975. He did so partly because the heavy U.S. bombing of Cambodia — more than three times the amount of bombing inflicted on Japan in World War II — had destabilized the country and inadvertently increased support for this extreme anti-Western communist group (Moss 2008, 19).

As is true in most communist countries,

> The Khmer Rouge also forbade the . . . practice of religion. They waged fierce class warfare and attacked family life and traditional classes and culture. . . . Besides the upper classes, the main victims

were ethnic minorities such as the Chinese and Vietnamese, the sick (many in hospitals were killed or driven into the streets), and Catholics and Muslims. Gruesome tortures often preceded death, and the Khmer Rouge often not only displayed an indifference to individual human life, but also engaged in sadistic behavior (2008, 19–20).

Pol Pot was influenced by Darwinism but indirectly as a result of the influence of China, the subject of this chapter. Nonetheless, it was "Pol Pot . . . [who] applied Darwin's ideas in the slaughter of a vast number of Cambodians" (Alexis 2007, 159). "What Pol Pot had in common with Mao and Stalin, and to a lesser extent some other communist leaders, was a belief that the restructuring of society and human life justified the taking of human lives. . . . and the ideas of nineteenth-century thinkers like Marx (1818–83), Darwin (1809–82), and Friedrich Nietzsche (1844–1900), as well as racist, nationalist, and imperialist ideas, were often used, properly or improperly, to justify such killings" (Moss 2008, 20, 34).

The result was "the Khmer Rouge brought about a more radical transformation of the country in a shorter period of time than their fellow communists in the Soviet Union or China had succeeded in doing (Moss 2008, 19). Ho Chi Minh, the leader of the Communist Party in Viet Nam, was also influenced by Darwin's ideas (Brocheux 2007, 38). Paul Johnson concluded that in

> the twentieth century, it is likely that over 100 million people were killed or starved to death as a result of totalitarian regimes infected with varieties of social Darwinism. But then Darwin himself had always insisted on the high percentage of destruction involved in breeding. . . . Nature, he believed is always profuse, in death as well as life. . . . At the time *Origin* was published, there were about 1,325 million human beings in the world. By the time Mao Tse-tung, last of the great "exterminators," died — having himself presided over the deaths of 70 million — the human total had risen to 3,900 million (Johnson 2012, 138).

Conclusions

The Chinese and Cambodian Holocausts were possible because Darwinism is more than a scientific theory: it is fundamentally a comprehensive worldview, a philosophical stance about the nature of all reality. The materialism that underpins the Darwinian worldview spawned scientific racism and eugenics in the West and revolutionary fervor in the East. The new generation must understand and recognize the significance of this fact and avoid uncritical acceptance of the philosophical roots of any science (Pusey 2009, 163). The number of Darwinists today in China is higher than in most nations — 74 percent compared to 56 percent in Russia and 52 percent in Spain and Egypt, according to one study. Yet few understand its contribution to their recent turbulent history (Stephenson 2009).

References

Alexis, Jonas. 2007. *In the Name of Education.* Maitland, FL: Xulon Press.

Azar, Larry. 1990. *Twentieth Century in Crisis: Foundations of Totalitarianism.* Dubuque, IA: Kendal-Hunt.

Benton, Gregor, and Lin Chun (editors). 2010. *Was Mao Really a Monster: The Academic Response to Chang and Halliday's Mao: The Unknown Story.* New York: Routledge.

Boorman, Howard L. 1963. "Mao Tse-tung: The Lacquered Image." *The China Quarterly* 16:1-55.

Brocheux, Pierre. 2007. *Ho Chi Minh: A Biography.* New York: Cambridge University Press.

Chang, Jung, and Jon Halliday. 2005. *Mao: The Unknown Story.* New York: Knopf.

Devillers, Philippe. 1967. *Mao.* New York: Schocken.

Dikötter, Frank. 1992. *The Discourse of Race in Modern China.* Stanford, CA: Stanford University Press.

Dirlik, Arif. 1989. *The Origins of Chinese Communism.* New York: Oxford University Press.

Fan, Fa-ti. 1998. "Book Review of *Lu Xun and Evolution.*" *Journal of History of Biology* 32(1):218–220.

Hsü, Kenneth. 1986. *The Great Dying: Cosmic Catastrophe, Dinosaurs and the Theory of Evolution.* New York: Harcourt, Brace Jovanovich.

Johnson, Paul. 2012. *Darwin: Portrait of a Genius.* New York: Viking

Karl, Rebecca E. 1998. "Creating Asia: China in the World at the Beginning of the Twentieth Century." *The American Historical Review* 103(4):1096–1118.

Kiernan, Ben. 2008. *The Pol Pot Regime: Race, Power, and Genocide in Cambodia Under the Khmer Rouge, 1975–79.* New Haven, CT: Yale University Press

Meisner, Maurice. 2007. *Mao Zedong: A Political and Intellectual Portrait.* Malden, MA: Polity Press.

Milner, Richard. 2009. *Darwin's Universe: Evolution from A to Z.* Berkeley, CA: University of California.

Moss, Walter. 2008. *An Age of Progress? Clashing Twentieth-Century Global Forces.* New York: Anthem Press.

Perloff, James. 1999. *Tornado in a Junkyard.* Arlington, MA: Refuge Books.

Pusey, James Reeve. 1983. *China and Charles Darwin.* Boston, MA: Harvard University Press.

———. 1998. *Lu Xin & Evolution.* Albany, NY: State University of New York Press.

———. 2009. "Global Darwin: Revolutionary Road." *Nature* 462:162–163.

Rankin, Mary B. 1971. *Early Chinese Revolutionaries: Radical Intellectuals in Shanghai and Chekiang, 1902–1911.* Cambridge, MA: Harvard University Press.

Ruse, Michael. 1986. "Biology and Values: A Fresh Look," in *Logic, Methodology, and Philosophy of Science,* by Marcus et al. Elsevier Science Publications.

Schwartz, Fred. 1972. *The Three Faces of Revolution.* Falls Church, VA: The Capital Hill Press.

———. 1985. "Demand for an Astronomical Sum in Reparations." *Christian Anti-Communism Crusade,* Feb. 1.

Short, Philip. 1999. *Mao: A Life.* New York: Henry Holt.

Sing, Lam Lai. 2000. *Mao Tse-Tung's Ch'I and the Chinese Political Economy with Special Reference to the Post-Mao Modernization Revolution.* Lewiston, NY: The Edwin Mellen Press.

Snow, Edgar. 1961. *Red Star Over China.* New York: Grove Press.

Stein, George J. 1988. "Biological Science and the Roots of Nazism." *American Scientist* 76:50–58.

Stephenson, Tony. 2009. "Darwin Survey Shows International Consensus on Acceptance of Evolution." *British Council,* www.britishcouncil.org/darwin.

Topgyal, Sonam. 1984. "Over 1.2 Million Died Under Chinese Rule." *Tibetan Review* 19(3):7.

Yahya, Harun. 2004. *Communist China's Policy of Oppression in East Turkestan.* Istanbul: Global Publishing.

Zhisui, Dr. Li. 1994. *The Private Life of Chairman Mao.* New York, NY: Random House.

Chapter 16

Darwinian Criminality Theory: A Tragic Chapter in History

Introduction

Darwinists once believed that individual human beings occasionally reverted, both physically and mentally, to a prehuman stage of evolutionary development. This person was called an atavistic throwback. As a result of this belief, the focus of Darwinian criminologists was on identifying the criminal type who should be imprisoned permanently to protect society, even if the particular offense committed was minor. Conversely, if a "non-criminal type" committed even a serious offense, it was an aberration, and therefore, they argued, imprisonment would serve no purpose.

Darwinian criminologists believed punishment must fit the criminal and not the crime. Criminologists widely adopted this theory to explain crime and, as a result, it influenced both public opinion and official policy. The "criminal physical type" stereotype is still very much with us, even though the theory of evolutionary throwbacks (atavisms) as a causative factor in criminality was empirically disproved decades ago.

The major influences Darwinism had on racism, the Holocaust, and World War II, all have been well documented in this volume and elsewhere (Weikart 2003). Racism influenced, or reinforced, by Darwinism especially was "a persistent theme of American and British anthropology" (Lewin 1987, 55). Less widely known is the adverse effect Darwinism has had on nearly every field of human endeavor and "nowhere was the triumph of scientific materialism more consequential than in the field of crime and punishment" including penology (West 2007, 42). Darwinian corrections theory developed partly because, once a theory is established in one discipline, it often is uncritically adopted into other disciplines. Scientists in most fields try to accommodate theories that they believe are well accepted in other fields, sometimes without adequate examination of them. This acceptance often occurs without full awareness of the debate that exists within the theory's own discipline.

Examples of fields in which Darwinism has been uncritically adopted with tragic consequences include not only criminology but also the whole fields of sociology and psychology. This fact "illustrates the enormous influence of evolutionary theory in fields far removed from its biological core. Even the most abstract scientists are not free agents. Major ideas have remarkably subtle and far-reaching extensions" (Gould 1977, 223). For example,

> the nineteenth-century preoccupation with the process of evolution reinforced the degenerationist association of socially problematic behaviors with reversion to a lower form of life. Charles Darwin's *Origin of Species* (1859) seemed to depict a titanic, ubiquitous struggle between primitive and complex organisms. In *The Descent of Man* (1871) Darwin explained that evolution creates hierarchies of intelligence, morality, and other human characteristics (Rafter 1997, 37).

Sociologists, in general, uncritically accepted Darwinism, especially after Comte published his *Polity* (Barnes 1948, 106–107). The acceptance of Darwinism in sociology was based on the reasoning that human

> social organization has developed as a result of his biological evolution — hence, social evolution is subsequent to but essentially parallel with, and presumably a product of, biological evolution. Individual human characteristics and behavior are therefore to

be understood as reflections of this common organic and biological inheritance, not freely and intelligently self-determined, but biologically determined (Vold 1958, 10).

The behavioral sciences were influenced by biological evolution to the extent that the study of human cultures and societies has been modeled by current biological evolution theories. This has been true for decades and has affected both theory and policy (Morris 1974). Weatherwax noted that as early as the late 1800s, "the principle of [biological] evolution, and its influence has carried over into the field of social problems and has had a profound influence on all thought" (1909, 42; see Gould 1977, 223). Darwinism not only caused these ideas to become mainstream but also to intensify speculation about evolution and humans' relationship to less complex organisms. Darwinism also shaped the work done in the natural sciences and by

> English sociologist Herbert Spencer, who coined the phrase "survival of the fittest." Such speculation intensified with the 1859 publication of *The Origin of Species*, in which Darwin argues that "the innumerable species, genera, and families of organic beings, with which this world is peopled, have all descended . . . from common parents." . . . Darwin's ideas seemed to be congruent with the notion of the criminal as an animalistic holdover from the primitive past. Passages in which Darwin remarks on "rudimentary, atrophied, or aborted organs," moreover, could easily be read as confirmations of Lombroso's reports of the criminal's snakelike teeth and other animalistic anomalies (Rafter 1997, 126).

Eventually it was realized that some applications of Darwinism (such as *social Darwinism*) caused a great deal of harm.

The History of Atavism

The idea of human atavism was first openly discussed by Darwin in 1871. An example is his suggestion that persons with the "worst dispositions, which occasionally without any assignable cause make their appearance in families, may perhaps be reversions to a savage state, from which we are not removed by very many generations" (Darwin 1881, 137). Since atavistic persons had degenerated not only behaviorally but also physically, it soon was argued that criminals could often be identified by *physical traits alone*. Abnormal dentition, asymmetry of the face, large ears, certain eye defects, "ape-like" facial features, and "inverted" sexual characteristics (homosexuality) were all viewed as physical evidence of an atavistic human and thus also a criminal type (Taylor et al. 1973, 41).

The atavism concept was a major line of evidence that Darwin used to support his theory, and evolutionists believed that a "reversion to a former state of existence," which was widely accepted in the late 1800s, can only be explained by the theory that humans

> descended from some ape-like creature, no [other] valid reason can be assigned why certain muscles should . . . suddenly reappear after an interval of many thousand generations, in the same manner as with horses, asses, and mules, dark coloured stripes suddenly reappear on the legs, and shoulders, after an interval of hundreds, or more probably thousands of generations (Darwin 1871, Vol. 1, 129).

He added that these cases of reversion are

> closely related to those of rudimentary organs given in the first chapter [of his book]. . . . Some parts which are rudimentary in man, as the os coccyx in both sexes, and the mammae in the male sex, are always present; whilst others, such as the supracondyloid foraman, only occasionally appear, and therefore might have been introduced under the head of reversion. These several reversionary structures, as well as the strictly rudimentary ones, reveal the descent of man from some lower form in an unmistakable manner (Darwin 1871, Vol. 1, 129–130).

Darwin concluded that atavism was "unmistakable" evidence for human evolution. Lyell even attributed genius in areas as diverse as religion, ethics, philosophy, and the sciences to atavism:

> The occasional appearance of such extraordinary mental powers may be attributed to atavism; but there must have been a beginning to the series of such rare and anomalous events. If, in conformity with the law of progression, we believe mankind to have risen slowly from a rude and humble starting point, such leaps may have successively introduced not only higher and higher forms and grades of intellect, but at a much remoter period may have cleared at one bound the space which separated the highest stage of the unprogressive intelligence of the inferior animals from the first and lowest form of improvable reason manifested by Man (1863, 504–505).

Exactly what caused this physical and mental regression or degeneration never was explained. Nonetheless, atavism was considered a major evidence of evolution for decades (Pal 1918). Atavism also shared both the respect and acceptance of Darwinists for decades and doubts became more frequent only after the 1940s. An early 1940 booklet argued that, while atavism was claimed to be one of the most compelling proofs for evolution and "an interesting phenomenon to the student of heredity," it does not provide

> evidence of evolution. If we had really descended from ape-like creatures, we might expect to find some of the characteristics of these ancestors appearing now and then among human beings. . . . This "proof" reminds us that within the last few years a scientist solemnly suggested that the present jazz craze was an evolutionary [atavism, causing a mimicking] development of the rhythmic movements of the jelly-fish (Pettit 1942, 82).

Atavism Applied to Criminology

The adoption of the evolution theory called "atavism" by the field of corrections turned out to be a tragic example of what can result from the uncritical acceptance of ideas from one field by another. The development of the now completely discredited human atavism theory had tragic consequences for thousands of persons (Rennevile 1995; Gould 1996). As noted, Atavism is the belief that certain physical traits can appear in humans that are the result of a biological "throw-back" to an earlier stage of our evolutionary history (Rennevile 1995). Related to Haeckel's "ontogeny recapitulates phylogeny" theory, atavism teaches that early human development involves passing through our evolutionary history. When this evolutionary development is blocked, the result is the birth of a more "primitive" human type (Lombroso-Ferrero 1911). The major source of this idea was Darwin, who wrote:

> With mankind, some of the worst dispositions, which occasionally without any assignable cause make their appearance in families, may perhaps be reversions to a savage state, from which we are not removed by very many generations. This view seems indeed recognized in the common expression that such men are the black sheep of the family (1871, Vol. 1, 173).

The primitive type involved behavior that was the result of natural selection, because at one time the behavior aided survival. Lombroso and other Darwinists included behavior that we call rape, plus parricide, infanticide, cannibalism, kidnapping, and other "antisocial actions found throughout the animal kingdom, as well as among human savages" were all selected (West 2007, 51). Noyes wrote, in the "process of evolution, crime has been one of the necessary accompaniments of the struggle for existence" (1888, 34). Crime now is wrong, many Darwinists then argued, because it no longer serves a necessary function in human society.

The atavism theory of crime causation was developed by the theorist whom many regard as one of the founding fathers of criminology, Cesare Lombroso (1835–1909), professor of psychiatry at the University of Pavia (Harrowitz 1994; Papa 1983; Simon 1990; Wolfgang 1961). Lombroso became one of the "most eulogized" scientists in history — until he realized the harm that his ideas caused. He then became one of the most attacked criminologists of his day (Cole 1995). Lombroso's views are discussed in depth in his 1876 book *The Criminal Man* in which he taught that "criminals are a form of evolutionary throwback to a more primitive human type" (Lindesmith et al. 1937). In the words of Rafter, Lombroso and his followers concluded that

> incorrigible offenders are "born criminals," apelike throwbacks to a more primitive evolutionary stage. Born criminals differ so radically from lawful people that scientists can identify them by their physical and mental abnormalities, just as physical anthropologists can identify members of different races by their physical characteristics (1997, 110).

Many behavioral scientists once accepted the belief that individual "throwbacks" or "degenerations" (referred to as *atavisms* by Darwin and *criminal anthropology* by those in corrections) caused a type of a moral prehuman to be born to "normal" families (Kurella 1910, 19). These researchers deemphasized the importance of both environmental and sociological factors in crime. They spent much time measuring various body parts, especially foreheads and brain cases, concluding that the closer the person physically resembled an ape, the greater the evolutionary and behavioral "regression."

Specific traits they looked for included "a smaller skull with certain traits found among animals, a taller body, handle-shaped ears, insensitivity to pain, acute eyesight, and left-handedness" (Wetzell 2000, 29). They believed this method was as scientific as the traditional *experimental versus control group* and other common research methods used in the behavioral sciences (Lombroso-Ferrero 1911). The ultimate source of this idea is from Darwin:

Whereas Lombroso's idea of measuring criminals' bodies and skulls derived from the anthropometric practices of contemporary physical anthropology, his interpretation of these characteristics as atavistic reflected the influence of Charles Darwin (Wetzell 2000, 29).

Gould concluded that Lombroso's theory was not just a

vague proclamation that crime is hereditary — such claims were common enough in his time — but a specific *evolutionary* theory based upon anthropometric data. Criminals are evolutionary throwbacks in our midst. Germs of an ancestral past lie dormant in our heredity. In some unfortunate individuals, the past comes to life again. These people are innately driven to act as a normal ape or savage would, but such behavior is deemed criminal in our civilized society (Gould 1996, 153).

Gould added that the supporters believed that this system made it easy to

identify born criminals because they bear anatomical signs of their apishness. Their atavism is both physical and mental, but the physical signs, or stigmata as Lombroso called them, are decisive. Criminal *behavior* can also arise in normal men, but we know the "born criminal" by his anatomy. Anatomy, indeed, is destiny, and born criminals cannot escape their inherited taint: "We are governed by silent laws which never cease to operate and which rule society with more authority than the laws inscribed on our statute books. [In conclusion, crime] . . . appears to be a natural phenomenon" (Gould 1996, 153).

This atavistic "degeneracy" was believed by many criminologists to cause the victims both to look more like an "animal" and also to behave "in more primitive and savage" ways than their civilized counterparts (Vold 1958, 28). These "animal-people" called "criminaloids" also were thought to be far more likely to become involved in criminal activities. Lombroso acknowledged that other factors exist, and that every criminal was not "born criminal," but estimated organic factors accounted for from 35 to 40 percent of criminal activity. He stressed that the congenital determinant was the principal cause, and environmental factors were one of the least important causes (West 2007, 51). To measure the level of "animal traits" in a person, scientists evaluated the various "physical characteristics of prison inmates" to identify certain features typically found in the criminal population. Among these characteristics . . . were shifty eyes, receding hairlines, red hair, strong jaws, wispy beards, and the like. Lombroso came to the conclusion that criminals are a form of evolutionary throwback to a more primitive human type (Robertson 1981, 183).

This theory was not an obscure view held by a few extremists, but probably was the most influential doctrine to emerge in corrections from the entire anthropometric tradition (Gould 1996, 165–172). Furthermore, Lombroso held a high position in the "brilliant epoch of positive study of the world" (Kurella 1910, v). In 1896, prominent French criminologist Dallemagne concluded that Lombroso's ideas and thoughts "revolutionized" corrections, and "for 20 years, his thoughts fed discussions; the Italian master was the order of the day in all debates; his thoughts appeared as events" (Gould 1996, 165). Gould adds that Dallemagne's observation about the widespread acceptance of atavism was accurate and, unfortunately, had a major influence on corrections:

> Criminal anthropology was not just an academician's debate, however lively. It was *the* subject of discussion in legal and penal circles for years. It provoked numerous "reforms" and was, until World War I, the subject of an international conference held every four years for judges, jurists, and government officials as well as for scientists (1996, 165–166).

Lombroso's Worldview

As a youth, Lombroso embraced "free thought" philosophy and Darwinism, rejecting the Church and its teachings. Lombroso was guided primarily by materialism and "by the Darwinian idea of the variability of races" (Kurella 1910, 12). The theory Lombroso developed became an "important criteria for judgment in many criminal trials. Again we cannot know how many men were condemned unjustly because they were extensively tattooed, failed to blush, or had unusually large jaws and arms" (Ferri 1897, 166–167, quoted in Gould 1996, 168–169). Mr. Ferri, Lombroso's chief lieutenant, wrote that a study of the

> anthropological factors of crime provides the guardians and administrators of the law with new and more certain methods in the detection of the guilty . . . [physical traits] will frequently suffice to give police agents . . . scientific guidance in their inquiries. . . . And

when we remember the enormous number of crimes and offenses which are not punished, for lack or inadequacy of evidence, and the frequency of trials which are based solely on circumstantial hints, it is easy to see the practical utility of the primary connection between criminal sociology and penal procedure (Ferri 1897, 166–167, quoted in Gould 1996, 168–169).

Lombroso's thinking is apparent in his discussion of crimes that he was called upon to solve, such as a case about two stepsons accused of killing a woman. After his examination, Lombroso declared (1911, 436) that one stepson was "the most perfect type of the born criminal; enormous jaws, frontal sinuses, and zygomata. . . ." This stepson "was convicted" in spite of the lack of evidence. In another case, based solely on circumstantial evidence, Lombroso argued for the conviction of a man accused of robbing and murdering a rich farmer. The evidence included testimony that the accused was seen sleeping near the crime and hid the next morning when the police approached. No other evidence of his guilt was given.

Lombroso's examination concluded that this man had "a physiognomy approaching the criminal type. . . . In every way, then, biology furnished in this case indications which, joined with the other evidence, would have been enough to convict him in a country less tender toward criminals" (1911, 437). Although he was acquitted, Lombroso felt he should have been convicted on the basis of biological evidence alone.

The Major Tragedy of the Darwin Atavistic Belief:
Its influence on Social Policy

As noted, Darwinian theory was used most prominently in corrections by Cesare Lombroso, who was trained in both psychiatry and biology. He obtained his atavistic beliefs from his academic training in evolution and his study of the works of

Charles Darwin, who connected modern humans with a nonhuman past through his theory of evolution. Lombroso had been involved for some time in the study of physical differences between criminals and normals, but his notion of atavism as a cause of crime emerged as a bolt from the blue during his autopsy of an infamous robber, whom Lombroso found to have skull depressions characteristic of lower primates (McCaghy 1976, 14).

Lombroso has been described as one of the best-known criminologists and the founder of the positivist corrections school, which applied the scientific method to study the cause of behavior (Klein 1996; Lentini 1981; Scartezzini 1981; Cole 1995). Professor McCaghy claims that his importance in stimulating

FRANK LESLIE'S
ILLUSTRATED
WEEKLY

A scene in the courtroom before the acquittal of Lizzie Borden, the accused, and her counsel, ex-Governor Robinson, 1893.

> research on the criminal is undeniable. . . . Lombroso's most important book was *L'Uomo delinquente* (*The Criminal Man*), first published in Italy in 1876. Here he presented his doctrine of evolutionary *atavism*. Criminals were seen as distinct types of humans who could be distinguished from non-criminals by certain physical traits. These traits . . . served to identify persons who were out of step with the evolutionary scheme. Such persons were considered to be closer to apes or to early primitive humans than were most modern individuals; they were throwbacks (atavists) to an earlier stage in human development (1976, 14).

In his book, *The Criminal Man*, Lombroso included a long series of anecdotes to prove that the *usual* behavior of all animals was criminal and amoral. Among the many examples that he provided were animals that eliminate sexual rivals by "murder," animals that killed out of rage (such as "mad" elephants), and other animals committing mass murder by going on stampedes, etc. He also used as "proof" examples such as ants that killed recalcitrant aphids and devoured them as "punishment." Lombroso even argued that the methods insectivorous plants used to procure food were the "equivalent of crime."

Having established to his own satisfaction that animals were "criminal" by our standards, he then proceeded to build a case for the view that humans who committed similar "crimes" also must have reverted back to their animal ancestry (Rafter 1997). Even the language used by atavistic criminals, Lombroso concluded, was similar to that of "savage tribes" and he argued that many onomatopoeias and personifications of inanimate objects, demonstrated this regression. Said Lombroso (1911, 225), "They speak like savages, because they are true savages in the midst of our brilliant European civilization." This conclusion, he believed, was

> not merely an idea, but a revelation. At the sight of that [criminal] skull, I seemed to see all of a sudden . . . the problem of the nature of the criminal — an atavistic being who reproduces in his person the ferocious instincts of primitive humanity and the inferior animals. Thus were explained anatomically the enormous jaws, high cheekbones, prominent superciliary arches, solitary lines in the palms, extreme size of the orbits, handle-shaped or sessile ears found in criminals, savages, and apes, insensibility to pain, extremely acute sight, tattooing, excessive idleness, love of orgies, and the irresistible craving for evil for its own sake, the desire not only to extinguish life in the victim, but to mutilate the corpse, tear its flesh, and drink its blood (Lombroso 1911, xiv–xv).

Other researchers explained the "primitive moral" concept in terms of psychology:

> Drawing on the evolutionary explanation of moral backwardness that criminal anthropologists had used before him, Goddard hypothesized that the "primitive" instincts "that lead the child to become what we loosely call a moral imbecile, ripen about the age of nine years; now if a child is arrested in his development at just about that time when he is a liar, a thief, a sex pervert, or whatever else he may be, because those instincts are strong in him. . . . Had he been arrested in his development a year or two sooner, he would not have been a moral imbecile (Rafter 1997, 138).

Importantly, "Lombroso's theory was not a work of abstract science. He founded and actively led an international school of 'criminal anthropology' that spearheaded one of the most influential late nineteenth-century social movements" (Papa 1983). Lombroso's "positive" or "new" school "campaigned vigorously for changes in law enforcement and penal practices" (Gould 1977, 225). Lombroso coined the word "criminology" to refer to the study of unlawful behavior, and it was largely due to his efforts that universities began teaching criminology classes. Lombroso and his many distinguished students also invoked biology to argue that punishment must fit the criminal, not the crime. Gould provides the following example:

> A normal man might murder in a moment of jealous rage. What purpose would execution or a life in prison serve? He needs no reform, for his nature is good; society needs no protection from him, for he will not transgress again. A born criminal might be in the dock for some petty crime. What good will a short sentence serve: since he cannot be rehabilitated, a short sentence only reduces the time to his next, perhaps more serious, offense. . . . The original Lombrosians advocated harsh treatment for "born criminals" (1996, 170–171).

Gould opined that this "misapplication of anthropometry and evolutionary theory is all the more tragic because Lombroso's biological model was so utterly invalid and because it shifted so much attention from the social basis of crime to fallacious ideas about the innate propensity of criminals" (1996, 170–171).

The atavistic criminal anthropology school evaluated many trivial human physical traits, including ears, to find evidence of atavism. For example, Beall (1894, 262) describes ears that formed an almost acute angle at the top, and contrasted to the "graceful curve which is characteristic of the normal ear." Beall concludes that this sharp ear form "is very common in those who are tainted with criminal proclivities or who incline to abnormality of some sort." Beall then gives an example of an ear that is a "coarse, unloving appendage to the human head [which] bespeaks a perverted or undeveloped mind. It is a mark of arrested or distorted development" (p. 262). After describing the criminal ear, the author concludes, "Such ears as these are a badge of inherited poverty of moral instinct," thus we should "study these placards which nature has erected and thus prepare ourselves intelligently to labor for the development of our race" (p. 262). This view implies that prison sentences should be based more on the ear type of the accused than on the crime — and unfortunately, sentences were often based more on morphology than behavior.

Women, Atavism, and Crime

The theory of women and crime that Lombroso developed also argued that female crime is explained by Darwin's atavistic theory:

Cesare Lombroso (1835–1909), one of the earliest criminologists to theorize about why women commit crimes, concluded that individuals develop differentially within sexual and racial limitations. He suggested that the human race ranged hierarchically from the white male, who was the most highly developed, down to the nonwhite female. Lombroso believed that women shared many traits with children and that they were morally deficient. He attributed their relatively small participation in crime to their lack of intelligence (Simon 1983, 1665).

Lombroso argued that even prostitution can be explained by atavism (Lombroso 1996). He reasoned that the

> precocity of prostitutes — the precocity which increases their apparent beauty — is primarily attributable to atavism. Due also to it is the virility underlying the female criminal type; for what we look for most in the female is femininity, and when we find the opposite in her we conclude as a rule that there must be some anomaly. And in order to understand the significance and the atavistic origin of this anomaly, we have only to remember that virility was one of the special features of the savage women. . . . The primitive woman was rarely a murderess; but she was always a prostitute, and such she remained until semi-civilised epochs. Atavism, again, then explains why prostitutes should show a greater number of retrogressive characteristics than are to be observed in the female criminal (Lombroso and Ferrero 1895, 111–112).

Lombroso and Ferrero also taught that women were less evolved than males, and from this idea came the view that women who behave like animals or just look "wild" is proof that these women are nearer to their animal origins. Consequently, they will have other anomalies that prove their atavistic origin, such as large jaws and cheekbones (Lombroso and Ferrero 1895, 112; Kline 1996). Atavism even explained the comparative rarity of the criminal type in women who congenitally "are less inclined to crime than men," partly because they are "by nature less ferocious than males" (Lombroso and Ferrero 1895, 110).

Other researchers then argued that women were more involved in some kinds of crime than males. For example, W.I. Thomas credited women with "superior capabilities of survival because they are farther down the scale in terms of evolution" (Klein 1996, 167). Lombroso's ideas on women and crime were very influential in the late 1800s and early 1900s, especially in Italy, France, and Germany (Bland and Doan 1998; Papa 1983; Renneville 1994). Many of his followers had very similar ideas on women and atavism.

In Klein's words, the road from Lombroso to our present view of criminals was "surprisingly straight" (1996, 162). His work influenced many accomplished criminologists, including one of Lombroso's most celebrated disciples, Enrico Ferri (1856–1929), who also was a disciple of Darwin (West 2007, 51). Other famous disciples of Lombroso include Eugenio Florian, Roberto Ardigo, Vilfredo Pareto, and W.I. Thomas (who wrote several important volumes on corrections in the early 1900s) (Scartezzini 1981; Lentini 1981).

Just how widespread the genetic atavistic theory of crime was is indicated by Weikart's claim that

> most eugenicists viewed criminality — or at least the tendency to criminality — as a hereditary condition, many eugenicists also suggested permanent incarceration for habitual criminals. Ribbert, for example, thought habitual criminals should be treated just like the mentally ill, permanently locking them away in asylums. Luschan agreed, since "crime in the great majority of cases is a hereditary disease" and therefore "the Criminal [*sic*] should only be considered as a pure lunatic, who is not responsible for his ill doings." Not holding criminals responsible for their actions, however, did not imply that they would get off scot-free. In fact, the new eugenics conception of incarceration made their "punishment" even worse than under the old system. Luschan called for "*the complete and permanent isolation of the criminal*," rather than the current system of temporary incarceration and then release, which allowed criminals to have children in between stints in prison. Luschan expressed faith that vigorous eugenics measures would ultimately eradicate crime from society (2003, 137).

A major Lombrosian solution to crime, especially born criminals, was to permanently remove them from society, which meant life imprisonment (West 2007, 52). A second solution was to prohibit atavistic people from breeding, as is obvious in Ribbert's ideas (Klein 1996, 161).

The End of the Atavistic Criminal Theory

The best-known early study to empirically evaluate atavism as a factor in causing crime was that of Charles Goring (1919). In his study, which then was considered to be a model of scientific and technical accuracy, Goring carefully compared approximately 3,000 English convicts with several large groups of Englishmen who did not have criminal records. The convicts he studied were all recidivists, and he assumed for this reason that most were of a "thoroughly criminal type." Goring also made comparisons with university undergraduates, officers in the British army, and hospital patients.

He found that "there were no more protrusions or other peculiarities of head among the prisoners than among the Royal Engineers" (Vold 1958, 53). Although Goring's work resulted in a major blow to the theory of atavism and crime, it took years to convince its many devoted followers that the theory was invalid. Atavism still persisted in the American penal code as late as the 1940s (Pick 1986). As Gould notes, Lombroso slowly retreated under the growing barrage of criticism for his theory; yet he never abandoned (or even compromised) his conclusion that crime is biological. Rather, he

> merely enlarged the range of innate causes. His original theory had the virtue of simplicity and striking originality — criminals are apes in our midst, marked by the anatomical stigmata of atavism. Later versions became more diffuse, but also more inclusive. Atavism remained as a primary biological cause of criminal behavior, but Lombroso added several categories of congenital illness and degeneration: "We see in the criminal," he wrote (1887, 651), "a savage man and, at the same time, a sick man." In later years, Lombroso awarded special prominence to epilepsy as a mark of criminality; he finally stated that almost every "born criminal" suffers from epilepsy to some degree. The added burden imposed by Lombroso's theory upon thousands of epileptics cannot be calculated; they became a major target of eugenical schemes in part because Lombroso had explicated their illness as a mark of moral degeneracy (1996, 164).

The empirical evidence against the theory, the daily contradictions to it, and even the lack of evidence were not the only reasons for the theory's ultimate downfall (Moran 1978). Another reason was that, although many researchers and criminologists realized the atavistic idea was fatally flawed, many looked to new biological hypotheses to explain crime. As a result, other theories that implied criminals were physically different from noncriminals, such as those of Sheldon et al. (1940), later came into vogue.

An important question is, "How did the theory of atavism come to take such a prominent place in corrections, complete with examples that convinced many professionals of the correctness of the theory?" Several hypotheses include:

1. Once a belief is established, its supporters can often find support for it if they look long and hard enough (Gould 1996, 1976). In researching a "criminal" population, one can often locate what appear to be good examples of offenders who had "ape-like" body characteristics. Unless a comparative group of noncriminals is used, only limited insight can be gained by this technique. Many examples of people who supported the theory were located among the criminal population, and it was assumed without data that comparable examples did not exist (or rarely existed) in the noncriminal population. Topinard noted that Lombroso did not say, "Here is a fact which suggests an induction . . . [rather his] conclusion is fashioned in advance; he seeks proof, he defends his thesis like an advocate who ends up by persuading himself . . . [Lombroso] is too convinced" (1887, 676).

2. Certain nationalities or races are, at times, more likely to be involved in crime because of their social environment, discrimination, or other reasons. These races include some which had the characteristics that were supposedly typical of an atavistic person. In America, white Anglo-Saxon Protestants were less commonly found among the convicted criminal populations compared to individuals who were members of minority groups such as Blacks, Armenians, and others because of these reasons. This explanation may account for many of the alleged atavistic examples, just as it may now account for the highly disproportionate number of Blacks in American prisons (Klein 1996).

3. Due to disease, health problems, poverty, etc., certain individuals may develop traits that were similar to the supposed atavistic persons. These traits, in turn, may make it more difficult to hold a job or even achieve social acceptance. As a consequence of these factors, it became more difficult for such persons to exist within society's laws. They may, then, be more likely to involve themselves in criminal behavior (Nachshon 1985).

Lindesmith and Levin document that the Darwinian theory of criminality rapidly spread to the criminology elite as a result of a number of factors that caused the acceptance of Lombrosianism [the theories of Atavism expounded by the famous criminologist Cesaro Lombroso] as a logical development of already existing tendencies in the social sciences. Chief among these was the spread of Darwinism. After the publication in 1859 of Darwin's *Origin of the Species*, Darwinian concepts not only swept through the biological sciences, but were also applied in a wholesale manner in the social sciences — in anthropology, political sciences, and sociology (1937, 667).

Lindesmith and Levin add that Lombroso's ideas, although not original, were attractive to

those who were preoccupied with Darwinism and its application to other fields of thought. In the same year that the *Origin of the Species* appeared, an anthropological society was founded in Paris and the next decades witnessed considerable development of interest in this field. . . . In general, it may be said that an increased prestige of the natural sciences and especially of biology led to the beginning of a series of importations from one or the other of these fields into the realm of the social sciences. Lombrosianism represents the first major importation of this character into criminology (1937, 667–668).

Lindesmith and Levin also note that the history of science includes periods where "myth and fashion and social conditions often have exercised an influence quite unrelated to the soundness of theories or to the implications of accumulated evidence" (p. 671). Referring specifically to the Lombrosian theories (notably atavism), they add that the widespread acceptance of the Lombrosian theory of crime represents a retrogression in the field of

criminology rather than a step in advance. The eclipse of the earlier work may perhaps best be explained as a result of shifting prestige values associated with the importation of social Darwinism into the social sciences, with the growing popularity, in the latter part of the 19th century, of psychiatric and other individualistic or biological theories, and with the isolation of American criminology from earlier European developments (p. 653).

In addition, Lindesmith and Levin conclude that the preoccupation of Lombrosians with Darwinism and their belief that the causes of crime were found in the biology of the criminal rather than in his relations to others led them to fail entirely to appreciate the importance of the type of historical research done by Avé-Lallemant and others. What Lombroso did was to reverse the method of explanation that had been current since the time of Guerry and Quetelet and, instead of maintaining that institutions and traditions determined the nature of the criminal, he held that the nature of the criminal determined the character of institutions and traditions (p. 661).

It also should be stressed that, although Lombrosian crime causation theories were very popular, they also were sharply criticized by some in his day. A number of 19th-century biologists recognized the racism inherent in Darwinism and discerned where the theory was leading science. Others realized that the evidences on which atavism was based were weak or even close to nonexistent. Consequently, Gould notes that Lombroso's atavism theory

> caused a great stir and aroused one of the most heated scientific debates of the nineteenth century. Lombroso, though he peppered his work with volumes of numbers, had not made the usual obeisances to cold objectivity. Even those great apriorists, the disciples of Paul Broca, chided Lombroso for his lawyerly, rather than scientific, approach (1996, 162).

Although Lombrosian authors later modified their theory to allow for the influence of social factors (even in the case of supposed fully atavistic criminals), the theory was accepted by many people long after it was proved wrong — and it still is accepted by some today as valid (Ghiglieri 1999; Lewontin 1999; Kaplan et al. 1998; Giddens 1991; Nachshon 1985; Faccioli 1976; Burman 1994). Klein, citing several examples, concludes that the ideas of Lombroso, Thomas, and others of this school still influence contemporary theorists of criminality (1996, 175).

Summary and Conclusions

Although atavisms were once commonly touted as a major proof of evolution, the subject today is considered a "dark period" in criminology (Brown 1986). Even though many judge Lombroso's work a "bizarre aberration," his conclusions followed logically from Darwinism and the positivists' philosophy of the late 19th and early 20th century (Pick 1986). Like vestigial organs, embryonic recapitulation, and nascent organs, the whole concept of atavism is an embarrassment to biological science today. Virtually all of the conditions formerly labeled "atavistic" now are recognized as belonging in the domain of medicine.

Atavism is yet another embarrassing chapter in the history of Darwinism, which, although disproved, is still very much part of our culture, and its "bitter fruit" still infects our society (Rafter 1997; Rosenberg 1974). Hicks documented that even Lombroso's atavistic criminal idea is also still widely accepted in our culture and in the minds of law enforcers. Examples he gives include the incorrect stereotype of a burglar as someone who has a "jutting lower jaw, broken nose, low forehead, and isn't bright" (Hicks 1986, 130–156). Hicks adds that while a police officer in training, and an anthropology graduate student then as well, investigators from Tucson, Arizona, invited them

> to view a new videotape on conducting interviews and interrogations. . . . My reaction to the tape — not shared by my companions — went from interest to disbelief as I watched the Army investigator explain how one can identify criminal types by the structure of the cheek bones, distance between the eyes, degree of eyebrow growth, composition of the nose and so on, all illustrated by large charts depicting typical criminal faces. I recall that eyebrows that do not separate but represent a more or less hairy continuum from one eye socket to the next indicated nefarious propensities. (My own eyebrows, I am ashamed to say, are connected.) . . . And the reactions of my companions, who had never heard of Lombroso? My boss was impressed. The detective commander wanted a copy of the tape. And the I.R.S. and the Army — I shudder (1986, 130–156).

The connection of criminology to Darwinism was complex and went beyond atavism:

> Many natural science findings suggested that evolution is purposeful, its goal an ever-higher civilization. If this is true, then it follows that the criminal must be primitive, a holdover from an earlier evolutionary stage. Some of Darwin's own statements appear to equate adaptation with progress. In the final pages of *The Origin of Species* he rhapsodizes that "from the war of nature . . . the most exalted object which we are capable of conceiving, namely, the production of the higher animals, directly follows." *The Descent of Man* (1871), in which Darwin applies his theory of evolution specifically to humans, argues that man's "intellectual and moral faculties" are

"inherited" and "perfected or advanced through natural selection." With nature itself apparently striving to advance civilization, surely progressive nations should help by getting rid of born criminals (Rafter 1997, 127).

Tragically, the theory still is reflected in modern theories of biological determination (Nachshon 1985; Micale 1995; Shotwell 1998; Rothenberg 1975) and even in some "feminist criminology" schools (Brown 1986; Klein 1996; Faccioli 1976).

The theory of atavism is a tragic example of the tendency for the behavioral sciences to uncritically apply Darwinism to their discipline. Although the theory of atavism lacks empirical support, it was still accepted uncritically for decades and was used in theory building by criminologists and others. A major reason it was accepted was because it relied heavily on the assumption that atavism had been proven empirically. Part of this tragedy is the harm that this theory has caused to scientific progress by misdirecting significant energy into nonproductive dead ends.

The far greater tragedy is the fact that the theory probably influenced the criminal conviction of thousands of innocent victims. In conclusion, Macbeth's words apply especially to atavisms: "When the first enthusiasm [of evolution] wore off and the bill for the damages came in, the biologist realized that things had gone too far. There had been bad science as well as bad sociology . . ." (1971, 57). Unfortunately, this came too late for the thousands of victims who received unjust imprisonment and execution, in part due to a theory of criminality based on 19th-century Darwinism.

References

Barnes, Harry Elmer, editor. 1948. *An Introduction to the History of Socialism.* Chicago, IL: University of Chicago Press.

Beall, Edgar. 1894. "Criminal Ears." *Phrenological Journal* Nov. 98(5):262–3.

Bland, Lucy, and Laura Doan. 1998. *Sexology Uncensored.* Chicago, IL: University of Chicago Press.

Brown, Beverly. 1986. "Women and Crime: The Dark Figures of Criminology." *Economy and Society* 15(3):355–402.

Burman, Erica. 1994. Review of "Antisemitism, Misogyny and the Logic of Cultural Difference: Cesare Lombroso and Matilde Serao" by Nancy Horowitz. *Feminist Review* 53:111–113.

Cole, George F. 1995. *Of Criminal Justice; Seventh Edition.* New York: Wadsworth Publishing Company.

Darwin, Charles. 1871. *The Descent of Man.* New York: Modern Library Edition.

———. 1881. *The Descent of Man.* London: John Murray. Reprinted 1896 by D. Appleton and Co. New York.

Faccioli, Franca. 1976. "Criminality Today (Part One)." *Critica-Sociologica* 37:6–16.

Ghiglieri, Michael P. 1999. *The Dark Side of Man: Tracing the Origins of Male Violence.* Reading, PA: Perseus. Reading, PA.

Giddens, Anthony. 1991. *Introduction to Sociology.* New York: W.W. Norton.

Goring, Charles. 1919. *The English Convict: A Statistical Study.* London: His Majesty's Stationery Office.

Gould, Stephen J. 1976. "Criminal Man Revived." *Natural History* 85(3):16–18.

———. 1977. "The Criminal as Nature's Mistake," in *Ever Since Darwin.* New York: W.W. Norton and Company.

———. 1996. *The Mismeasure of Man.* New York: W.W. Norton and Co.

Harrowitz, Nancy. 1994. *Antisemitism, Misogyny and the Logic of Cultural Difference: Cesare Lombroso and Matilde Sero.* Lincoln, NE: University of Nebraska Press.

Hicks, Robert D. 1986. "Criminal Eyebrows." *The Nation* 237(8):130, 156.

Kaplan, Carina V., and Myriam I. Feldfeber. 1998. *The Construction of Subjectivities under Educational Policies of Social Selectivity: The Meritocratic Logic.* Paper presented at the International Sociological Association.

Klein, Dorie. 1996. "The Etiology of Female Crime," in *Criminological Perspectives; A Reader.* Edited by John Muncie, Eugene McLaughlin, and Mary Langan. Thousand Oaks, CA: Sage Publications, p. 160–182.

Kurella, Hans. 1910. *Cesare Lombroso, a Modern Man of Science.* Translated from the German by M. Eden Paul. New York: Rebman.

Lentini, Orlando. 1981. "Organicism and Social Action from Ardigo to Pareto." *Quaderni-di-Sociologia* 29(2):192–215.

Lewin, Roger. 1987. *Bones of Contention.* New York: Simon and Schuster.

Lewontin, R.C. 1999. "The Problem with an Evolutionary Answer." Review of *The Dark Side of Man: Tracing the Origins of Male Violence* by Michael P. Ghiglieri. *Nature* 400:728-729.

Lindesmith, A., and Levin, Y. 1937. "The Lombrosian Myth in Criminology." *American Journal of Sociology* 42:653–71.

Lombroso, Cesare. 1887. *L'homme Criminel.* Paris: F. Alcan.

———. and William Ferrero. 1895. *The Female Offender.* London: T. Fisher Unwin. Reprinted by Rothman, Littleton, CO, 1980.

———. 1911. *Crime, Its Causes and Remedies.* Boston, MA: Little Brown.

———. 1996. "The Criminal Type in Women and Its Atavistic Origin," in *Criminological Perspectives: A Reader.* Thousand Oaks, CA: Sage Publications.

Lombroso-Ferrero, Gina. 1911. *The Criminal Man, According to the Classification of Cesare Lombroso, Briefly Summarized by His Daughter Gina Lombroso-Ferrero, with an introduction by Cesare Lombroso, illustrated.* New York: G.P. Putnam.

Lyell, Charles. 1863. *The Antiquity of Man.* London: John Murray.

Macbeth, Norman. 1971. *Darwin Retried.* New York: Dell Publishers.

McCaghy, Charles. 1976. *Deviant Behavior.* New York: Macmillan.

Micale, Mark. 1995. Review of "Anti-Semitism, Misogyny, and the Logic of Cultural Difference: Cesare Lombroso and Matilde Serao" by Nancy Horowitz. *Modernism/Modernity* 2(3):185–186.

Moran, Richard. 1978. "Biomedical Research and the Politics of Crime Control: A Historical Perspective." *Contemporary Crises* 2(3):335–57.

Morris, Henry. 1974. *The Troubled Waters of Evolution.* San Diego, CA: Creation Life Publishers.

Nachshon, Israel. 1985. "Neuropsychological Aspects of Violent Behavior: Hemisphere Function." *Crime and Social Deviance* 13:37–64.

Noyes, William. 1888. "The Criminal Type." *Journal of Social Science*, April, 24:32–34.

Pal, S.B. 1918. "An Ectromelus: An Atavistic Relapse." *Journal of Mental Science* 64(266):268–71.

Papa, Emilio R. 1983. "Social Sciences, Positivism, and Political Engagement in the European Debate on the Italian School of Criminal Anthropology (1876–1900)." *Critica-Sociologica* 67:90–113.

Pettit, William H. 1942. "Evolution," in *Heresies Exposed,* edited by William Irvine. New York: Loizeaux Brothers.

Pick, Daniel. 1986. "The Faces of Anarchy: Lombroso and the Politics of Criminal Science in Post-Unification Italy." *History Workshop* 21:60–86.

Rafter, Nicole Hahn. 1997. *Creating Born Criminals.* Chicago, IL: University of Illinois Press.

Rennevile, Marc. 1994. "The Anthropology of the Criminal in France." *Criminologie* 27(2):185–209.

———. 1995. "Biological Theories of Criminal Behavior." *M-S (Medicine Sciences)* 11(12):1720–1724.

Robertson, Ian. 1981. *Sociology.* New York: Worth Publishers.

Rosenberg, Charles E. 1974. "The Bitter Fruit: Heredity, Disease, and Social Thought in Nineteenth-Century America." *Perspectives in American History* 8:189–235.

Rothenberg, Robert. 1975. *The Complete Book of Breast Care.* New York: Crown Publications.

Scartezzini, Riccardo. 1981. "Late Nineteenth-Century Research: The Vagabonds by Florian and Cavaglieri." *Quaderni-di-Sociologica* 29(2):216–235.

Sheldon, W.H., S.S. Stevens, and W.B. Tucker. 1940. *The Varieties of Human Physique.* New York: Harper and Row.

Shotwell, David A. 1998. "A Perspective on Delinquency." *The American Rationalist* 43(3):10–11.

Simon, Donatella. 1990. "Origins of Collective Psychology in France and Italy: Problems of Juridical & Criminal Sociology." *Studi di Sociologia* 28(4):507–517.

Simon, Rita James. 1983. "Women and Crime," in *The Encyclopedia of Crime and Justice,* edited by Sanford Kadish. New York: Macmillan and Free Press, p. 1664–1669.

Taylor, Ian, Paul Walton, and Jack Young. 1973. *The New Criminology.* London: Routledge and Kegan Paul.

Topinard, Paul. 1887. "L'Anthropologie criminelle." *Revue d'Anthropologue.* 3rd series 2:658:691.

Vold, George. 1958. *Theoretical Criminology.* New York: Oxford University Press.

Weatherwax, Paul. 1909. *Plant Biology.* New York: Macmillan Co.

Weikart, Richard. 2003. *From Darwin to Hitler: Evolutionary Ethics, Eugenics, and Racism in Germany.* New York: Palgrave Macmillan.

West, John G. 2007. *Darwin Day in America: How Politics and Culture Have Been Dehumanized in the Name of Science.* Wilmington, DE: ISI Books.

Wetzell, Richard F. 2000. *Inventing the Criminal: A History of German Criminology, 1880–1945.* Chapel Hill, NC: University of North Carolina Press.

Wolfgang, Marvin E. 1961. "Pioneers in Criminology: Cesare Lombroso (1835–1909)." *The Journal of Criminal Law and Criminology* 52(4):361–391.

Chapter 17

Darwinism and the 20th-Century Totalitarianism Holocaust

Introduction

The acceptance of Darwinism and the loss of the basic Christian influence in society were both major factors in the rise of Nazism, fascism, communism, and ruthless capitalism (see Azar 1990; Bergman 1999; Bergman 2001). These movements caused numerous wars, conflicts, and slaughters that lead to the deaths of hundreds of millions of persons. Professor Azar wrote that all of the "vicious ideologies of the first half of the twentieth century — Communism, Fascism, Nazism — paid homage to evolution" (1990, 218).

It is difficult to postulate how differently history would have unfolded if the Darwinian revolution never had occurred, but the evidence indicates that if Marx, Stalin, Hitler, Mao Tse-tung, and other totalitarian leaders had believed (and acted on) the Christian creationist theistic worldview, they would not have accepted atheism, materialism, and absolutism or have influenced the slaughters that dominated the 20th century. Rummel, in his mammoth three-volume study of the last century's mass murderers, concluded that at the top of the list were Stalin, Hitler, and Mao Tse-tung, in that order (2008, 8).

The historical evidence indicates that before becoming converts to Darwinism, Marx, Stalin, Hitler, and Mao Tse-tung all accepted the Christian teaching that all humans were brothers because they were all descendants of Adam and Eve (Medvedev 1989). If they had continued to embrace Christian creationism, they would not have become leaders of the anti-Christian totalitarian movements that ideologically opposed Christianity. For these reasons, Darwinism was likely an important factor in the deaths of an estimated over 250 million persons and the enormous suffering inflicted on more than a billion people. The tragic influence these Darwin converts had in world history can be estimated by reviewing the death toll of just two movements, the German and communist holocausts. Darwinism had

> been used to provide intellectual support to a multitude of cruel and vicious policies. Causes which have been justified by Social Darwinism include slavery, imperialism, racism, genocide, the Holocaust, Fascism, Communism, war, and not helping the poor, to name but a few. Where previously there was no clear intellectual justification for most of these causes, Darwin provided one, and . . . his justification had the backing of many reputable scientists of his day. . . . among historians with no axe to grind this is not controversial, although it is rarely expressed this directly, that Darwin must be listed as one of those responsible, along with numerous Nazis, for the Holocaust (Holden 2000, 2–3).

A common objection to the conclusion that Darwinism had an important influence on the Nazi and communist holocausts lies in the fact that, as far as we know, Darwin was a good husband and father, opposed slavery, and never actively openly opposed Christianity. The fact is, "Darwin was the first Social Darwinist," and the argument that you "can't blame him for the Holocaust" because "as a person he was not such a bad guy" is erroneous because "unless you are going to claim Darwin was a deeply stupid man (an opinion I certainly don't hold), he must have known the use his theory would be put to. Darwin's personal qualities also seem irrelevant" (Holden 2000, 4).

Many cruel sadistic tyrants have their good qualities. Hitler loved animals, especially his dog Blondie, and could be very nice to his mistress, children, and certain friends. Thus, absolving Darwin for the crimes of other Social

Darwinists is not unlike Dr. Frankenstein claiming the killing spree by the monster he created had nothing to do with him (Holden 2000, 4). Holden also concluded that Darwin "clearly" anticipated the uses to which his theory would be applied, and that Darwin was a racist who knew full well

> the alleged "perversion" of his theory, and his theory DID result in a lot of suffering (the only question being how much we can attribute to him, which is historically unanswerable with precision), then although I hesitate to use the term, judged by its historical impact it seems to me [to] be quite reasonable to call Darwinism evil. Especially since the theory is basically dogma and can not as claimed explain the origin of species . . . if the theory was true, one could hardly criticize it, as any attempt to censor science is dead wrong, and if that is the way the universe is, we just have to get used to it (Holden 2000, 4).

Although Darwin's goal in developing his evolution worldview was very clear from his writings, he rarely openly or directly challenged the Scriptures or Christianity because he felt that an indirect approach was far more effective (Perloff 1999, 152). In 1873, he wrote to his son that openly opposing Christianity was far less effective than a "back door" approach:

> Last night Dicey and Litchfield were talking about J. Stuart Mill's never expressing his religious convictions, as he was urged to do so by his father. Both agreed strongly that if he had done so, he would never have influenced the present age in the manner in which he has done. His books would not have been text books at Oxford, to take a weaker instance. Lyell is most firmly convinced that he has shaken the faith in the Deluge far more efficiently by never having said a word against the Bible, than if he had acted otherwise. . . . I have lately read Morley's *Life of Voltaire* and he insists strongly that direct attacks on Christianity (even when written with the wonderful force and vigor of Voltaire) produce little permanent effect: real good seems only to follow the slow and silent side attacks (quoted in Himmelfarb 1962, 387).

Darwinism and World War I

Less well known is the important contribution of Darwinism in causing World War I. On the list of "Big" causes is "Social Darwinism" partly because "Social Darwinism . . . stimulated imperialism, which in turn justified the expansion of armies and navies" (Hamilton and Herwig 2003, 16). In the 1870s and 1880s, the philosophy of Darwinism spread throughout the Western world, "where it exerted a considerable influence, before reaching its apogee in the radical racialist theories of National Socialism (the Nazis)" (Wehler 1985, 179).

German Nazi death camp Auschwitz in Poland, with the arrival of Hungarian Jews in the summer of 1944.

One of many turn-of-the-century examples of the voluminous literature devoted to popularizing Social Darwinism is the 1913 literary opus written by General Bernhardi titled *Vom Heutigen Kriege*. This book expounded the thesis that war was a biological necessity because it helped to rid the world of the less fit.

This view of war was "not confined to a lunatic fringe, but instead won wide acceptance especially among journalists, academics and politicians" in Germany (Carr 1979, 217). These views were dominant at the highest echelons of the German government and intelligentsia. At the outbreak of World War I, the German chancellor, Bethmann-Hollweg, shared the widespread belief that a conflict between the superior and inferior races was inevitable (Carr 1979, 216–219). In 1912, the German monarch even referred to World War I as a Darwinist "selectionist racial war" against the Slavs and other "inferior" races (Kellogg 1917). Holden notes that the

> widespread and complacent attitude that war was inevitable, natural, and beneficial in weeding out the inferior races, is generally cited as one of the many causes of the first world war by careful authors. An American, Colonel House, was appalled by the attitude of resigned complacency and bellicosity he saw when he visited Europe in 1913, and which was to a very large extent the fault of Darwin's writings. Further evidence of how seriously Social Darwinism was taken at the turn of the century is provided by the propaganda issued by the Pan-German league and other groups within Germany (2000, 1).

For this reason, the loss of life and property caused by World War I also should be included as part of the estimated death toll caused directly or indirectly, in part, by the Darwinism movement.

The Influence of Darwinism on History

One way that the tragic influence of Darwinism on history can be estimated is by reviewing the losses related to wars, including the communist and the Nazi conflicts. In reviewing the data that follows, although some nations may exaggerate their losses in order to encourage sympathy — or even to justify building a stronger military defense — in many cases the actual tragedy is probably greater than most estimates because the full effects of a major war cannot be known until decades after the fighting ends. Battle wounds that do not result in immediate loss of life often shorten it. Soldiers can die from war-injury complications as long as 20 or more years later, such as the man who died almost 30 years after a bullet was lodged in his neck during World War II. The bullet could not be removed safely and slowly shifted, causing death years later. This and many other similar war-related fatalities were not counted as such. In a study of murder by governments, Rummel concluded that power kills and absolute power is far more likely to kill. He concludes that 170 million persons were murdered by the government mass murders that he studied (2008, 1–2).

The Cost of World War I

The financial loss and the loss of lives was far greater in the 20th-century wars than in all of the over 5,300 major formal wars catalogued during the previous 5,000 years combined. A conservative estimate of the number killed in Western wars alone for the last three centuries illustrates this fact:

Century	Estimated lives lost
18th	3,000,000
19th	5,000,000
20th	160,000,000
Total	168,000,000

One Harvard study that evaluated the 902 major wars that occurred between 500 B.C. and A.D. 1918 concluded the number of combatants and casualties involved in World War I was seven times larger than all of the 901 previous recorded wars combined (Foster 1945, 6). Germany's losses in World War I were estimated at 1,824,000 dead and 4,247,600 wounded; Russia's losses were 1,664,800 dead and 3,784,600 wounded. The total dead from all fighting for World War I was over 23 million (Roberts et al. 1979, 153), and casualties both from military action and war-caused disease and famine deaths was estimated at over 40 million (Hersch 1931).

The Cost of World War II

The total direct and indirect cost of World War II was four times greater in extent than World War I — and cost around four trillion dollars in 1945 (Foster 1945, 6). These losses must be viewed in terms of Hitler's inhumanity.

The human lives lost in World War II from both military action and war-distributed disease is estimated at over 65 million, larger than the size of the under-18 population living in the entire United States at the time (Grattan 1949; Wright 1942, 245). Germany lost 6.9 million soldiers on the Soviet front, and an estimated 27.5 million Soviet citizens died battling German troops. In addition, millions of fatalities related to the war, including the 1.5 million who died of hunger in Leningrad due to the German blockade in their determination to eliminate the city population. The total number of people who died from war-related hunger and illness alone was estimated at approximately 12 million.

As to Hitler's designs for his former ally, Russia, "Hitler never offered excuses for his massacres" but

> gave orders that Leningrad should be leveled to the ground and the entire population massacred, and he reserved a special fate for Moscow. Not one person was to be left alive and not one stone was to be left standing on another, and the rubble of the city was to be concealed under a vast lake. The Sonderkommandos were under orders to kill men, women, and children, and those who showed signs of squeamishness at the prospect of killing women and children were to be severely punished . . . Jews, Poles, and Russians were subhuman and did not deserve to live (Payne 1973, 67).

In Germany, fully half of all adult males were killed or wounded (Freed 1970). The official American fatality number for World War II was 402,339, and the direct cost to America alone was estimated at $263 billion (the amount is the dollar value of the time; source: U.S. Government Statistics).

The term "holocaust" usually refers to the Nazi murder of European Jews, but Germany is not the only civilized nation that has indulged in massive slaughters of its own population (Rabinowitz 1979). Actually, several major slaughters in history were more massive than the Jewish Holocaust, all of which were triggered by communist governments (Azar 1990). Since

World War II, humans have fought over 130 wars, including Vietnam, the longest one in U.S. history until Afghanistan (Morrow 1982, 88).

The Death Toll of Communist Movements

Until recently, the four major written histories of the Stalinist era were Roy Medvedev's *Let History Judge* (1989), Robert Conquest's *The Great Terror* (1968), Antonov-Ovseyenko's *The Time of Stalin* (1981), and Alexander Solzhenitsyn's *The Gulag Archipelago* (1974). Antonov-Ovseyenko's *The Time of Stalin*, according to Stephen Cohen (1981, viii), professor of Soviet politics at Princeton, is one of the more important recent works on the communist holocaust.

Antonov-Ovseyenko, the only child of a martyred Soviet founding father, was both a witness and a historian of Stalinism. His father, a noted Bolshevik revolutionist who led the party seizure of the Winter Palace in October of 1917, served in the nascent Soviet government and rose to commander and political chief of the Red Army. Antonov-Ovseyenko estimates the number of deaths (shown in Table I) during the first 30 years of Soviet rule was 81 million (1981, 210–213):

Table I: The Number of Deaths in the First 30 Years of Soviet Rule

Communist Civil War fatalities (including the victims of war-related famine and the execution of "class enemies")	16,000,000
Fatalities caused by the collectivization of agriculture (including deaths by government-induced famine, deportations, and executions)	22,000,000
Purges during the late1930s	19,000,000
Killed during the war (by mass deportations, camp deaths, preemptive executions, exemplary executions, etc.)	15,000,000
Executions and repressions after the war	9,000,000
	Total 81,000,000

The Death Toll of Modern Communist Revolutions

According to a 1983 Foreign Affairs Research Institute report, modern "communistic" revolutions were the cause of about 140 million deaths. The report included all premature deaths from execution, man-made famine, imprisonment, deportation, slave labor, and civil and international warfare. The coalition counted 46.2 million Asian, 45 million Soviet, and 3.6 million European victims of communism from 1917 to 1967, reaching the fairly comprehensive sum of 139,917,700 deaths. Dolot (1985) claims the Ukrainian communist holocaust cost 7 million lives.

The Chinese communist death toll far exceeds that caused by the Axis war, both before and during World War II. Walker (1971) estimated as many as 63 million persons died as a result of Chinese communism from 1927 to date (see Table II).

Table II Some Communist Death Tolls

Conflict	Range of Death Estimates
First Civil War (1927–36)	250,000 to 500,000
Fighting during Sino-Japanese War (1937–45)	40,000 to 50,000
Second Civil War (1945–49)	1,200,000 to 1,250,000
Land reform prior to "Liberation"	500,000 to 1,000,000
Political Liquidation Campaigns (1949–58)	15,000,000 to 30,000,000
Korean War	500,000 to 1,234,000
The "Great Leap Forward" and the Communes (1958–59)	1,000,000 to 2,000,000
Struggles with minority nationalities	500,000 to 1,000,000
The "Great Proletarian Cultural Revolution" and its aftermath (1965–1969)	250,000 to 500,000
Deaths in forced labor camps and frontier "development"	15,000,000 to 25,000,000
"Anticrime" campaign (1983 to present)	500,000 to 1,000,000
TOTAL RANGE OF ESTIMATES	34,800,000 to 63,534,000

Schwartz (1972, 1985) claims that Mao Tse-tung's "Great Cultural Revolution" holocaust alone was responsible for some 29 million deaths, as well as the disruption of the lives of 600 million people. In a study using primary documents, Chang and Halliday claim that Mao was "responsible for well over 70 million deaths in peacetime, more than any other twentieth-century leader" (2005, 3). While some dispute this number, the other figures provided are still in the multimillions (Benton and Chun 2010). Sonam

Topgyal (1984, 7) estimated that the Chinese murdered 1,278,387 persons during their 33-year rule of Tibet alone.

Specifically, 174,138 Tibetans died in prison and labor camps, 156,758 were executed, 432,607 died fighting, 413,151 died of starvation, 92,731 of torture, and 9,002 of suicide. Only six of the more than 7,000 active monasteries located in the Himalayas before the 1950 Chinese takeover remain. During one three-year period alone, the Red Army killed or lost through desertion close to 150,000 of its own soldiers for disobeying orders. Almost as many were killed in action, assumed captured, or invalided out of the army (Chang and Halliday 2005, 296).

Other Communist-Produced Holocausts

Dr. Schwartz's research foundation claimed that over two million persons were killed by the Pol Pot Cambodian government. *Facts on File* (February 20, 1981) quoted a February 5th United Nations human rights panel report that concluded the five-year-long Pol Pot regime genocide was "without precedent in our century, except for the horror of Nazism." When the communists took control of the country in April 1975, millions were killed, including entire villages and communes, pregnant women or women

German fighter planes (Heinkel He 111s) that went into service in 1937.

who had just given birth, the elderly, entire families, newborn babies, and even mental patients (February 2, 1979, *Facts On File*).

The number of Cambodian men and women massacred from 1975 to 1978 is as high as 3 million (Sihanouk 1980, 77; Hawk 1982, 21). Sihanouk, Cambodia's first head of state after the revolution (he resigned on April 2, 1976), believes this estimate is exaggerated but agreed that the number was high and "the remaining five million Khmers were barely holding on after three years of forced labor, hardships of every variety and suffering . . . unparalleled in all of human history."

These "slaves," the author reminds us, were doctors, students, and highly trained civil servants. Many of these who fled traveled through mine fields in a desperate attempt to reach the border, but barely one-tenth made it. The rest died, were captured, or were murdered. The elimination of so many competent personnel rendered the nation's industrial and military complex virtually useless.

With War Comes Disease and Famine

One disastrous consequence of war is not only the direct killing but also the spread of disease both among humans and domestic animals (especially cattle) by soldiers. War commonly causes major disruptions in both the economy and food production and distribution, resulting in food shortages and famines. World War I caused "appalling mortality from disease" (Goldthorpe 1978, 25). In the West alone, the 1918 influenza outbreak caused over 40 million deaths. Although Western governments later took vigorous action to deal with the plague, the war caused much of the flu problem and greatly impeded improvement in civilian living standards for decades.

Famines were sometimes a deliberate ploy by a government to pressure recalcitrant people into acquiescing (Dolot 1985). Antonov-Ovseyenko claims the 1932 Soviet holocaust was an artificially produced famine (1981, 64). Stalin's forced famine collectivization and his liquidation of the Kulaks cost close to 22 million lives. In an attempt to summarize the deaths that resulted from the communist holocaust due to government-caused disease and famine, one of the most extensive studies by persons who had access to the formerly top secret Soviet archives produced the following estimates:

Nation	Estimated Deaths
U.S.S.R.	20 million
China	65 million
Vietnam	1 million
North Korea	2 million
Cambodia	2 million
Eastern Europe	1 million
Latin America	150,000
Africa	1.7 million
Afghanistan	1.5 million
The international Communist movement	about 10,000
	Total 100 million

Source: Courtois, et al. (1999, p. 4)

Since 1970, One in Every Four Nations Has Been at War

Forty-five nations — a fourth of the world's countries — were involved in a war since the 1970s, most involving communism. Communist conflicts since 1900 add up to a loss of over 200 million lives — almost the entire population of the United States, the fourth most populous nation today. Most of the bloodiest of these conflicts involved communist takeovers, including

Cambodia — civil war involving 200,000 Vietnamese, Cambodian troops vs. 63,000 guerrillas; four million dead since 1970.

Indonesia — guerrilla war involving 269,000 troops vs. 6,500 nationalist rebels; 100,000 to 250,000 dead since 1975.

Afghanistan — civil war involving 100,000 rebels vs. 140,000 Soviet and Afghan troops; about 100,000 dead since 1978.

Philippines — guerrilla war involving 112,800 troops vs. thousands of communist rebels; 50,000 dead since 1972.

Vietnam — conventional war involving 300,000 Chinese troops vs. 200,000 Vietnamese; 47,000 dead since 1979.

El Salvador — guerrilla war involving 10,000 Marxists vs. 25,000 troops; over 30,000 dead since 1977.

Guatemala — guerrilla war involving 6,000 leftist rebels vs. 30,600 troops; 12,000 to 22,000 dead since 1982.

Ethiopia — guerrilla war involving 250,000 Ethiopian troops vs. 45,000 Eritrean communists; close to 30,000 dead since 1962. (From *The Center for Defense Information*'s "World at War" report, 1980).

According to Sampson (1978), over 25 million persons have been slaughtered in mostly communist wars since 1945 — as many fatalities as occurred in both the world wars. Wright estimates that at least 10 percent of all deaths in modern civilization can be attributed to war (1942, 246). Since 1945, not more than 26 days existed in which a hot war was not occurring somewhere in the world, and most of these wars were communist inspired (Sampson 1978)! The total *indirect loss* of life from war-related disease and injury since 1945 is probably another 20 million. An example of the still continuing effects of communism is as follows:

Forty years ago, Cambodia was the most developed and cleanest nation in Asia. Phnom Penh was a showcase city with public services, promenades, and city gardens. Then, in 1970, the country was plunged into [war] . . . between Marxists and government forces. . . . When the Marxist Khmer Rouge forcibly took control of the nation in 1973, the nation rapidly deteriorated to a Third World wasteland (Dabel 2000, 29).

As a result, vast tracts of farmland stood idle, and nearly four million land mines were still hiding in rice paddies, preventing agriculture and other development. Almost daily, farmers were

killed or maimed by the anti-personnel devices that were planted during fighting more than 20 years ago. . . . Despite these devastating political and economic problems, it is the HIV/AIDS infection rate that may destroy the people. By the end of this year, health officials expect 40,000 full-blown cases of AIDS in Cambodia. . . . Health officials say 250,000 Cambodians are already infected with HIV. The number grows by 100 people per day. When Cambodia's 7,346 "commercial sex workers" (the politically correct term for "prostitute") were surveyed, 43 percent tested positive for HIV. "Commercial sex workers" and their customers account for the spread of nearly all cases of HIV/AIDS in Cambodia (Dabel 2000, 29).

The Jeanne d'Arc school on fire at Frederiksberg, 1945.

More recently, 31 "major armed conflicts" in 27 countries have been fought in the world since 1994! The Darwinian and anti-Christian revolutions that influenced these wars and holocausts have cost tens of millions of lives, *much* of our wealth, and have brought abject poverty to the lives of many of the world's masses. Over 60 percent of the world's population now lives in poverty, and about half of these in life-threatening poverty, with 400 million on the edge of starvation.

The additional money required to achieve adequate levels of food, healthcare, and housing to the world's population was estimated a few years ago at around 20 billion dollars. This huge sum was approximately what the world spent at the time either for war, or the preparation for war, every two weeks, most of which until recently involved communist conflicts. It now costs over 25 billion dollars annually to take care of America's war-injured, much of this at Veterans Administration hospitals at government expense.

Putting This in Perspective

Darwinism is only one factor, although a critically important factor, that led to fascism, communism, capitalism, and cold-blooded tyranny. Other factors aside from Darwinism were important in the development of 20th-century totalitarianism-inspired holocausts, but this review focuses only on the influence of Darwinism. Darwinism was widely accepted in England, France, and the United States — none of which developed totalitarianism systems like those in Germany, Italy, or Russia. For this reason, we must also look to other factors to fully explain the development of totalitarianism.

Communism was a product of not only Darwinism but also of the so-called "enlightenment" thinkers and a particular social system and history. Many historical factors predated and influenced the growth and development of Darwinism. For example, the works of Kant, Hegel, Comte, and especially those thinkers who were part of the so-called "enlightenment," with its emphasis on extreme rationalism and the inevitability of "progress" all had an important impact on Western thought. Darwin in many ways has followed in the footsteps of these thinkers, and later, Marx, Nietzsche, and others were important. The so-called "rationalism movement" also was critical and had a profound impact on Western Europe and Christianity in the late 1600s.

Nevertheless, Darwinism was a critically important step in the process that led to totalitarianism, but nationalism and the drive for power and for empires were also both important. Conversely, the fierce nationalism and imperialism that infected Europe during the 18th and 19th centuries also helped to lay the foundation for, and the acceptance of, a particular form of Darwinism.

Under Lenin and Stalin, the U.S.S.R. became a bloody "evil empire," partly because Russian communism was materialistic, atheistic, and absolutistic. Darwinism, though, was also important in Russia. Stalin did not starve six million Ukrainian Kulaks to death because he was a Darwinist, but rather his immediate reason was because they resisted collectivization, and the confiscation of their grain supplies helped to feed the residents of Moscow. Darwinism, though, clearly helped him and his government to justify his yearnings for national glory and collectivization, especially by helping to negate the influence of Christianity.

The obvious motivations of power, wealth, and glory, are important factors in expanding national territory, but *even here* Darwinism was important because the European nations were expanding their influence and territory "overseas in Asia, Africa, and the Pacific. It was somehow taken for granted that it was right for them to do this because the European white man was inherently superior to people of darker skins and should take over as a matter of course" (Asimov 1977, 89–94). Asimov adds that this worldview was "made 'scientific' by the works of . . . Herbert Spencer, who applied the views of evolution, first elaborated by the English naturalist Charles Robert Darwin, in 1859, to society." It was Spencer who

A young African American in Chicago in a study of race relations and race riots.

coined the phrase "Survival of the fittest" and in 1884 argued, for instance, that people who were unemployable or burdens on society should be allowed to die rather than be made objects of help and charity. To do this, apparently, would weed out unfit individuals and strengthen the race. It was a horrible philosophy that could be used to justify the worst impulses of human beings. A conquering nation could destroy its enemy (as the Americans destroyed the Indians) because it was "more fit," and it could prove it was "more fit" because it destroyed its enemy. Indeed, the exploitation of the rest of humanity by white Europeans could be made to seem a noble gesture — as the superior Whites reached out to help the inferiors on other continents by employing them as servants and allowing them to live on scraps (Asimov 1977, 89–94).

He added that large numbers of citizens in the United States "were affected by the Spenserian philosophy and who ached to have the United States help spread the blessings of imperialism, especially since the 'end of the frontier' in 1890 seemed to leave American expansive energies with little to do at home" (Asimov 1977, 89–94).

Another important factor in causing the Holocaust was the anti-Semitic programs and bigotry that was deeply entrenched in European culture long before Darwin. Hitler found many normal "Christian" Germans receptive to his anti-Semitic harangues and legislation, partly because Christianity had lost much of its life and influence in Germany and much of Europe. Darwinism reinforced existing prejudices against Jews, but this was not the only factor causing the Holocaust.

The loss of Christian influence and the corruption of the Church also were critically important. The early Christian Church was strongly opposed to violent conflicts and consistently supported helping the weak and less powerful (Bainton 1960; Nuttall 1971; Marrin 1971; MacGregor 1954). The Scriptures clearly stress that we are to "pursue the things which make for peace and the building up of one another" (Romans 14:19, NASB). Christians are commanded to "be peaceable with one another . . . support the weak, be long suffering toward all and work against the tendency for one to render injury but, on the contrary, always pursue what is good toward all" (1 Thessalonians 4:13–15 paraphrase). This clear teaching repeated throughout the Scriptures is in contrast to the communist and totalitarian philosophy, which stresses violent revolution and a dictatorship of the proletariat as the "scientific" solution to human problems.

Theologians generally explain these passages as referring to the dictum that we, as individuals, are to pursue peace and love our enemies (Matthew 5:44). These Scriptures focus on individual personal relationships, their application is not limited to interpersonal conflicts but also applies to intergroup conflicts. Had Hitler, Stalin, Marx, and the others not rejected biblical Christianity for a secular Darwinian "enlightenment" secular worldview, they could not have accepted the inhumanity inherent in the Nazi/communistic systems they led, and the hundreds of millions of lives lost in the holocausts reviewed above would never have occurred. In the end, the book Darwin wrote set forth a theory of biological origins that

> had no economic or political implications. But though many might go so far as to concede that God created the world through a long process of evolution, the end result of Darwin's theory has been the killing of tens of millions of innocents. He therefore became the spiritual father of the greatest mass-murderer in history (Wurmbrand 1986, 86).

References

Antonov-Ovseyenko, Anton. 1981. *The Time of Stalin: Portrait of a Tyranny.* New York: Harper and Row.

Asimov, Isaac. 1977. *The Golden Door: The United States from 1856 to 1918.* Boston, MA: Houghton Mifflin Company.

Azar, Larry. 1990. *Twentieth Century in Crisis: Foundations of Totalitarianism.* Dubuque, IA: Kendal-Hunt.

Bainton, Roland H. 1960. *Christian Attitudes toward War and Peace.* New York: Abingdon Press.

Benton, Gregor, and Lin Chun, editors. 2010. *Was Mao Really a Monster: The Academic Response to Chang and Halliday's Mao: The Unknown Story.* New York: Routledge.

Bergman, Jerry. 1999. "Darwinism and the Nazi Race Holocaust." *CenTech J.* 13(2):101–111.

———. 2001. "The Darwinian Foundation of Communism." *T.J. Technical Journal* 15(1):89–95.

Carr, William. 1979. *A History of Germany 1815–1945.* New York: St. Martin's Press.

Chang, Jung, and Jon Halliday. 2005. *Mao: The Unknown Story.* New York: Knopf.

Cohen, Stephen. 1981. Introduction in Anton Antonov-Ovseyenko, *The Time of Stalin: Portrait of a Tyranny.* New York: Harper and Row.

Conquest, Robert. 1968. *The Great Terror.* New York: Macmillan Company.

Courtois, Stephene, Nicolas Werth, Jean-Louis Panne, Andrzej Paczkowski, Karen Bartosek, and Jean-Louis Margolin. 1999. *The Black Book of Communism; Crimes, Terror, Repression.* Cambridge, MA: Harvard University Press.

Dabel, Greg. 2000. "The New Killing Fields." *World,* March 18, 15(11):29–30.

Dolot, Miron. 1985. *Execution by Hunger.* New York: Norton.

Foster, Freling. 1945. "Keep Up with the World." *Colliers,* September 29, p. 6.

Freed, Leonard. 1970. *Made in Germany.* New York: Grossman Publishers.

Goldthorpe, J.E. 1978. *The Sociology of the Third World.* Cambridge, MA: Cambridge University Press.

Grattan, C. Hartley. 1949. "What the War Cost." *Harpers,* April, p. 76–79.

Hamilton, Richard F., and Holger H. Herwig. 2003. *The Origins of World War I.* New York, NY: Cambridge University Press.

Hawk, David. 1982. "The Killing of Cambodia." *The New Republic,* November 15, p. 17–21.

Hersch, L. 1931. "Demographic Effects of Modern War," in *What Would Be the Character of a New War?* London: Interparliamentary Union.

Himmelfarb, Gertrude. 1962. *Darwin and the Darwinian Revolution.* New York: W.W. Norton.

Holden, Ted. 2000. "Is the Theory of Evolution a Source of Racism and Evil?" Unpublished Manuscript.

Kellogg, Vernon. 1917. *Headquarters Nights.* Boston, MA: Atlantic Monthly Press.

MacGregor, G.H.C. 1954. *The New Testament Basis of Pacifism.* Nyack, NY: Fellowship Publications.

Marrin, Albert, editor. 1971. *War and the Christian Conscience.* Chicago, IL: Henry Regnery Company.

Medvedev, Roy. 1989. *Let History Judge. The Origins and Consequences of Stalinism.* New York: Columbia University Press.

Morrow, Lance. 1982. "The Metaphysics of War." *Time,* May 17, p. 88.

Nuttall, Geofrey. 1971. *Christian Pacifism in History.* Berkeley, CA: World Without War Council.

Payne, Robert. 1973. *Massacre; The Tragedy of Bangladesh and the Phenomenon of Mass Slaughter throughout History.* New York: Macmillan.

Perloff, James. 1999. *Tornado in a Junkyard; The Relentless Myth of Darwinism.* Arlington, MA: Refuge Books.

Rabinowitz, Dorothy. 1979. *About the Holocaust.* New York: The American Jewish Committee.

Roberts, Ron, and Robert M. Kloss. 1979. *Social Movements.* St. Louis, MO: C.V. Mosby

Rummel, Rudolph J. 2008. *Death by Government.* New Brunswick, NJ: Transaction Publishers.

Sampson, Anthony. 1978. "Want to Start a War." *Esquire,* March 1, p. 59–69.

Schwartz, Fred. 1972. *The Three Faces of Revolution.* Falls Church, VA: The Capital Hill Press.

———. 1985. "Demand for an Astronomical Sum in Reparations," *Christian Anti-Communism Crusade,* Feb. 1.

Sihanouk, Norodom. 1980. *War and Hope; The Case for Cambodia.* New York: Pantheon Books.

Solzhenitsyn, Alexander. 1974. *The Gulag Archipelago.* New York: Harper and Row.

Topgyal, Sonam. 1984. "Over 1.2 Million Died Under Chinese Rule." *Tibetan Review* 19(3):7.

Walker, Richard. 1971. *The Human Cost of Communism in China.* Washington, DC: U.S. Government Printing office; p. 15, see Schwartz, 1972, updated by the *Conservative Digest,* April, 10(4) and *The Christian News,* April 30, p. 12.

Wehler, Hans-Ulrich. 1985. *The German Empire, 1871–1918.* Translated from the German by Kim Traynor. Dover, NH: Berg Publishers.

Wright, Quincy. 1942. *A Study of War.* Chicago, IL: University of Chicago Press.

Wurmbrand, Richard. 1986. *Marx and Satan.* Bartlesville, OK: Living Sacrifice Book Company.

DARWIN

The Dark Side of Charles Darwin

978-0-89051-605-8 | $13.99

THE DARK SIDE OF CHARLES DARWIN

JERRY BERGMAN

A CRITICAL ANALYSIS of an ICON of SCIENCE

Persuaded by the Evidence

A unique and interesting collection of true stories from Christians – each sharing his personal journey to find the Biblical truth of a six-day creation! From scientists to youth ministers!

978-0-89051-545-7 | $13.99